To Edward
will best wish.

Denis

2007

GW00401343

A LIVING STONE
SELECTED ESSAYS AND ADDRESSES
by
MICHAEL PRIOR CM

**edited with an introduction
by
Duncan Macpherson**

LIVING STONES
of the Holy Land Trust

A LIVING STONE
Selected Essays and Addresses
by Michael Prior CM

First published 2006 by
Living Stones of the Holy Land Trust
(Regd. Charity no. 1081204)

10-digit ISBN 0-9552088-0-7
13-digit ISBN 978-0-9552088-0-5

The Revd Professor Michael Prior CM died suddenly in July 2004. Vincentian
priest and academic, he was also a stalwart, fearless and vocal supporter of the rights
of Palestinians, and a founder and chairman of *Living Stones*. The reaction to his
death has been one of deep sadness and loss. Such has been the strength of the
response of his many friends and colleagues, coupled with a powerful wish to see his
name and work perpetuated, that *Living Stones* has decided to establish a memorial
educational fund in his memory. Details are available from *The Living Stones of the
Holy Land Trust* (regd. charity no. 1081204), 1 Gough Square, London EC4A 3DE.

Produced by Melisende
London EC1N 8QU

Editor: Leonard Harrow
Printed at the Cromwell Press, Trowbridge, England

CONTENTS

Note: the original details of works published in this collection are prefixed by an asterisk [*] in the Bibliography.

MICHAEL PRIOR,
THE MAN AND HIS MESSAGE
Duncan Macpherson

'My life has been singularly poor in outward happenings. I cannot tell much about them, for it would strike me as hollow and insubstantial. I can understand myself only in the light of inner happenings. It is these that make up the singularities of my life, and with these my autobiography deals.'
(Carl Gustav Jung, *Memories, Dreams, Reflections,* Collins and Routledge Kegan Paul, London, 1963, 19.)

Alas, Michael, unlike Jung, left no autobiography. However, the words of Jung, quoted above, impressed Michael enough for him to have written them into the inside cover of his academic diary for 1988-89. The inner happenings making up the singularities of Michael's life must remain largely a matter of conjecture even to those closest to him. The outward happenings—the publications, the unflagging advocacy for the poor and the oppressed, the human warmth, jocundity and sheer irrepressibility of the man—strike those who knew him as far from 'hollow or insubstantial.'

Vincentian priest, Scripture scholar, teacher, musician, linguist, poet, liberation theologian, peace activist and advocate of Palestinian rights: Michael Prior was all of these. The many people who mourn him will remember him differently, but for all of them he will be remembered as a friend. Michael had a great gift of friendship—so much so that even people who only met him once or twice counted themselves his friends and experienced a genuine sense of sorrow at their loss.

In this brief biographical introduction to some of Michael's many essays and addresses a picture emerges of a life that combined qualities of joyful, almost anarchic exuberance with all the seriousness of the scholar, the devotedness of the priest and the just anger of the revolutionary. From his early days in Cork he excelled at everything to which he set his hand, but he decided to devote his considerable talents to his life in a religious community dedicated to the service of the poor. It was this community that enabled him to pursue his studies in Dublin, Rome, Jerusalem and London, equipping him as a teacher and as a scholar of some standing in the academy of biblical scholars.

His interest in Scripture led him to visit the land of the Bible and these visits gave him a focus in his commitment to advocacy on behalf of the poor and oppressed. Michael not only became an eloquent supporter of the rights of Palestinians, he also engaged with the difficult question of the way in which the Bible was interpreted to justify their expropriation and oppression. At the same time as administering a department of Theology and Religious Studies he continued to pursue scholarly research and to campaign vigorously on behalf of the Palestinian people. Gradually he was to close the gap between academic theory and political engagement, developing a rare model of morally and politically committed scholarly discourse, paying particular attention to the land traditions of the Bible.

Inevitably Michael's ideas occasioned some controversy and criticism. Temperamentally, however, Michael relished nothing better than an argument in which he could embarrass individuals and institutions that he considered to be callous and dishonest over issues in which he was sure that he had right on his side. This controversy led him to some fruitful exploration of the controverted issue of the relationship between anti-Zionism and anti-Semitism. At the conclusion of his life he had been a prime mover in an exciting new research project focusing on the Holy Land as a multi-disciplinary study with particular focus on the role of fundamentalism in Christianity, Judaism and Islam. His untimely death cut short his work but the issues he raised continue to demand answers and the causes he engaged continue to need the support not only of dedicated Christians like Michael, but of all people of good will.

EARLY LIFE, EDUCATION AND VOCATION TO THE PRIESTHOOD

'My native wit and curiosity for learning received every opportunity for development.' (Private notes by Michael Prior)

Michael was born in the 'rebel county' of Cork on the fifteenth of March 1942. His mother Eileen Hourihan, a Cork girl, was one of nine children.

In 1932 she married James Prior, an officer in the Garda, from Ballinamore in County Leitrim. Ballinamore means 'Mouth of the Big Ford,' and is situated at the ancient frontier between the province of Ulster and the rest of Ireland. Michael was the youngest of five: his eldest brother Patrick Peter (1935), who died in childhood, John (1937-1985), James (1939-) and his sister, Nuala (1940-). Michael recalled that his father was the authority-figure in the house but that his mother was the one who really exercised it. Michael was devoted to his mother and remembered her fondly as 'the most selfless person I have ever known. I cannot ever remember her acting out of self-interest.'[1]

Michael attended the local convent infant school of St Vincent's, run by the Sisters of Charity. There he was taught Latin by one Sr Christopher and joined his brother James as an altar server at the convent. Even as a child Michael was fascinated by the drama of the ritual of the Mass. James and Nuala recall that they and their brother John were persuaded to kneel while Michael 'celebrated Mass' vested in one of his father's blue Garda shirts in the kitchen of their home, substituting biscuits and lemonade for bread and wine and sometimes burning incense grains, purloined from the convent chapel, on the jets of the cooker.

Michael's secondary schooling was at Our Lady's Mount, North Monastery in Cork for which he earned a scholarship. The school was staffed by the strongly nationalistic Irish Christian Brothers who gave the lessons in the Irish language. Here he excelled in several sports, playing for his school in the all-Ireland Hurling championship. He was also assiduous in his studies, sometimes getting up at four in the morning to study. Like many intelligent young Irishmen of his generation Michael decided to test his vocation to the priesthood and he applied to join the Congregation of the Mission; a world wide community of priests founded by Saint Vincent de Paul (1581-1660) and living under vows, committed to 'prefer the service of the poor to everything else.' However, before he embarked upon this next stage in his career he decided to earn some money for books and he spent an enjoyable summer of 1960 in England, staying with his brother James in Wolverhampton and working as a bus conductor on the local buses.

Those who knew Michael during his teenage years attest to his boundless enthusiasm. He was a lively and a humorous companion with

---

[1] Unpublished autobiographical notes.

a great zest for life, a gift for music and languages and a keen follower of every kind of sport. He also had enthusiasm for popular music, rugby football, soccer, and in female companionship, all interests normal for a boy of his age. However Michael left the joys of youth, along with the smoking of cigarettes, at the door of the seminary when he joined the Vincentians. Often throughout his life he would surprise and please by offering, from memory, lusty renderings of the entire repertoire of the various top twenty pop songs recorded up to 7 September 1960, the day when he was admitted to the Congregation of the Mission. Subsequent hit-songs were unknown territory to him. Life in the novitiate at that time was rigid and demanding in other ways, especially to someone with Michael's fierce independence of spirit and anarchic sense of fun. Contemporaries of Michael from that period recall finding him a little larger than life and they enjoyed making fun of his Cork accent. On one occasion Michael was told that he should obey his superiors in any matter that was not against his conscience even if it seemed to him unreasonable. To this Michael replied by asking with some vigour whether he should obey if told to plant cabbages upside down!

During the entire period of his novitiate home visits were forbidden and even when his father died in 1968 he was not allowed to stay with his mother when he was allowed back to Cork to attend the funeral. However in retrospect Michael felt a debt of gratitude to the Vincentians and in 1985 he gave a speech in which he claimed for himself that 'As well as imbibing the gentle sprit of Vincent de Paul I learned many lessons in goodness from my confreres, with whom I have always lived in peace and with great joy.' He also took the opportunity to express gratitude for the educational opportunities that he received: 'The Vincentian community enabled me to study in four universities and one other centre of Higher Education, in four different countries, in Dublin, Rome, London and Jerusalem.'[2]

The first of these opportunities for university study came after a year of spiritual formation with the Vincentians in Dublin and at Saint Joseph's in Blackrock in Dublin for the study of philosophy, in which he gained a distinction. He was then sent to University College Dublin study for a BSc degree at majoring in Experimental Physics, minoring in Mathematics. In 1964 he embarked on theological studies at the

---

[2] Unpublished notes from a speech at a celebration after the occasion of being awarded his doctorate in 1985.

Angelicum University in Rome and at Holy Cross College in Clonliffe, obtaining the degree of BD *(cum laude)* before his ordination as a Catholic Priest on May 31 in 1969 at the hands of Dr John Charles Mcquaid, Archbishop of Dublin.

Earlier that year Michael published an article that tells us a lot about the no nonsense approach and the realism that he brought to his apostolate. 'What is called for is true *aggiornamento*, not only at the institutional level but also at the individual one. Each of it is part believer and part atheist, in that there are areas of life, which go along without our religious beliefs affecting them: the draught of liturgy we drink in on Sunday does not spill over into the rest of the week. Mass for many people is not a symbolic expression of their commitment to Christ, but is merely one more activity, which the climate of the moment regards as desirable. We need to integrate the human and the divine in ourselves first of all and then proceed to do it in our society.' [3] His friend and confrere Father Fergus Kelly comments that Michael spent the next thirty-five years of his life trying to integrate the human and the divine.[4]

One of the first masses as a priest was for the Sisters of Charity in Peacock Lane in Cork, the community that had provided his first school education and from whose orchards he and his brother James had once stolen apples. From the beginning of his priestly ministry Michael always felt obliged to engage in advocacy for the outsider and the underdog. At that time the sisters also ran a Magdalen laundry, part of the now notorious system, operative in Ireland until the 1990s, whereby unmarried mothers and young girls thought to be of doubtful sexual morals, were placed under the care of women's religious communities who labelled them as 'penitents' and set them to work in the laundry. Typically of the young Father Michael, he insisted that those he referred to as 'the ladies from the laundry' should be allowed to come to his celebratory Mass.

Immediately after his ordination he studied German at the Goethe Institute in Dublin, and Prien in Germany, spending the summer of 1970 as an assistant pastor in the town of Hochstadt. On his return from Germany he studied Semitic Languages at the Institute of Semitic

---

[3] 'Faith and Secular man,' *Evangelizare,* Dublin, Easter 1969. Cited by Fergus Kelly CM in *Colloque,* Winter 2005, 178-9.

[4] Fergus Kelly CM in *Colloque,* Winter 2005, 179.

languages under Dermot Ryan, later Archbishop of Dublin, before returning to Rome to the Pontifical Biblical Institute to study for the Licence in Sacred Scripture or LSS, which he was to pass *summa cum laude,* The last year of his studies at the Biblicum provided the opportunity for him to participate in a two-week study tour pilgrimage in the Holy Land with 31 other students under the leadership of Professor Richard Mackowski, SJ. Returning to Ireland in 1972 he became Director of Students and Master of Novices at the Vincentian Seminary in Dublin and he continued in this role until 1975. This proved a difficult role. The Catholic Church was trying to adjust to the changes brought in by the Second Vatican Council and, in common with other religious communities; the Vincentians were experiencing a cultural and spiritual upheaval. Michael had acquired a taste for scholarship and would have preferred to continue his studies. However his unhappiness during this time in Dublin was mitigated by the opportunity to function as a visiting Lecturer in Biblical Studies at All Hallows College, the Mater Dei Institute and at Carysfort Teacher Training College. In 1973 he shared the 1973 prize for Young (under 35) Theologian of the Year in Ireland for an essay on 'The Episcopal Virtues of 1 Tim 3.1-7'.

TEACHER, SCHOLAR AND ADVOCATE OF THE POOR

In 1975 Michael was appointed to the staff of Bishop Ullathorne School in Coventry, a secondary school under the pastoral care of the Vincentians. It was here, with the encouragement of his confreres, that he later claimed to have sharpened his interest in continuing higher study; 'keeping my hand in scholarship while I lived in the intellectually, emotionally and spiritually stimulating environment of 77 Kenilworth Road, Coventry, in the company of Hugh Murnaghan … and of Diarmuid Moran who is smiling down on us from heaven.'[5]

Michael remained in Coventry until September 1977 when he was appointed to the staff of the Department of Theology and Religious Studies at Saint Mary's College Strawberry Hill. Saint Mary's is the oldest Roman Catholic institution of higher education in England and had been founded in Brook Green in Hammersmith in 1850 to train

---

[5] *Ibid.*, 1985.

male teachers for the growing numbers of poor Catholic children. In 1899 Vincentians had been invited by the Catholic bishops of England and Wales to taken charge of the administration of the college, which had moved to Strawberry Hill in 1925. In 1977 there were some nine Vincentians on the staff and a further five living as part of the community in the historic gothic castle of Walpole House. Michael could not have imagined then that at his death he would be the last Vincentian on the staff of Saint Mary's.

The teachers in the department at that time included four priests and three lay people including the present writer. My first impression of Michael was of a large, jovial man with a shock of white hair. He seemed to combine qualities of warmth and openness with bluntness of expression and a sometimes-disturbing love of banter and argument. During his years at Saint Mary's his love of biblical scholarship expressed itself both in his teaching and his writing. As a teacher, diligent students found him supportive and stimulating. One student later said of him 'my love of things academic started in Michael's classes. He was a truly inspirational and passionate teacher and also a lovely, funny man. I can honestly say he played a foundational role in my life. I think of him often with respect and fondness.'[6] Another recalls Michael 'starting a Monday morning scripture lecture, by singing 'My father was a wandering Aramaean ...' accompanying himself on the guitar. I thought to myself at the time, this was a wonderfully novel way of teaching the Old Testament.'[7] However, Michael did not suffer fools gladly and students who had not prepared their work would often feel the edge of his tongue. On such student later confessed that without Michael she might not ever have made the effort to gain her degree. 'He told me I was "just a dosser." I burst into tears and he asked me if crying proved that I was not a dosser.'

Michael himself could never have been called a 'dosser.' During the 1970s and 80s in addition to a full teaching programme he set out to popularise biblical scholarship through several series of articles in magazines and newspapers including the Dominican, Dublin-based, publication *Scripture in Church*, the Bible Reading Fellowship publication *Word in Worship*, the German language *Heute* and the popular Catholic weekly, *The Universe*, and in 1977 he began an editorial collaboration

---

[6] Dr Laura Williamson, teaching in the School of Law, Glasgow University.
[7] Mark Brennan.

with me as joint executive editor of *Scripture Bulletin*, the successor to *Scripture* as the journal of the Catholic Biblical Association of Great Britain. At the same time he decided to engage in doctoral research and, returning to his earlier interest in I Timothy, he enrolled for a PhD at King's College, London to write a thesis entitled *Second Timothy: A Personal Letter of Paul*. In 1985, after a sabbatical year in Jerusalem, he successfully completed the degree. In 1987 he became head of the Department of Theology and Religious Studies at Saint Mary's and continued as such for the next ten years. Michael relished the work involved. In Fergus Kelly's words, 'He loved the world of academia—of inter-departmental struggles, of syllabi and assessments and examinations and all the inter-relationships of life that go to make a college like St. Mary's such a vibrant, living organism.'[8]

Under Michael's leadership as head of Theology and Religious Studies the department was to develop new programmes including an MA in Religion and Education, a single honours BA in Theology, single honours in Theology and Religious Studies, and a Masters programme in Theology and Religious Studies. He also stimulated a growth in research activity within the Department through the introduction of regular research seminars, and the promotion of publishing. As part of his commitment to public theology, he also promoted a number of series of public lectures. Warmly supportive of students and colleagues Michael frequently drove the College management to distraction with lengthy, well argued, but often inflated, written demands for greater resources of staffing and finance for the work of the department.

In addition to his teaching, writing and the work he did as a priest in support of the College Chaplaincy, he also served as a part time chaplain to gypsies and travelling people in London (1977-83) becoming actively involved in political advocacy on their behalf. Father Fergus Kelly summed up Michael's approach to the Vincentian option for the poor as follows: 'If you were serious about the living, the living word of God, you had to get out there and be with the poor, whether it was the travelling community in London, or the Palestinian people of the Holy Land.'[9] One of the avenues of Michael's concern for the oppressed was

---

[8] Fergus Kelly CM, at Michael's memorial Mass, 30 July 2004.
[9] *Ibid.*

in poetry. In an unpublished poem he penned in Christmas 1982 Michael saw a parallel between the Holy Family and the homeless travellers in the London Borough of Ealing:

> In the beginning was the silence of the evicted
> Moved by hundreds of functionaries to begin their trek
> To Waltham Cross, or Edinburgh, or Manchester or anywhere
> outside Ealing Borough
> Since there was no room for them at the inn
> But the wounded did not oblige
> And wander in the desert
> To be moved on from the side of the road
> As garbage is swept by a street cleaner.

His particular interest in the social implications of Christianity also involved him in working with Justice and Peace groups and functioning as regional chaplain to the West London Society of St Vincent de Paul. He was a member of CND and he was instrumental in setting up a College Amnesty group. Michael also followed closely the unfolding of events in Northern Ireland. Despite his Christian pacifist commitment, in his frequently vigorous debate on the issues no one was left in any doubt of his political sympathy for the Irish republican cause. However it was the issue of Palestinian that was to engage him most. In the words of the Palestinian priest and educator Father Elias Chacour, 'He understood very well the statement of the Lord Jesus when he said: Everything you do to one of these little ones, you do it to me. This is where his commitment to the Palestinian cause came from.'[10]

THE PILGRIM AND THE LIVING STONES

Michael's interest in issues of justice and peace in the Holy Land was first stirred in the seminary during the Six-Day war of June 1967. He later recalled how TV pictures and reports of Arab-Israel war conveyed to him that he 'was observing a classic David versus Goliath conflict,' with diminutive, innocent Israel repulsing its rapacious Arab predators:

---

[10] Father Elias Chacour, Ibillin, Galilee (memorial tribute).

'The startling, speedy, and comprehensive victory of Israel produced surges of delight in me.'[11] However during his first study visit to the Holy Land in 1972 he sensed something wrong in what he regarded as the 'obvious *Apartheid* of Israeli-Arab society'. Nine years later in 1982, he agreed to come with me on a student study tour in which our party had been invited to stay with Palestinian students at Bir Zeit University. Along with the rest of the party Michael and I were radicalised by the experience, witnessing at first hand curfews and house demolitions and meeting young men who had been tortured and held without trial. In particular a meeting with a family whose house had been demolished in the village of Beit Sahour, the traditional site of the 'Shepherds Field' moved Michael to pen verses in the cause of the dispossessed:

> While shepherds watched their flocks by night
> A mile away the soldiers
> Dynamite the inn of the little family
> Whose fifteen year old, like David,
> Threw a stone at the Israeli Goliath,
> But without David's success.
> For his crime against the mighty
> The lowly are rendered homeless
> And pitch their tent
> Beside the empty tomb.
> The grandeur of the mother ennobled by suffering;
> The two children standing uncomprehending
> And the father with jaded resignation
> Begins to raise a covering
> Over the foundations.[12]

Even at this time however, Michael had no doubts about the legitimacy of the Jewish State or of Israeli occupation in the light of Israel's security needs. In 1983 and in 1985 dance troupes from Bir Zeit University came as guests of the Saint Mary's Students Union, on the first of two tours of Britain, performing traditional Palestinian dance at a number of universities in Britain. Michael entered into these events

---

[11] Prior 1999. *Zionism and the State of Israel: A Moral Inquiry*. London and New York: Routledge, 1999.

[12] This poem together with the earlier poem on the Ealing travelling people was published in *Scripture Bulletin*, XIII, No. 1, London, 1982, 1.

with gusto, chauffeuring the dancers in one of the College minibuses and offering renderings of Palestinian nationalist songs spontaneously translated into Irish. However it was only during the course of his sabbatical year spent in the École Biblique et Archéologique de Jérusalem (1983-84) that he began to raise questions about the role of the biblical narrative of promise and possession of land in the expansionist activity that he witnessed.

Just before his return Michael was obliged to deal with a problem in relation to his editorship of Scripture Bulletin. Michael became joint editor of *Scripture Bulletin* in 1980. When I decided to resign as the other joint editor I had assumed that Michael would simply take over as editor. His characteristically forthright advocacy of the Palestinian cause in the editorial columns of *Scripture Bulletin* may have been a factor in a brief dispute over his future editorial position. Wisely, however, the committee of the Catholic Biblical Association of Great Britain agreed that he should serve as executive editor on his return from his sabbatical year and he continued in that post until 1989, remaining a member of the editorial board and subsequently serving two terms as Chairman of the CBA between 1995 and 1998 and again from 1998.

In 1984 Michael played a leading role in setting up Living Stones, 'an ecumenical trust seeking to promote contacts between Christian communities in Britain and those in the Holy Land and in neighbouring countries.' Michael was happy to observe the way in which such contacts almost invariably enlisted sympathy and support for the Palestinian cause. He returned to the Holy Land with another student group in 1985 and by that time his political analysis had began to crystallise into a radical critique of Zionism. The fact that Living Stones was from the beginning non-political was for Michael an irritating limitation and although he continued to lead Living Stones until his death he sought other platforms where he could engage in more overtly political campaigning, not only against the Israeli occupation but also against Zionist ideology as a whole.

Michael was opposed to what he called the 'hegemonic discourse' in which Church and Academy allowed a place for discrete criticism of the Israeli occupation and human rights violations but, in the name of 'balance', ruled out of court any critical discussion of the original Zionist project. In a climate where many liberal commentators sought to combine concern for the Palestinians with support for Israel, Prior insisted on the 'original sin' of 1948 (as against the fashionable theory that depicted Israel as 'falling from grace' subsequent to the occupation of the territories in 1967).

Michael seized every opportunity to express his support for the Palestinians in the popular media; on BBC Radio 4, on Radio Telefis Eirann, various American and other foreign radio stations and once, in 2000, on BBC TV to commentate on Pope John Paul II's visit to Bethlehem. He was also in demand at academic conferences at numerous venues in Britain, Ireland, the US, Finland, Russia. Jordan, Iran and, of course, in Jerusalem, at conferences organised by Sabeel, the Palestinian Liberation Theology institute set up by his friend, Canon Naim Ateek.

Throughout the last twenty five years of his life the magnetic attraction of the Holy Land for Michael continued unabated. From 1983 onwards he led numerous study tours and pilgrimages to Israel or to Israel, Jordan and the Occupied Territories. Those who participated in these were provided with the fruits of his biblical scholarship, his profound Christian spirituality and his political analysis in equal and undivided measure. During the first 1991 war in the Gulf, 'Operation Desert Storm', he was an active member of the 'Christian Coalition for Peace in the Gulf'. In the same year he was arrested during a peace march from Jerusalem to Amman. Israeli police were certainly nonplussed by this large white-haired Irishman singing the Psalms in Hebrew while he was detained in the police stations of Jericho. When they told him that he was allowed one telephone call he replied that he wanted to ring the Pope!

NEW TESTAMENT SCHOLAR

The demands of administration have often diverted departmental and faculty heads from personal scholarly research, let alone political activism. Not so with Michael Prior. Michael became dedicated to the proposition that academic scholarship could be both committed and serious. Always serious, the level of commitment increased with each of the four phases of Michael's scholarly work: first phase as a scholar of the historical critical approach to the Bible; the second as exegete and contextual theologian; the third phase moved him into the perspectives of contemporary liberation theology and the fourth into consideration of the ethical consequences of the land traditions of the Bible.

Michael established his reputation as a historical critic with the publication of his doctoral thesis in book form, in a prestigious series, in 1989. His *Paul the Letter Writer and the Second Letter to Timothy* received significant academic attention with reviews in some twenty international journals, in six languages, exerting considerable influence on New Testament discourse at an international level. It opened up new avenues of research into the nature of Paul as an epistolographer, as well as on appropriate methods of studying the Pauline letters. It alerted the scholarly community to the issues of co-authorship of most of the Pauline Letters, and pioneering the study of the implications of that reality for the concept of Pauline authorship, emphasising the distinctive nature and the epistolary context (e.g., ecclesial, or private) of each of the Pauline letters.

Several scholars applauded Michael's insistence on the necessity of separating 2 Timothy from the other Pastoral Letters and the implications of that insight were to have a major impact on the study of the Pastoral Epistles. This seminal work anticipated by two years the publication of Randolph Richards' *The Secretary in the Letters of Paul* (1991), and its findings stimulated Jerome Murphy-O'Connor's 1994 study, *Paul et l'Art Epistolaire* (*Paul the Letter Writer* 1995), and, as acknowledged by the author in a private communication, Lance Pierson's *In the Steps of Timothy* (1995). In the *Anchor Bible* Commentary on the Pastoral Epistles the late J D Quinn considered that Michael's translation and interpretation of 2 Tim 2.14 fundamentally changed the understanding of the epistolary context of the letter—a view accepted in the latest revision of the Jerusalem Bible. Other scholars applauded Michael's methodology and the boldness of his argument.[13]

CONTEXTUAL EXEGETE AND THEOLOGIAN

Michael's work as an exegete of the Bible was given a new direction by the context in which much of it was carried out—in the Holy Land. After his first study visit to the Holy Land in 1972, he spent 1983-84 in the École Biblique, returning there virtually every year since, and spending

---

[13] The work is referred to in George W Knight's *Commentary* (1992), and in Prof Frances Young's *Theology of the Pastorals* (1994), which applauds '... a fascinating case being made for re-reading it as a plea to Timothy to join Paul quickly because it looks as though he is going to be acquitted and the mission to Spain will be on the agenda after all. This involves some unconventional exegesis, of which much seems quite plausible' (p. 140). Philip Towner's *Commentary* (1994) refers to it in several places (e.g., pp. 15, 33, 35, 50).

his last sabbatical year at Bethlehem and Tantur in 1996-7. In his leadership and co-leadership of more than ten student study visits he combined archaeological, biblical and religious study with the ideals of Christian pilgrimage. As such he was an 'ongoing witness to the systemic oppression of the indigenous population, to "legitimise" which, appeal was made to the Bible.'[14] Michael responded to this by placing himself at the forefront, at the international level, in the development of a discourse challenging conventional views on the Holy Land.

In 1993 Michael was asked to be the liaison between the Steering Committee for the 1993 Cumberland Lodge International Seminar on *Christians in the Holy Land* and the Jerusalem Church. This involved meetings in Jerusalem with the three Patriarchs and other church leaders, theologians and academics. Michael went on to compose the preface and serve as chief editor of the published papers, including his own major article on 'Christian Pilgrimage to the Holy Land, in Antiquity and Today'. Launched both in London and Jerusalem, its publication led to the convening of further international conferences, stimulated the birth of a Palestinian Liberation Theology, and helped in the establishment of a specialised academic imprint (Melisende, London) which has published some twenty books on the subject since 1995. *Christians in the Holy Land* was reprinted in 1996, and an Arabic translation was published in 1998, in a strikingly interfaith enterprise. His 'Pilgrimage to the Holy Land, Yesterday and Today' in *Christians in the Holy Land* was described as 'the most comprehensive and authoritative account of the Christian Church in the Holy Land. Including the most recent research findings of sociologists, and the most up-to-date and informed comments of theologians and other scholars, it was to become an essential element in the study of religion in the Middle East.'[15]

LIBERATION THEOLOGIAN

In the words of his friend Peter Miano, it was in the context of Palestine

---

[14] Prior, unpublished papers, 2002.

[15] 'There is an absorbing essay on pilgrimage to the Holy Land, its history and purpose and how, in our own day, it could be carried out with more sensitivity towards the feelings of the indigenous Christians in Jerusalem and elsewhere in Palestine. Its author, Dr Michael Prior ... is among the pioneers of the "Living Stones" idea of pilgrimage, which encourages the traveller to be concerned more with people than with things.' (Michael Adams, *The Tablet*, 4 March 1995).

that Michael 'became disenchanted and impatient with the moral emptiness of mainstream biblical scholarship.' [16] With his reputation as a New Testament scholar firmly established Michael was anxious to move on to explore liberationist interpretations of Scripture.

The fruit of his new avenue of study was evident in articles in *Scripture Bulletin* and elsewhere, which focused on the Sermon of the Mount and on the 'preference for the poor' in Luke's Gospel. This latter was developed more fully in his *Jesus the Liberator, Nazareth Liberation Theology (Luke 4.16-30) (The Biblical Seminar 26)* in 1995. Sheffield Academic Press described it as a 'wide-ranging and radical enterprise, uniting a respect for the methods of New Testament study with a commitment to social change enlivened by its values ... Sensitive to the concerns of biblical scholarship, this challenging exegesis respects the faith perspective that the Word of God is alive and active, and calls for a response in every generation.' One review manuscript by Dr Kevin Rafferty of All Hallows, Dublin, commended the book for its 'outstanding contribution to contemporary contextual biblical exegesis'. Moving beyond the dominant historical-critical method Michael stressed the need for liberationist reader-criticism of the Gospel and for due attention to the contemporary political challenge of the teaching of Jesus. Reviewed in eight international journals, this interpretation had some influence in liberation theology circles and at the interface between biblical scholarship and contemporary society, as well as within the academy of biblical scholars.

MORAL CRITIC OF THE LAND TRADITIONS OF THE BIBLE

Michael continued to write both popular and scholarly material on Scripture but at the same time he was beginning to see the Bible as part of the problem of the world's ills rather than as part of their solution. 'This book should carry a health warning!' was his frequent comment. His solidarity with the Palestinians led him to feel increasingly uncomfortable with those parts of the Old Testament that seemed to

---

[16] Peter Miano, 'Toward a Reconsideration of Christian Zionism', *Living Stones Magazine*, Summer 2005.

provide precedent, and so to justify, the modern expulsion and oppression of the Palestinians.[17] It became clear to him that the narrative had fuelled virtually every form of militant colonialism emanating from Europe, providing allegedly divine legitimisation for Western colonisers in their zeal to implant 'outposts of progress' in 'the heart of darkness'. His article, 'The Bible as Instrument of Oppression' followed.[18] An examination of the existing scholarly writing on the subject of the land traditions of the Bible did not impress him. Convinced of the active or passive collusion of much Western biblical scholarship in the oppression of the Palestinian people, he developed this thesis in his *The Bible and Colonialism. A Moral Critique,* finally published in 1997. The original title was to have been *The Land of Israel, God and Morality* but the Sheffield Academic Press suggested a title that would reflect the wider discussion of the relationship between biblical hermeneutics and the appropriation of the land traditions of the Bible in history. Here he examined the way in which the narrative of the Exodus and the Conquest had been utilised to justify colonialism in Latin America, South Africa and, of course, Palestine. Working against a background of bullet-fire and in the shadow of tanks—the research was completed in Bethlehem-Jerusalem—added certain intensity to his research on the militaristic texts of the Bible.

In an unpublished letter to the Principal in 2003 Michael wrote that he had 'discovered' that the seminal studies of W D Davies were not only seriously defective but were, by his own admission, politically motivated. Walter Brueggemann had confessed that studies on 'the land' characteristically stop before they get to contemporary issues of land in modern Israel Palestine. Neglectful of moral considerations, much biblical investigation reflected the Euro-centric perspectives of virtually all western historiography, and in the case of W F Albright, traces of its racism. The Bible, for some, 'was *the idea* that *redeems the conquest of the earth.*'[19]

Aware of the challenge that his approach offered to the traditional understanding of the inspiration of Scripture Michael was

---

[17] 'In 1993 I felt obliged to revisit the biblical narrative from the perspective of "the land". What struck me most was that the divine promise of land was integrally linked with the mandate to exterminate the indigenous peoples. The implications of the existence of such moral dispositions, presented as mandated by the divinity, within a book which is canonised as Sacred Scripture, invited the most serious investigation' (Prior, unpublished papers, 2003).

[18] Prior, unpublished papers. 2003.

[19] Later Michael moved to extend the study of the relationship between the Bible and

nonetheless reluctant to suggest alternative ways in which problematic texts might be read. Trained, as he was in the historical critical method, Michael was uneasy with anything that smacked too much of allegorising approaches or interpretations that might not have been in the minds of the human authors.

In the early 1990s Michael proposed the establishment of a Middle East Centre, and later a Centre for Arabic, Islamic and Middle East Studies in St Mary's, with hopes of external funding. He also collaborated in efforts to establish Prophet Elias College, Ibillin, Galilee, on a university footing through Surrey University. The opportune time for such projects, however, had not arrived. Meanwhile he availed himself of the invitation to establish Religious Studies as an academic discipline in Bethlehem University.

In 1996-97, Michael took his second sabbatical year as visiting Professor of Theology in Bethlehem University. In the aftermath of the Oslo Agreement and the setting up of the Palestinian authority in Gaza and in parts of the West Bank Israel it was now possible for the first time since 1967 to train Palestinian pilgrimage and tour guides. Michael enthusiastically set about developing and teaching a programme to train Palestinian tour guides at Bethlehem University. During his tenure he created a network of co-operation with institutes in the Holy Land and designed and planned a programme of Religious Studies as a university degree course, unique in the Palestinian sector, and one of the few in the Arab world. At the same time he fulfilled the role of a scholar-in-residence at Tantur Ecumenical Institute for Theology, Jerusalem. Here in November of 1996 Michael gave a public lecture on 'The Moral Problem of the Land Traditions in the Bible', and managed to arouse some controversy when the then rector intervened to recommend commitment to academic 'balance' in Christian approaches to the Israeli-Palestinian conflict. Michael replied by asking whether this balanced approach should always apply in the same way between the oppressor and the oppressed, between the rapist and his victim. He also preached a partisan and highly political

---

colonialism to embrace the Irish context, the findings featuring in a preliminary way in a chapter for a work in Gaelic.*An Bíobla agus an Leatrom. Staidéir Comparáideach ar Úsáid an Bhíobla sa Pholaitíochtsa Mheiriceá Laidineach, in Éirinn, san Afraic Theas, agus sa Phalaistín* ('The Bible and Oppression. A Comparative Study of the Use of the Bible in Politics in Latin America, Ireland, South Africa and Palestine'). Maigh Nuad: An Sagart (2003).

homily in front of various ecclesiastical and academic dignitaries at the Christmas Midnight Mass at the University, delighting some and embarrassing others in equal measure.[20]

Michael's sabbatical was rudely interrupted by his being rushed into the Hadassah Hospital for urgent angiogram and angioplasty operations. Fortunately the treatment was a complete success and Michael was soon enjoying himself writing humorous verses about his operation[21] and amusing the Palestinian employees of the hospital by naming his bedpan and the urine bottle after two formerly terrorist Israeli prime ministers, 'Shamir' and 'Begin' respectively! On his return to Saint Mary's in testimony of his recovery he gave a concert of classical guitar music and songs in the music room. He had already e-mailed the Principal of Saint Mary's resigning as Head of Department so as to focus on his research and he now devoted much of the time in which he was not teaching to completing his historical and ethical critique to Zionism. This represented a partial shift in the focus of his scholarly interest away from the Bible towards the study of political ideology and modern history. However the appeal to biblical authority and precedent meant that his critique of Zionist ideologues constantly returned to the discussion to biblical themes.

Michael's magisterial work was finally published in 1999 under the title of *Zionism and the State of Israel: A Moral Inquiry*. In this work Michael located Political Zionism within the imperialist culture of 19th-century European nationalisms, rather than in the biblical narrative. The first part of the book traces the development of Zion from its secular origins in Herzl as an anti-religious movement in the 1890s to the sacred 'Zionism' endorsed today by Jewish and Christian religious right-wingers. The book goes on to examine the responses to Zionism by Christians of various stripes both before and after 1948 and 1967 and to critique the biblical justification for Zionism. Proceeding from a position of extreme scepticism towards the historicity of this part of the Old Testament the

---

[20] The text of his homily included the following: 'I pass by the checkpoint between Bethlehem and Jerusalem twice a day, with all of the privileges of being a foreigner, I boil with anger at the humiliation, degradation, and oppression which the colonizing enterprise of Zionism has inflicted on the people of this region. I wonder to myself how long this tyranny is going to last. Where is the Glory of God in all of this, and where does one taste some of God's peace?'

[21] The surgeon was a Dr Hisham and the verses reflecting on the experience of instruments expanding inside him was entitled 'Hisham's Balloon.'

book goes on to deplore the failure of biblical scholars to include the perspectives of the human rights discourse on their discussion of the biblical notion of the land tradition.[22] The main section of the book seeks to demonstrate that the expulsion of the Palestinians, far from being a consequence of the Nazi Holocaust or of the fortunes of war in 1948, had been planned by the founding fathers of Zionism from the beginning. The last section of the book addresses the myth that anti-Zionism is based upon anti-Semitism or anti-Judaism as it traces the history of Jewish anti-Zionism, both secular and religious. It exposes the foundational myths of the State of Israel and points to a way forward that does not espouse apartheid and ethnic cleansing. Historian, and author of three books on the subject, David McDowall considered this 'profoundly disturbing book' to be 'the best demolition job on the moral legitimisation of Israel that I have seen.'

Meanwhile, in February 2001, in collaboration with his friend and colleague, Dr Nur Masalha, a Palestinian historian resident in the UK and recently appointed Research Fellow in the Theology and Religious Studies Department at St Mary's College, Michael made the proposal to establish a centre for Holy Land Studies. This led to the establishment of the Holy Land Research Project with Michael as Chair and Nur Masalha as Director. After an initial small grant to establish the project in 2001, they managed, in 2003, to obtain a major grant of £167,313 from the Arts and Humanities Research Board to direct a research project, 'A Comparative Study of Jewish, Christian and Muslim Fundamentalist Perspectives on Jerusalem, and their Implications'. Dr Nur Masalha then became the senior Research worker, employing a further research worker resident in the Holy Land. Michael's first research fieldwork for this project was in Jerusalem in March 2003. The project convened workshops, conferences, and sponsored lectures and led to the establishment of an internationally applauded and refereed journal, *Holy Land Studies, A Multidisciplinary Journal* (Continuum), of which he became editor.

This multi-disciplinary journal which appears twice yearly draws upon expertise from various disciplines including history, culture, politics,

---

[22] One sympathetic Evangelical commentator comments that 'It behoves those who take a more conservative approach to biblical scholarship and historiography to offer an equally robust refutation of the Zionist reading. However they are more likely than Prior to be able to engage in debate biblical literalists who defend a Zionist reading.' http://www.christchurch-virginiawater.co.uk/articles/zionismprior.htm.

religion, archaeology, sociology and discusses a range of topics including the issue of 'two nations' and 'three faiths'; conflicting Israeli and Palestinian perspectives; social and economic conditions; Palestine in history and today; ecumenism and interfaith relations; modernisation, religious revivalisms and fundamentalisms; Zionism and Post-Zionism; the 'new historiography' of Israel and Palestine, etc. The uniqueness of this journal lies in the fact that it brings together diversified discourses that are conventionally kept separate.[23]

The first issue of *Holy Land Studies* appeared in 2002. Ilan Pappé of Haifa University and Yasir Suleiman of Edinburgh joined Michael on a small working editorial board together with Nur Masalha as Associate Editor and Book Review Editor. A much larger advisory board of distinguished international scholars and writers included Edward Said, William Dalrymple, Salim Tamari, Bernard Sabella and Noam Chomsky. The first issue included articles on Post-Zionism, the two-state solution, Maimonides, and an article by Michael Prior entitled 'Ethnic Cleansing and the Bible: A Moral Critique'. Subsequent subjects discussed in the pages of the journal have included Israel's Bedouin population, competing Israeli and Palestinian historical narratives, appreciations of the work of Edward Said after his death in 2003, Christian, Jewish and Muslim fundamentalisms, the situation of Palestine refugees in Lebanon and Jordan, Anti-Zionism and Anti-Semitism, exploration of parallels between Israel/ Palestine and the situations in South Africa and Northern Ireland and, finally, several scholarly appreciations of the life and thought of Michael Prior after his death in 2004.

The uniqueness of this journal lies in the fact that it brings together diversified discourses and disciplines that are conventionally kept separate. The only unifying factor is the historical or geographical link with the Holy Land of Israel Palestine. The subjects discussed in the articles so far are quite diverse but there is an understandable preponderance of topics relating more directly to the present political conflict. Under its new editor, Nur Masalha, we can expect it to

[23] Other members of the Editorial Committee were Ilan Pappé (Haifa) and Yasir Suleiman (Edinburgh). And the International Advisory Board included Edward Said (New York), Dan Rabinowitz (Jerusalem), Timothy Niblock (Exeter), Naseer Aruri (Massachusetts), David Burrell (Notre Dame), Thomas L Thompson (Copenhagen), Thomas Mullins (Harvard), Samih Farsoun (Washington DC), Rosemary Radford Ruether (Chicago) and Noam Chomsky (Massachusetts). After Michael's death, Nur Masalha became editor as well as Director of the Holy Land Research Project.

continue on the intellectually rigorous and wide-ranging course begun in collaboration with Michael Prior.

At the time of his death in July 2004 Michael had begun to prepare a book on Christian Zionism (to be co-edited with Nur Masalha) with the proposed title of *Holy Land, Unholy Alliance. Christian Zionism, the US, and the State of Israel* as well as a major study on *The Bible and Zionism* that he has hoped to be ready for the press in 2005.

A FEARLESS CAMPAIGNER

Michael once wrote, revealingly, 'I don't think I have fears. I don't expect to meet superpersons more problematic than the self I perceive.'[24] Michael's absence of fear served him well in his commitment to the cause of the Palestinians, which aroused consistent opposition, particularly over the last fourteen years of his life. Fortunately Michael thrived on opposition. Knowing them to be unfair, he shrugged off imputations of anti-Semitism. In 1990 an article in *The Jewish Chronicle*[25] identified Living Stones as being at the core of a campaign 'driving a wedge between the Church and Israel.' The author of the article interviewed Michael in his office at Saint Mary's describing him as 'a Cork-born, white haired and ostensibly genial academic.' In the course of the interview Michael shocked the interviewer by avoiding the word 'Israel', referring to 'the Land' instead. The only exception being when he referred to Israel as either 'the lapdog of the US or its rottweiler'. According to the hostile account of the conversation he had said this 'with the air of having coined something profound.' He then went on to give his account of a meeting in the Houses of Parliament of the Israel Advisory Group of the Council of Christians and Jews to which he had been invited 'apparently by mistake'. 'Unsurprisingly', the interviewer comments 'his account of the meeting differs from that of the pro-Israeli participants. Their recollection is that they spent the entire session defending Zionism while Prior accused them of being tools of the Israeli establishment. Asked for his opinion of the CCJ, Prior produced a five-page memorandum written,

---

[24] Unpublished notes made during a Summer School of the London Institute of Psychosynthesis at Stowe School in 1988.

[25] Jenni Frazer, 'Driving a Wedge: the Church and Israel,' *Jewish Chronicle*, 11 May 1990, 30-31.

he said, for his own purposes as an aide-memoire. The Israel Advisory Group he said 'appeared to see itself not only as an uncritical supporter of the policies of the State of Israel but as a highly organised pressure group ...'

In his account of the Israel Advisory Group meeting to his friends Michael claimed that he had been scandalised to find that its main business had been concerned with how to silence embarrassing critics of Israel in the religious media. *The Jewish Chronicle* article, together with the fact that he had been dis-invited from the committee and that it was then suspended, all occasioned him mischievous amusement. For years afterwards he loved to describe himself as 'ostensibly genial' and was delighted to think that Zionists saw a group like Living Stones, with no financial resources whatever, as being ideologically significant.

Michael was always impervious to accusations of anti-Semitism, knowing them to be false. Jews who were active in the peace movement excited Michael's admiration and he had a particular regard for anti-Zionist Jewish intellectuals, whether secular or religious. In the early eighties he collaborated with the anti-Zionist Israeli activist Dr Uri Davis, then living in London, and invited him to join the committee of the newly formed committee of Living Stones. In the late 1980s he was particularly impressed by the views of the Jewish American writer and academic Marc Ellis, offering him friendship and Vincentian hospitality when he visited London.[26] In his *Zionism and the State of Israel* Michael also drew on the arguments of other Jewish scholars, including Chaim Bermant, Noam Chomsky, Israel Shahak, Stan Cohen and others. Later in 2001, when forming the editorial board of the new interdisciplinary Holy Land Studies, he invited the celebrated Israeli dissident academic Ilan Pappé to serve actively on the editorial board.

Although friends could sometimes hurt Michael, he relished taking on institutional Goliaths. In 2002, the Jesuit Holy Cross College in Massachusetts withdrew a lecture invitation. Writing to the president of the college on his return he reproached the college for preventing him from contributing to a discussion on critical issues of Israel-Palestine: '...

---

[26] Ellis argued that Jews ran the danger of becoming 'everything we loathed about our oppressors' (*Tablet* 27.2.1988). Ellis spoke movingly of the ecumenical bargain by which Jews traded silence about past persecution in return for Christian silence over present violations of Palestinian rights.

the American public is singularly seriously, misinformed. Part of the reason for such misinformation is the failure of academic leaders, religious leaders, and the media to address critical questions of justice and peace in the region. Rather than give a lead in such matters, your Church- and College-institution has submitted to intimidation from people hostile to the discussion of historical truth, justice, and academic freedom, issues, which are a feature of my work. In so doing, your College has, in my estimation, betrayed its religious and academic mission in the interests of conformity to external bodies, which have no such aspirations.'[27]

Michael found further irony in the fact that it was a Jesuit-led institution dedicated to the veneration of the Holy Cross that had withdrawn the invitation. In a letter of protest Michael contrasted the College's behaviour in this matter with the heroic witness to truth, justice and freedom exemplified by the Jesuit martyr, Ignacio Ellacuría. 'Adapting the exhortation of St Ignatius, your Founder, who exhorted his disciples to go on their knees at the foot of the Cross and ask, "What have I done, what am I doing, what will I do for Christ crucified?", Fr Ellacuría urged Christians today to reflect on the conditions of the poor and ask, "What have I done, what am I doing for the people on the cross, and what will I do to uncrucify them, and have them raised?" It is such sentiments that motivate me in my pursuit of truth and justice, in a presumed atmosphere of academic and ecclesiastical freedom.'[28]

Michael's research has emphasised the moral imperative within biblical and theological studies, pursuing significant truth-questions, with a sensitivity to, and moral concern for the social consequences of the use of the biblical narrative as an instrument of oppression. As Michael expressed it 'I have engaged in biblical research with the spirit of what Elisabeth Schüssler Fiorenza recently calls an "ethics of accountability", i.e., with a concern for exposing "the ethical consequences of the biblical text and its meanings", especially when these have promoted various forms of oppression, not least through "colonial dehumanisation", and for making their findings known to a wider public' (*Rhetoric and Ethic. The Politics of Biblical Studies*, 1999, pp. 28-29).

---

[27] Letter to the Very Revd Michael C McFarland, SJ, President, College of the Holy Cross, Worcester, Massachusetts, 1 December 2002. (http://www.al-bushra.org/hedchrch/jesuit.html)..

[28] *Ibid.*

The academic strength of Michael's argument and his tenacious courage in giving expression to unwelcome ideas not only aroused opposition, it also helped to win him an internationally respected place in academic discourse.[29]

This made fact made his last major controversy the harder to understand. Since 1972 his major contribution had included his four monographs, four books that he had edited or co-edited, contributed chapters to seventeen books, and written numerous articles in a variety of journals, national and international, eleven biblical-liturgical articles and commentaries, and some thirty popular articles in national and international journals. He had also reviewed numerous scholarly books in national and international journals, edited two journals and served on the editorial board of three other publications.

On his resignation as Head of Department, Michael began to plan for the setting up of a research centre on Holy Land Studies at Saint Mary's and made application for the status of a Professor of the University of Surrey to head up this project. His application was supported by Professor Jerome Murphy-O'Connor, OP, of the École Biblique in Jerusalem, Professor James O'Connell of the Bradford School of Peace Studies and Philip Davies, Professor of Biblical Studies at Sheffield. Astonishingly Michael's work was considered too partisan and the initial application was turned down. In his lengthy correspondence with the College and University authorities Michael correctly pointed out that his research had more than adequately taken into account a wide range of evidence and countervailing perspectives in his work. Correctly he suspected that he had been expressing a moral critique of *apartheid* in South Africa or human rights violations in the Soviet Union there would have been no such problem. However, what had proved unacceptable was criticism of Israeli policies and, even more fundamentally, of Zionism itself. Eventually Michael was able to vindicate his reputation against those unable to distinguish between unscholarly partisanship and morally committed scholarship. The awarding of the professorship just a few months before his death involved the recognition that he had brought the Church, no less than

---

[29] Professor Heikki Räisänen, New Testament professor at the University of Helsinki, estimated Michael to be 'one of the most important scholars in today's Britain', and who in singling out his work in the context of Israel, insisted that 'a moral evaluation of biblical texts and of their interpretation is indispensable today.' *Beyond New Testament Theology*, 2000, 207.

the Academy, into dialogue with his view. His work had become well known within all sectors of the Christian community in the Holy Land also, and widely known internationally among scholars and other writers on the Holy Land.

Sadly the full flowering of his research projects would remain unfulfilled. Michael was up a ladder in his garden, pruning a tree when he fell to the ground. His cleaner found him at about 2pm on 22 July 2004. He had suffered a severe head injury and the inquest, held on 15 November, returned a verdict of accidental death.

The unexpected suddenness of his death compounded the sense of great loss experienced by the many people who loved and esteemed him. Among the many tributes that were offered the things most frequently mentioned were his gift of friendship, his moral tenacity and his unwavering commitment to the cause of the oppressed. Michael was also a considerable biblical scholar and an acute political historian. In both areas he raised more questions than he answered. While it is legitimate to describe Michael as a liberation theologian his expertise lay primarily in Scripture rather than in systematic theology. Likewise, despite his passion for political argument, Michael was not a politician. As with his discussion of questions of biblical hermeneutics, he died without offering practical solutions to the political issues that he raised. Michael often criticised what he regarded as the sometimes morally and politically 'shambolic' failures of the Palestinian leadership. However, in April 2004 he visited Ramallah and clearly felt great pleasure at being photographed with Arafat, expressing his personal solidarity with him in his suffering and isolation. Had Arafat asked Michael to give him practical advice on the way forward it is unlikely he would have received much in the way of specific practicable advice. Michael was a prophet but he had little interest in the kinds of compromise involved in the practice of politics as the 'art of the possible'.[30]

Despite his radicalism and his detailed knowledge of post-colonial theory he had very little background in Marx, Marxism, or other radical social analysis that one might have expected in a liberation theologian. His considerable strengths lay in the areas of historical and textual criticism and in the ability to engage in an ethical critique of injustice. Had he lived another ten or twenty years he might have tied up

---

[30] 'Politics is the art of the possible.' Otto Von Bismarck, remark, August 11 1867.

some of the loose ends in his theology of biblical inspiration or political analysis. The chances are that he would not. When challenged he would often argue that his task was to identify the problem and he was happy to leave it to others to propose the answers. By temperament he was suited to the role of prophet rather than of reconciler or political fixer. Nevertheless his prophetic inspiration was one that derived directly from Old Testament prophets and from the one who preached good news to the poor in the synagogue of Nazareth.

A few weeks before his death the eighteenth International Catholic-Jewish Liaison Committee met in Buenos Aires and, among other things, expressed the view that anti-Zionism and anti-Semitism were synonymous terms. It also referred to the 'struggle against terrorism' in a way that completely ignored the context of the injustice suffered by the Palestinians. Michael immediately penned an article for *The Tablet*. His final article in *The Tablet* appeared some twelve days after his death.[31] It seems likely that, in the interests of 'balance', the piece might have been refused, but in the context of Michael's tragic accident it was decided to include his article. Predictably, Michael's comments excited a heated correspondence in the letter columns of the paper—an outcome that Michael would have relished had he lived!

His last words to me in a telephone conversation the day before his death were that what was needed was a new forum for Jewish-Christian dialogue that did not involve political pre-conditions but allowed anti-Zionist Jews and anti-Zionist Christians to be party to the conversation. 'Go for it! We'll do it!' he said. Not everyone who mourned Michael shared Michael's faith or his politics. But Michael's faith and Michael's friendship were robustly inclusive. He was the kind of Catholic who was at ease with Christians of other traditions, with believers in Judaism and Islam, with agnostics and atheists. He would be happy for everyone to follow him as far down the road as they are able, preaching good news for the poor and liberation for captives: 'Go for it! We'll do it.'

Michael Prior, priest, scholar and activist: born Cork, 15 March 1942; ordained priest 1969; Senior Lecturer in Theology and Religious Studies, St Mary's College, Strawberry Hill 1977-97, Head of Department 1987-97, Principal Lecturer 1997-2002, Senior Research Fellow 2002-04, Professor of Bible and Theology 2004; died Osterley, Middlesex, 21 July 2004.

---

[31] This article appeared in 'A Disaster for Dialogue,' *The Tablet*, 31 July 2004.

ACKNOWLEDGEMENTS

On behalf of the Living Stones Trust I would like to express appreciation to the Provincial of the Congregation of the Mission (Province of Ireland, England and Scotland), Father Kevin O'Shea, for his encouragement and help in this publication. Thanks are also due to all those other Vincentian fathers who have helped with information and reminiscences of Michael as a member of the Vincentian community.

Particular thanks are due to Michael's sister, Nuala Mulcare, and to his brother James Prior for their help with information on Michael's early life and to the former principal of Saint Mary's College, Father Desmond Beirne CM, Dr Paddy Walsh of the Institute of Education, University of London, Dr Nur Masalha, Julia Head and the other many friends and former colleagues from the years spent by Michael at Saint Mary's College.

Appreciation is especially due to the Prior family for making this publication possible through its generosity in inaugurating the Michael Prior Memorial Fund to be administered by the Living Stones Trust. Finally I wish to express my gratitude to Leonard Harrow of Melisende Publishing and to David Toorawa, vice-chair of Living Stones, for their work in helping to prepare the text for publication.

REVISITING LUKE[1]

> *This early, rather technical, article illustrates Michael's*
> *engagement with the historical critical method as applied to Luke*
> *and the synoptic question.* (Scripture Bulletin, 1976)

At the end of the last century, at a time when many physicists believed that all of the laws of physics had been discovered, Michelson concluded:

> The more important fundamental laws and facts of physical science have all been discovered, and these are so firmly established that the possibility of their ever being supplanted in consequence of new discoveries is exceedingly remote ... Our future discoveries must be looked for in the sixth place of decimals.[2]

Little did he suspect that within twenty years the world would witness epoch making discoveries of the nature of matter, and widespread application of these discoveries to our everyday lives. Up to very recently there was an analogous confidence in the area of Gospel studies. Beginners

---

[1] The main works cited in this article are:

What is a Gospel? The Genre of the Canonical Gospels, by Charles H Talbert. Pp. xi + 147 *(SPCK,* London, 1978).

The Evangelists' Calendar. A Lectionary Explanation of the Development of Scripture, by M D Goulder. Pp. xiv + 334 *(SPCK,* London, 1978).

Tradition and Design in Luke's Gospel. A Study in Early Christian Historiography, by Jothn Drury. Pp. xiii + 208 (DLT, London, 1976).

The Birth of the Messiah. A Commentary on the Infancy Narratives in Matthew and Luke, by Raymond E. Brown, 8.S. Pp. 594 (Geoffrey Chapman, London, 1977).

An Adult Christ at Christmas. Essays on the Three Biblical Christmas Stories, by Raymond E Brown, SS. Pp. viii + 50 (The Liturgical Press, Collegeville, Minnesota, 1978).

Perspectives on Luke-Acts, ed., by Charles H Talbert. Pp. ix + 269 (T & T Clark, Edinburgh, 1978).

The Gospel of Luke. A Commentary on the Greek Text, by I Howard Marshall. Pp. 928 (The New International Greek Testament Commentary, The Paternoster Press, Exeter, 1978).

[2] Quoted in F K Richtmyer, E H Kennard, J N Cooper, *Introduction to Modern Physics* (New York, 1969), p. 43.

learned very quickly that their initiation rite into NT scholarship demanded a profession of faith in the dogmas: (a) Mark was the first written Gospel; (b) this was used by Matthew and Luke, but independently of each other; (c) Matthew and Luke both used another source, Q, for about 200 of their verses, mostly dealing with sayings of Jesus; (d) that a gospel is an unique literary genre in the ancient world, and has nothing in common with Greco-Roman biographies in particular; (e) that the material of the gospels consists of separate units of the deeds and words of Jesus as preserved in the early communities, and that these were gather into written records and finally used by the authors of the gospels, and that by examining the way the authors used their sources we can discover the different theologies of the authors. It is becoming increasingly clear that the foundations on which this received wisdom rests are much less secure than ever suspected.

LUKE A BIOGRAPHY?

In the nineteenth century there were several attempts to get behind the Christ of the Christian Creed to the Jesus of first century Palestine, to recover his message, to uncover his actions, to compose a 'Life of Jesus' from the material available in the gospels. The advent of Form Criticism, with its concentration on the separable elements of the gospel material made it appear that the most one could see of Jesus was a series of snapshots from his life which one had to interpret without the help of details of time and occasion.[3] Schweitzer summed up the situation in this celebrated passage:

> Formerly it was possible to book through-tickets at the supplementary-psychological-knowledge office which enabled those travelling in the interests of the Life-of-Jesus construction to use express trains, thus avoiding the inconvenience of having to stop at every little station, change, and run the risk of missing their connection. This ticket office is now closed. There is a station at the end of each section of the narrative, and the connections are not guaranteed.[4]

---

[3] The metaphor was used by F W Beare in his lecture, 'The Quest of the Historical Jesus: Resumed or Bypassed?' at the Sixth International Congress on Biblical Studies, Oxford, 1978.

[4] *The Quest of the Historical Jesus* (ET, third edition, London, 1954), pp. 331f.

Bultmann's scepticism about ever being able to recover from the gospels even the faintest picture of the deeds and words of Jesus as he lived in Galilee and Judea in the years AD 30-33 frustrated the hope of ever being able to view the gospels as biographies in any sense.[5]

Against this background, C H Talbert's designation of the gospels as biographies in the Greco-Roman sense marks a departure from the present-day consensus. To adapt C F Evans' metaphor[6] the Alexandrian librarian would have catalogued Mark and John with the Type B biographies which aim at dispelling 'a false image of the teacher' and provide 'a true model to follow' (p. 94). They would share a shelf with Xenophon's *Memorabilia,* Philodemus' *Life of Epicurus,* Philostratus' *Life of Appolonius of Tyana* and Porphyry's *Life of Pythagoras* (from among the lives of the philosophers), and Isocrates' *Busiris,* Nicolaus of Damascus' *Life of Augustus,* Tacitus' *Agricola,* and Pseudo-Callisthenes' *Life of Alexander* (from among the lives or rulers). Mark, then, presents a true picture of the church's Saviour for the disciples to follow, and 'was written in terms of the myth of immortals' (p. 134), while John wrote his account in terms of a descending-ascending redeemer figure. Matthew's Gospel would have been catalogued among the *Type E* biographies which validate, or provide the key to the teaching of the philosopher or ruler, and would be on the same shelf as Porphyry's *Life of Plotinus,* Andronicus' *Life of Aristotle,* and Philo's *Life of Moses,* all of the which are concerned with the teaching of the master and the exegesis of that teaching. An assistant to the librarian might, perhaps, be forgiven for classifying Matthew with *Type B* biographies, since it also is concerned to protect the true image of the Church's Lord. Finally, Luke-Acts, because it deals with the life of Jesus (gospel) and his continued presence in the work of his successors (Acts) would join, among others, the anonymous 3rd-century BC *Life of*

---

5   'I do indeed think that we can know almost nothing concerning the life and personality of Jesus, since the early Christian sources show no interest in either, are moreover fragmentary and often legendary' (*Jesus and the Word,* ET, London, 1958, p. 14). This historical scepticism, however, was not extended to include the message of Jesus, but even here 'we have no absolute assurance that the exact words of this oldest layer (i.e., what is left of his sayings after the critic has excluded Hellenistic elements, and items added in by the church) were really spoken by Jesus' (*ibid.* p. 17), for even this may be the result of a complicated historical process.

6   C F Evans, *The New Testament Gospels* (1965), p. 7fl, asks how a 2nd-century librarian in Alexandria would classify Mark. Librarians, however, are not infallible judges of genre: not so long ago a book entitled *The Paschal Mystery* was catalogued with the novels in a city library!

Aristotle, and Diogenes Laertius' *Lives of Eminent Philosophers (Type D).*
Talbert, therefore, situates the gospels very firmly and very precisely in
the literary category of ancient biography—the framework which gave
the canonical gospels their form and structure.[7] Already in 1915 C W
Votaw[8] attempted to place the canonical gospels within the category of
ancient biography,[9] but his presentation of possible Greco-Roman parallels
to the gospels was not enthusiastically received[10] and it is only in very
recent times that the question is being opened up again.[11] H Talbert
attributes the neglect to the influence of Barth with his stress on the
transcendental qualities of the gospels as the unrivalled Word of God, but
more especially to Bultmann who denied significant generic links between
the gospels and Greco-Roman biographies, because, (a) the gospels are
'mythical', whereas the biographies treat their subjects in human terms;
(b) the gospels are cultic, in fact 'expanded cult legends' which derive
from a community gathered in worship, whereas ancient biographies
were simply literary works with no connection with worship; (c) the
gospels emanate from a world-negating community, whereas the
biographies come from world-affirming communities. Talbert argues in
turn that Bultmann is wrong each time, and that the canonical gospels in
their outer form (mythical structure), their function or setting (cult) and
their world attitude are sufficiently close to Greco-Roman biographies
that they can be classified together.

---

[7] The other two types into which Talbert classifies ancient biographies do not concern us
here: *Type A* which sets out to provide the reader with a pattern to copy, and *Type C* which
discredits the subject.

[8] Originally published in the *American Journal of Theology, vol.* 19 (1915), pp. 54-73, 217-249,
and reprinted in the Facet Books Biblical Series-27 (Fortress Press), Philadelphia, 1970),
pp. viii + 64.

[9] 'The earlier Dialogues of Plato, in their biographical material, correspond in a general way
to the Gospel of Matthew and Luke ... A limited measure of parallelism may be said to
obtain between the First Book of Xenophon's *Memorabilia* and the Gospels of Matthew
and Luke, while the other books of the *Memorabilia,* and the later Dialogues of Plato ...
sustain a tenuous parallelism with the Gospel of John.' Votaw, *op. cit.,* p. 249 (62).

[10] E.g., Bultmann, *The History of the Synoptic Tradition* (ET, Oxford, 1963): 'What analogies (to
the form of the Gospel) can be suggested? There are none in the Greek Tradition; for
there is no point in considering ... the Hellenistic biography' (p. 371f), at which he
relegates Votaw to the third place in a footnote of three items. Further, he concludes: 'The
analogies that are to hand serve only to throw the uniqueness of the Gospel into still
stronger relief ... It is thus an original creation of Christianity' (p. 373f).

[11] Moses Hades and Morton Smith, *Heroes and Gods* (New York, 1965); several other tentative
studies noted by Talbert on p. 22.

On the face of it is difficult to maintain that the early church had to invent its own genre, quite unrelated to contemporary patterns, to communicate its experience of Jesus[12]—after all it did not invent the art of epistle writing or the genre of apocalyptic. Is it not impossible to communicate in an altogether unfamiliar literary genre? However, one must have considerable reservations about Talbert's methods and results. Is Bultmann's triple criterion of similarity in form, use, and attitude sufficient for assigning works to the same literary category? Even if a case can be made for similarities in these areas, are not the differences more obvious? Much of Talbert's evidence is impressive, but certainly not as convincing as he makes out: in the first part of his argument, 'Mythical Structure-I' the ancient authors he cites are much later than the canonical gospels, and his dealing with this difficulty is unsatisfactory (p. 43); the differences between what is known of early Christian worship and the cultic setting of the Greco-Roman biographies are far greater than their similarities; the section on the world-negating/affirming aspect is the weakest part of the book-in any case two works of similar world-attitude ought not to be put in the same literary category for this reason alone. The book is thought-provoking, but in the course of reading it one would never guess that the Gospels had anything to do with a Jewish background.

LUKE A LECTIONARY?

Michael Goulder more than compensates for Talbert's neglect of the Jewish background to the gospels. His *The Evangelists' Calendar is* the most exciting contribution to biblical scholarship in many decades. In his view the designation of a gospel as a book is the basic error.[13] Rather it is a

---

[12] H Riesenfeld, *The Gospel Tradition and its Beginnings* (London, 1957: 'In the history of religion and of literature alike a Gospel is something wholly unique . . . To the Gospels as a whole there is no known parallel or analogy' (p. 5). Perrin *(What is Redaction Criticism?* London, 1970): 'The literary form 'Gospel' is the unique product of early Christianity and as such must be held to be characteristic of a distinctive element in early Christian faith' (p. 75).

[13] With characteristic humour—a feature of the book—Goulder dismisses Schürmann's suggestion that Theophilus paid for the publishing of Luke-Acts, and Dibelius' view that Luke wrote with an eye to the book-market, as well as to the Christian community, thus: 'Did one walk down the Argiletum and say to a bookseller, 'Good morning. A copy of Horace's *Satires,* please. Oh, and have you *The Acts of the Apostles?* By Dr. Lucas, of

collection of reflections of a Christian preacher recording events and teachings from the life of Jesus in a sequence determined by the material of the synagogue-church readings on the Sundays or feasts. It comes as no surprise that the early Christian assemblies recalled at Passover time the events of the Passion and Death of Jesus, and at Easter the Resurrection Appearances, and that the Apocalyptic Discourses were used in the period leading up to Passover. Goulder's argument, however, is not so much that these communities used the Gospel material in this way, but that the liturgical recalling of the life of Jesus was the very womb out of which each of synoptic gospels was born: 'If Luke's Gospel may quite likely have been read as a series of stories, could it have been developed as a series of stories?' (p. 6). His conclusions concerning the origin of the synoptic gospels are that:

(a) Mark made the first attempt to provide a liturgical series of readings, beginning in the October New Year, and running as far as Easter;

(b) Matthew filled out this half year, from Easter to Easter, and in so doing concentrated on the Jewish Festivals of Pentecost (The Sermon on the Mount, Mt. 5-7), New Year (Mission and Repentance Discourse, Mt 10-11), Atonement (Forgiveness and Jonah, Mt. 12), Tabernacles (Harvest Parables, Mt. 13), Dedication (Transfiguration and Church Law, Mt. 17-19), and Passover (Pharisees, Readiness for Parousia, Mt. 23, 24-25), the intervening chapters being the readings for the Sabbaths;

(c) Luke, who in his Prologue acknowledges that 'many', or 'others' *(polloi)*, including at least Mark and Matthew, had undertaken to compile a narrative of the deeds and words of Jesus from eye-witness and preaching sources, set out to provide in *liturgical* order an annual series of readings for his gentile church. This was superior to Mark's attempt which ran for only half the year (since 'there is no sale for a six-and-a-half-month lectionary', p. 245), and more relevant than Matthew's with its conservative Jewish-Christian emphasis on the Jewish feasts with their eight-day sets of readings.

Corinth'?' (p. 1). However, the importance of preaching for the formation of the Gospel material was so emphasized by Dibelius that I H Marshall can say: 'In the beginning was the sermon' is an apt summary of his approach' *(Luke: Historian and Theologian,* Exeter, 1970, p. 49)-in fact, this work, with its judgement very favourable to the reliability of Luke as historian, is ignored by Goulder in line with his disinterest in what Jesus said and did.

The following, then, are the stages which yielded our canonical Gospels:

> (i) from the year after the Crucifixion the Church remembered the Passion of Jesus at Passovertide—that the Passion accounts were the first to take shape is generally recognized;
>
> (ii) the preceding Sabbaths were used to recall Jesus' prophecies of return-Christ's return was expected at Passover;
>
> (iii) there was complete freedom for the remainder of the liturgical year, with the choice of Jesus—material being suggested by the readings from the Law and the Prophets;
>
> (iv) since new converts were to be received at Eastertime, it became necessary to have suitable readings and instructions, beginning from around the feast of Dedication, 'material on the Christian Way, told in the context of Jesus' journey up to Jerusalem' (p. 245);
>
> (v) the felt need to provide a continuous story of Jesus' ministry was answered by Mark in Rome—and he was familiar with the Petrine traditions. Matthew and Luke improved his scheme as explained above.

So much for the exciting conclusion. Goulder recognizes that his thesis takes a big leap, but suggests that sometimes scholarship advances by the consideration of big leaps and soaring possibilities (p. ix). His thesis demands that we know the themes of the Jewish festival readings, and the readings of the intervening Sabbaths in the 1st century AD;[14] that the churches of the evangelists celebrated the Jewish feasts and used the synagogue lections; that some external check must be found for his divisions of the Gospel material; and, finally, having fixed a gospel pericope to a particular feast day or Sabbath there be 'striking correlations' between the synagogue reading and the Jesus-pericope in the case of the festivals, and 'much more than random correlation' for Sabbath readings.

---

[14] That there was a fixed cycle, annual or triennial, of readings at the New Testament period is denied by M McNamara: 'To postulate any cycle, be it annual, triennial or of some other sort, for Palestine goes beyond the evidence at our disposal. Theories based on any such cycle are founded on very insecure premises' (*Targum and Testament,* Shannon, 1972, p. 47). According to le Déaut (*The Spirituality of Judaism,* Religious Experience Series, vol. 11, R Le Déaut, A Jaubert and K Hruby, Wheathampstead, 1977, p. 36) the cycle became fixed only in the 2nd and 3rd centuries AD.

Right down to the 2nd century AD, according to Goulder, the Liturgy of the Word in the synagogue consisted of a reading from the Torah followed by its Aramaic paraphrase, then from the Prophets, etc., and a corresponding Targum, lasting 'perhaps an hour and a quarter in all, spent listening', which, he says, is wearisome and unedifying (p. 52f.). The solution to this difficulty was to spread the readings over a three-year cycle in place of the one-year. If this argument cannot stand, the whole thesis collapses, for it demands that the synagogue readings were precisely fixed in an annual cycle which began in the month Nisan, our mid-March to mid-April.[15]

Goulder next divides Luke's Gospel into 84 sections, being guided in the task by the divisions of Codex Alexandrinus, Bodmer P[75] and the logic of the gospel. Following Matthew's example Luke celebrated Easter on the third Sunday of the year (after 14 Nisan), the Easter Octave on the fourth, and began with the material of 1: 15-25 on the fifth Sunday of the year, for which the annual cycle reading was Gen. 23-25: 18. The Torah reading (Sidra) on the sixth Sunday was Gen. 25: 19-28: 9, and Luke shows the fulfilment of this Sidra (with Esau and Jacob struggling in womb of Rebekah, etc.), with John leaping in the womb of Elizabeth (Lk 1: 26-56) —the only two instances in the Bible of children leaping in the womb. There is an impressive correlation of content, and coincidence of names, rare words and phrases for Sidroth 2, and 4-12 'which it would be rash to ascribe to accident' (p. 82). On the other hand the absence of a Lukan parallel for Sidra 1 (Gen 1-6: 8) and 3 (Gen 17-17) is an embarrassment for the lectionary theory, but then Goulder make no claim that the reconstructed lectionary cycle 'explains every

---

[15] Not everyone will be convinced by this refutation of Ch. Perrot's evidence for the late fixing of the standard triennial and annual cycles at about 200 AD *(La Lecture de la Bible dans la Synagogue,* Hildesheim, 1973), and when he refers to L Morris' *(The New Testament and the Jewish Lectionaries,* London, 1964) demolition of Aileen Guilding's triennial-cycle theory *(The Fourth Gospel and Jewish* Worship, Oxford, 1960), he ought to have pointed out that Morris rejects all theories based on a fixed cycle in NT times: 'the fundamental reason for postulating a number of different cycles is that the evidence is not clear enough to establish any one cycle as generally accepted ... The evidence as we have it seems to indicate that the early Christians were more like Free Churchmen (who read from the O and NT regularly, but do not use a lectionary) than those who follow a lectionary ... at the beginning of the Christian era there were no fixed lessons ... It is scarcely an exaggeration to say that everyone who has written on this subject seems to have a different idea from everyone else ... Their handling of the evidence in some of its aspects will seems to most to be more ingenious than convincing' (Morris, p. 19, 24, 25, 26, 47).

detail of the structure of each of the three Synoptic Gospels' (p. 18). He claims to have a plausible explanation for Luke's deviation from Mark's order: having followed Mark's order diligently from 1: 1-15 (Lk 3: 14: 15), Luke 4: 16-30 promotes Mark's account of the rejection at Nazareth (Mk 6: 1-6). The reason: the thirteenth Sidra is Ex 1-6: 1 which describes Moses' forty years in Midian, his being sent to his people and their disobeying him (cf. Acts 7), and what more suitable 'echo' than Jesus, another Moses, being rejected by his own. Luke continues to follow Mark's order, with one small reversal, from Lk 4: 31-6: 19, after which he interpolates his Sermon on the Plain, the cure of the Centurion's slave and the raising of the widow's son at Nain (so suitable for the beginning of the New Year Festival which is about to begin, Lk 7: 18-35 being the New Year material), and then, so suitably for Atonement Day the story of the woman whom Jesus forgave (Lk 7: 36-50), echoing Lev 16-18, the Atonement Day Sidra with ch. 18 focussing on sexual sins— Luke brought Mk 14: 3-9 forward, then, because he 'needed her for Atonement' (p. 86). Luke again follows the order of Mark from Lk 8: 4-9: 17 Wk 4: 1-6: 44), with some exceptions—and Lk 8: 4-21 is so suitable for Tabernacles (The Sower, etc.), but only for a one-day celebration (unlike Mt's ch. 13 spread over the eight days of Tabernacles) which was enough for any Gentile Church. Next, why the Lukan omission of Mark 6: 45-8: 26? 'Mark's eight Dedication lessons are seven too many' (p. 90)!, since the Lukan Church had reduced the Jewish eight-day festival to one. Lk 9: 18-50 follows Mk 8: 27-9: 40, but why does he desert him from 9: 51-18: 14? Because the Lucan journey narrative was the Christian counterpart of Deuteronomy, and was used three times more intensively that hitherto, at the rate of eleven chapters in as many weeks-the catechumens met three times during the week for an instruction on what the whole church would hear the following Sunday. This was the Christian catechumenate (ch. Lk 1: 4 in which Theophilus is promised to be told the full truth of the things in which he had been *catechized),* after which the catechumen was baptized at Easter.

Encouraged by the range of correlations, and by the success of the lectionary theory is accounting for some hitherto unexplained difficulties of Luke's order, Goulder presses on to investigate the use of the rest of the OT in the first century synagogue, in the hope that the readings from the Law and the Prophets may also offer correlations. At this point he throws caution to the wind and offers 'an attempt to interpret the whole of Scripture as liturgical, in origin and use' (p. 131), the NT epistles being the only exception, in that their origin was not liturgical, although their use was. He fixes a Histories cycle of readings, and discerns credible parallels for twenty-five out of the fifty-four weeks, bringing the total Lukan/OT parallels to forty-nine. Isaiah as we have it is the collection of prophetic statements used in the cult in the course of the year, and the Writings, too, grew to maturity in the matrix of worship. Chapter 8 extends his thesis in *Midrash and Lection in Matthew by* now using the prophetic lections, and here he finds plausible parallels for the citation formulae in either the Sidra or the Haphtarah. With regard to the NT epistles, he argues that they already had para-canonical status in the liturgy alongside the OT in the 1st century. The common elements between Matthew and Paul, then, can be explained by positing the view that Matthew knew Paul's letters from their place in the liturgy and included part of the Apostle's teaching in his Gospel: Romans for Easter onwards fitting the Genesis Sidrot, Corinthians suiting Exodus, and so on in order of length, ending with Thessalonians for Passover—which, of course, is the order of the epistles in our Bibles. Moreover, the parallels tend to cluster around the festivals: Rom 12-14 and the Sermon on the Mount at Pentecost; I Cor with the New Year material in Mt 10-11; Ephesians with Matthew's Dedication chapters 16-19; 1 Thes 2 with Mt 23, and 1 Thes 3-5 with Mt 24-25 for Passover.

And on to the final chapter, dealing with Mark. Immediately there are problems. Codex Alexandrinus, the main external basis for the divisions of the Gospels has only forty nine divisions: and how can one fill out the Jewish Sabbaths and feasts with so little? Goulder opts for Mark beginning at the New Year feast (month of Tishri, our mid-September to mid-October), and ending at Passover-Easter. This accounts for the expansion of Mark by Matthew, most of which is found in the first eleven chapters of Matthew-from chapter 12 onwards Matthew follows Mark's order very closely. Why did Mark not record Jesus' Sermon on the Mount? Simply because he had no Pentecost (p. 244)! Setting Mark's divisions alongside the fixed OT readings reveals some striking coincidences: Mk 1 has the coming of God's Kingdom for New Year; Mk 2 presents Jesus as God's viceregent forgiving sins, for Atonement; Mk 3-4 has its Harvest parables for Tabernacles; Mk 7-9 has its Qorban and Transfiguration for Dedication; and the Apocalyptic Discourse, Mk 13 preparing the way for the Passion Narrative. The intervening Markan sections fill out the Sabbaths between the festivals, and altogether the correlations between the Markan readings and those of the OT are striking in many cases, e.g., Mk's Leper at 1: 40-45 occurring on the second Sabbath in the month of Tishri, for which the Sidra is Lev 14-15, The Leper.

This work is immense in its scholarship. It radically questions so much of what is taken as secure in biblical scholarship. It will force scholars to examine more carefully the possibility of regarding the Bible as the written record of the recitation of the Word in the liturgy. On the positive side the thesis looks much more natural than those which consider the gospels to have been written with all the research paraphernalia of a scholar writing a doctoral thesis. The public worship of the community seems a more likely womb from which the Scriptures were born than a library compartment hermetically sealed from the outside world by double-glazed tomes. Goulder reacts against the view of the evangelists seen 'in the guise of Oxford scholars, poring over their sources, meticulously piecing together the evidence of various documents',[16] but he will surely by joined to the ranks of those who say 'the gospels are linked with lectionaries'[17] and can offer no other explanation for their conclusions other than that they have read their sources with 'liturgical spectacles'.[18] Those who have a high regard for Luke's interest in the events of the life of Jesus will not be happy to see this question ignored—they will wonder whether the authority of the Scriptures depends hardly at all on the authority of Jesus, but only on the homiletic ingenuity and imagination of the author. New Testament scholarship needs to be liberated from the limitations it sets itself in each generation-this is the age of Redaction Criticism, where the scholars' attention focusses on the qualities of the redactor as author, and on the life-setting of the authors' communities, but this is done in such a way as to ignore the setting within the historical

---

[16] Morna Hooker, 'In his own Image?', in *What About the New Testament? Essays in Honour* of *Christopher Evans,* ed. by M Hooker and C Hickling (London, 1975), p. 29.

[17] R G Finch, *The Synagogue Lectionary and the New Testament* (London. 1939) argued that the readings in the synagogue services lie behind most of the New Testament; P P Levertoff's Introduction to Matthew in A *New Commentary on Holy Scripture,* ed., by C Gore, H L Goudge and A Guillaume(London, 1928) argued the case for Matthew; Guilding, *op. cit.,* presents the case for John; P Carrington, *The Primitive Christian Calendar* (Cambridge, 1952) relates Mark to the Jewish lectionary tradition.

[18] Hooker, *op. cit.,* p. 38.

ministry of Jesus. In the end there will have to be some kind of rapprochement between those who seen most of the Gospels rooted in the ministry of Jesus, and those who ascribe much to the literary or homiletic imagination of the evangelists and their churches. At times Goulder is driven more by the momentum of his enthusiasm than by the power of the evidence—he seems at times to be afflicted with Midas' gift that everything he touches becomes liturgical gold. One must have the most serious reservations about his starting point.[19] One must recognize that where a theory exists facts are found to abound. Nor can one be altogether swept along by the many successes of the thesis, since others before him have been equally enthusiastic about their results.[20] However, despite being left with many questions unanswered we feel that Goulder's basic instinct is right, even if at several places the reconstruction is more fantastic than one can bear.[21]

LUKE: *GAUDIUM ET SPES?*

Acknowledging some dependence on Goulder's earlier work[22] John Drury accounts for the construction of Luke's work in this way: Luke presided at the weekly Christian assembly at which there were three readings: one from the OT; one from Matthew or Luke, and one, perhaps, from Paul's Letter to the Corinthians. Luke was the preacher, and when he preached he expounded the texts, linked them, and related them to the

---

[19] That the Jewish Lectionary was established as a one-year cycle in this period, and was so used by the Christian communities is highly questionable since it finds almost no support among the experts.

[20] Carrington assured his readers that the facts fitted his theory 'like a glove' (*op. cit.*, p. 26), while Guilding saw in her work 'the clearest possible proof of the influence of the *three-year* lectionary system on the pattern of the Gospel' (*op. cit.*, p. 50).

[21] The book is written with great clarity, and many touches of humour. At each stage of thee argument there are charts, and very helpful tables, eight in all, building up the picture as the evidence is brought forward. Table VIII brings all the findings together. Pp. 17f. summarize the book, and on p. 16 Goulder invites chose whose reading time is limited to move on to the last chapter after he has read pp.17f. It would be a pity to follow his advice since there are so many great insights in the intervening pages. Finally, the critic who dismisses Goulder because of the weakness of his starting point is going to have trouble explaining away the extraordinary parallels between the Gospel pericopes and the proposed OT readings. Must the building be demolished because its foundations are suspect, or does the excellence of the building guarantee the security of the foundations?

[22] Midrash and Lection in Matthew (London, 1974).

needs of his community (like any good homilist).[23] The readings and homily were followed by prayer and the Eucharist. But Luke was no monk: and he was as much at home in the marketplace and at the dinner-parties of the privileged as he was in the eucharistic assembly. When he went to his desk to compose his gospel he had before him his OT scrolls, his Christian writings and, perhaps, his own sermon notes, and from these he wrote the first thoroughgoing exposition of the relation between Christianity and unecclesiastical experience—a kind of 'Gaudium et Spes',[24] Christianity in dialogue with the Modem World of the first half of the second century.[25] In Drury's estimation Paul was so dazzled by the Cross that he saw all that preceded it (with the exception of Abraham's faith) as darkness. Mark improved on Paul in that he presented this Cross as the outcome of Jesus' life for which John's ministry was a preparation. Matthew went further still: he added didactic material to Mark, and showed very explicitly that Jesus was the fulfilment of OT expectations. Luke also presents Jesus as fulfilling OT prophecy but he does so in a more subtle and smooth way, so much so that the modern reader might miss some of the resonances. Unlike C K Barrett[26] and, as we have seen C H Talbert, Drury places Luke firmly within the tradition of Jewish historiography with its great love of midrash and story.[27] He sees the LXX as a major source for his gospel, especially in his Infancy Narrative where Drury finds that 'septuagintal words and phrases are as thick on the ground as autumn leaves' (p. 49).[28] After Luke 2, however, the LXX has to compete with Mark as Luke's main source for narrative and with

---

[23] This way of exegeting the Scriptures is sometimes termed 'midrash', a word which is used in biblical studies with a great variety of meanings (cf. Renée Bloch's article 'Midrash' in *Dictionaire de la Bible, Supplément* (Paris, 1957) which lists about ten different types of biblical interpretation which she classifies as 'midrash'), with the result that 'the word as used currently in biblical studies is approaching the point where it is no longer really meaningful' (A G Wright, *The Literary Genre Midrash,* New York, 1967, p. 21f.).

[24] This is the title of Vatican Council II's 'Pastoral Constitution on the Church in the Modern World', arguably the most significant of the Council's documents in that it addressed itself 'not only to the sons of the Church ... but to the whole of humanity' (par. 2), *The Documents of Vatican II,* ed. W M Abbott (New York, 1966), p. 200.

[25] This proposal is so out of keeping with the findings of the majority of scholars that it must be described as eccentric. Because of the importance of the dating for interpretation Drury ought to have amassed very considerable evidence to justify his position.

[26] 'His fellows are Polybius and Plutarch, Josephus and Tacitus,' in *Luke the Historian in Recent Study* (Epworth, 1961, p. 9).

[27] Drury estimates Luke to be 'one of the greatest narrative midrashists' (p. 12).

[28] He examines sixteen Septuagintal phrases in Lk 1-2 in Appendix A, pp. 185f.

Matthew as the main source for his teaching. The source for Luke's special material is right under the nose of source critics: the OT itself. Indeed! For example, this is the genesis and development of the incident which results in his account of the raising of the Nain widow's son (Lk 7: 11-17): Mark's record of the raising of Jairus' daughter (Mk 5) is 'a shadowy source' (p. 71), which he embellishes through a midrash on 1 Kgs 17 (Elijah restored the life of the Zarephath's widow's son). While paying lip-service occasionally to the possible historicity of what is peculiar to Luke he explains the Parable, or story as he prefers to call it, of the Prodigal Son as having as its source Mt 21: 28-32, which Luke developed through a midrash on Deut 21, with help from Sir 33, 1 Kgs 8, Hos 2, Ex 10, etc. In the same way he accounts for the Good Samaritan as having its source in Mt 22: 34ff and its present form in Luke's midrash on 2 Chron 27. The reader expects from an author who castigates NT scholars for their neglect of Luke as an historian more evidence for his dismissal of Jesus as a story-teller comparable to Luke.[29]

Luke was determined to make Mark 'more historically consecutive' (p. 83), and he and Matthew were so successful that 'Mark subsequently fell out of esteem and practically out of use in the Church.' (p. 83). Any explanation of Gospel origins has to contend with many problems. Drury attributes to Luke's respect for history his omission of the material in Mk 6: 45-8: 26: he excludes the healing of the Syro-phoenician's daughter and of the deaf man in Decapolis because he knows that the mission to the gentiles was not part of the ministry of Jesus, but was the great business of the Church (Acts), and 'Luke's is the least gentile gospel of all the synoptics' (p. 98), a view that will scarcely gain the approval of the scholarly community! Luke omits the cure of the blind man at Bethsaida (Mk 8: 22-26) since he wishes Peter's Confession (Lk 9: 18-20), Mk 8: 27-29) to follow the feeding of the five thousand (Lk 9: 10-17, Mk 6: 30-44), just as he has the Emmaus disciples recognizing Jesus only after he had broken the bread. For his Passion Narrative Luke

---

[29] On changing from reading history to theology Drury was led 'to a certain bafflement' in that 'History was much pondered and invoked in New Testament studies but practised in a less pervasive and delicate way' (p. xii). His fascination for a midrashic interpretation tends to force conclusions on the evidence. His failure to mention I H Marshall's important study, *Luke: Historian and Theologian* (Exeter, 1970) betrays a serious weakness in the work. Although Marshall puts more stress on Luke as theologian he does show that the two roles go together. Cf. C J Hemer, 'Luke the Historian', in *Bulletin of John Ryland's Library*, Vol. 60 Autumn 1977).

redacted Mark.[30] In line with a growing number of scholars Drury discards the hypothesis of Q, and argues instead for Luke's use of Matthew on the basis of the similarity in order between Lk 3: 74: 13 and Mt 3: 74: 11, their placing of the Sermon at a similar point, and the order of the material within the Sermon itself, all of which would be difficult to explain on the view that Matthew and Luke used a common source, but independently of each other. Like Evans and Goulder, Drury seeks Lk 9: 51-18: 14, the Way to Jerusalem narrative, as based on Deuteronomy, which is 'the string on to which Luke threads teaching material from Matthew and from his own resources' (p.140).

For a work that professes to enquire into Luke's gospel with the nose of a historian there is an unfortunate agnosticism on the very question of historicity. Early in the book, on the basis of some similarities between Ephesians and Luke, and between the Pastorals, Hebrews and Luke[31] the author argues for a common life-setting for all four. On the one hand, one could without difficulty catalogue a much more impressive collection of differences between them, and on the basis of the same methodology make a stronger case for a difference in outlook. Secondly, even if one is swayed by the marshalling of elements of similarity the conclusion that all four must therefore be placed at the end of the first century rests on a range of assumptions that must be challenged by any historian. The reasons advanced for suggesting the first half of the second century as the date of composition are particularly weak.[32] By accepting this date, of course,

---

[30] Vincent Taylor, *The Passion Narrative of St. Luke*, (Cambridge, 1972), sees in Luke's account of the Passion the strongest case for a non-Markan source for this gospel: 'There is good reason to maintain that Lk 22: 14-24 is part of a larger whole' gospel, composed AD 60-65 and found by Luke at Caesarea (AA 21: 8), (p. 125f.).

[31] S G Wilson, *Luke and the Pastoral Epistles* (London, 1979), makes a strong case for Luke as the author of the Pastorals, arguing from similarities in language, themes, and techniques in compilation. As we shall see J D Quinn takes the same view, adding that the Pastorals are the third volume of the Lukan trilogy. C P M Jones, 'The Epistle to the Hebrews and the Lucan Writings', in *Studies in the Gospels,* ed. D E Nincham (Oxford, 1957), argues that Luke and Hebrews 'stand together as forming a solid block' (p. 142), and that there is a 'family likeness' between them (p. 143); cf. H W Montefiore, *The Epistle to the Hebrews* (London, 1964), p. 1, who writes of a number of points of contact between Luke and Hebrews; Origen reports a tradition that Luke the author of the Gospel and the Acts also wrote Hebrews (Eusebius, HE VI 25, quoted in E Hennecke, *New Testament Apocrypha, Vol. 1 [ET,* London, 1963], p. 53f.).

[32] J A T Robinson, *Redating the New Testament* (London, 1976), shows up the weaknesses of the methodological principles employed in dating the NT material. There is little in Luke that demands a date later than 70 AD.

the author removes Luke from the historical ministry of Jesus by at least three generations, and this may well account for the extraordinary statement from a historian that 'Little will be said here of the factual value of Luke's work' (p. 12). Unless redaction critics pay more attention to the relation of the gospels to the historical ministry of Jesus their readers may be forced into opting for a form of gnosticism in which Luke, rather than Jesus, is proclaimed as Lord!

LUKE AND JESUS' ORIGINS

Another occupational hazard of redaction critics is to have one's judgement under such captivity to a particular theory that much of the evidence is ignored. Hans Conzelmann in presenting his theology of Luke effectively ignored the first two chapters of Luke, even though he claims to be 'concerned with the whole of Luke's writings as they stand.'[33] In the verdict of Paul S Minear, 'If Conzelmann had taken full account of the nativity stories ... his position would have been changed at several major points.'[34] Surveying the situation in 1966 Minear noted the concentration on Lucan studies in the previous decade, and particularly the 'almost phenomenal' number of essays dealing with the first two chapters. More especially he concluded that so many studies of the Gospel ignored chapters 1 and 2, and that studies on these chapters did not relate them to the rest of the gospel.[35] Raymond E Brown's recent commentary certainly avoids this criticism: Luke 1-2 serve the same purpose in relation to the rest of the Gospel as do AA 1-2 to the remainder of Acts—just as AA 1-2 provide a transition from Jesus to the Church, so Lk 1-2 serves as a transition from the story of Israel to that of Jesus.[36] The stories of the conception and birth of Jesus are the most popular of all the Gospel material, with the possible exception of the crucifixion, and yet they are the least plausible from a historical point of view. Brown polarizes scholarship on this question into two camps, one holding strongly to the

---

[33] *The Theology of Saint Luke*, ET, London, 1960, (p. 9).

[34] Paul S Minear, 'Luke's Use of the Birth Stories', in *Studies in Luke-Acts,* ed. L E Keek and J L Martyn (London, 1968), p. 121.

[35] *Ibid.*, p. 111.

[36] Raymond E Brown, *The Birth of the Messiah* (London, 1977), p. 242f.

historical character of the material, and the other dismissing it as full of folklore, and hence unworthy bearers of the Gospel message. He sees three phases in the scholarly attitude to these chapters, (a) the recognition that the Infancy Narratives[37] differ significantly from the body of the Gospels, (b) the problem of historicity when it is realized that Matthew and Luke differ so much, leading finally to the conclusion that, (c) they are vehicles of the evangelists' theology, rather than statements of history. Brown suggests that every serious reader of the material will go through these three stages in turn.[38]

The 'Gospel of the Origins of Jesus Christ'[39] is the final stage of the development of the Gospels backwards from the oldest Christian preaching (cf. AA 2: 22, 32; 3: 14-15; 4: 10, 10: 39f; 1 Cor 15: 3f.) which was concerned with the death and resurrection of Jesus as the enthronement of Jesus as Son of God, followed by its development into the Passion Narratives, leading to an interest in the deeds and words of Jesus. Mark advanced this 'Christological Moment' to the baptism at which Jesus is proclaimed to be the beloved Son, although Jesus' true identity is kept from the disciples during his lifetime (cf. Mk 9: 2-8; 15: 39). Matthew presents Jesus as recognized as God's Son by his disciples during the public ministry (Mt 14: 23, not in Mk 6: 51f.; Mt 16: 16, not in Mk 8: 29), and together with Luke reveals his identity as early as at his conception.[40] In this way Brown affirms the theological value of the accounts, and finds in them a theology that is 'as profoundly Christian and as dramatically persuasive as the last two chapters, the story of the passion and resurrection.'[41]

---

[37] Brown recognizes the limitations of the title, since both first chapters deal with conception and pregnancy rather than infancy, Lk 2: 41-52 deals with Jesus at the age of twelve, and Mt. 2: 13-23 can scarcely he called narrative.

[38] P. 26.

[39] This is the title preferred by Brian M Nolan, *The Royal Son of God. The Christology of Matthew 1-2 in the Setting of the Gospel* (Orbis Biblicus et Orientalis 23, University of Fribourg, 1979), because it 'both connects Matthew 1-2 with the dramatic history of Jesus the Messiah ("Gospel"), and points up its characteristic subject matter in a comprehensive way ("Origins")', p. 113. He examines the merits and inadequacies of other designations: Birth Narrative, Infancy Gospel, Prologue, *Vorgeschichte,* Pre-Baptism (Narrative) Cycle, etc., pp. 108-113.

[40] R H Fuller. 'The Conception/ Birth of Jesus as a Christological Moment' (*Journal for the Study of the NT* 1 [1978], 37-52) argues that Brown's explanation is 'an oversimplification of the christological development behind the infancy narratives in their final form', p. 38.

[41] Brown, p. 38.

With this emphasis on theological considerations interest in questions of historicity fades somewhat, but by no means disappears.[42] If it is granted that the evangelists were not writing history we must enquire into the particular style of their method. The term 'Midrash' is widely applied in this context, even though as we have indicated in note 23 the word is used with a great variety of meaning.[43] There is nothing in the Infancy accounts to suggest that the evangelists were primarily interested in exegeting a text, or several texts of Scripture with a view to making them relevant to the circumstances of the present. Their primary concern, to judge by the overall thrust of their finished product, was to show that from the moment of his conception Jesus was the Son of God and of Davidic descent, conceived through the power of the Holy Spirit. Luke's work is his own composition, using some elements of historical information and popular tradition[44] around which he arranges his material with one eye looking into Israel's past (where we see reflections of Abraham and Sarah, Samson and Samuel, and hear the echoes of the canticles of Hannah, Leah and David) and one eye to the future (the preparatory role of the Baptist, the decisive role of the Spirit both in the life of Jesus and of the Church, the angelic appearances of Acts, etc.).[45]

---

[42] In his *An Adult Christ at Christmas* Brown notes that he deliberately placed the attention to questions of historicity late in his *Birth*, 'lest they get out of focus' (p. 5). He notes eleven points shared by both accounts, and argues on that basis for the existence of a common infancy tradition earlier than either evangelist's work, and thus weighing 'on the plus side of the historical scale' (p. 34f.): the parents are Mary and Joseph; Joseph is of Davidic descent; angelic pronouncement of forthcoming birth; the conception is not through intercourse, but through the Holy Spirit (Appendix IV discusses the Virginal Conception—both Matthew and Luke regarded this as historical, but Brown concludes that the 'scientifically controllable' biblical evidence leaves the question of historicity unresolved, p. 527); the angels direct that he be named Jesus, and that he is to be Saviour; the birth takes place after the parents come together; the birth is at Bethlehem, in the reign (days) of Herod the Great, and the child is reared at Nazareth.

[43] In an excellent section on Midrash, Nolan, *The Royal Son of God*, criticizes the rigidity of confining 'Midrash' to an exegesis of a text, on which grounds one would have to remove the Infancy Narratives from that genre, since they concentrate on Christ, and on the OT: 'Midrash is more accurately thought of as an attitude to scripture and to life which ... is based on the biblical text *and its application*, and which assumes a variety of literary expressions. Neither of these two aspects of midrash—experience and composition—may be suppressed' (p. 55f.).

[44] Note 2, p. 498, gives as examples of historical information the names of the Baptist's parents, and of popular tradition the angelic annunciation pattern.

[45] Since the work is a thorough commentary on the four chapters only the briefest outline has been given there. The book is justifiably being hailed as a major contribution to

PERSPECTIVES IN LUKE–ACTS[46]

J B Tyson draws attention to the turbulence within gospel source scholarship. To show the diversity of opinion he focusses on four attempts to solve the synoptic problem, those of Streeter,[47] Farrer,[48] Griesbach/ Farmer,[49] and Lindsey.[50] Variations on these are supplied by Butler, Parker, Leon-Dufour, Gaboury, Benoit-Boismard, Goulder, Dungan and Rosche.[51] Against a background of such confusion Tyson criticizes the prevailing redaction criticism method which is entirely based on a theory of literary dependence of one evangelist on the work of another. He calls for a new approach for Luke-Acts, in which the whole work is examined in its arrangement of material, its attention to plot, the kind of reader implied, etc.—a procedure which will illuminate Luke, even if it does not solve the Synoptic Problem.

Schuyler Brown embarks on such a programme. He examines some suggested 'purposes of Luke-Acts' to see if they are consistent with

---

Gospel studies—it is the first modern commentary to treat the two narratives together, and the first to do so using all the modern techniques of biblical scholarship of which Fr Brown is a highly regarded exponent. His other book, *An Adult Christ at Christmas*, is a more popular presentation of his main argument with an exegesis of Matthew 2: 1-23; Luke 2: 140; and Luke 2: 41-52.

[46] *Perspectives on Luke-Acts* is the result of study undertaken by the Journal of Biblical Literature Luke-Acts Group in the period 1972-78. The following are the articles we select for comment: J B Tyson, 'Source Criticism of the Gospel of Luke', pp. 24-39; S Brown, 'The Role of the Prologues in Determining the Purpose of Luke-Acts', pp. 99-111; R J Karris, 'Poor and Rich: the Lukan *Sitz im Leben*', pp. 112-125; A A Trites, 'The Prayer Motif in Luke-Acts', pp. 168-186; and J D Quinn, 'The Last Volume of Luke: The Relation of Luker-Acts to the Pastoral Epistles', pp. 62-75.

[47] B H Streeter, *The Four Gospels* (London, 1924): Mk is the earliest, and was used by Mt and Lk, but independently, and these also had a common source, Q.

[48] A M Farrer, 'On Dispensing with Q', in *Studies in the Gospels,* ed. D E Nineham (Oxford, 1957): Mk was used by Mt, and both were used by Lk.

[49] The modern version of Griesbach: W R Farmer, *The Synoptic Problem* (Dillsboro, 1964): Mt the first, used by Lk and both used by Mk.

[50] R L Lindsey, *A New Approach to the Synoptic Gospels* (Jerusalem, 1971): Luke combined a Primitive Narrative (a Greek translation of a Hebrew or Aramaic original, PN) and Q; Mk combined PN and Lk, and Mt used PN, Q, and Mk.

[51] Cf. also Bernard Orchard, *Matthew, Luke and Mark* (Manchester, 1976), R W Longstaff, *Evidence of Conflation in Mark? A Study of the Synoptic Problem* (Montana, 1977), and J J Griesbach, *Synoptic and Text-Critical Studies 1776-1976,* ed. by B Orchard and T R W Longstaff (Cambridge, 1978), for the growing support for a Mt Lk Mk order. On the other hand, John M Rist, *On the Independence of Matthew and Mark* (Cambridge, 1977), rejects any hypothesis of literary dependence between Mt and Mk, the similarities being accounted for by common oral traditions.

the stated aims of Lk 1: 34. He finds the evidence ambiguous. He concludes that the prologue of Luke could be so interpreted as to offer support to the view that Luke-Acts is primarily concerned with the evangelization of the non-Christian world, or alternatively that is was aimed at protecting the community from heresy. He perceptively suggests that this double tendency in the prologue may reflect two circles of readers, and invites further study of Luke's life-setting.

As if taking up the challenge, R J Karris attempts to discover this life-setting through an examination of one of the Lukan themes: poor and rich. He concludes that the real problem in the Lukan community was the presence of its rich members: Lk 18: 18-30 and 19: 1-10 deal with the possibility of a rich man ever being a true Christian; AA 2: 41-47 and 4: 31c-35 show how riches prevent a man from helping the poor; Lk 12: 13-34 and 14: 16-24 show the rich that they are too attached to their possessions; 16: 1-31 focusses on the need to give alms, etc. Secondly, Karris sees strong evidence for persecution as a feature of the life of the Lukan group (Lk 6: 24-26; 14: 25-33). In this view Luke is more a gospel for the rich than for the poor.

A A Trites examines the prayer-motif in Luke-Acts. Luke-Acts does inculcate the practice of prayer but this is the result of the author's primary concern which is to show that God directs history through prayer, as can be seen in the life of Jesus and that of the Church. The article gives a most enriching analysis of the practice of prayer and the teaching on it in both Luke and Acts, showing its importance, the prominence of praise, the example of Jesus, the need to engage in it continually, the fidelity of the early church and its place in the life of its leaders.

Jerome D Quinn takes up again his thesis that Luke is the author of the Pastoral Epistles (see note 31). He argues his case on the basis of linguistic similarities, common material and theological relationships. They form the third volume of the trilogy Luke-Acts-Pastorals. They belong to the category of the 'non-real-letter', i.e., letters with directives for the readers allegedly coming from an authenticating authority, with the added intention of satisfying the curiosity of the readers by giving biographical information about the supposed author. Luke, then, sought to give further security to Theophilus by rehabilitating the Pauline apostolate and teaching—Paul had been allowed to fall into oblivion, his letters being read by no more than one or another church. The author, then, in the eighties attempted to restore Paul to favour, and did so by transmitting his work and teaching to his children. It was the final volume of the trilogy that was the catalyst for collecting the Pauline letters in the period 90-100. Luke-Acts-Pastorals also stimulated other writings, among which Luke was counted to give the four gospels. Acts then became a sort of Deuteronomy concluding the Pentateuch of Gospels/Acts. This is a very ingenious reconstruction and therefore requires a lot of demonstration. To demonstrate that Luke is the author of the Pastorals would in itself involve several assumptions: e.g., that similarities in language, thought-pattern, and theology between two works demands the same author, and that differences do not rule out the same author; that a theory of pseudonymity is preferable to one involving a secretary. Furthermore evidence has to be produced to place the Pastorals so late. Nor is it clear that Luke made an outstanding success at rehabilitating Paul. If he wished to do that surely he would have been familiar with the letters of Paul, would have used them in Acts, and would have produced more obviously authentic Pauline letters than the Pastorals. Quinn will offer a more comprehensive case in his Anchor Bible commentary under preparation. Meanwhile he calls for a review of the technique of pseudonymity—it is high time that the whole question of letter writing was looked at again[52] and invites a new look at Luke-Acts in the light of its epistolatory ending.

PUTTING IT TOGETHER

In the first major commentary on the Greek text of Luke since Creed's in 1930, I H Marshall reflects all the movements in biblical studies since that time, and gathers together, from the four winds, every worthwhile contribution to Lukan studies, allows it its say, and evaluates it. He supports Luke's use of Mark, and also, with less confidence, the Q hypothesis, and denies any large-scale creation of material by the author. He accepts the traditional view that Luke, the companion of Paul, is the author, and that he wrote at a date not far from 70 A.D. He sees a twofold purpose in the work: to secure the faith of the committed and to appeal to a wider audience. He prefers to regard all of these views as operating models, or

---

[52] E.g., the possibility that different co-workers were allowed more freedom in the actual writing of the letters, with the signature of Paul coming as a seal of approval—cf. the composition of Papal Encyclicals and Bishops' Pastorals.

paradigms, which satisfactorily account for the massive evidence provided in the commentary, rather than as conclusions. Throughout the work Marshall reflects his confidence in Luke as a faithful historian. He agrees with Schürmann that the tradition history of Luke 1-2 is still wrapped in darkness (p. 48), and he prefers to keep an open mind on the historicity of the material recorded in them. In fact he tends towards leaving many other questions open. His comments on the Emmaus story are typical of his approach: he reports scholarly opinion on the literary links with the feeding of the multitude, and on the features it has in common with the story of the Ethiopian eunuch (AA 8: 26-40); he mentions the difficulties in squaring the story with history, summarizes the various attempts at separating the Lukan additions to a traditional source, and concludes that the story is not Luke's creation, but has a basis in tradition and probably in history. There are times when the reader would hope for a closer examination of some of the elements of historicity, but the limitations in this area spring from the nature of the sources than from a weakness in method. Marshall shows how it is possible to draw together what is best in scholarship at a time of great productivity in Lukan studies.

THE WAY AHEAD

There is little likelihood that the Synoptic Problem can ever be settled[53] and this author takes the view that a working-hypothesis based on literary dependence of one evangelist on the Gospel of another creates more problems than it solves. It is better, therefore, to withhold judgement on a source theory and proceed to examine each of the Gospels in its own uniqueness. More attention will be given to describing the *Sitz im Leben* of Luke. Perhaps when the fever for the search for sources subsides, and when more light is shed on Luke's adaptation of the life of Jesus to his own community, we may hope that attention will be given to the relevance of Luke's Gospel to the life of the community in this generation.

---

[53] In the forthcoming Cambridge Griesbach Conference, August 1979, papers will be read on a theology of each of the synoptics in turn based on the order proposed by Griesbach.

JESUS' TEACHING
ON THE MOUNT

Written for Scripture Bulletin *in 1988, this essay reveals Michael the scholar searching out the practical application of the teaching of Jesus*

The teaching of Jesus recorded in the Gospel of Matthew, chapters 5-7, is among the best known of his sayings. It appears to be the most popular, and most frequently discussed section of the Bible, and this has been the case from the beginning of Christianity.[1] Who has not heard of 'turning the other cheek', 'loving enemies', 'almsgiving, praying and fasting in secret', the 'Our Father', 'seeking first the kingdom of God', 'not being anxious', 'not judging', and 'walking the straight and narrow'?

But the fact that it is so familiar does not mean that it is the best understood section of the teachings of Jesus, nor that its teachings are put into practice on a large scale. Even after two thousand years of investigation the Sermon continues to intrigue, stimulate, and baffle people.[2]

A few years ago an American lecturer did an interesting experiment. He changed the rather churchy language of the Sermon into a more contemporary form, abbreviated it, and then presented it to students of the humanities in a university, asking them to comment on it. Most of them did not recognize the sayings to have come from Jesus. Among the names suggested as the source were Karl Marx, Gandhi, Hitler, Malcolm X, and 'some loopy-leftie'. When asked if they thought the principles could be put into practice, most said 'no', and some said 'yes', but only in an ideal world.

Closer to home, I carried out my own enquiry. I invited university students of religious studies to read Matthew 5-7, and some

---

[1] 'No portion of the Scriptures was more frequently quoted and referred to by the Ante-Nicene writers than the Sermon on the Mount' (Kissinger, W.S. 1975. *The Sermon on the Mount. A History of Interpretation and Bibliography*. American Theological Library Association 3. Metuchen: Scarecrow, *9.6*).

[2] While no full-scale history of interpretation has been attempted there is much useful information in McArthur, H.K 1960. *Understanding the Sermon on the Mount*. New York: Harper, Kissinger 1975, and Baumann, C. 1985. *The Sermon on the Mount: The Modern Quest for its Meaning*. Macon: Mercer University Press.

days later I asked them to answer in one sentence each the questions 'What is your reaction to having read the Sermon?', and 'What is the relevance of the Sermon on the Mount?'

The reactions ranged from 'I enjoyed it' to 'I was perplexed'. It was experienced as 'giving a guide to life', and giving 'hope to the ordinary person in the street', on the one hand, and being an account of 'how Christians must live, or of 'how Jews should live', or of 'how Jesus gave a deeper meaning of the laws and the prophets', on the other.

The range of answers on the relevance was even wider: 'still applicable today'; 'pointing to a more worthwhile lifestyle'; 'impracticable'; reaffirming the more important Old Testament laws'; 'expanding the commandments'; 're-instating the laws of Moses'; 'reinforcing the Ten Commandments'; 'changing the old teachings'; 'insisting on an interior goodness', etc.

Is it not very interesting that there is such diversity of understanding and interpretation? The fact is that when people are given the liberty of doing so they witness to a great variety of reactions to the Sermon, and register a great diversity of views concerning its relevance. Moreover, most of the questions which have engaged scholars down the centuries come to the surface: Is the Sermon addressed to Jews, or Christians, or to everyone? Does it continue the teaching of Moses, or replace it? Does its distinctiveness reside in its appeal to dispositions, and not mere external behaviour? Is it attractive but impossible? Is it merely an ideal to strive after, without any hope of being achieved? Or is the teaching mere nonsense in this real world?

THE SERMON IN HISTORY

Understanding the demands of the Sermon has always been a problem. The history of interpretation illustrates a great variety of responses. The early Fathers of the Church saw the demands of the Sermon as applying to all believers, but it is clear that from an early period the practicability of applying them to life was questioned.[3] In the Middle Ages there began to grow up a two-tier kind of Christianity, with the commandments

---

[3] Note the presence in many early *MSS* of *eikei* ('without cause') in Jesus' prohibition of anger in Matt 5: 22. This probably reflects the attempts by copyists to soften the demand of Jesus.

applying to all, but counsels only to some (e.g., St Thomas, Summa *Theol.* 1, IIae, cvii-cviii).

For such reformers as the followers of Thomas Münzer, the Melchiorists, Mennonites, etc., the Sermon was the norm for every Christian. The more moderate of them settled for the separation of Church and state, espoused love and non-resistance, and rejected oaths and violence. A Christian must separate himself from the state, since 'saints' cannot have any truck with 'sinners'.

Menno Simons asked:

> How can a Christian defend scripturally retaliation, rebellion, war, striking, slaying, torturing, stealing, robbing and plundering and burning cities, and conquering countries? (quoted in Kissinger 1975, 33).

He saw the Sermon as a charter for true Christian living, and he held that a believer's chief concern must be to pattern his life after the teaching and example of Jesus even though the price would be martyrdom. For the Quakers, too, war and revenge could not be reconciled with Christian practice.

In his attempt to steer a course between the Roman canonists who espoused a two-tier Christianity and the radical reformers who demanded an uncompromising withdrawal from the world, Luther was driven to distinguish between two kingdoms: the secular, and the divine. Only the divine could be ruled by the Commandments and the Sermon. A Christian could legitimately go to war, or sit on a judge's bench, not as a Christian, but only as a member of secular society.[4] Zwingli and Calvin went further. They supposed that one could rule a city on the basis of the Sermon, and tried it in Zurich and Geneva.

In their different ways both Luther and the radical reformers witness to the difficulties involved in trying to live out the demands of the teaching of the Sermon in the real world.

The influential American theologian, Reinhold Niebuhr, approached the problem with the honesty and pragmatism one associates with American intellectuals. He drew a very sharp distinction between the individual and society. He claimed that the Sermon had nothing to

---

[4] J Pelikan, ed., 1956, *Luther's Works*, Vol. 21: *The Sermon on the Mount and the Magnificat*. St Louis: Concordia, p. 113.

say about political morality. Pacifists, he claimed, evaded the messiness of politics and contracted out of society. The unselfish love of the other which is behind the Sermon is impossible in our existence. Nevertheless, while the Sermon's demands are impossible of fulfilment, they reveal in every situation the possibility of a higher good.[5]

The German, Dietrich Bonhoeffer, saw the problem as one of keeping the commands of the Sermon: what the world needs is people doing the Sermon, rather than just interpreting it:

> To deal with the word of Jesus otherwise than by doing it is to wrong him. It is to deny the Sermon on the Mount and to say No to his word. If we start asking questions, posing problems, and offering interpretations, we are not doing his word. ... The Sermon on the Mount is there for the purpose of being done (Matt 7: 24ff.) (Bonhoeffer, in Kissinger 84f).

Some scholars objected that the Sermon portrays Jesus as speaking in figurative language. He did not intend people to understand him literally. He trusted his hearers to interpret his message properly.

THE TRUE INTERPRETATION?

How is one to decide which, if any, of these views is correct? One must hope that an examination of the text of the Sermon would offer some clue. But, as in many things in life, the answer one comes out with is very much dependent on the questions one poses. Is one to examine the Sermon on the Mount on its own, or should one first consider the place of the Sermon in the wider context of the whole of Matthew's Gospel?

---

[5] In his *Moral Man and Immoral Society,* New York: Scribner (1932), Niebuhr insisted that the differences between individuals and groups were such that the Sermon was relevant only to the former, and could not be brought to bear on such matters as social justice. Later in the famous chapter on 'The Relevance of an Impossible Ethical Ideal', he argued that, while the demands of the Sermon are impossible to fulfil in our historical existence, they offer a higher ideal in every situation, and thus provide an impetus to higher moral living. (1935. *An Interpretation of Christian Ethics.* New York: Harper).

THE CONTENT OF THE SERMON

The Sermon on the Mount deals with the blessedness of those in the kingdom (5: 3-16), Jesus' interpretation of some of the Hebrew Laws (5: 17-48), practical instructions for living (6: 1-7: 12), and the challenge to a dedicated lifestyle (7: 13-29). It covers such subjects as murder, anger, and adultery of the heart, and forbids divorce, oaths, retaliation, and hatred. It deals with the three characteristic pieties of the Pharisees, and counsels on how properly to give alms, pray, and fast. It gives instruction on how to behave towards God, and one's neighbour. It ends by issuing a necessary choice, either to opt for the narrow road that leads to life, or the wider one that leads to destruction. 'Some sermon!' you might well say. In the past it was generally believed that the material in the Sermon was delivered by Jesus on one occasion. The disciples sat down (5: 1), Jesus opened his mouth (5: 2), and at the end the crowds were astonished at his teaching (7: 28). But most scholars nowadays consider the 'sermon' to be a collection of key teachings of Jesus spoken on several occasions. It is rather a pity that we continue to refer to it as a 'sermon' when the text itself calls it a 'teaching' (Matt 5: 2; 7: 28).

The material in the Teaching on the Mount can be seen to cluster around some key areas of life, and it is not unlikely that the Gospel writer put together into one teaching session blocks of material which were the substance of teachings given on different occasions. Different scholars have imposed their own pattern on the Teaching, and what follows is my amplification of the pattern suggested by Jack Dean Kingsbury.[6]

THE STRUCTURE AND THEME OF THE TEACHING

JESUS ASCENDS THE MOUNTAIN TO TEACH (5: 1-2)

PART 1

Introduction. On Those who Practise the Greater Righteousness (53-16)
('blessed are ...'; 'salt'; 'light')

---

[6] 'The Place, Structure, and Meaning of the Sermon on the Mount within Matthew' in *Interpretation* 41 (1987) 131-43, p.136. The entire vol. 41 (no.2) of *Interpretation is* devoted to the Sermon, and the articles by Guelich, Cahill, Lischer, *et al.*, are most illuminating.

PART 2

On Practising the Greater Righteousness Toward the Neighbour (5: 17-45)
(fulfilment of Law/Prophets;
reconciliation; No lustful glance/divorce/oaths/retaliation;
love enemies)

'YOU, THEREFORE, MUST BE PERFECT AS YOUR
HEAVENLY FATHER IS PERFECT(SA8)

PART 3

On Practising the Greater Righteousness Before God
(6: 1-18)
(almsgiving; praying; fasting)

PART 4

On Practising the Greater Righteousness in Other Areas of Life (6: 19-7: 12)
(NOT storing up/being anxious/judging/throwing pearls;
BUT Ask/Seek/Knock)

'SO WHATEVER YOU WISH THAT MEN WOULD DO
TO YOU, DO SO TO THEM;
FOR THIS IS THE LAW AND THE PROPHETS'(7: 12)

PART 5

Conclusion: Injunctions on Practising the Greater Righteousness (7: 13-27)
(Gate narrow/way hard; good fruit/bad fruit; doing/saying
Father's Will)

'AND EVERYONE WHO HEARS THESE WORDS OF
MINE, AND DOES NOT DO THEM WILL BE LIKE A
FOOLISH MAN WHO BUILT HIS HOUSE UPON THE
SAND: AND THE RAIN FELL, AND WINDS BLEW
AND BEAT AGAINST THE HOUSE, AND IT FELL:
AND GREAT WAS THE FALL OF IT'(7: 26f.)

HAVING FINISHED JESUS DESCENDS FROM THE MOUNTAIN (7: 28-8: 1)

The Greater Righteousness?

In this arrangement, Jesus is presented as teaching a greater righteousness. What is this Greater Righteousness? It is a righteousness exceeding both that of the Scribes (5: 17-48), and of the Pharisees (6: 1-18). it is the righteousness of the Kingdom of Heaven (6: 19-7: 12). It is issued as a challenge to choose well (7: 13-27). The abstract concept of 'the greater righteousness' is best understood in terms of human behaviour.

THE ONE WHO LIVES OUT THE GREATER RIGHTEOUSNESS

is 'poor in spirit', in that he trusts not in himself, but in God; 'mourns' on recognizing the distress of the world; has no clout in the world's terms; has his heart set on the good things which only God can bring about; is merciful; is undivided in his allegiance to God; mends the brokenness of God's world; and is faithful to God's righteousness to the point of suffering persecution.

Because of his good behaviour he does for people what salt does for food; and he brings God's promised light to those who sit in darkness.

He brings to their state of completion the instructions give through Moses and the Prophets by eschewing killing, and making it up with his brother; not even glancing at a woman with lust in his heart; respecting the indissolubility of marriage; not taking oaths; not retaliating; loving his enemy; in a word, by being perfect, as his heavenly Father is perfect.

When he gives alms, prays, and fasts he does so without ostentation.

He lays up treasures in heaven; his life is full of light; he
serves God rather than possessions; he does not get anxious
about life but trusts in God, like the birds and the lilies;

He does not judge people harshly; he does not waste the
treasures of his life by apostasy; in his need he asks/seeks/
knocks, and is provided for;

He does for others what he would wish done to himself this
is the law and the prophets.

He must not underestimate the difficulty of preferring the
good to evil, but must stick to the straight and narrow; not
be deluded by false prophets who bear no worthwhile fruit;
and do more than pay lip-service to the Lord.

Even prophesying, casting out demons, and doing mighty
works will not be enough.

Nor is it enough to hear the words; the Teaching is there for
the doing.

Kingsbury sums up as follows: 'The 'greater righteousness' is
that style of life intended to be the mark of disciples of Jesus ... The
'greater righteousness', then, is the quality of life which is indicative of
disciples who make up the church. It is behaviour that comports itself
with living in the sphere of God's kingdom (5: 20; 6: 33) ... It is love
toward God and love toward neighbour that constitute the heart of the
greater righteousness' (Kingsbury, 136f).

Those who practise the greater righteousness form the new
community of God's eschatological people: those who live in, and call
others to the eschatological rule made real by becoming disciples of
Jesus.

WHO CONSTITUTE THIS COMMUNITY?

It would appear from the flow of Matthew's story that it is 'the people'
whom Jesus began to invite to 'repent for the kingdom of heaven has
drawn near' (Matt 4: 17), and who witnessed his widespread teaching/
preaching/healing (Matt 4: 23ff.), and the fishermen whom he invited

to become fishers of men (Simon/Peter and Andrew) and follow him (and James and John) (Matt 4: 18-22). On closer examination, however, such a conclusion has its problems.[7]

Similarly, the view that it is the disciples just called who constitute the community is not without its problems, for in addition to those who endure persecution 'on my account' (Matt 5: 11), there are 'false prophets' in sheep's clothing who do not bear good fruit, and even those who prophesied/cast out demons/did many mighty works in his name he calls 'workers of lawlessness' (Matt 7: 15-23).

If, then, neither 'the crowds', nor 'all the first disciples' fits the bill, who are the recipients of the Teaching? Whom else does Matthew have in view? Is it the members of his Church? One must conclude that it is the implied readers of Matthew's Gospel.[8] The implied reader, then, has presented to him the delivery of the Teaching of Jesus in a dramatic fashion, as the words of the Messiah Son of God, who speaks of future sufferings for disciples, and of disciples turned workers of lawlessness. But who are the implied readers?

THE SERMON FOR TODAY

While the determination of Jesus' audience, or Matthew's intended readers is an important one for the question of the interpretation of the Teaching, and of its relevance today, it is not the only question.

Lest it might appear that the concentration on the 'implied reader' contributes towards fixing the meaning of the text it must be stressed that the intention of the author does not determine the meaning of the text. It is, of course, very likely that the author had some particular

---

[7] Although the crowds are presented as favourable to Jesus at times, as early as chapter 11 he censures them as 'this (evil) generation' that repudiated both John the Baptist and himself (Matt 11: 7-19). Moreover, they join in with their leaders in calling for his crucifixion (Matt 27: 20-26, 38-44).

[8] There are indications in the Gospel that Matthew was sensitive to his readers. In Matt 27: 8 the author remarks that the field bought with Judas' money is known as the Field of Blood 'to this day'. Similarly, 'to this day' false rumours are spread that Jesus did not rise from the dead (Matt 28: 15). And at Matt 24: 15 the author abruptly interrupts the narrative by saying 'Let the reader understand!' These references make it clear that the author consciously moves beyond the time of Jesus' lifetime, and writes from the standpoint of a later period looking back at Jesus.

intention as he embarked on his writing, and in the absence of access to the author's stated aims the critic is left to deduce from the text the intention of the author. But even if it were possible to discover that intention we would not have arrived at the meaning of the text. The fact is that the text of the Teaching, like any other literary text, can have a multiplicity of meanings, to be calculated from the meanings deduced by the variety of readers.

For that reason, no amount of historico-critical investigation of Matthew's use of his sources, and the nature of the Matthean Church can solve the question of the meaning of the Sermon for today. Even in Matthew's own day the Sermon could not have had one agreed meaning. Matthew may have had one meaning, but common sense rules out the possibility that this one meaning would coincide with the meaning which each individual hearer/reader drew from the text, The hope of uncovering the meaning of the text by enquiring only into the historical setting is therefore illusory.

Because Matthew's presentation of the Teaching of Jesus is in a book which is available for both private and public reading, the Teaching is directed at anyone who reads or hears it.

But that is not the whole picture. One must not be satisfied with extracting this very powerful Teaching of Jesus from the totality of the Gospel of Matthew. Matthew does not present Jesus merely as a wonderful teacher. The Teaching must be seen against its immediate background in the Gospel (4: 17-11: 1) wherein the narrator presents Jesus as proffering salvation to Israel through his ministry of teaching, preaching, and healing (4: 23; 9: 35; 11: 1). Clearly, the so-called 'Sermon' is the example *par excellence* of this facet of Jesus' activity. But Jesus' delivery of the Sermon on the Mount is not the climactic event in Matthew to which all else is subordinate. It must be seen also within the framework of the whole Gospel of Matthew. At this point one has to face into the question of discovering the plot of the Gospel.

The plot in Matthew, according to Kingsbury, is the element of conflict which pits Israel against Jesus. The climax, then, is not the Sermon on the Mount or any of the discourses, but the narration of the passion (p.133). We propose that the climax is reached only at the very end of the Gospel when the Risen Jesus gives to the Eleven the mission to all the nations, on a mountain in Galilee (28: 16-20). The promise to be with the disciples to the end of the age brings to a completion the prediction stated in the Emmanuel passage at the beginning of the Gospel (1: 23). The Gospel of Matthew, then, is framed by the assurance of the perpetual presence of God through his emissary, Jesus Messiah.

Those who had survived the traumatic days with Jesus as he suffered and died were now given the assurance of his permanent presence with them to the end of the age. His presence is not merely that of a great Teacher. Matthew's Jesus is not just a second Moses, or a wonderful Lawgiver.[9] For Matthew, the deliverer of the Teaching on the Mount is not the 'Teacher', but the 'Son of God'.[10] He is nothing less than God's mouthpiece. And that is the major reason the Teaching is so important. In it one learns of God's intentions.

People respond to the Teaching in many different ways. This variety is reflected not only in the history of interpretation, but also in people's responses in our own day. For some it is a call to the most heroic moral living. Many see it as an ideal to strive for, or as a framework within which to make one's moral choices. It leaves others quite unmoved. It is possible to interpret the Teaching in a thousand different ways. However, working one's way through the possibilities may serve only to evade the task of putting it into practice.

Although it may never be possible to put the demands of the Teaching fully into practice, we all know people who by the quality of their lives demonstrate that the effort is not without some success. The Teaching should be more than an ideal. It should serve to spur one on to a higher kind of moral living. Loving is superior to hating. Peace is preferable to war. Respect and reverence for others is more admirable than their exploitation. However, the success with which individuals put the demands of the Teaching into practice is not matched by nations, or even societies.[11]

---

[9] However highly Matthew esteems Jesus' teaching, he is never addressed as 'teacher' or 'rabbi' by persons of faith, but only by Judas, opponents, and strangers.

[10] For Matthew Jesus is Christ, conceived in Mary 'of the Holy Spirit' (1: 18, 20), on whom the Spirit descended at his baptism (3: 16), which Spirit enabled him to cast out demons, thus bringing about the kingdom (12: 28). His intimacy with the Father is unique-He is the source of all that has been delivered to him (11: 27), including, of course, his teaching (7: 27f.).

[11] In his introduction to Tolstoy's *The Kingdom of God is Within You* (ET 1905: Noonday Press, USA 1971), Kenneth Rexroth joins forces with Tolstoy in complaining that 'The great churches have indisputably compromised the simple ethics of the Gospels, and yet, Protestant and Catholic, they have always represented the Christian ethic as extraordinarily

THE SERMON IN SECULAR SOCIETY

Obviously, the Teaching on the Mount has especial relevance to anyone who claims to be a follower of Jesus. Even if it is conceded that the application of the Teaching on the Mount to the world of politics is not practicable, it can surely be insisted that the Teaching provides guidelines by which communities of believers, at least, ought to live out their daily lives. If the attitudes of the Teaching cannot be expected to infuse the Reagan-Gorbachov discussions, they ought to permeate the lifestyle of the local Christian community at least. Communities which claim to live in discipleship of Jesus must recognize in the Teaching a statement of the demands which the members of the community place upon each other. The Teaching suggests attitudes which ought to be the hallmark of the local Christian community, and it does so in a manner which recognizes the reality of people living the Christian life within a community of believers. Christian communities in which the practice of the high ideals of the Teaching is not apparent have good reason to examine their consciences.

But what are the implications of the Teaching for the world of secular affairs? Clearly, an individual is in more control of his life than he is of society. Yet society itself is composed of individuals, and its values derive to some extent from those of the individuals who compose it. The least that can be expected of disciples of Jesus is that they promote in public life the values which the Teaching of Jesus proposes. Central to this perspective is the treatment of others with that combination of compassion, forgiveness, and love which is characteristic of God himself (cf. 5: 48). The intention to treat others in the manner one would wish them to treat oneself (7: 12) has profound social and political implications. Such a disposition offers the most serious resistance to the idolizing of the divisions of the human family on the basis of nationality, creed, race,

---

difficult and unpleasant. It is nothing of the sort. Many Buddhists and most Quakers, many simple monks and nuns, millions of humble housewives who attend daily Mass or Wednesday Prayer Meeting, live this way with ease and joy' (pp. ixf.). It must be pointed out that such people are often sufficiently secure in their identity and circumstances that they do not have to deal with the problem of exercising the virtues of the Teaching in the market-place, nor do they attempt to organize society in general along the moral code of the Teaching. Were they constrained to act like the rest of men their success in applying the Teaching on the Mount to the realities of life would be no greater than that achieved by members of the great Churches.

or wealth. William Lloyd Garrison's declaration of sentiments adopted by the Boston Peace Convention in 1838 offers a timely correction to excesses of nationalism or sectarianism:

> Our country is the world, our countrymen are all mankind. We love the land of our nativity, only as we love all other lands. The interests, rights, and liberties of American citizens are no more dear to us than are those of the whole human race.[12]

Even the most corrupt of human societies can be subverted by goodness and love. The Golden Rule of doing to others what one would wish others to do to oneself might well find expression in the houses of parliament and foreign offices throughout the world. It can be brought to bear both in local affairs, and in international conflicts. The world is badly in need of love and reconciliation.[13]

The enormity of converting the world from one's own parish is reduced by practising what has been called 'the theo-politics of small steps': sowing love where there is hatred, pardon where there is injury, building bridges where there are chasms, etc., and in every way living as an instrument of peace.

People respond to the Sermon in terms of their own idealism and moral uprightness. Tolstoy said, 'As I read these rules, it seemed to me that they had special reference to me and demanded that I, if no one else, should execute them.'[14] He was equal in his condemnation of state and Church: one must choose between the Sermon on the Mount, and the Church; and Christianity in its true meaning destroys the state.

---

[12] Quoted in Tolstoy 1905, 7.

[13] The German Orthodox Jewish scholar, Pinchas Lapide, writes: 'Reason today dictates carrying the Golden Rule out of the house of God into parliaments and foreign-offices ... from social welfare through disarmament conferences to the settling of international conflicts. For today the love of neighbour and the ministry of reconciliation are not platitudes or mere embellishment of a pious sermon, but the urgent dictates of an urgently needed strategy of conciliation ... The world clock sounds the passing hours. Our time of probation is running out. It is already late' *(The Sermon on the Mount. Utopia or Program for Action?* ET 1986. New York: Orbis, 1986, p.142).

[14] *My Religion,* 1884, vol. XVI *Complete Works,* p.10.

Conclusion

The interpretation of the Teaching of Jesus Which best does justice to Matthew is that which recognizes in it the revelation of God the Father's will. The way of life described in it, which we have called 'the greater righteousness', is life lived to the full. The alternative lifestyle falls short of what is desirable, and at least in some sense possible. Anyone who hears/reads the Teaching is invited to strive to become the kind of person it describes, to love God perfectly and one's neighbour as oneself. For Matthew the ever-present Jesus Messiah is the paradigm.

The choice need not be an all-or-nothing one. Such a posing of the options is less than likely to prove very helpful. A more enlightened manner of interpreting the Teaching is to regard it, not as law to be obeyed, but as statements pointing to an excellence of moral living which invite the reader/hearer to consider, weigh up, and to implement in one's personal and political life in proportion to one's moral fibre and generosity of spirit. The degree to which they are implemented in one's personal and political life is a measure of the extent to which God's end-time rule is effective in oneself and in society. The inadequacy of the implementation confirms the realization that God's Kingdom has yet to come in its completed form, and gives the recitation of the Lord's Prayer a renewed sense of urgency.

The reader is left in no illusion about the demands of discipleship. The path will not be smooth. Trespasses will be committed. Temptations to give up the effort will be persistent. But the reader who absorbs the whole Gospel of Matthew encounters the One who by his actions shows the way, and is encouraged by the constancy of his companionship (Matt 28: 20).

It is fitting that these reflections should be presented on 25 January, the Feast of the Conversion of St Paul, and of the founding by St Vincent de Paul of the Congregation of the Mission. Each of these disciples of Jesus underwent an experience of inner transformation, and this 'conversion' propelled them to live a lifestyle akin to that described in the Teaching their Master delivered on the Mount.

PAUL ON 'POWER AND WEAKNESS'

This essay in Pauline scholarship explores a key Christian antithesis and ends with an illustration of the theme from the Palestinian experience. (The Month, 1988)

Before proceeding to all analysis of the occurrence of 'power/weakness' in Paul, it is well to situate his reflections against a more general contemporary Jewish background. Paul the Jew could not conceive of power, except in terms of his 1st century Jewish perspective, and the modifications of that traditional perspective in the light of the life of Jesus, and his experience of the Gospel. What distinguishes Paul from the Jews who did not recognize Jesus as Messiah is his attitude to Jesus as the agent of God's power.

'POWER' AND 'WEAKNESS' TERMINOLOGY

The predictable way of discussing the question of power/weakness in Paul is to examine the terminology in his letters.[1] A simple analysis of the 48 occurrences of the noun *dynamis* (power, might, strength), shows that it appears in each of the letters, except 1 Timothy, Titus, and Philippians emon. It is clear that Paul, like any zealous Jew, acknowledges that the source of all power is God.[2] Another aspect of the Pauline understanding of 'power' is gauged by noting that he contrasts 'power' with '(mere) talk' (1 Corinthians 4: 19f.; cf. 1 Thessalonians 1: 5, and 2 Timothy 3: 5).

---

[1] See D A Black, *Paul, Apostle of Weakness: Astheneia and Its Cognates in Pauline Literature* (American University Studies: Series 7, Theology and Religion 3). New York/ Bern / Frankfurt: Lang 1984.

[2] Eight Pauline texts refer explicitly to 'the power of God' (Romans 1: 16; 1 Corinthians 1: 18, 24, 2: 5; 2 Corinthians 6: 7; 13: 4 twice; and 2 Timothy 1: 18). Paul uses the phrase 'the power of the (holy) spirit' twice (Romans 15: 3, 9; cf. 1 Corinthians 2: 4; Ephesians 3: 16; 1 Thessalonians 1: 5). We meet 'the power of the Lord (Jesus)' in 1 Corinthians 5: 4, and in 2 Corinthians 12: 9 we meet the only NT occurrence of 'the power of Christ', and 'power' and 'weakness' together.

While 'power' is contrasted with 'timidity,' in 2 Timothy 1: 7, in 2 Corinthians 12: 9 we have that characteristically Pauline way of recognizing power in weakness, and in 1 Corinthians 15: 43 we read that the body which is sown in weakness (physical death.) is raised in power (resurrection).

An overview of Paul's use of the noun *astheneia* (weakness) reflects Paul's unusual understanding of weakness. While the conventional sense of (physical) weakness is apparent in, e.g., Romans 6: 9; 8: 26, one notices a clustering of the term in certain parts of the Corinthian correspondence (1 Corinthians 1: 25ff; 2: 3; 2 Corinthians 10: 10; 12: 9; 13: 4). We shall return to this matter.

'POWER' AND 'WEAKNESS' IN THE PAULINE LETTERS
Methodological Considerations

So far we have drawn attention to the presence of the terms 'power' and 'weakness' in the Pauline Corpus, without paying any attention to the context of each letter. Although it is very common among biblical theologians this method has many drawbacks.

Considerable distortion can arise if the Pauline Corpus is viewed as offering a systematic exposition of Pauline thought. As well as taking account of the peculiar nature of the composition of the letters,[3] one must respect the full context of the relationship between the authors and the recipients of the letters. The major source of information is the letters themselves, which, in addition to being only one side of the epistolary contact, may be a very poor indication of the totality of the picture.

Paul exercised his influence among the Christian communities in several ways. He founded the churches in Galatia, Thessalonika, Philippians and Corinth. Thus he exercised a profound, life-transforming and permanent effect on the members, influencing their spiritual,

---

[3] See my treatment of the fact that the majority of the so-called Pauline Letters were co-authored, and that several of them were written with the help of secretarial assistance, in M Prior, *Paul the Letter Writer and the Second Letter to Timothy (JSNTSS)*, Sheffield 1988.

[4] See Bengt Holmberg, *Paul and Power. The Structure of Authority in the Primitive Church as Reflected in the Pauline Epistles*, Philippians adelphia: Fortress 1980, pp.70-73.

intellectual, ethical, and social lives.[4] Secondly, he exercised his authority by sending his representatives (e.g., Timothy, sent to Thessalonika, Philippi and Corinth; Titus, sent twice to Corinth). Thirdly, he exercised his authority through the letters, through which, as is clear in Romans, he hoped to influence the belief and behaviour of the recipients. Finally, in several of his letters he shows himself to be determined to visit the community, and thereby, further exercise his authority.

Unfortunately the letters give an altogether inadequate picture of the critical stage of the founding of the churches, and of the very complex web of relationships between the Apostle and the churches. But they are our major source of information, and we must make the best of them and Paul's views on power and weakness is the theme that is represented very unevenly in the letters.

1 and 2 Thessalonians, 1 Timothy and Titus

In 1 Thessalonians there is no sustained reflection on power/weakness, and no mention of the Cross, nor of the suffering of Christ. This is true also of 2 Thessalonians, and 1 Timothy. In Titus there is no discussion of power/weakness, and no mention of suffering, although there is an allusion to the suffering of Christ (2: 13f; cf. 3: 6).

The Captivity Letters

Paul is a prisoner when writing to Philippians (1: 1, 10, 13, 23), but there is no mention of suffering, nor of the suffering of Christ, nor is there any reference to weakness. While there is reference to power in Colossians (1: 11), or to the Cross (1: 20, 22), and to Paul's sufferings (1: 24), there is no reference to weakness. While there are several references to 'power' in Ephesians (1: 19f; 3: 7; cf. 3: 20f.), there is no sustained treatment of a power/weakness theme.

While writing to the Philippians Paul was not only in prison (1: 7, 13f, 16f.), but was in a situation of some danger (1: 20.26; 2: 17). However, there is nothing about 'weakness'. On the contrary, he claims to have learned to be content in whatever state he found himself, and the source of his security is 'he who strengthens me' (4: 11 ff.).

The theme of suffering is very prominent in 2 Timothy, as is also the power/weakness theme. Paul appeals to his own experience of suffering as an example of how Timothy should behave in the face of imminent persecution (1: 9-12; 2: 9f). The experience of his own chains, and his fears for the fidelity of Timothy focus his attention on suffering. Clearly he takes consolation in the death/life pattern of Christ Jesus (2: 11ff.). Not only had Paul been rescued by the Lord from the sufferings he had endured in the past (3: 11), but most recently, in the face of his being abandoned by all others, the Lord had stood by him and given him power to proclaim the word fully (4: 16f.).[5]

Romans

Here the discussion of power and weakness in the sense used elsewhere takes a minor place in the more general discussion of the power of the Gospel as compared with that of the Jewish Law. For Paul the source of power is the Gospel. This basic perception is stated in a well-defined fashion in the two verses in the Letter to the Romans which many people regard as being the key verses of the whole letter (Romans 1: 16f.): 'For 1 am not ashamed of the Gospel for it is the power *(dynamis)* of God for salvation to every one who believes ...'

GALATIANS

The substance of Paul's major apologia in Galatians is that his Gospel is from God (1: 1, 12, 16). The theme of weakness appears in his reminder that it was because of a bodily ailment that he preached the gospel to them at first; and though his condition was a trial to them, they did not scorn or despise him, but received him as an angel of God, as Christ Jesus (4: 13-16).

A key to understanding his thought lies in the claim that his only boast is in the Cross of Jesus Christ, 'by which the world has been crucified to me, and I to the world. ... for I bear on my body the marks

---

[5] See my construction of the circumstances of 2 Timothy in Prior 1988.

(ta stigmata) of Jesus' (6: 14-17). The most likely interpretation of this NT *hapax legomenon* is that Paul is referring to the physical scars which he received in the course of his missionary activities in that region (Acts 14: 6.2l; Galatians 4: 13; 2 Timothy 3: 10f; 2 Corinthians 11: 25).[6]

While there is no sustained power/weakness theme, for the first time we have prominence given to Paul's bodily ailment, and this appears to have been a source of difficulty while he was with them.

1 CORINTHIANS

We are left, then, with Paul's letters to the Corinthian church.[7] His dealings with the Corinthian community were tempestuous, although this is much more obvious in 2 Corinthians than in 1 Corinthians. Any discussion of the theme of power/weakness in these letters must take place within the wider context of the relationship between Paul and the Corinthians, insofar as that is known. The two letters available to us are only part of a larger correspondence between the Apostle and the Corinthian church and, further, since other factors intervened between the writing of the two we must be careful to respect the epistolary context of each of the letters in turn.[8]

---

[6] See the detailed discussion in John S Pobee, *Persecution and Martyrdom in the Theology of Paul.* (*JSNTSS* 6), Sheffield, 1985, pp.94ff.

[7] The interpretation of the Corinthian correspondence is seriously dependent upon the integrity of the letters. While 2 Corinthians is certainly a compilation of (two) letters, the challenges to the literary unity of 1 Corinthians have not been successful. See J Murphy-O'Connor, 'Interpolations in 1 Corinthians', *CBQ* 48 (1986): 81-94. See also the more general discussion of the integrity of the Corinthian correspondence in R P Martin, *2 Corinthians* (Word Biblical Commentary 40), Waco: Word Books, 1986, pp. xl-iii.

[8] In c. AD 50-51 Paul established the church at Corinth (Acts 18), and in the period 51-54 he wrote the community a letter (Letter A, now lost—see 1 Corinthians 5: 9). In 54 he wrote again, having heard oral reports about their problems (1 Corinthians 1: 11) (Letter 13, our 1 Cor). In (spring) 55 he paid an emergency visit to Corinth, and was confronted by his opponents, and had to leave in a hurry (2 Corinthians 1: 15ff). In (summer) 55 Paul wrote again (the 'tearful' letter C of our 2 Corinthians 2: 4; 7: 8, now lost). In (autumn) 55 he received word that the Corinthians had undergone a change of heart, and lie dispatched to them letter D (2 Corinthians 1-9), stating that he was pleased and confident. In 56 he received word that the Corinthians' attitude had taken a turn for the worse, and he wrote Letter F (our 2 Corinthians 10-13). He later visited the city and wrote from there to the Romans (Martin 1986, p. xlvi).

The context of 1 Corinthians

Paul exercised considerable influence over the Corinthian Christians. He was their father in the gospel (1 Corinthians 4: 15; cf. 1 Corinthians 9: 1f; 2 Corinthians 10: 14; 11: 2). In addition to expressing his authority through this letter, he had already sent his emissary Timothy, and was planning to visit them again (1 Corinthians 4: 15-19; 11: 34; 16: 2-11). He invoked his authority, by encouraging imitation of himself (4: 16; 11: 1), and by issuing instructions on how to deal with various matters.

The first encounter with the theme of power/weakness is in the context of the debate on *sophia* (wisdom). The wisdom of the world is contrasted with that of God. The key element in the discussion is the Cross as the reference point. Secondly, Paul appeals to the social/intellectual mix of the Corinthian Christians, reminding them that not many were wise according to the flesh, etc., but that God chose the foolish ones of the world, etc., to shame the wise, etc. Thirdly, he reminds them of his preaching among them in the past. He came, not in lofty words of wisdom, and he proclaimed nothing except Jesus Christ and him crucified (1 Corinthians 2: 1f.). He confesses that he came among them in weakness, fear and much trembling (2: 5). While he had imparted wisdom, it was not the wisdom of the world, but the hidden wisdom of God (2: 8).

He next appeals to the activity of the Spirit of God. God revealed the secret through the Spirit (2:10, 13). By virtue of the gifts they have received they are puffed up (4: 7). In the light of what follows it appears that they must have despised the apostle who, by comparison, was a spectacle to the world (4: 9f.). A litany of deprivation follows (vv. 11 ff.). Later on, in a different context, Paul protests that 'to the weak I became weak, that I might win the weak. I have become all things to all men, that I might by all means save some' (1 Corinthians 9: 22).

While it seems at first sight that the major problem underlying 1 Corinthians is the existence of factions in the community there (Paul's, Apollo's, Cephas', Christ's—1 Corinthians I: 10ff; cf. 3: 6, 21: 4-6), on closer examination it appears that the more, fundamental issue at stake is the nature of Paul's authority, and the content and style of his proclamation of the gospel. His message was that of the crucified Christ, which was not a matter of human wisdom, but was the power of God (1 Corinthians 1: 18). Such is the stress in chs. 1-4 on the contrast between Paul's preaching of the word of the Cross and the wisdom of the world that one must suspect that there was considerable dissatisfaction in the community with both the content and manner of his proclamation (cf. Corinthians I: 9-27).[9] There is sufficient evidence to infer that the very apostleship of Paul was in question (1 Corinthians 9: 1-12; cf. 1:1, 12: 4: 1-5, 8-13, 14-121; 5: 1-2).

Nevertheless, at this stage there is no question of total hostility between Paul and the Corinthians, and the mood of the letter is conciliatory, and, notwithstanding the vehemence of chs.5-6 and 9, even cordial. While the first four chapters, and chapter 9 in particular, give the strong impression that the authority of Paul was the main bone of contention for the Corinthian community, the remainder of the letter reveals the extent of Paul's *confidence* in his authority vis-à-vis the Corinthians. Subsequent events show that this confidence was misplaced. We note, however, that 1 Corinthians offers little or no evidence (1 Corinthians 9: 1,1) to suggest that the differences with Paul result from the community having been invaded by outsiders. Outsiders did come later, and as we shall see, the mood of 2 Corinthians is all together more troubled.

2 CORINTHIANS
The context of 2 Corinthians

2 Corinthians is both the paradise and the despair of the commentator (Martin 1985, x). It contains the fullest and most passionate account of what Paul meant by apostleship.

It is clear that between Paul's departure from Corinth (Acts 18: 8) and the writing of 2 Cor, the relations between Paul and the Corinthians had deteriorated very badly. He had paid an unexpected visit (2 Corinthians 2: 1-4). Moreover, the community in Corinth had been visited by outsiders, and the vehemence of Paul's language in 2 Corinthians 10-13 makes it likely that their criticism of Paul had some support among the Corinthians.

---

[9] The basic stance of Gordon D Fee's commentary is that the historical situation in Corinth was one of conflict between the church and its founder, rather than one of conflict between different factions in Corinth *(The First Epistle to the Corinthians* (NICNT), Grand Rapids: Eerdmans, 1987, p. 6). It is, however, important not to allow subsequent developments to colour our reading of the situation at the time 1 Corinthians was written. In particular, the background to the vigorous confrontation in 2 Corinthians 10- 12 is the activities of Paul's opponents who have come into the community from the outside.

Everything in 2 Corinthians must he read against the most bitter attack being made on Paul the person, and Paul the apostolic minister. He defends himself vigorously against these attacks, partly, perhaps on a human plane, but more especially because he realised that no less than the authentic interpretation of the gospel, as he saw it, was at stake. Paul saw his person and his proclamation of the gospel as inextricably bound together.

The first part of 2 Corinthians reflects what must have been one of the most distressing experiences of Paul's life. He had been personally opposed and insulted by an individual or group in the Corinthian church. He was taunted with insincerity and duplicity (1: 17), accused of making promises he did not fulfil, and of arrogantly asserting authority he did not possess. Chapters 1-7 attempt to explain and justify Paul's actions in the light of his ministry.

We note in 2 Corinthians the emphasis on the afflictions which befell the faithful disciple of Jesus (1: 3-8; 4: 8-13; 6: 4-10; 7: 5). This is presented within a context of Paul's apostleship being criticized (see 2: 7; 3: 5; 4: 1-5). However, there is no treatment of the theme of power/weakness in chapters 1-7, nor in chapters 8-9.

Chapters 10-13 reflect a new threat, occasioned by the arrival of Judeo-Christians. From Paul's sarcastic criticism of what he contemptuously calls 'the super-apostles' we can attempt to construct a picture of their character. Their roots were Jewish (11: 22)—so are his, and more so. Since they were critical of his physical appearance (10: 10) we conclude that theirs was more impressive. In particular, they were skilled in the art of rhetoric, and boasting of their achievements (11: 12-18), and were acknowledged by Paul himself to be his superiors in eloquence (11: 6). They, unlike Paul, were professionally maintained by their admiring Corinthian followers (11: 7-11; 12: 14-18). Perhaps Paul's appeal to his own mystical experiences was occasioned by the high esteem attached to those of the super-apostles (12: 1-10). Although Paul claims to more than match them in some of their qualities, he shifts the focus away from his own self-sufficiency to that of God's sufficiency (cf. 2: 16: 3: 6). Paul regards his authority to derive from the power/weakness of the Cross, rather than from the manifestations of the Spirit present in both the superapostles and himself.

In all, we see that Paul was accused of vacillation (1: 17f, 23), pride and boasting (3: 1, 12; 5: 12), lack of success in preaching (4: 3), physical weakness (10: 10), 'rudeness' of speech, deficiency in rhetorical skill (11: 6), being an ungifted person (4: 7-10; 10: 10; 12: 7-10; 13: 9), dishonesty (12: 16-19), posing as a 'fool' (5: 13; 11: 16-19; 12: 6), and lack of apostolic standing (11: 5; 12: 12). Above all, he is held to be a deceiver (4: 8) and a charlatan (10: 1), a blatant denier of the power of the Christian message (13: 2-9).

What led him to his reflections on power in weakness?

THE ORIGIN OF PAUL'S THEOLOGY OF POWER/WEAKNESS
Crucified Messiah?

An outstanding feature of Paul's thought is his interpretation of the death of Jesus by crucifixion. He must have had to reassess the normal categories of strength/weakness in the light of Jesus' death-resurrection. Was this the catalyst for his remarkable fusion of strength and weakness in, e.g., 1 Corinthians 12?

In addition to his assessment of the place of suffering and crucifixion in the life-pattern of Christ he doubtless shared at least some of the admiration for the dedication to the point of death which characterized at least some strands of Jewish piety.[10] Paul attempted to address the scandal element of the crucifixion by interpreting Jesus' death, not only as a surrender of self to God (Galatians 2: 20; Ephesians 5: 2, 25; Philippians 2: 7f; cf. Romans 15: 3), but as efficacious for atoning for 'our sins' (Galatians 1: 4; Romans 3: 25; 8: 3; cf. 1 Timothy 2: 6; Titus 2: 14).

It should not come as a surprise that 'weakness' should not be distant from 'strength' in the thought-patterns of one whose Lord, in whom the fullness of the deity existed, suffered the despicable death of crucifixion. The power of God's resurrection of Jesus could never allow the ordinary interpretation of total weakness in death by crucifixion to

---

[10] See, e.g., the Book of Daniel, and 1 Maccabees 2: 60; 4 Maccabees 13: 9, 16: 3; Hebrews 11: 34; *Enoch* 91-104. Jewish regard for martyrdom is reflected also in Sirach 2, *Wisdom of Solomon 2*; 1QS 8A; 1QH 2: 12ff, *Assumption of Moses* 3: 1; 8: 1, 5, 9: 6, and the *Martyrdom of Isaiah*. It is difficult to imagine that such a widely known martyr theology would not have left some mark on the assessment of Jesus' death by his disciples, and one might well expect that this Jewish reverence for martyrs may have influenced Paul's theological reflections on the death of Jesus, and on the sufferings involved in the apostolate. See 'A Theology of Martyrdom in Judaism', in Pobee 1985, pp. 13-46.

hold sway. We submit that Paul's apparently paradoxical reflections on strength and weakness, had, as one of its foundations, the historical crucifixion and resurrection of Jesus. This was the core of his wisdom (1 Corinthians 2: 1f.).

Paul's Own Persecutions?

It must be suspected that Paul's life experience would colour his theological reflections. The crucifixion-resurrection of Jesus underpins also the sufferings attendant upon being a disciple of Jesus, and an apostle. Suffering and persecution take on a new meaning in the light of Jesus' death-resurrection (Romans 5: 1-11; 2 Corinthians 1: 3-7; 4: 14). In 1 Corinthians 4: 9 Paul compares the life of an apostle to that of men condemned to death in the arena. It is likely that this description, together with the reference to fighting the beasts in Ephesus (1 Corinthians 15: 32) are not to he understood as more than figurative language by which Paul described the life and death struggle which attended the execution of the apostolic ministry.

Paul himself met with formidable persecution, as the extended apologia of 2 Corinthians 11: 23-33 makes plain. He had experienced a variety of difficulties: imprisonments, beatings, a stoning, shipwreck, danger from rivers, etc. The memory of this litany of problems issues in his posing the rhetorical question: 'Who is weak, and I am not weak?' He goes on, 'If I must boast, I will boast of the things that show my weakness' (2 Corinthians 11: 29f; cf.1 Thessalonians 2: 2, 15). Inevitably, the one who experiences persecution is, in social terms, weak, compared with the physical strength of the persecutor.

CONCLUSIONS

I propose as one of the conclusions of this study that Paul's views on power/weakness arose out of his dealings with the various communities with which he had contact. The critical element in his thoughts derived from quite specific contexts.

Galatians : Bodily Ailments as Paul's Weakness

The scars on Paul's body, which resulted from various stonings, etc. ('the stigmata of Jesus'), instead of weakening Paul's claims, serve to authenticate his apostleship. They show his belonging to Jesus and his devoted service to his master.

Paul's strength /weakness is demonstrated in his persistence in preaching the Gospel in the midst of afflictions.

1 Corinthians: Paul's Message and Method as his Weakness

The emphasis in 1 Corinthians on countering the Corinthian view of being 'spiritual beings' suggests that some of the excesses of the community lay in their evaluation of the gifts of the Spirit, and their consequent devaluation of the less spectacular. To people who ignored the significance of the body (6: 12-15), and denied the resurrection of the dead (15: 12), who treasured the gift of tongues above all other gifts (12-14), who believed that they had already arrived in the company of angels (13: 1), who approved of sexual immorality (6: 12-20), while denying sexual relations within marriage (7: 1-6), the memory of Paul as a preacher of Christ crucified, in a manner lacking the finesse of rhetorical skills was not likely to command respect. Moreover, the fact that he insisted on working at the demeaning job of tentmaking/leather-working (Acts 18: 3; cf. 1 Corinthians 4: 12; 1 Thessalonians 2: 9; 2 Thessalonians 3: 8), and refused their financial support lowered him in their estimation as an apostle (9: 1-19). It is in this light that one must understand Paul's insistence on the cross, and on his weaknesses. In the view of the Corinthians, by comparison with them he had a long way to go.

2 Corinthians: Paul's Persecution as Power/Weakness

The climax of Paul's reflections on power/weakness is reached in chapters 11 and 12. He argues that although his pedigree surpasses that of the 'superapostles', paradoxically his real boast is in his weakness (11: 30). In the midst of even ecstatic experiences he was brought down to earth by a 'thorn in the flesh', 'an angel of Satan', to harass him and keep him from being too elated (12: 7). He is alluding to the many tribulations he encountered in the course of his ministry. The Lord himself assured him that the Lord's power is made perfect in weakness (12: 9). For that reason Paul can put up with all kinds of weaknesses, insults, hardships, persecutions, and calamities, 'for when I am weak, then I am strong' (12: 10). The weakness of which Paul boasts was the result of the persecutions he encountered in the preaching of the Gospel. The same kind of weakness brought about the crucifixion of Jesus (13: 4), and subsequently the death of Paul himself.

Paul recognized that the persecutions attendant upon the preaching of the Gospel were a necessary 'weakness' in the witness to the Christ crucified. To experience the same 'weakness' as the Lord was a privilege. Paul's theology of the Cross was more in harmony with the life-death of the Crucified One, than was the reliance of the super-apostles on eloquent words, extraordinary deeds, and impressive spiritual experiences.

What I am suggesting, then, is that the development of Paul's (theological) reflections on power/weakness derives from his dealings with the Corinthian community in particular, and arises from the nature of his relationship with them. They are not the result of his theoretical reflections on the ignominious crucifixion-death of Jesus, and its divine vindication by resurrection alone. Nor are they the result of his positive assessment of sufferings in the light of some traditional Jewish appreciation of suffering and martyrdom. Rather they derive from Paul's defence against the attack made upon him by elements of the church in Corinth who denigrated him, and called his apostleship into question. Paul saw that the calling into question of his apostleship on the grounds of unimpressive speech, inadequate miracle working, and modest spiritual experiences called the sufferings and crucifixion of Christ himself into question also.

Paul's experience of opposition and persecution had given him a feeling of empowerment in the midst of oppression. Only people who know by personal experience this kind of empowerment can understand Paul at this point.

These theoretical reflections were in my mind before I paid my recent visit to the occupied West Bank of the Jordan. I conversed with people who had been brutally beaten, whose houses had been bulldozed, whose refugee camp had been constantly placed under curfew. Their intellectuals describe the experience of the *intifada* as one of empowerment in oppression. Their power in weakness manifests itself in their determination not to cower, in their unity of purpose and sacrifice, and in their certainty of success in the face of formidable odds. Shattered limbs, broken skulls, houses reduced to rubble, all bring forth a power in weakness. These people without exception would understand the secret of Paul's sense of power in weakness, and would support him in his disagreements with the super-apostles of Corinth.

JESUS AND THE
EVANGELIZATION OF THE POOR

Here Michael develops themes from his 1995 Jesus the Liberator and argues, 'there is no legitimate theology that is not politically involved.'(Scripture Bulletin, 1996)

The Gospel of Luke is commonly regarded as 'the gospel of the poor'. Richard Cassidy's assessment is typical: 'An unmistakable feature of the Jesus described in Luke's account is that he displays a specific and consistent concern for the sick and the poor' (1987. 2). Cassidy cites the Nazareth synagogue scene (4. 18-19), the banquet of poor, maimed, etc. (14. 12-14), the reference to diseases and infirmities (14. 21), the parable of Lazarus, (16. 19-26), all of which are peculiar to Luke. In addition he highlights Luke's references to Jesus' concern for less regarded groups, such as Samaritans, Gentiles, women, and tax-collectors. But, are the poor in Luke's gospel to be identified with the hungry, those who weep, the sick, those who labour, those who bear burdens, the last, the simple, the lost, the sinners? In the first instance it is prudent to distinguish between Jesus' attitude to the poor, and that to tax-collectors and sinners (see Prior 1995: 163).

THE SCENE IN NAZARETH

In what is virtually the first scene of the Galilean ministry, Luke 4. 16-30 situates Jesus in the context of his own town in lively discussion with his own people, in their synagogue. The Nazareth scene is presented with an abundance of dramatic and literary skill. There is no mention of a reading from the Law, nor of the other elements of the service. Jesus' Old Testament text is from Isaiah (61. 1-2b and 58 .6). The use of Isaiah 61, with its emphasis on the poor (cf. Luke 7.22), ushers in a new order, which Jesus describes as the acceptable year of the Lord (Luke 19.9; cf. 23.43—see Prior 1994). Insofar as the brief Lucan account reflects what actually happened, it could do no more than summarize the lively debate which ensued. The core of Jesus' message is that the good news of Isaiah 61,

81

originally directed at the consolation of the returned exiles from Babylon, is transposed into good news for all who are oppressed.

The Isaiah text as recorded by Luke is free of any reference to that exclusiveness which is a feature of many religious traditions. Ethnicity and 'nationalism' are being challenged. The introduction of Isa 58. 6 ('to set at those who are oppressed) into the Isa 61 text intensifies the social implications of Jesus' message of freedom, due to the particular social emphasis within Isa 58. Moreover, Jesus declares the moment of liberation to be today. The Lucan Jesus' radical re-interpretation of the concept of election, challenging the notion of God's choice of one specific people, is intensified by his appeal to the example of two of the great Hebrew prophets. Jesus' focus on the Isaiah texts, with their absence of any reference to a preference for one race or nation, is reinforced by the references to Elijah and Elisha. From this point on, as the Lucan Gospel unfolds, Gods chosen ones will include the poor, the blind, the lame, the Samaritan, the Gentile, the tax-collector, the sinner, etc. This revolutionary message is good news for the outsider, and a great disappointment to those who trusted in ethnicity and tradition to give them their status. It did not go down well with the audience in his hometown.

POOR AND RICH

A survey of the occurrence of *ptochos* in the New Testament shows that *the poor* are the opposite of the rich (Luke 6. 24; Luke 16. 20, 22; 2 Cor 8. 9; James 2. 2, 3; however, see Rev 3. 17). Moreover, the path to discipleship for the rich ruler of Luke 18. 22 is to sell all that he has and give to the poor - compare Zacchaeus who gave half of his goods to *the poor* (Luke 19. 8). The evangelization of the poor is of the same order as the liberation of prisoners, the restoring of sight to the blind, the freeing of the oppressed (Luke 4. 18), the healing of the lame, lepers, and the deaf, and the raising of the dead (Luke 7. 22). Finally, the poor are classed with the non-rich, the maimed, the lame, and the blind (Luke 14. 13; cf. Luke 14. 21), perhaps because, while they exhibit quite distinct disabilities, they reflect different modes of disadvantage in society (see Prior 1995: 170-71).

It is significant to examine also the use of the term which expresses the other end of the spectrum. While *plousios* (a rich person) occurs in Matthew three times (19. 23, 24; 25. 27), twice in Mark (10. 25; 12. 41), not at all in John, it occurs eleven times in Luke. Elsewhere in the New Testament it occurs in 2 Cor 8. 9; Eph 2. 4; 1 Tim, 6. 17; James 1. 10, 11; 2. 5, 6; 5. 1; and Rev 2. 9; 3. 17; 6. 15; 13. 16. Statistics alone, then, suggest that Luke has a particular interest in the rich. Luke's Jesus is critical of the *rich* man who brought forth plentifully, and who was tempted to eat, drink, and be merry (12. 16). He also criticizes the host who invited only *rich* neighbours (14. 12). But it is in those passages in which he contrasts the rich with the poor that his teaching is at its starkest (Beatitude/Woe of 6. 20, 24, and a *rich* man and Lazarus at 16. 19, and the poor widow who gave her all, Luke 21. 14). Luke records incidents which reflect a total selfishness (the rich ruler of 18. 22-25), and a total selflessness (the poor widow of 21. 14), separated by the example of Zacchaeus who gave half his possessions away (Luke 19).

Luke's arrangement of his narrative in 18. 18-19. 10 is particularly revealing. It consists of the dialogue with the rich ruler (18. 18-30), a passion prediction (18. 31-34), the healing of the blind beggar near Jericho (18. 35-43), and the conversion of Zacchaeus (19. 1-10). Having acknowledged Jesus to be a 'good teacher', the rich ruler grows sad when he learns that inheriting eternal life demands that he sell all that he has, and give to the poor. Zacchaeus, on the other hand, who already gives half his goods to the poor, receives Jesus with joy, and with him salvation. Between the two accounts of rich men and their dealings with Jesus we have the passion prediction and the healing of the blind beggar near Jericho. Hamm sees in the literary arrangement,

> 'a kind of narrative triptych, with the center panel being the story of a literal cure of a blind man, and the two wing panels being the stories of two men blinded by their riches, one of whom, the rich ruler, is not freed by his encounter with Jesus, and the other, Zacchaeus, who is open to the gift of salvation (19.9)'(Hamm 1986. 464).

The placement of the passion prediction as a kind of hinge between the first and central panel, however, makes the triptych image rather forced. Nevertheless, it is clear from the narrative that the rich ruler of 18.18-30 needs to be cured of a kind of blindness associated with his wealth, while Zacchaeus has already given half his goods to the poor. Let the reader understand!

Putting these reflections on the theme of the rich in Luke side by side with his remarks on the poor leaves one in little doubt that when Luke speaks of *poor people* he means people who are lacking in the essentials for subsistence. But one is never poor only in a material sense. Material poverty involves loss of dignity, status, and security, and, in a society sensitive to questions of ritual purity, uncleanness.

Various attempts have been made to identify more clearly the circumstances of the community in which Luke composed his work. Why does Luke portray Jesus as being so concerned with the poor and the rich? Scholars have proposed various answers. According to Cadbury Jesus' focus was on the rich, and their responsibility to give alms, rather than on the alleviation of the lot of the poor as such (1966: 262-63). Degenhardt argues that the admonitions to abandon wealth are given only to the travelling apostles, missionaries, wandering preachers, and resident community leaders, etc. (1965: 214-15). He argues that Luke confronted *Gentile* Christians, who because of their background, had little time for the poor (pp. 221-23). Dupont takes the view that the beatitudes of Luke are addressed to the Christian community, while the woes are addressed to those outside that community, i.e., blind Israel (1973: 149-203).

Karris challenges the view of Dupont that the beatitudes and the woes cannot be addressed to the same community (1978. 115). He concludes that Luke is more concerned with possessors, than with the poor (p. 116). He holds that the summaries of Acts 2. 41-47 and 4. 31-35 are of major significance, and that they show that the ideal of friendship, so rarely found in secular society, is found in the Christian community, because Christians treat each other as friends. The function of these summaries, then, is to try to bring the Gentile Christians in his community to a sense of the Christian/Jewish concern for the poor. Luke's Christian community consists of 'propertied Christians who have been converted and cannot easily extricate themselves from their cultural mindsets. It also consists of Christians in need of alms. Luke takes great pains to show that Christians treat each other as friends and that almsgiving and care for one another's welfare isthe essence of the Way. If the converts do not learn this lesson and learn it well, there is danger that the Christian movement may splinter' (Karris 1978: 117).

Philip Esler summarizes the circumstances of the Lucan church as follows: Luke's community, living in a hellenistic city of the Roman

East in the period 85-95, experienced difficulties both from within and without. Its membership was mixed, and included people from the opposite ends of the religious and social spectra. Prior to their embracing the Christian Way some had been pagans, and others conservative Jews. Some were from the richest echelons of society, while others were beggars. The fact that the members of Jewish origin shared table fellowship with those of Gentile origin further exacerbated the problems which the Jewish Christians were having with the synagogue. The social mix of the community also contributed to the internal tensions of the Lucan community:

> The presence within the same group of representatives from the glittering elite and from the squalid urban poor was very unusual in this society and created severe internal problems, especially since some of the traditions of Jesus' sayings known to the community counselled the rich to a generosity to the destitute quite at odds with Greco-Roman attitudes to gift-giving (Esler 1987: 221).

This situation spurred on one of the leaders or intellectuals in the community, whom tradition named Luke, to re-interpret the traditions of Jesus in such a fashion as to reassure the different groups within the community by answering their problems.

On the social front Luke intensified the preference for the poor which was in the traditions available to him, and which went back to Jesus himself. He also introduced a paraenetic motif, warning the rich that their way to salvation depended on their generosity to the poor. Luke's theology, then, was motivated by the religious, social and political forces active in his own community. The relevance of Luke, Esler concludes, derives from the fact that he exercised such liberty in re-interpreting the traditions in order to address the real needs of his own community, and not merely from the appeal of so much of his theology, with its interest in such contemporary themes as rich and poor.

> The freedom with which he has moulded the gospel to minister to the needs of his community constitutes a potent authority for all those struggling to realize a Christian vision and a Christian life-style attuned to the social, economic and political realities of our own time'(Esler 1987: 223).

These various attempts help one to understand the world of the author of Luke-Acts. But even if the historical-critical method of investigation had been completely successful in illuminating the past, the curiosity of the human mind and heart would not have been satisfied. For Christians, the Bible is the book of the Church, and church people desire more than an unearthing of the past. Church people, not unreasonably, expect their religious tradition to illuminate the context of their present and future lives. Each new engagement of the believer with the text of the Bible unleashes a new encounter. It is not sufficient to discover how the person and teaching of Jesus Christ was significant in 1st century Nazareth, Jerusalem, or some hellenistic city in which Luke-Acts may have been composed, but how it is consequential today in Strawberry Hill, Sarajevo, etc. One should not attempt to evade facing major contemporary issues by expending all one's interpretative energies on questions about the past.

THE CHALLENGE FOR TODAY

Theology is constantly tempted to ignore history in favour of eternity, and to confine the salvation which the Gospel offers to the private and individual dimension. The Lucan text is an obvious one for developing a theology of liberation. One of the lessons taught by the practitioners of liberation theology is that experience *(praxis)* is the primary element in theologizing. Exegesis of a text dealing with the evangelizing of the poor should begin with the personal experience of the poor (cf. Prager 1991). In a corresponding fashion, authentic exegesis of Luke 4.16-30 should derive from a saturation in the experience of the under-class.

To profess faith in Jesus Christ is to say that his message and significance is central to one's values, gives one's life its fundamental character and direction, shapes one's understanding and vision, is the norm for evaluating oneself and others in our world, gives grounding to one's hopes and fears and aspirations, and informs one's conscience, affections and loyalties (see MacNamara 1988: 2-3). The invitation to profess faith in Jesus Christ, then, may require that one turns one's personal and community world on its head. While the emphases of each of the evangelists diverge, they are at one in requiring of the reader repentance *(metanoia)*. Whereas Matthew and Mark open the public ministry of

Jesus with the call to repentance, Luke proclaims the good news to the poor in the synagogue of Nazareth.

Responding to the invitation to repentance is not merely a matter of words, and no sensitive reader can fail to be alerted to the social obligations implied in the Lucan call to repentance (Luke 3. 10-14). It is difficult to avoid the conclusion that discipleship of the Lucan Jews demands frugality, and, if one has possessions, the alienation of them in favour of the poor. It is impossible to escape the conclusion that the Lucan theme of rich and poor must leave any Christian community fundamentally disturbed in the face of serious inequalities of wealth and social security in its own community.

A Lucan Christian ought not to possess more than is absolutely necessary for survival, as long as others are in need. It would be a scandal if the dress and meals of disciples of the Lucan Jesus were closer in quality to those of the Rich Man than to those of Lazarus. The Lucan theme of rich-poor invites its readers to alienate its riches in favour of the poor. Readers are left free to respond in proportion to their moral generosity and perhaps in the light of their political analysis. The concept of *evangelizing the poor* involves both theory and practice. In addition to getting the rhetoric right, one is presumed to effect some action, or programme of action, in favour of the poor person. What kind of betterment of the poor person is required to constitute evangelization? At this point one must acknowledge the radically different context of the Christians in Luke's church, and that of Christians today.

The inspired documents of the Early Church reflect a context in which followers of the Christian Way were in a minority, and were without any significant political power. The same cannot be said of the Christians of any period since Constantine. If the most that was required by Luke in his context was that the rich members of his community should come to the aid of the poor ones, and that they should live frugally, much more is required of Christians today if they submit themselves to the power of Luke's invitation.

Whether or not a Christian, or group of Christians, lives frugally is not a phenomenon of absolute significance, and is probably a matter of marginal interest to the poor. The poor do not require Christians to adopt the destitution of their lifestyle. In any case, because biblical scholars and all church officials are secure members of the empowered class, their 'practice of poverty' can never be more than a gesture. In our western society, at least, Christian leaders and exegetes can never share the degradation of the poor.

What the poor can with justification require is that Christians use their power in their favour. Modern Christians true to the picture presented by Luke are invited to subvert, rather than underpin those cultures which produce poverty, and ignore the plight of the poor. The modern Lazarus is not likely to be impressed should Dives imitate his life-style, even to the point of having the sores of his body licked by dogs. A Christian society which rests content with the life-style of the rich man of Luke 16, and allows Lazarus to languish, cannot expect to fare any better than the man who dressed in purple and feasted sumptuously every day.

Readers attracted to the ideal of the evangelization of the poor, may be expected to respond to Luke's invitation with enthusiasm To respond absolutely puts one in a position of radical discipleship—that will always be a minority response. Turning one's back on the poor leaves the rich one sad. Fortunately, as the discipleship of Zacchaeus shows, half-measures are better than none.

LUCAN LIBERATION AND LIFE

One of the major achievements of the challenge which liberation theologies have offered to Western dominated theology is its insistence that authentic theological reflection cannot be divorced from the social and political realities of life. It is only when theology involves itself with the realities of the conditions of people, and particularly those in oppression that it can be seen to offer a new order.

Nevertheless, liberation rhetoric is not sufficient. Liberation requires great people who can elevate into concrete political programmes the ideals of liberation theologies. Such a task is beyond the ability of exegetes alone, and will require collaboration with theologians, economists, politicians, etc.

The Church must pursue the goal of the liberation which Jesus ushered in. His message contained the seeds of revolution. But to see the Gospel as addressing only individual people, and in a private fashion is to guarantee its social irrelevance. However, Jesus did not leave a clearly worked out strategy whereby his disciples would transform, the world. It is up to the ingenuity of his disciples to carry the message forward, so that it becomes a light to the world, the salt of the earth, and the leaven that transforms the world in all its parts. In Jesus' new society God's favour is poured out on the underclass.

But from being a society which looked to the transformation of the world, the Christian Church has had to accommodate itself to a long life in history. From being an agent of radical reform, it came to be the major stabilising factor in the Roman Empire, within a few hundred years, and behaved like all imperial, or state religions in propping up the current present structures. In most parts of the world today Christians have access to the power structures of society. The Lucan Jesus invites them to subvert all oppressive patterns in society, so that the human family can live in equality and mutual respect.

CONCLUSION

The New Order ushered in by Jesus of Nazareth challenges those who encounter it to participate in the liberation of the oppressed. The task is formidable. The pervasiveness and ubiquity of evil in the world tempts one to abandon the struggle to continue to bring the Kingdom about, and leave things to God to sort out at the end of time. This cannot be a legitimate Christian option. The liturgy of Good Friday invites Christians to grapple with the perplexity of apparent disaster: to face into the reality of dreams which have become nightmares, of visions which have never come off the drawing-board. They are invited to die with Christ, to enter the tomb with the spirit-less corpse of Jesus, bringing 'our body's labour, our spirit's grief, our selfish hearts, our failing faith, our daily toil, the plants in our heart's poor soil, all that we start and spoil, each hopeful dream, the chances we have missed, the graces we resist' (from Kevin Nichol's hymn, 'In Bread we Bring you, Lord').

The Christian Church, which comes and stays together precisely because of Jesus has a critical role to play if it is to be true to its Master. But meanwhile, it must itself be subjected to the conversion involved in being evangelized. The Christian Church, if it is faithful to its founder from Nazareth, should be at the forefront of transformation, not only by offering the world the liberation rhetoric of Luke 4. 16-30, but by contributing to the development of goals and strategies by which the poor can experience the blessedness of the Gospel. Jesus' ministry acted out the programme of reform announced in Nazareth, as he testified for John the Baptist, 'Go and tell John what you have seen and heard: the blind receive their sight, the lame walk, lepers are cleansed, and the deaf hear, the dead are raised up, poor people are evangelized' (Luke 7. 22).

In God's Kingdom the poor will be enriched, captives will be set free, the blind will have their sight restored, the oppressed will be freed, and the longed-for year of God's favour will be ushered in. The liberation Jesus inaugurated in Nazareth was not a national liberation, but rather a liberation for all. His message of release from bondage, however, does not automatically eliminate the interracial barbarisms in Sarajevo, the scandalous starving in Somalia, or restore the dignity of a people trodden down by various forms of structural oppression.

Jesus' message is an invitation to join the company of those committed to a better future, of a New Order of The Kingdom, wherein we have

> .... Festivals at which the poor man
> Is king and the consumptive is
> Healed; mirrors in which the blind look
> At themselves and love looks at them
> Back; and industry is for mending
> The bent bones and the minds fractured
> By life. It's a long way off, but to get
> There takes no time and admission
> Is free, if you will purge yourself
> Of desire, and present yourself with
> Your need only and the simple offering
> Of your faith, green as a leaf
> (R S Thomas, *The Kingdom*)

Alas, much more is required than the purging of one's individual malice! There is no legitimate theology that is not politically involved. The political theology which derives from the teaching and example of the crucified Lord of history exposes the institutionalized selfishness espoused by nation states and international economic communities. But the poor and exploited will not congratulate the Christian Church merely for exposing injustice. Appropriate political action must derive from theological reflection which is focused on the programme, 'He sent me to evangelize the poor', and is enlivened by the vision, 'See, I make all things new' (Rev 21. 5). The preacher in the Nazareth synagogue offers an ethic which is distinctive. His call is to bring about God's New Order within the reality of life. Only when 'the blind receive their sight, the lame walk, lepers are cleansed, and the deaf hear, the dead are raised up, poor people are evangelized' (Luke 7. 22) can the Church be at peace with its Founder, the Nazareth preacher, and its Lord.

REFERENCES

Cadbury, H J. *The Making of Luke-Acts*. London: SPCK, 1927.
Cassidy, R J *Jesus, Politics and Society: A of Luke's Gospel* New York: Maryknoll (Orbis), 1978.
Degenhardt, H.-J. *Lukas, Evangelist der Armen: Besitz und Besitzverzicht in den lukanischen Schriften: Eine traditions- und redaktionsgeschichtliche Untersuchung.* Stuttgart: Katholisches Bibelwerk, 1965
Dupont, Jacques. *Les Béatitudes*. Études Bibliques. Paris: Gabalda, 1958(I), 1960 (II) 1973 (III).
Esler, Philip F. *Community and Gospel in Luke-Acts*. SNTSMS 57. Cambridge: Cambridge University Press, 1987
Hanim, D. 'Sight to the Blind: Vision as Metaphor in Luke.' *Biblica* 67 (1986) 457–77
Harris, R J. 'Poor and Rich: The Lukan *Sitz im Leben*', in *Perspectives on Luke-Acts,* ed C H Talbert. Edinburgh: T&T Clark, 1978, 112–25
MacNamara, V. *The Truth in Love. Reflections on Christian Morality*. Dublin: Gill & Macmillan, 1988.
Prior, M. 'Isaiah and the Liberation of the Poor (Luke 4. 16–30)', *Scripture Bulletin* 24 (1994) 36–46.
Prior, M. *Jesus the Liberator. Nazareth Liberation Theology (Luke 4. 16-30)*. Sheffield: Sheffield Academic Press, 1995.
Prager, J P. The Poor as the Starting Point for Vincentian Studies: A Liberation Hermeneutic.' *Vincentiana* 1991 (no 2): 140–145.

REVISITING
THE PASTORAL EPISTLES

This major article for Scripture Bulletin *in 2001 reviewed Michael's major doctoral research findings in the light of subsequent scholarship.*

The publication of Monsignor Jerome D Quinn's commentary on the First and Second Letters to Timothy,[1] twelve years after his death, brings to the academy the full fruits of his engagement with the Pastoral Epistles (henceforth PE). Quinn, a past president of the Catholic Biblical Association of the USA, former editor of the *Catholic Biblical Quarterly*, and a former member of the Pontifical Biblical Commission, had been engaged, since 1966, in writing the Anchor Bible commentary on the PE. I have a special interest in the publication, both personal and professional. It also provides an opportunity to revisit an area that occupied my scholastic attention for many years.

I followed Mgr Quinn's course in the Pontifical Biblical Institute, Rome in 1971-72. His refreshing style encouraged one to interrogate scholastic assumptions. To that end, parallel to his lectures, he had us contrast two commentaries on the PE, which drew opposite conclusions from the same evidence. C K Barrett, an expert in the language and thought world of 1st-century Christianity, argued that the PE were pseudepigraphical letters, written by a disciple after Paul's death (possibly in the period AD 90-125), and incorporating fragments of genuine Pauline letters, while J N D Kelly, a specialist in the 2nd century, concluded that they were genuine letters of Paul.[2]

While the Anchor Bible commentaries were intended for the general reader they were to be written with the most exacting standards of scholarship. Few of the volumes in fact could be read by the general

---

[1] Jerome D Quinn and William C Wacker, *The First and Second Letters to Timothy. A New Translation with Notes and Commentary* (The Eerdmans Critical Commentary), Grand Rapids, Michigan, Cambridge, UK: Eerdmans, 2000.

[2] C K Barrett, *The Pastoral Epistles* (Oxford: Clarendon, 1963) and J N D Kelly, *The Pastoral Epistles* (London: A&C Black, 1963).

public, and most provided their authors with a license to dazzle readers with their exegetical skills. That Quinn's commentary would match the most technical in the series was reinforced by the determination to publish it in two volumes. Quinn had been invited to write in 1966, and it was already 1972, with no end in sight.

In addition to attributing the PE to the author of Luke-Acts, Quinn proposed that they constituted the 'third roll' of the trilogy Luke-Acts-PE. The block of three 'unreal', pseudepigraphical letters was intended to be read as an epistolary appendix extending the narrative of Luke-Acts to encompass Paul's imminent death. Quinn was not the first to suggest that Luke had written the PE, but that they constituted the third volume of the author's literary production was a bold hypothesis indeed. The order of composition was Titus, 1 Timothy and 2 Timothy, with the sixty-six words long Tit 1.1-4—out of all proportion to the short letter that follows—functioning as a preface to the whole collection. As a postgraduate student I considered his thesis to require more convincing supporting evidence than he appeared at that time to be able to provide.

There was a chasm between Quinn's impressive, detailed analysis of words and his imaginative reconstruction of the origins of the letters. Nevertheless I was so impressed by the breadth, depth, thoroughness and imaginative character of his exegesis that I wrote my final *Tessina* ('The Episcopal Virtues of 1 Tim 3.1-7') also under his direction. My subsequent difficulty in making progress on the social setting of 1 Tim 3.1-7, without having taken a position on the authenticity of the PE, led me to further research on the question of authorship.[3]

Already by 1976 Mgr Quinn had suffered a severe heart attack in Alice Springs. While he recuperated with me in September 1987, after another heart attack in Oxford, he read the manuscript of my book, *Paul the Letter Writer and the Second Letter to Timothy*, subsequently published in 1989. Given Quinn's poor health, I doubted that his commentary would ever see the light of day. After I had sent him a copy of my book on 8 May 1989, the attorney for his estate informed me that Mgr Quinn had died on 13 September the previous year, and that the administrator of his estate would put it in the library of the St

---

[3] I proposed a model of Paul as an epistolographer following the patterns of letter writing of his day, a study which culminated in my doctoral thesis, 'Second Timothy: A Personal Letter of Paul' (Kings College, London University 1985).

Paul Seminary. I wondered what would be the fruit of all his work on the PE.

Philip Boelter graciously saw the first volume, *The Letter to Titus*, through to publication in 1990, as volume 35 of the Anchor Bible series. As if offering an *apologia* for his novel reading of the letters Quinn insisted that 'Scholarship advances … with the individual insights and analysis of its practitioners, not by majority vote' (p. xiii). Its introduction to and translation of all three letters are reproduced in the second volume, for which William C Wacker reworked the 1,442 pages of Quinn's manuscript, from 1 Tim 4.6 to the end of 2 Timothy-Quinn had completed the work as far as 1 Tim 4.5. Understandably, there is no attempt to take account of the literature on the PE which has appeared since 1988. But somewhat surprisingly, this second volume inaugurates the Eerdmans Critical Commentary series—there is no indication as to the fate of what was to have been Vol. 35a of the Anchor Bible series. The commentaries on Titus (1990) and this new one on First and Second Timothy (2000) mark the culmination of Quinn's contribution to biblical scholarship. It should be set in a historical perspective.

FROM AUTHENTICITY TO PSEUDONYMITY

Since the 19th century up to quite recently scholarship on the PE has been dominated by the question of the identity of their author(s)—despite the fact that, except for some doubts in the 2nd century, their Pauline authenticity was unquestioned until the 19th century. Questions such as, by whom were they written, when, to whom, for what purpose, etc.— reflecting the typical concerns of the historical critical method—eclipsed other legitimate questions, such as ones concerning their theological content. Moreover, some of the academic debate reflected Reformation polemics, with the Catholic constituency applauding what they found in the PE because it mirrored a theology and church governance with which it was familiar.

In some circles on the Protestant side it was not unusual until recently to consider the PE to witness to a Christianity which sought little more than to live comfortably in the world: Christian life had become 'routinised': it had lost its charismatic enthusiasm and had become 'bourgeois', producing a distinctly 'middle-class' Christian culture, which was a corruption of the earlier (invariably Pauline) kind of Christian polity. These letters written two or three generations after Paul's death, then, were not only different from, but also inferior to the genuine letters of Paul, being a corruption of his charismatic message, accommodating it to a period which was distinguished by a systematisation of doctrine, a deadening of faith, and an encasement of the Spirit who blows where he wills. The PE reflected the period of 'early Catholicism', which, in the judgement of some not enamoured of the practices of the Roman Catholic Church, represented a sad declension from the apostolic (i.e., Pauline) Gospel. The PE, then, produced a Gospel that was not only post-apostolic in time but also sub-apostolic in standard. Some of the more recent scholarship, however, judges the PE to reflect a coherent theological and ethical perspective rooted in some particular ecclesial context in time and place, rather than a merely meta-historical context disengaged from particularities of space and time.[4]

The modern challenge to the Pauline authenticity of the PE began in the 19th century. Friedrich Schleiermacher—the first to publish a rejection of the Pauline authorship of one of the PE—argued that 1 Timothy, because of its un-Pauline style and vocabulary, the difficulty of fitting its personal circumstances into the known life of Paul, and the nature of the opposition presupposed in it, could not have been written by Paul. Nevertheless, pseudonymous authorship in no way detracted from the authority of the work, which was established by its content, rather than by its authorship.[5] J G Eichhorn claimed to have anticipated Schleiermacher's conclusion, and added that Titus and 2 Timothy—since all three were considered to stand together—also were written, not by Paul, but by a clever forger after his death. Again, that they were pseudonymous did not detract from their authority, since they were in agreement with apostolic doctrine.[6] Later, F C Baur argued that the heretics implied in the PE could not be situated within the apostolic period, but fitted well with 2nd-century Gnosticism. Hence, the PE were written by 2nd-century Paulinists as part of their defence against the Gnosticism of the 2nd century.[7]

---

[4] See especially Frances Young, *The Theology of the Pastorals* (Cambridge: Cambridge University Press, 1994).

[5] *Über den sogennanten ersten Brief des Paulus as den Timotheus* (Berlin, 1807).

[6] *Einleitung in das Neue Testament*, Vol. 3 (Leipzig, 1814).

[7] *Die sogennanten Pastoralbriefe des Apostels Paulus aufs neue kritisch untersucht* (Stuttgart/Tübingen, 1835).

H J Holtzmann's work quickly established itself as the classic statement of the case against the Pauline authorship of the PE: they could not be fitted into the known life of Paul; the traditions about a Pauline mission to Spain should be dismissed; the implied situation of the addressees was contrary to the historical reality; the opponents were not the Judaisers of Paul's time, but 2nd-century Gnostics; but, above all, the vocabulary and literary style of the letters told against their presumed Pauline authorship. A follower of Paul did not hesitate to call his hero from the grave to come to the aid of the 2nd-century Church in its hour of need. By creating a fictitious correspondence from Paul to Timothy and Titus the author instilled in the readers of the PE the assurance that his pattern of church government enjoyed the support of 'Pauline' authentication.[8]

Despite Holtzmann's 'definitive argument' against it, however, the authenticity of the PE was defended widely over the following thirty years. It was P N Harrison's study which shifted the balance in Anglo-American scholarship against the traditional view. Although he presented other arguments also,[9] his use of statistics and graphs in discussing the distinctive vocabulary of the PE gave his argument the appearance of 'objectivity', if not indeed 'mathematical exactitude'. Most critically, he argued that the vocabulary of the PE was not only distinctive but reflected a period later than that of Paul. No less than 175 of the 848 words of the PE's vocabulary do not occur in the New Testament. He pointed out that 93 of that 175 occur in either the Fathers or Apologists, asserting that that showed that they belonged to the working vocabulary of the 2nd century.[10]

---

[8] *Die Pastoralbriefe kritisch und exegetisch behandelt* (Leipzig, 1880), 109-10, 157-59, 276.

[9] Harrison's argument deals with the question of the chronological framework of the Pastorals, their polemics, their doctrine, their ecclesiastical organisation, and psychological factors, which, when taken together, 'are almost overwhelming and decisive' (*The Problem of the Pastoral Epistles*, Oxford: Oxford University Press, 1921, 60).

[10] Harrison's scholarship at this point is fundamentally flawed, since it can be verified readily that no less than 95 of 'the distinctively 2nd-century 175 words' occur, several frequently, in the writings of Philo of Alexandria, who died some twenty years before Paul. Indeed as early as 1929 F R M Hitchcock showed that at least 153 of the 175 words occur in extant writings from before 50 AD ('Tests for the Pastorals', in *Journal of Theological Studies* 30: 272-29). Nevertheless, despite additional evidence fatal to his insistence on a 2nd-century provenance for the PE, Harrison was unrepentant in 1964, when he modified some of the structure of his 1921 work, leaving its sandy foundations untouched (see his *Paulines and Pastorals*, London: Villiers Publications). It should be acknowledged that Harrison's critical argument for placing the PE in the 2nd century, namely that concerning its allegedly 2nd-century vocabulary, has no validity whatever, and that that part of his argument should have been withdrawn from the discussion long ago.

Despite their 2nd-century provenance, however, Harrison asserted that the PE contained a 'notable quantity of definitely Pauline matter bearing the unmistakable stamp of the apostle'. These genuine Pauline fragments, taken from brief notes addressed by the Apostle at various times, were put together by a Paulinist some fifty years after Paul's death, and form part of the texts of 2 Timothy and Titus.[11] But some continued to argue for the authenticity of the PE.

By the 1980s, the obstacles to accepting the traditional view of the Pauline authorship of the PE focused on the perceived irreconcilability between them and the recognised letters of Paul, in matters of language, literary style, theological perspective, church organisation, the nature of the opponents, and the difficulty of situating their biographical details within Paul's known life. To these internal criteria could be added the alleged evidence of p[46], the Chester-Beatty papyrus, which was taken to witness to the absence of the PE from this, the earliest collection of Paul's letters.[12] Three hypotheses contended for support: a minority view that the PE are genuinely Pauline; a view of diminishing support that, while pseudonymous, they contain fragments from genuine Pauline letters; and the most popular hypothesis that they are altogether pseudonymous, written after Paul's lifetime by someone claiming his authority.

The task of those espousing the genuineness of the letters was formidable, since there was a detailed Pauline framework into which they would have to insert the evidence of the PE. Moreover, they had to account for the host of differences between the PE and the Paulines, in both content and language. Usually this was attempted by arguing that Paul wrote the PE close to the end of his life, reflecting a period of missionary activity after he had been released from his first imprisonment in Rome, for which missionary activity, of course, there is considerable evidence.[13] Invariably differences in vocabulary and language were accounted for by supposing that Paul allowed more freedom of expression to his secretary, not least while he was in prison (2 Timothy).

---

[11] *The Problem of the Pastoral Epistles*, 68, 87, 93, 103-7.

[12] Jeremy Doty refutes this conclusion, and argues that the author of p[46] (c. AD 200) either did include the three letters, or intended including them, but miscalculated the space required ('p[46] and the Pastorals: A Misleading Consensus?', in *New Testament Studies* 44[1998]: 578-90).

[13] See my *Paul the Letter Writer and the Second Letter to Timothy* (Sheffield: Sheffield Academic Press, 1989), 66-90.

Given their unspoken assumptions, and their failure to deal with a host of objections, it is surprising that fragments theories ever gained currency. They were, of course, a moral 'safe haven': while allowing considerable pseudonymous invention, they incorporated genuine Pauline elements, always, allegedly, for the highest of motives. In concluding that the question of authorship lies between those supporting their authenticity and those espousing pseudepigraphy David Cook judged that 'the intermediate ground occupied by the defenders of the fragment hypothesis proves to be rather a no man's land not suited for habitation.'[14]

That the PE are pseudonymous letters, written by a disciple of Paul in the post-apostolic period for the highest of motives, is the most popular view among scholars, with 80-90 percent support, according to Raymond E Brown.[15] Such support, as in most cases of academic consensus, is not the result of each scholar investigating the matter afresh, but of accepting someone else's work, which one has had neither the time nor the inclination to interrogate. Hypotheses of pseudepigraphy in general are attractive since their reconstruction of the past does not have to fall within a clearly delineated historical context, of time, space or occasion. They are characteristically vague in their putative historical settings for the PE. While Quinn is somewhat more forthcoming than others in suggesting a historical context for the pseudonymous PE his hypothesis also has its share of assumptions and unprovable assertions.

---

[14] 'The Pastoral Fragments Reconsidered', in *Journal of Theological Studies* n.s. 35(1984): 120-31. Nevertheless, in a revised version of the fragments theory James D Miller's recent study argues that neither Pauline nor pseudonymous authorship can adequately account for the origin of the PE, since they lack the characteristics of written narrative prose: lacking a developed argument they wander through a variety of topics, centring on none (*The Pastoral Letters as Composite Documents*, Cambridge: Cambridge University Press, 1997). They are best explained as composite documents by a compiler, based loosely upon genuine notes from Paul to his co-workers. Miller detects an 'authentic core' in each letter—in 1 Timothy, 1.1-7; 1.18-20; 3.14-15; 6.20-21, which, when read consecutively, form a 'plausible' note—consisting of the original Pauline notes which form the loose framework for the rest of the material. A 'school', analogous to that at Qumran, which was dedicated to the preservation and creative transmission of religious texts, may have 'splintered' the notes and produced the PE, in the interests of training and caring for church leaders. His argument fails to convince. Where, for one problem, is the evidence in Qumran for the composition of a pseudonymous letter allegedly from the Teacher of Righteousness?

[15] *An Introduction to the New Testament* (New York/London: Doubleday, 1997), 668.

THE SIGNIFICANCE OF QUINN'S COMMENTARY

The introduction to the commentary on 1 and 2 Timothy, which reproduces that of the 1990 volume (*Titus*), outlines Quinn's overall analysis of the letters and summarises his evidence for his hypothesis. Just as other collections of letters—a popular literary genre in Roman political life—were assembled by an admirer of the writer, and passed on to subsequent generations because of their enduring value, so also the PE. Sometimes a collection of letters was prefixed to another work (as in the seven letters within the Book of Revelation, etc.), or inserted within a text (as in Jer 29, etc.), or added at the end.[16] Quinn asserts that:

> The appearance of compositions in the epistolary form within a larger work of instructive history signalled the genuineness, the credibility, and the authority of what was going to be or had been narrated. A cluster of letters intensified these impressions.

The PE, then, were read as a collection in the second, or indeed the 1st century, being considered by their presenter at least to be an authoritative message from a significant personality from the past.

Moreover, Timothy and Titus:

> are less actual historical individuals than paradigmatic persons...who furnish the pattern of what the continuing Pauline apostolate is and does. They are models of Paul and models for believers as they are designated to carry on the apostle's work, carry out his commands, imitate his sufferings, teach his gospel and practise it themselves, preside at the liturgy, receive material support for their ministerial work, and choose other men who will in their turn share their apostolic ministry.

The opponents also have a typological character. The PE were received and read, then, not as individual letters from the Paul of history, but as a 'characterisation' of the great apostle and his teaching for the

---

[16] Unfortunately the evidence for this critical assertion is not reproduced in the commentary. Instead Quinn directs the reader to his article, 'The Last Volume of Luke: the Relation of Luke-Acts to the Pastoral Epistles', in *Perspectives on Luke-Acts* (ed. C H Talbert, Edinburgh: T&T Clark, 1978), 62-75.

new generation—for Quinn, the letters were written in the period AD 80-85, and most likely in Rome.[17] Even more assumptions follow.

The ignominious death of Paul, condemned by Roman law, was a source of embarrassment to the early Christians, who consequently attempted to play down his person, his teaching and his ministry. A disciple, wishing to counter this tendency and 'rehabilitate' Paul, composed the PE pseudonymously. That Paul's condemnation to death was a source of scandal to Christians strikes me as an unlikely assumption, given the centrality of Jesus' crucifixion in early Christian preaching, not to speak of its role within Pauline theology, as well as Paul's discourse in Philippians on his own possible death. Furthermore, why should the author of the PE issue his *apologia* for Paul by writing letters in Paul's name to individuals, rather than, as was his custom, to communities? And why three, with two (1 Timothy and Titus) sharing much in common? Quinn's assertions are replete with assumptions: 'The PE as a collection would have been received and read not as individual letters from the Paul of history but as a 'characterization' of the great apostle and his teaching for the new generation'(p. 20).

For Quinn, the PE emphasise the unity of Christian believers, Christian links with their past, especially with the Pauline apostolate and its teaching. They also prepare Christians for the future—with the 'catholic church' and the catholic canon of Scripture pitted against the Gnostics and the followers of Marcion—and for the even further removed eschaton. Such hypotheses, of course, account for some of the relevant data, but involve a host of hidden and uprovable assumptions. But in the ethereal culture of theories of pseudepigraphy Quinn's overall hypothesis is, as least, as possible as a range of others.

But whatever one's misgivings about Quinn's general hypothesis, the two volumes constitute a major commentary on the Greek text, and are a welcome addition to the literature on the PE. The detailed comments on each verse are a model of exact scholarship, reflecting the author's exceptional erudition not only in matters of biblical studies but in the wider culture of the 1st century. Quinn's attention to detail, and his insistence on availing of the insights of all the scholars who preceded him, marks out his commentary as the most learned one since the two-volume commentary of Ceslaus Spicq.[18] It is a monument to the memory

---

[17] *The First and Second Letters to Timothy*, 8-9, 15-16, 19-21.

[18] *Les Épîtres Pastorales* (Paris: Gabalda, 1969, revised).

of a scholar who dedicated much of his life's work to a commentary on the PE. Moreover, the academy owes a great debt to each of the stalwarts, Philip Boulter (*Titus*) and William C Wacker (*The First and Second Letters to Timothy*), who saw the massive works through to publication.

The wealth of learning and detail in the Notes and Comments will ensure that Quinn's commentary will be consulted for generations to come. Inevitably scholars will differ here and there on the details. A more pressing question, however, concerns the relation between the comments on the separate verses, which are most enlightening, and the overall picture summarised in the introductory material: do the detailed notes and comments provide additional and adequate academic support for the bold hypothesis by which the author accounts for the production of the PE? I wish to indicate some of the reservations I have to accepting his hypothesis.

THE SEDUCTION OF PSEUDONYMITY

Invariably theories of pseudonymity are proposed on the basis of assumptions, which are not always explicit. Their plausibility would be less problematic if one could show that the practice of composing pseudepigraphic *letters* was common, and that the PE were just one more example. In reality, however, such letters are rare, and where there is evidence for them they differ from the PE. Moreover, unlike hypotheses which argue for Pauline authenticity, which have to fulfil very exacting conditions (specificity of place, time and occasion, etc.), theories of pseudonymity pass the test of scholarly verifiability very lightly: all that needs to be done is to propose that some unknown person, on some unknown occasion, and for some supposed, unverifiable purpose, produced his own theological viewpoint under the guise of Pauline letters. Hence, such hypotheses, however bizarre, are virtually impervious to disproof.[19] The evidence Quinn provides to support his hypothesis is not sufficient to convince this reader. The notes and commentary, however

---

[19] Limitations of imagination are the only obstacle to innumerable possible hypotheses of pseudepigraphy. Richard I Pervo, for example, suggests that the PE constitute an 'epistolary novel', for which no real epistolary context is necessary ('Romancing an oft-neglected Stone: The Pastoral Epistles and the Epistolary Novel', in *The Journal of Higher Criticism* 1[1994]: 25-47).

replete with impressive lexicographical learning, do not press home the assertions offered in the Introduction. Nor are the multiple difficulties attending the hypothesis really addressed. Moreover, it does not appear to be necessary even to consider the moral implications of pseudepigraphy and the possibility of deceit.

Hesitations based on moral reservations concerning the acceptability of pseudepigraphy are easily assuaged. It is sufficient merely to assert, without evidence, that the pseudonymous authors always worked from the highest motives. Such theories are thus brought into a safe theological sanctuary, preserving both the moral integrity of the author and the (Pauline) authority of the pseudepigraphon. But, on what grounds can one be sure that the author was a *pedisequus* (follower) of Paul (Harrison), who, operating throughout with genuine pastoral zeal, passed on what Paul 'had dictated' in his lifetime, presenting it later as what should obtain for the church of the pseudepigrapher's day?[20]

On what historical and academic basis can one presume on a type of pseudonymity which was 'innocent, sincere and honest…not [the fruit] of malice or cowardice, but rather of modesty and natural timidity'?[21] On what grounds can one assume that 'When the pseudonymous writings of the New Testament claimed the authorship of the most prominent apostles … this was not a skilful trick of the so-called faker … but the logical conclusion of the presupposition that the Spirit himself was the author',[22] or, that the pseudonymous writer considered his master to be alive in heaven addressing a new audience from the clouds, so to speak?[23] Could one so easily rule out the possibility that the letters came from the hand of an unscrupulous church official, a 'clever forger', or a liar, however noble— perhaps even 'a liar, and a fluent liar therewith' (as Rudyard Kipling's Pagett, MP)—who, writing in Paul's name to invoke his authority, did not hesitate to distort his teaching in the interests of advancing his own 'early

---

[20] Such is the view advanced by Norbert Brox in what was then the most impressive statement of the pseudonymous provenance of the PE (*Die Pastoralbriefe*, Regensburger Neues Testament, Regensburg: Pustet, 1969).

[21] Thus A Deissmann, *Bible Studies. Contributions chiefly from Papyri and Inscriptions to the History of the Language and Literature, and the Religion of Hellenistic Judaism and Primitive Christianity* (Edinburgh: T&T Clark, 1903), 15.

[22] Thus K Aland, 'The Problem of Anonymity and Pseudonymity in Christian Literature of the First Two Centuries', in *Journal of Theological Studies* 12(1961): 39-49, 44-45.

[23] Thus K Koch, 'Pseudonymous Writing', *The Interpreter's Dictionary of the Bible,* Supp. Vol., 1976: 712-14, 713.

Catholic' type of Christianity,[24] and who was now languishing in the other place finally lamenting his indiscretion, or still defiantly rejoicing in the comprehensive success of his deceit?

Unspoken assumptions that pseudepigraphical letters were innocent and morally acceptable in the post-apostolic period are scarcely ever questioned, despite significant evidence from antiquity pointing in the opposite direction. Indeed, in no case can it be deduced with certainty that pseudepigrapha were executed with no intention to deceive. On the contrary: having examined both Christian and non-Christian documents, L.R. Donelson concluded that, 'We have no known instance of a pseudepigraphon recognised as such which acquired prescriptive and proscriptive authority as well. If discovered, it was rejected.'[25] There is abundant evidence to show that no writing known as pseudepigraphical was ever accepted as authoritative in the early church.[26] Nevertheless, Raymond Brown could claim:

> One of the Pauline 'school' of disciples took it upon himself to write a letter in Paul's name because he wanted it to be received authoritatively as what Paul would say to the situation addressed. Such a situation makes sense if one supposes that Paul was dead and the disciple considered himself an authoritative interpreter of the apostle whose thought he endorsed. Attribution of the letter to Paul in those circumstances would not be using a false name or making a false claim that Paul wrote the letter.[27]

---

[24] Thus D N Penny, 'The Pseudo-Pauline Letters of the First Two Centuries' (unpublished doctoral dissertation (Emory University, 1979).

[25] L R Donelson, *Pseudepigraphy and the Ethical Arguments in the Pastoral Epistles* (Tübingen: Mohr, 1986), 11. The widely accepted argument advanced by D Meade that within the Old Testament there was a tradition of pseudonymous literature in which traditions were supplemented, interpreted and expanded in the name of earlier authors is hardly relevant to the discussion of the PE (*Pseudonymity and Canon*, WUNT 39, Tübingen: Mohr-Siebeck, 1986, 17-43); see further Stanley E Porter, 'Pauline Authorship and the Pastoral Epistles: Implications for Canon', in *Bulletin for Biblical Research* 5(1995): 105-23, 116-18.

[26] The Muratorian Canon rejected both the *Letter to the Laodiceans* and the *Letter to the Alexandrians* because they were suspected of being forgeries. Tertullian in the 3rd century tells of the author *of 3 Corinthians* (mid-2nd century) being removed from the office of presbyter (*On Baptism* 17); according to Eusebius (*H.E.* 6.12.1-6) Bishop Serapion in c. 200 rejected the Gospel of Peter, and Bishop Salonius rejected Salvatian's pamphlet written to the church in the name of Timothy.

[27] *An Introduction to the New Testament*, 586.

While it may be reassuring to assume that a pseudonymous author did not consider himself to be engaged in an enterprise of deception, but was merely following an accepted religious practice, there simply is no evidence to support such a benevolent conclusion. Moreover, to say that the pseudonymous writer deceived nobody in his own lifetime is an unproven assertion. What is certain is that he did deceive all subsequent generations up to very recent times. Nevertheless, despite all of its attendant problems, pseudonymity has become virtually a way of life among New Testament scholars, whose appetite for it grows by what it feeds on.[28] It is no longer necessary even to argue the case, it being sufficient merely to assume it.

SCHOLARSHIP MOVES ON

Several commentaries and scholarly works on the PE have appeared since Mons. Quinn's death in 1988, and attention has moved somewhat from concentrating on the question of authenticity to an examination of their content. Throughout the period of my own academic engagement with the PE (1971-87) I was constantly frustrated by the sterility of much of the scholarship, which did little more than repeat the results of earlier scholarship. Accordingly as scholars embraced hypotheses of pseudepigraphy more easily 'the sky was the limit' for the exercise of the imagination. I determined to examine the practice of Pauline authorship afresh. Three aspects of 'Pauline' epistolography in particular demanded attention, since in the excitement of pursuing various hypotheses of pseudeipgraphy the academy had not noticed some distinctive facts of Paul's practice: the fact of co-authorship, the undoubted use of secretarial assistance, and the ecclesial nature of the correspondence. In addition, I proposed a more fluid notion of 'Pauline authorship' against which to evaluate the authenticity of the PE, and argued for the genuineness of 2 Timothy, for which I suggested a novel provenance. Space permits me here only to summarise the evidence. The detailed argument is available elsewhere.[29]

---

[28] J A T Robinson, *Redating the New Testament* (London: SCM, 1976), 186.
[29] See my *Paul the Letter Writer and the Second Letter to Timothy*.

Co-authorship and the Pauline Letters

One of the most striking factors which separates the 'Pauline Letters' from the body of ancient epistolography is the fact that in eight of the thirteen letters more than one person's name occurs in the place reserved for authors.[30] Co-authorship of letters is very much the exception in antiquity. Although each of the vast majority of extant papyrus letters is written by one person a small number is clearly co-authored.[31] Moreover, in those cases, with the single exception of *P.Ryl.* 131, the first person pronoun is always in the plural, clearly indicating that they are intentionally co-authored. The practice in antiquity, then, was that where more than one person was named in the prescript of a letter it was co-authored.

Unlike the bulk of ancient letters Paul's letters display a very high proportion of co-authored ones. Nevertheless, while scholars pride themselves on the attention they pay to the social and literary context of the New Testament texts they pay scant attention to the remarkable prominence of co-authorship in the Pauline corpus, even ten years after I first drew attention to the fact. Nevertheless, one detects some evidence of a shift in the direction of according it some attention. Whereas in 1990 Jerome Murphy-O'Connor considered my judgement that there was co-authorship in (some of) the undoubtedly Pauline letters to be 'a provocative thesis', by 1995 he was an ardent advocate of that position.[32] Indeed, the fact of co-authorship in most of Paul's letters is so obvious that it defies explanation how exegetes continue to ignore it. The matter demands attention.

---

[30] Galatians is written in Paul's name and in that of the unnamed brothers with him (1.1-2). Sosthenes is named with Paul in 1 Cor 1.1, and Timothy figures with him in 2 Cor 1.1, Phil 1.1, Col 1.1, and Phlm 1, while Silvanus and Timothy are named with Paul in 1 and 2 Thess 1.1.

[31] Among the papyrus letters these include *P.Oxy.* 118; 1033; 1672, *P.Haun.* 16, *P.Amh.* 33; 35, *B.G.U.* 1022, *P.Gen.* 16, *P.Thead.* 17; *P.Ryl.* 131; 243; 624; *P.Tebt.* 28, *P.Magd.* 36; *P.Ross.-Georg* 8. Among the Royal Hellenistic letters only two were written by more than one person (Letters 9 and 35 in C Bradford Welles, *Royal Correspondence in the Hellenistic Period. A Study in Greek Epigraphy*, New Haven, 1934). The *Apochrypal Letter to Paul* was written by Stephanas and four presbyters.

[32] Contrast the tentative comment in his review of my *Paul the Letter Writer and the Second Letter to Timothy* (*Revue Biblique* 97 [1990]: 294-95) with the detailed treatment of the subject in his *Paul the Letter-Writer. His World, His Options, His Skills* (Collegeville: Liturgical Press, 1995), 16-34.

Unfortunately, the criteria that would allow us to estimate the contribution of each member of the co-authoring team are not available. What is certain, however, and more certain than any hypothesis of Pauline pseudepigraphy, is that co-authorship did take place, and this fact alone should dilute the prevailing certainties concerning the style and language of Paul as an epistolographer. Moreover, two additional factors also undermine the normal presumptions about Pauline authorship.

Paul's use of secretaries

We know from the letters themselves that Paul (and his co-author[s])[33] employed secretarial assistance for at least six of the thirteen letters,[34] and that in one case the secretary, Tertius, sent greetings in his own name (Rom 16.22). The question arises as to how 'Paul' operated, and how much of each letter was written by 'him', and how much by the secretary. Randolph E. Richards has devoted a full monograph to the question.[35] Having already investigated the matter myself, I was well aware of the difficulty in moving from speculation as to what secretaries might have contributed to the 'Pauline Letters' to a firm conclusion as to what is likely to have been their actual contribution. For that reason I anticipated that Richards' admirable energies would produce modest assured results. I was not surprised. Indeed, Richards is not able to go much further than to conclude that because an editorial role for a secretary was very common in antiquity, it is likely to have been the case for Paul's letters also. There is no significant shake-up of the conventional wisdom surrounding the 'Pauline Corpus'.

One can speculate, on the basis of the various uses of secretaries in antiquity, as to how 'Paul' employed such assistance. We do have a great deal of evidence as to how Cicero comported himself, but 'Paul' was no Cicero. It is impossible to say how much liberty 'Paul' allowed his amanuenses. 'He' may have premeditated a letter, with or without writing notes, and, having made corrections, dictated it to an amanuensis who wrote syllable by syllable, perhaps, as Spintharus did to Cicero's dictation,

---

[33] From this point on one should understand 'Paul' to refer to Paul and his co-author(s).

[34] Rom 16.22; 2 Thess 3.17; 1 Cor 16.21; Gal 6.11; Col 4.18 and Phlm 19.

[35] *The Secretary in the Letters of Paul* (Tübingen: J C B Mohr, 1995).

or by the use of some form of shorthand, which would seem to have been necessary for Tiro. But, 'Paul' may have been as disdainful of dictation as was Quintilian.

What is clearer, however, is that even members of the upper classes who employed secretaries insisted on writing intimate personal letters in their own hand. Cicero apologised for writing to Atticus in somebody else's hand (*Ad Att.* II, xxiii, 1). Similarly, Seneca wrote to friends in his own hand (*Ad Luc.* XXVI, 8). Julius Caesar, too, wrote in his own hand to Cicero (Suetonius *De Vita Caes.*, *Julius* LVI, 6), and Quintilian commended the skill of calligraphy, precisely for its importance in writing to friends (I, 28-29). If it is permissible to situate Paul in the known practices of letter-writing in antiquity it is not unreasonable to suspect that his personal letters—and only the PE fall into that category— were written by himself, without the aid of a secretary.[36]

Ecclesial correspondence

A third striking feature of the letters of Paul is that they are communal, rather than individual, both at the level of sender and receiver. In every letter other than the PE, 'Paul' writes to at least one local community. The fact that the letters to different local communities were subsequently gathered, and published as a collection for posterity further reflects their public character. That the PE are addressed to individuals rather than to communities, then, separates them further from the other Paulines. And since they purport to be written by Paul alone they are in a double sense 'personal letters'.[37]

BREAKING THE STEREOTYPE OF PAUL AS LETTER-WRITER

One must take serious note, then, of three interlocking variables which unfreeze the stereotypical picture of Paul as an epistolographer writing alone and unaided: the fact of the co-authorship of most of the 'Pauline Letters'; the fact of secretarial assistance in their composition; and the

---

[36] See further my *Paul the Letter Writer and the Second Letter to Timothy*, 45-50.
[37] *Ibid.*, 50-57.

fact that most of the letters purport to be ecclesial, only the three PE being private. Moreover, one cannot but be impressed by the important place of Timothy in the 'Pauline Corpus', whether as co-author (2 Corinthians, Philippians, Colossians, 1 and 2 Thessalonians, and Philemon), or emissary (1 Cor 4.17; 16.10-11). It should not be surprising, then, that the PE should exhibit differences from the other Paulines which in the main were co-authored (in several cases with Timothy), used secretarial assistance, and were intended for communal use.

Moreover, each of the three PE deserves the application of the same kind of methodology one brings to bear on the other letters of Paul, that is, that each reflects a unique epistolary context. There is, for one example, no internal evidence to suggest that the three letters originated from the same place and time, or that they should be read as a literary unit.[38] On the contrary: the similarities in some of the contents argue against their constituting a literary unit, unless one is particularly excusing of authorial repetition. In my *Paul the Letter Writer and the Second Letter to Timothy* I respect the unique epistolary context of each one, and demonstrate that Second Timothy is quite distinct from the other two, and, responding to the standard objections to its Pauline character, that it is a genuinely Pauline letter, for which I argue a novel provenance and occasion.

Although overturning entrenched scholastic positions is difficult in the extreme, there are indications of some movement away from the earlier presumptions. In his review of my *Paul the Letter Writer and the Second Letter to Timothy* Murphy-O'Connor judged the argument to be 'a systematic slaughter of sacred cows ... [and] a remarkable achievement. It changes the way we look at the problem of the Pastorals, and it raises new questions concerning the Pauline corpus'.[39] Philip Towner agrees that 'If the Pastorals are in fact uniquely Pauline in this way, some (at least) of the differences between them and the rest of the Paulines not only are to be expected but are actually entirely logical.' He adds that my work demonstrates how far from 'assured' is the case for pseudonymity, and that if an amanuensis enters the equation, vocabulary, idiom, and

---

[38] See P H Towner, 'Pauline Theology or Pauline Tradition in the Pastoral Epistles: The Question of Method', in *Tyndale Bulletin* 46 (1995): 287-314, 301-302.

[39] *Revue Biblique* 97(1990): 294-95. See also Murphy-O'Connor's *Paul the Letter-Writer. His World, His Options, His Skills*, 17-19, 35, 38, and his *Paul. A Critical Life* (Oxford: Clarendon, 1996), 357-68.

theological expression can no longer be used in any precise way to determine the Pauline authorship of the letters ascribed to him. If sole Pauline authorship is considered, differences between the Pastoral Epistles and the other (co-authored) Pauline epistles may well signify authenticity.'[40] Craig S Wansink also accepts the basic thrust of my thesis about the authenticity and occasion of 2 Timothy.[41] On the other hand, J D G Dunn follows the common pattern of ignoring the clear evidence pointing in the direction of co-authorship.[42]

The reality is that however disappointing to one's presumptions, the evidence, as distinct from the speculation, is overwhelming that the conventional assumptions of Pauline authorship are fundamentally defective. Probably because of the uniquely honoured position of Paul in the history of Christian reflection the suppositions that he wrote his letters unaided, after the fashion of an isolated scholar writing entirely on his own, break down completely when the clear testimony of his practice is allowed to take its natural place within that of ancient epistolography. However unsatisfactory it is to be unsure in assessing the extent of Paul's own part in the composition of the letters bearing his name (and that of others) we ought not to abandon the clear evidence of his own testimony to shared epistolographical activity, together with secretarial assistance in all non-personal letters. In general, when writing to ecclesial communities Paul wrote with others, while in the sole case of the doubly personal correspondence of the PE, he wrote alone. As for the difference in style and content between a letter to an individual and one to a community one profits from contrasting Ignatius of Antioch's letter to the church in Smyrna with that to its bishop, Polycarp.[43]

The whole question of what one means by Pauline authorship of the letters, then, must be revised fundamentally, since virtually every scholarly conclusion is vitiated by the failure to take seriously the facts, and not mere hypotheses, of co-authorship and the use of secretaries in most of the 'Pauline Letters', as well as the distinction between the ecclesial

[40] Philip Towner, *1-2 Timothy & Titus* (The IVP New Testament Commentary Series, Leicester: InterVarsity Press, 1994.), 34-35. See also his 'Pauline Theology or Pauline Tradition in the Pastoral Epistles: The Question of Method', in *Tyndale Bulletin* 46(1995): 287-314.
[41] *Chained in Christ. The Experience and Rhetoric of Paul's Imprisonments* (JSNTSS 130, Sheffield: Sheffield Academic Press, 1996), 16, 67-68, 136, 203.
[42] *The Theology of Paul the Apostle* (Grand Rapids MI/Cambridge: Eerdmans, 1998).
[43] See my *Paul the Letter Writer and the Second Letter to Timothy*, 53-57.

letters in that Corpus, and the private ones we call the PE. Hypotheses based on imagination and few facts should not easily displace reconstructions that respect the acknowledged Pauline epistolary practice. In matters of historical research fact should have primacy over theory, evidence over ideology.

Moreover, contrary to the method applied to all other NT letters, it is still customary to lump the three PE together as 'a collective whole', as though they reflected the same context:

> They presuppose the same false teachers, the same organization, and entirely similar conditions in the community. They move within the same relative theological concepts and have the same peculiarities of language and style.[44]

This perspective is facilitated by the imposition of the assertion—it can never be more than that—that they are 'unreal' pseudonymous letters, for which no verifiable epistolary context has to be deduced. However, methodologically, every effort ought to be exerted in the attempt to identify a real epistolary context for each letter, since it should be presumed that each has its own *raison d'être*.[45]

Taking his cue from my research, Murphy-O'Connor draws attention to over thirty elements in which something in 2 Timothy is missing in both 1 Timothy and Titus, or where something shared by them is absent from 2 Timothy. He concludes that the cumulative effect of these arguments is disastrous for the hypothesis of the unity of the Pastorals, since many of the elements go deep into the personality of the authors and their sociological perspectives.[46]

---

[44] W G Kümmel, *Introduction to the New Testament* (London: SCM, 1975), 367. Similarly, 'The three letters belong together, because only together do they make sense. The heart of their theology is only understood properly if their pseudonymity is acknowledged' (Frances Young, *The Theology of the Pastorals*. London: SPCK, 1994, 142).

[45] Luke T Johnson applauded my decision to treat 2 Timothy in isolation from 1 Timothy and Titus (review of my *Paul the Letter Writer and the Second Letter to Timothy* in *Catholic Biblical Quarterly* 53[1991]: 339-40). Later, he concluded that in the case of 2 Timothy 'there is as much to be said in favor of reading it as an authentic composition by Paul, as there is in favor of regarding it as a 2nd-century pseudonymous production' (*Letters to Paul's Delegates 1 Timothy, 2 Timothy and Titus*. Valley Forge, Pennsylvania: Trinity Press International, 1996), 103.

[46] See Murphy-O'Connor, '2 Timothy Contrasted with 1 Timothy and Titus,' *Revue Biblique* 98 (1991): 403-18.

A close examination of the texts of the PE shows clearly how different 2 Timothy is from the other two, particularly on the critical question of the letters' purposes. I argue that in 2 Timothy Paul, far from being weighed down by the fear of his impending death (4.6-8), was confident of being released from imprisonment in Rome, and was preparing for the next stage of his missionary activity: 'so that *through me* the proclamation of the Gospel would be *brought to its completion*, and that *all nations* would hear it' (4.16-18). With that purpose in view Paul framed the letter with a statement of his desire to see Timothy (1.4), which was now given an added urgency to come immediately, and before winter if possible (4.9-21). Paul wanted Timothy to come to Rome, not to provide personal comfort, but to form part of the mission-team he was assembling. Sadly, the Roman Church, of whom he earlier had had such hopes for furthering the spread of the Gospel to Spain (Rom 15.24), could not be relied on for the necessary help.

Paul's alternative strategy involved constituting a mission-team, which would include Luke who alone remained faithful, and Mark who was useful to him *eis diakonian*, i.e. in furthering the work of evangelisation (2 Tim 4.11). Paul, therefore, was more concerned about Timothy than he was about the doctrinal and ethical deviations of some putative false teachers: Timothy's personal fidelity to the Gospel, both as a disciple and a co-worker, was vital if Paul's hopes for his world-wide mission were to be realised. Hence, he appealed to Timothy to be mindful of the roots of his faith (1.5) and to rekindle the gift of God which he had received through the laying on of Paul's hands (1.6). It is my contention that the text of 2 Timothy provides an abundance of textual support for such an exegesis ('a drawing out of the meaning'), and is free of the obstacles to Pauline authenticity which are detected in 1 Timothy and Titus. In the case of 2 Timothy, at least, there is no need to seek refuge in an hypothesis of pseudepigraphy whose starting point (*eisegesis*, i.e., 'a reading into') is the assumption that it is not a 'real letter' with a unique epistolary context.[47]

---

[47] The case is argued more thoroughly in my *Paul the Letter Writer and the Second Letter to Timothy*. For a critique of the applications of statistical analysis to the 'Pauline Letters'— even that of Anthony Kenny which places 2 Timothy as near the centre of the Pauline letters as 2 Corinthians—see 25-35. For a variation on my reconstruction of 2 Timothy see Murphy-O'Connor, *Paul. A Critical Life*, 356-57.

LIVING STONES:
A RETREAT WITH
PALESTINIAN CHRISTIANS

This 1989 article for New Blackfriars *records Michael leading a 'retreat through pilgrimage' to the Holy Land with fellow Vincentian pilgrims.*

We are told in the First Letter of Peter: 'Come to him, to that living stone rejected by men, but in God's sight chosen and precious, and like living stones be yourselves built into a spiritual house, to be a holy priesthood, to offer spiritual sacrifices acceptable to God through Jesus Christ.'

In 1984 Christians in the village of Ibillin, in Galilee, said to a British group of pilgrims that visitors to the Holy Land should not confine themselves to visiting the ancient shrines of past ages; they should also visit the 'living stones' of the Land. From this originated the setting-up of an ecumenical organization in Britain called 'Living Stones'.

Last year a group associated with this organization, but predominantly made up of Vincentians (namely, priests of the Congregation of the Mission, founded by St Vincent de Paul), decided to make 'a retreat through pilgrimage' in the Holy Land. It was my conviction that the Land, its peoples, and its history combine to provide an extraordinarily powerful context in which to 'make a retreat'. What would be unique about this one was that it would include meetings with indigenous Christians, living in the throes of the *intifada*.

Some idea of what that meant both for the group and for the Christians that the group met is best conveyed in the words of some of those Christians.

In Nazareth, Canon Riah Abu El-Assal* said:

> There can be no Christian presence in the Land of the Holy
> One without the Christian community in the world. Therefore,
> wake up, Christians, before it is too late!
> We lost some 30 percent of our people in 1948. Today we

---

* Canon Riah, Anglican parish priest in Nazareth, later became the Anglican Bishop in Jerusalem [Editor].

make up 2.3 percent of the population. We were quite influential. We were servants of the community, and we have, under God, done well. But the presence of Christians in the Land of the Holy One is really threatened, both in Jerusalem and throughout the Land. There is an increase in those who emigrate for different purposes, and the number of those who are so disappointed and frustrated by what some Christians in the West say and preach about the State of Israel as the fulfilment of Old Testament prophecy, that they leave.

He spoke about the 800,000 to 1 million visitors who came in a normal year, and most of whom were Christians:

They do not know that we exist. How can we be expected to believe that they pray for us? When they come here they are misled about what is going on in His Land. The so-called holy shrines mean very little to us Christians. What matters are the *living stones,* and hence your visit is very important, and is a source of strength to me and the Christian community. Many of the Christian visitors to Nazareth are not aware that there are Arab Christians. They believe that all Arabs are Muslims, and all Muslims are Arab. There are ten million Arab Christians in the Middle East. When the Christian visitors get off their buses and stay here 30 to 60 minutes at the most, I say to them, 'Wake up! Jesus stayed here 30 years, can't you stay here 30 minutes more?'

Canon Riah spoke about the need for a Christian *aliyah,* a 'return home' of the local Christians. In Jerusalem in 1967 there were about 21,000 Christians and now only 6,800, most of them old. But as Arab Palestinians they were not protected:

We have been sacrificed for many years on the altar that was inscribed with 'Mercy for the Jews'. I have the right to appeal to the consciences of the German people, not only to compensate us, but to atone for what has happened to us Arab Palestinians as a result of their treatment of the Jews. We are not in a position to pay for the sins of others.

He pointed out how, as Arab Palestinians, they had been

discriminated against–especially by expropriation of land (more than 50 percent in Nazareth) and denial of educational opportunities, as well as numerous day-to-day restrictions. He mentioned that he himself was under a travel ban:

> I have been accused of advocating armed struggle, which I did not, because I am a non-violent person. I strongly believe that violence breeds more violence, and bloodshed breeds bloodshed. The reason for my being banned is that they do not want the likes of you people to hear what I have to say. I have told the Minister of the Interior, 'I will not be restrained, even if I have to be crucified.'
>
> I have a wish for the future that the two states of Israel and Palestine may become a federation of two states, with open borders. Then, we will become a blessing. So I believe. The Jews have suffered, the Palestinians have suffered too. They have proved themselves to be hardworking, we too. They were prepared to die for their cause, so, too, the Palestinians. It is now time to challenge both to live for the same cause, the cause of peace, and the cause of justice.

Father Chacour, of Ibillin, was quite as forthright:

> The bad fact is that the victims of the concentration camps are now practising some of the same methods they experienced in Germany and elsewhere. We try to build bridges with Jews and others, provided that they acknowledge that we cannot accept any status than to be their equals.

He, too, spoke about how they had suffered from the confiscation of their best land, how their numbers had dwindled. But he had hope too:

> We are living now in a very tense period of our Palestinian history, but very promising also. It's true that every day several martyrs are killed in the Occupied Territories during the *intifada. You* translate it very badly into English as 'uprising'. It is not 'up, and it is not 'rising'. It is an *intifada*. The word *intifada is* used in the Gospel by the Lord Jesus, when he says to you, 'If you go to a house, and you give them peace, and they don't accept that peace, go out, and before you leave,

shake your feet so that no dust remains on your feet.' This is the *intifada*. It is 'shaking away the occupation'. It is not against the Jews, not against the army, not against Israel. No. It is saying to the Jews, 'We do not want you to be occupying us. We don't want to be your servants or slaves. We want to be at home in our own country.

He said he hoped that the Churches 'will never dare to speak against one side, but for a solution for both sides, for justice for both sides.' But the Israelis had killed some very moderate Palestinian Christians and had jailed Mubarak Awad, the Chairman of the Centre for Non-violence and a devout Christian:

What do the Israelis refuse? The PLO? Moderate Palestinians? Non-violent Palestinians? Or simply the existence of the Palestinians?

In Jerusalem, the Latin Patriarch, Monsignor Michel Sabbah, also spoke of the difficulties of the moment, but there was a strong note of optimism in what he said as he contemplated the present distress. And that could even be said of a very different man, the Reverend Audeh Rantisi, the deposed Deputy Mayor of Ramallah, whom some of the group saw. Audeh can trace his ancestry to the building of the church of St George in Lydda in the fourth century; his ancestors were priests in that church. The story of his own sufferings as a refugee personalized the tragedy of the Palestinian people. But he said:

How can we bear the sufferings of Christ? It is by bearing the suffering of people, and striving for the right of God in the lives of human beings. That's what we are here for. We do pray. But prayer is not only kneeling.

He spoke about the brutal means used by the Israelis to suppress the *intifada,* and we asked him if he feared for his own life. He replied:

We are the servants of the Lord, standing for the rights of human beings, and the right of God in the lives of people. Therefore, we do not fear.

115

He was asked if this meant that he was confident that in the long run they would win, and he answered: 'Christ said, "I am the Way, the Truth, and the Life," and Christ is with us, and we shall arrive.' But he was critical of Christians in Europe:

> European Christians are quiet about what is going on here. Because they won't dare speak out, on account of their guilty conscience. But I do believe that, if they keep quiet, they will suffer from a doubly guilty conscience. The British are responsible. If you want to pay for damage done, pay out of your own pocket. Don't have us pay.

Audeh stressed that he always differentiated between Judaism and Zionism. 'Zionism has deprived the Jewish people of their own spiritual inheritance,' he said. His closing words were:

> It is time for Israel to think positively, and not depend on its muscle strength. Because already Israel has lost much morally. And I ask every nation that loves Israel to hasten to the situation, and help Israel out of this immoral situation, that true peace may come to this land. For from 1948 until now Israel has never had peace, because the peace of Israel depends upon the peace of the Palestinians. And I say, 'Blessed are the peacemakers.' We have peace-keepers, and we have no peace to keep! We need people today honest with God and with themselves, who have guts and speak up for peace.

Last of all in Jerusalem we met Bishop Kafity, the Anglican Bishop in Jerusalem. He said to us:

> You have chosen to come to us during an uprising. An uprising is not a strange event in Jerusalem, or the Holy Land. Because the first uprising that shook the world took place in Jerusalem, the Resurrection. And this uprising is a kind of extension of the resurrection of the new life. It's not just a political protest by the people against an occupying force.

He believed it was not 'the throwing of stones, or petrol bombs, or tear gas bombs, or roadblocks' that was important about the uprising:

What I hope you will discover is the spirituality of the uprising. There is a new spirituality among Muslims and Christians, one drawing them together. The other new element of the uprising is that it is forward-looking. For a long time the Palestinians have been backward-looking: 'Why am I a refugee? Why have they taken my house, etc.' We looked back at what happened to us, and we were mourning the situation. We were, so to speak, in the negative. The uprising has put us into the positive.

On Sunday the group went to the Arabic Mass in the Basilica in Bethlehem. It was very moving to hear the young people, many of them wearing crutches, sing their hymns.

And finally, the group made its way to the Latin Patriarchate Seminary in Beit Jala, just outside Bethlehem. The town was recovering from a curfew, declared to prevent a public demonstration at a Requiem Mass for a young Catholic shot by the soldiers. We prayed together with the seminarians, some from Nazareth, some from Madaba, and other villages on both banks of the Jordan. We sang hymns, they in Arabic, and we in English.

To visit the Holy Land at that time and in this way was a special privilege. The solidarity of the suffering Palestinians, on both sides of the Green Line, was astonishing. It would appear that the common experience of oppression is creating a nation. One young Palestinian intellectual put it this way: 'You might expect that the oppression would weaken us. On the contrary, we feel empowered.' But oppression and suffering cannot have that effect if that is all there is–oppression and suffering. In the words of Bishop Kafity:

> The uprising is a new spirituality among the people of the Land, saying 'No' to all kinds of oppression. Not saying 'No' to a Jew because he is a Jew. This uprising is not racist. The people are saying 'No' to a structure in their own land which is not of their choice, and, like the Resurrection, they are trying to bring about a new life, a new hope.

Surely here was a message which we could carry into our own lives.

THE *INTIFADA*:
A CHRISTIAN PERSPECTIVE

Written for the The Month *in 1990 this represents one of Michael's first forays into a political theology of the Palestinian struggle.*

On December 1987 an Israeli vehicle ploughed through a truck in Gaza killing four Palestinians, and injuring seven others inside who were returning from work in Israel. The following day some four thousand inhabitants of the Jabaliah refugee camp protested at the killing, and youths began to throw stones. This event signalled the beginning of what may prove to be one of the most significant events in the history of the Palestinian people this century. Within a short time the whole population of the West Bank and Gaza began to erupt in protest against the twenty year old Israeli occupation. A new word, *intifada,* entered the English language.

The Arabic word *intifada* suggests more than 'uprising'. It means 'shaking off', and designates the Palestinian eruption which attempts to shake off the oppressive occupation. It also means, 'to recover, to recuperate, to jump to one's feet'. My ear drums still reverberate with the proclamation by a Christian minister of the saying of Jesus as recorded in Matthew 10. 14, *unfudu 'l-gubara en arjulikum* ('Shake the dust from your feet').

INTIFADA—JUMPING TO ONE'S FEET

The events which followed were reported widely in the Western media, at least until Israeli censorship made reliable information less accessible, and the events in China and Eastern Europe assumed greater news value. At first the resistance to the Israeli occupation of the West Bank and Gaza seemed to be little more than the spontaneous stone-throwing protest by youngsters against local grievances—with the reversal of roles of David and Goliath this time. But soon it became clear that a new order was being born. The agenda was being set not by the PLO veterans abroad but by the women, children and young people within the Occupied Territories. In the matter of resistance to the occupation the traditional authority structure of Palestinian society was being reversed: women and children were in the front line; the elders, the traditional leaders of the society, were less relevant to the growing mass resistance movement.

Very quickly local leadership began to emerge, and a new way of life developed. What strikes the visitor most, perhaps, is the daily closure of shops except for three hours in the morning. The Palestinians buy only the basics, mostly just food and medicine. They import virtually nothing, and have developed a whole new system of self-reliance.

THE ISRAELI RESPONSE

The Israeli efforts to restore the *status quo* were brutal in the extreme. Unarmed civilians were shot dead in their hundreds. Thousands were treated for serious wounds. Thousands more were rounded up and put in administrative detention—and reports about the conditions in the Ansar III Military Detention Centre suggest the most serious violations of human rights, as well as violations of international law. Hundreds of houses were demolished. All Palestinian institutions of learning were closed down. Palestinian leaders were deported, a fact which even caused the US administration to vote against Israel at the United Nations for the first time since 1981. Curfews were imposed on whole towns—one refugee camp in Gaza was under curfew for 174 days in the year. The Israeli boast that it was 'the only democracy in the Middle East' was looking more and more fragile, and Israel was quickly losing friends amongst the international community.

VIA DOLOROSA IN JALIZOUN CAMP

On my first visit to the region during the *intifada* I went to see what life was like in a refugee camp on a Friday, while some colleagues were processing through the Way of the Cross in Jerusalem. At the site of her bulldozed house a mother told me that her sixteen-year-old boy was said to have thrown a molotov cocktail at the soldiers. That was not true— nothing was proved against him, she insisted, and added, 'Here you are guilty before you are considered to be innocent.' She protested that she was not afraid of such cowardly tactics: 'Israel is implanting the seeds of hatred in the minds and hearts of youngsters, and old people. They came at one o'clock in the morning, threw our belongings out, and bulldozed the house. This is what the gestapo used to do. They are copying what was done to them.' Defiantly, she exclaimed, 'P-L-O, IS-RAEL NO!'

Outside her tent, and beside her bulldozed house, a young girl explained that the soldiers came at one in the morning: 'They bulldozed the house even before there was any chance to see a lawyer—they do this all the time!'

Everybody appeared to be a victim of the *intifada*. I spoke to a grandmother, two of whose sons, and two grandsons are in prison. I met a young man who had lost his eye after being hit by a rubber bullet. A mother introduced me to her son who had lost his mind after being beaten in prison. Her other son showed me the bullet wound in his leg. I was invited into the house of a refugee who had been in prison for more than nine years. His daughter sang for us:

> 'Children of Palestine
> those who were driven out,
> and those who have stayed in.
> The children who have gone out have never
> forgotten the smell of the country.
> Palestine restores the soul,
> and gives life.'

On the wall of the house of this Muslim refugee family, with its ceiling of corrugated iron, there was a picture of Mary with Jesus.

EMPOWERMENT IN OPPRESSION

Bethlehem and its surrounding villages have had their own share of killings, maimings and beatings. It took me some time to understand why so many young people at Sunday Mass in Bethlehem were on crutches. A neighbouring village had been put under curfew in case the Requiem Mass and funeral for a Christian youth shot dead by the military might cause public disorder. Nevertheless Palestinian intellectuals and the leadership of the Churches to whom I spoke left me in no doubt that the experience of the *intifada* was one of empowerment in oppression.

All the people I spoke to agreed that the *intifada* had changed everything. The Palestinians had had enough of the occupation and wanted to shake it off. Muslim and Christian Palestinians were united in this determination—Christian Palestinians long for an independent Palestinian State, as do their Muslim brothers and sisters. Furthermore, the Christian Arabs in Israel whom I met were completely behind their suffering brothers and sisters in the Occupied Territories.

CHRISTIAN RESPONSES

One of the results of the *intifada is* the increased politicisation of the Christian churches in the Holy Land. To this can be coupled a new awareness of the situation of the Palestinians in the churches in the West. Many Christians in the West have seen enough for themselves to be very distressed by what is happening in the Holy Land.

My own growth in the understanding of these events is not untypical of that of many Western Christians. I remember my sense of exhilaration at the efficiency of the Israeli Defence Forces in the Six-Day War, and I was fully in support of the interests of the State of Israel. But when I visited the country for the first time in 1972 I began to sense immediately that some variant of an apartheid system operated in Israel and the Occupied Territories. It was only then that I began to become aware that the very birth of the State of Israel was effected at great cost to the indigenous Arab population. Somehow I avoided seeing inside the refugee camps, and in my zeal for archaeology and the investigation of biblical sites I was left with little opportunity to meet the victims.

DELEGATION OF BRITISH CHRISTIANS

In March 1989 the ten member Delegation of the British Council of Churches visited Israel, Jerusalem and the Occupied Territories of the West Bank and Gaza, and produced its report later that year.[1] It is clear

---

[1] *Impressions of Intifada. Report of a British Council of Churches Delegation to Israel and the Occupied Territories,* March 1989. Available from BCC, InterChurch House, 35-41 Lower Marsh, London SEI 7RL.

from the report that the members of the delegation went with open ears, minds and hearts. Section 1 begins with a quote from Michel Sabbah, the Latin Patriarch: 'While the *Intifada* lasts it is more dangerous for the Israeli people than the Palestinians. To save the Jewish world, peace is necessary. When Arabs and Jews become friends then Israel will have secure borders' (p. 1). Of the reality of life under the occupation an Arab Christian priest says, 'Occupation is always a corrupting situation both for occupier and occupied. A wooden cage or a golden cage is still a cage' (p. 2).

The Delegation was struck by the leadership roles assumed by the Palestinian women, as well as by the virtually universal support for the *intifada* among the population. They detected a genuine and sincere desire for peace, a determination to establish a Palestinian state alongside the State of Israel and an acknowledgement of PLO leadership. The *intifada,* the Delegation claims, has brought to the surface the underlying paternalism of Israeli society towards the Palestinians.

DELEGATION OF PALESTINIAN CHRISTIANS

The Middle East Council of Churches sent a delegation to Britain in November–December 1989. It met the leadership of the churches in Britain and other interested groups. It was led by the Anglican priest, and deposed Deputy Mayor of Ramallah, Audeh Rantisi. He stressed that the *intifada* had united the Palestinians as never before. 'I have seen many people being killed, and many injured, and others deported. I have seen homes being demolished.' He pleaded that now was the time for the Israelis to settle the problem—it would be more complicated later when this generation of young people has grown up. 'My main message is that Christians should come to understand the reality, and the seriousness of the situation in the Holy Land, and that they should pray for true peace, peace based on justice.'[2]

Rantisi's personal history is a microcosm of the Palestinian problem. On Sunday 11 July 1948 at 2 pm, when he was eleven, he and his family were driven from their hometown, Lydda, never to return again. For three days the inhabitants of Lydda and surrounding villages

---

[2] From the *Sunday* programme, BBC Radio 4, 3 December 1989.

walked without food or water, and some four thousand died from exhaustion and starvation. When they got to Ramallah there was not enough room to accommodate the refugees. Initially they slept under trees, and later thirteen people lived in the tent with which his family was provided. The second major upheaval occurred in the 1967 Six Day War, since when Ramallah has been under Israeli occupation.

Since the *intifada* Rantisi has been threatened with his life, and has had his car burnt. He has been interrogated by the military authorities no less than twelve times. While I was having lunch with him in Ramallah a refugee (a Muslim incidentally) from Jalizoun Camp called on him to come to visit the camp, since two more houses had been demolished. Despite the tragic circumstances he lives under every day, he is a man of peace and reconciliation. His message, and that of the delegation, left British Christians in no doubt that Palestinian Christians shared in the aspiration for an independent Palestinian state. This message comes loud and clear from both the leadership and the rank and file of the Christian churches in the Occupied Territories.

THEOLOGIES OF LIBERATION, PALESTINIAN AND JEWISH

Among the most significant contributions to theological reflection on the Israeli-Palestinian question are the works of the Palestinian Anglican, Canon Naim Ateek of St George's, Jerusalem,[3] and of the American Jew, Professor Marc Ellis.[4] Both made extensive lecture tours of Britain in 1990.

Ateek stresses that both Jews and Palestinians seek peace. When Jews talk of peace, they invariably speak of 'peace and security'. When

---

[3] Naim Stifan Ateek, 1989, *Justice and Only Justice. A Palestinian Theology of Liberation*. New York, Maryknoll: Orbis.

[4] Marc Ellis, 1987, *Toward a Jewish Theology of Liberation*. New York, Maryknoll: Orbis. More recently, 1990, *Beyond Innocence and Redemption. Confronting the Holocaust and Israeli Power*— the third subtitle is *Creating a Moral Future for the Jewish People*. He has written on the subject in *The Tablet* ('Jewish-Christian Impasse' 20 January, 'The Wrath of Israel' 16 June, 'End this Dialogue' 30 June 1990), *New Blackfriars* ('Theology and the Palestinian Uprising: A Jewish Perspective', Vol. 69, June 1988: 257-270), *The Month* ('Is there a Jewish Theology of Liberation?', Vol. 21, July 1988: 752-759) etc. The summary of Ellis' views and the quotations in this article are from his Public Lecture in the House of Commons, 19 June 1990.

Palestinians talk of peace, they speak of 'peace and justice'. But the Jewish insistence on security is the result of the experience of living in the West, and only secondarily of its experience in the Arab world. Nevertheless, Jews need security, as much as Palestinians seek justice, since they have suffered such dislocation in their original homelands.

Ateek's life story encapsulates the Palestinian problem. His family was expelled from its home in Beisan (Beth Shean) on 12 May 1948. He can recall with great precision what happened on that day, almost minute by minute. The whole population of 6,000 Arabs was expelled, the Muslims being sent across the Jordan, and the Christians to Nazareth which had not yet been occupied by the Zionists. On the declaration of the State of Israel he found himself condemned to second-class citizenship. On his first visit back to Beisan in 1958 he saw that the Anglican church had become a storehouse, the Roman Catholic one had become a school, and the Orthodox one had been left to rot. His family was not allowed to go into its own house, not even just to take a look. Some short time later his father suffered a stroke from which he later died.

Some forty years after the establishment of the State of Israel, Ateek's spirit has not been devoured by hatred or despair. He has a prophetic dream which has matured through the different stages of his life history. He now accepts the existence of the State of Israel in his Palestine, not as of right, but as of need, 'since the elimination of Israel would mean greater injustice to millions of innocent people who know no home except Israel' (p. 164). Any genuine solution, he insists, must pass the test of two sayings of Jesus: 'So whatever you wish that men should do to you, do so to them; for this is the law and the prophets' (Matt 7.12), and, 'You shall love your neighbour as yourself' (Mark 12.31).

TWO STATES SIDE BY SIDE

His solution moves out from the major premise: Palestine is a country for both the Jews and the Palestinians. Although the ideal would be the creation of one united democratic state for all Palestinians and Jews, he concedes that the existence of the Jewish State is a requirement for Jews. The minor premise is the creation of a Palestinian state, alongside the State of Israel in the West Bank and Gaza, in which all inhabitants would live as first-class citizens. Ateek insists that the security and well-being of

Israel demands the creation of a Palestinian state. With the two states living side by side the way would be open to fostering the patient work of reconciliation.

His dream of peace goes beyond the federation of the states of Israel and Palestine, and would include Lebanon and Jordan in a Federated States of the Holy Land. Jerusalem would have to be united, but shared as a city holy to Judaism, Islam and Christianity. Ideally it should become the federal capital of a United States of the Holy Land, with Beirut being Lebanon's capital, Amman Jordan's, a West Bank town Palestine's, and Tel Aviv Israel's. Micah's apocalyptic vision for Jerusalem (Mic 4.14) completes the picture. In his Strawberry Hill Public Lecture Ateek spelled out the stages more fully.[5]

PEACE MAKING

Ateek's solution has the quality of magnanimity and simplicity. He writes as a pastor, not as a politician. His scenario appears to leave out the designs of Syria, Iran and Iraq, and the growth of fundamentalist Islamic nationalism. Nevertheless, anyone who dismisses it as simplistic and unworkable should face up to the consequences of Israel pursuing its present intransigent policies. Israel will never be secure until it makes peace with its 150 million Arab neighbours, and peace with the Palestinians should be its immediate priority. The first requirement for any real progress is that the present Israeli leadership should now go. His new vision demands the stimulation and imagination of younger people. So much from a Palestinian Christian Arab perspective.

---

[5] Canon Ateek delivered the lecture 'The Holy Land —A Vision for the Future' on 8 May 1990 in St Mary's College, Strawberry Hill. He concluded that ideally Jews, Muslims and Christians should live together in one state. More realistically, since the Jews insist on a Jewish state, the best solution is to have two states. The two states should relate to one another in peace. He sees four stages of progress towards a final settlement: Stage 1: Palestinan State; Stage 2: Confederation with Jordan; Stage 3: Federation of Holy Land States: Lebanon Israel, Palestine, Jordan; Stage 4: Jerusalem as Federal Capital of the United States of the Holy Land.

A DESTRUCTIVE POLICY

In a prodigious output of books, articles and lectures, Professor Marc Ellis has charted a way out for Israel which respects the high moral traditions of Judaism, and enables the Jewish people to create a moral future. He sees the Jewish people today as facing the greatest crisis of its history since the destruction of the Temple in 70 AD. Only this time it is the Jews who have power, and that power is being used to disperse, to dislocate, to maim, to humiliate, and to destroy another people—the Palestinian people.

He sees the 1980s as perhaps the most shameful decade in the history of the Jewish people. The policy of the State of Israel, he believes, is to end the indigenous Palestinian presence and culture in historic Palestine.

A NEW JEWISH THEOLOGY?

As a Jewish theologian, he raises questions as to how Jewish theology might either legitimate this oppression, or help Jews to face the reality of what they have become. They might then change, since the end of the indigenous Arab culture in historic Palestine means for him the end of the Jewish tradition as we have known it.

Holocaust Theology has guided Jews for the last twenty years. But, according to Ellis, because of the questions it refuses to ask, and the questions it cannot ask, it is leading the Jewish community on the road to betrayal. Jewish suffering in the Holocaust has been seen as mandating its new empowerment, especially since 1967. Until recently no mention was made of the cost of that Jewish empowerment, especially to the Palestinians.

Ellis considers it vital to go beyond Holocaust Theology which never confronts the most important question, namely the cost of Jewish empowerment. He asks, 'How do we move to a new Jewish Theology which expresses the deepest aspirations of our people, one which faces the history we are creating with an honesty—I would say a brutal honesty—which represents the crisis which confronts us?' The way forward, he sees, is to recover and revive Jewish theological traditions which might lead to a new Jewish Theology relevant to the Palestinian crisis.

THE TRADITION OF DISSENT

He calls for a renewal of the tradition of dissent as represented by such as Martin Buber and Hannah Arendt who believed in a renewed and augmented Jewish community in Palestine. They sought a Jewish homeland, not a Jewish state, because they considered that a Jewish state would dominate the Palestinians and ultimately dominate the Jews. They believed in an essential equality that would be a litmus test for any Jewish community in Palestine.

Ellis sees the need to recover also the insights of non-Zionist and anti-Zionist Jews, whether religious or secular, who do not see Jews as constituting a nation, but as called to live in liberal democracies and contribute to them. The role of oriental (Sephardic) Jews in Israel is also important. These see Israel as dominated by European Jews, and ask the question, 'Are we with the Europeans, or ultimately with our Arab neighbours?'

Ellis charges that the recovery of this tradition of Jewish dissent is vital for the future of Israel. It is, apparently, very hard to find in Jewish thought today, and it has lost every battle with Jewish state power in Israel.

The other fundamental question which Ellis poses to modern Jewry revolves around the question of how Jews are going to use their suffering. It can be used as a blunt instrument against the Palestinians. Alternatively it can be used by way of solidarity with all who are struggling towards justice, and especially the Palestinian people. He fears that the Holocaust is being trivialised as a justification for bullying another people.

RECOVERING SYMBOLS

Ellis invokes another Jewish tradition which Jews would revive with profit, which he calls the inclusive liturgy of destruction. This involves recovering the symbols of Jewish peoplehood, especially its suffering in history. Persecuted Jews in the past, whether in Warsaw or Buchenwald, related their suffering to that of the past, whether the destruction of the Temple, or the exile from Spain. In that way they found meaning in their suffering. It became a form of resistance. This recalling of past suffering is not just a history, but a liturgical recounting of that history. The novel dimension now, of course, is that the Jewish liturgy of destruction is in danger of involving the destruction of another people, the Palestinians.

Happily there are many dissident Jewish voices criticising such policies of the Israeli government, and many inside Israel itself. Some Jewish Israelis go so far as to compare the Israeli treatment of the Palestinians with the Nazi treatment of the Jews, and Ellis sees many of the Israeli policies as comparable with those of the Nazis.[6] Some hope lies in the Jewish intuitive desire to be neither victim nor oppressor. This attitude is consistent with what is deepest and best in Jewish history. It is completely natural to express. But if Israel represses or suppresses such basic dispositions it will use its history as a blunt instrument to oppress not only another people, but its own people as well.

ADMISSIONS

Ellis argues that recovering the tradition of dissent and the inclusive liturgy of destruction demands of Jews the following admissions:

> First, what we as Jews have done to the Palestinian people since the establishment of the State of Israel in 1948 is wrong. Second, in the process of conquering and displacing the Palestinian people we, as Jews, have done what has been done to us over two millenia. Three, in this process we are becoming everything we loathe about our oppressors. Everything. Four, it is only in confrontation with state power in Israel, Jewish state power in Israel, that we as Jews can move beyond being victim or oppressor. Fifth, the movement beyond victimisation and oppression can only come through a solidarity with those whom we have displaced, that is, solidarity with the Palestinian people.

Ellis' final message to Christians in the West:

> We need neither a heightened silence nor a paternalistic embrace. What we need from Christians is a critical solidarity.

---

[6] Professor Israel Shahak of the Hebrew University, Jerusalem, himself a victim of Nazi persecution, writes of the Nazi-like violence employed by the police, borderguards, etc. He refers to the 'Nazification of the State of Israel and the expulsion or extermination of the Palestinians' (quoted in Ateek, 213).

We are adults. Stop speaking to us like children. Confront us with our history as we have confronted you. The logic of Zionism, if it can be completed, is no Palestinians. We will not be able to stop Israeli state power by ourselves. We need the help of our former enemies, Christians in the west, who have transformed their tradition partly because of understanding what they did to us. We need a critical solidarity which doesn't let us off the hook.

TALKS ABOUT TALKS

The various posturings within international politics concerning talks about talks must not distract attention away from the fundamental problem of the region which is the price that the Palestinians have had to pay for the encroachment on their land by Zionists from the diaspora. The creation of the State of Israel was not brought about without the destruction of some 400 Arab villages, and the exodus, and sometimes expulsion of some 880,000 Arab inhabitants. At least a further 300,000 left Palestine as a result of the 1967 Six Day War. There can be no question of a just solution to the problem unless these refugees are allowed to return to their former homes, or adequately compensated in accordance with international law. There can, of course, be a pragmatic solution, based on compromise by the parties concerned.

Secondly, the role of external forces must be recognised. Western support for the development of Zionism had little to do with wanting diaspora Jews to settle in the land of their ancestors in accordance with the proclivities of some traditions of Jewish piety. A convenient way of ensuring the growth and expansion of Western imperialism was to support incipient Zionism in its proposal to create a client Jewish settler state in Palestine. This would have the effect of preventing the growth of pan-Arab nationalism on the break-up of the Ottoman empire, and would of course also serve the purposes of the sponsor national states. The creation of a Jewish state in Palestine, financed by Jewish millionaires, and supported by Western bodies, would be an ideal solution to the designs of the interested European partners.

British Interests

In particular Britain determined to guarantee its own interests in controlling the eastern flank of the Suez Canal as a guarantee of its efficient commerce with India. That, and the containment of the designs of the French, was the motive behind the Balfour Declaration of 1917. This committed Britain to do the impossible, to facilitate the establishment in Palestine of a national home for the Jewish people, 'it being understood that nothing shall be done to prejudice the civil and religious rights of the existing non-Jewish communities in Palestine ...' When Britain could no longer contain the situation which it had allowed to develop, it washed its hands, and laid the problem at the door of the United Nations.

United States Financing

Nor has it been out of any spirit of altruism or philanthropy that the United States has largely financed, and continues to finance the Zionist State. Of the US 11.8 billion dollars international aid budget in 1990 Israel is to receive some 4 billion, that is more than 30 percent of the total.[7] When Senator Bob Dole proposed that a mere 5 percent of the whole budget be given to the emerging nations of Eastern Europe and elsewhere supporters of Israel were in consternation. They could not use the ubiquitous charge of antisemitism, and the well worn argument that Israel was the only democracy in the Middle East was beginning to show signs of terminal wear. Going too was the same need for the US to have a strategic ally in the face of Russian expansionism, now that the Soviet Union was having enough trouble containing matters within its own borders.

However, an ingenious solution was at hand. In October 1989 Washington had yielded finally to persistent Israeli pressure to restrict immigration of Soviet Jews. Up to that time some 94 percent of Soviet Jews who left the USSR did not go to Israel, and the majority went to the United States. Now that the US doors were closed, the majority of

---

[7] Although 3 billion dollars is the figure cited by the media, the recent reports of the US Congressional Research Service, brought to public attention by Republican Senate Minority Leader Bob Dole on 1 May, show that the real value of US military and economic aid to Israel is closer to 4 billion dollars per annum.

emigrating Soviet Jews would have to go to Israel against their real wishes. It is only a matter of time before US money will be used to finance the settlement of Soviet Jews in the West Bank. In this way the Soviet Union by providing the people, and the US by providing the funds would only delay the inevitable calamity caused by the demographic factors which undermine the security of the Zionist designs on Palestine.

Israel's only hope

The long-term security of the State of Israel is a matter of justifiable concern. Its future depends on whether it can build bridges with its Arab neighbours. If it attempts to annexe the West Bank and Gaza, and strengthen its control of South Lebanon it can only postpone its ultimate demise. Paradoxically the Palestinians are the key to its survival. If their legitimate aspirations are respected there can be some hope for a future peace. To accommodate the Palestinians Israel will have to change fundamentally. It must end the occupation. It must participate in the creation of a Palestinian state. It must make at least some reparation to the Palestinian people for the injury done. It must allow some Palestinians to return to their homeland.

It is only by acknowledging that it is destined to live among Palestinians and in an Arab world, and acting accordingly, that Israel can ever be secure. The hawks who argue for the annexation of the West Bank and Gaza, and the 'transfer' of the Palestinian population to the east bank of the Jordan condemn Israel to an impossible future. Should Israel refuse to make friends with the Arab neighbours which surround it, it is going to disappear, whether in ten, twenty, thirty or fifty years. Israel has only one way forward. The Palestinians have offered an historic compromise. It is in the long term interest of Israel to support the creation of a Palestinian State adjoining Israel. With the passage of time, relations between the two states could improve, since the prosperity of each would depend on the other. A negotiated solution which satisfies both Israel and the Palestinians is likely to reduce the major source of conflict in the whole region.

PALESTINIAN CHRISTIANS AND THE
LIBERATION OF THEOLOGY

As the title suggest, this article, written for The Month *in 1993, sees the Palestinian struggle as having relevance for the presuppositions of Christian theology.*

Two encounters I had recently in Palestine present a picture of church life among Palestinians that is very different to what we are accustomed in the West. One concerns an account of a Roman Catholic Mass, which took place in the largely Christian village of Beit Sahour, by the Shepherds' Field, near Bethlehem. An American nun, Sr Elaine, told of the aftermath of the murder of Antoine, a student at Bethlehem University, at the hands of Israeli soldiers: 'Antoine's body was brought to the Latin Church, and placed before the altar, with blood all over his clothes, running on to the floor. The priest said Mass, and the people wailed. After the funeral the people processed to Antoine's home, as is the custom. But the soldiers fired tear gas, and broke up the procession.' Sr Elaine sought refuge in great fear.

In my formal interview with a major Jerusalem church leader, my first question was, *How is the church here today?* He replied, 'We live here in a context of violence, which goes on.' *Are you hopeful for the peace process?* 'Yes, I am hopeful.' *Do you really believe that Israel will withdraw from the Occupied Territories?* 'I *A Living Stone—Selected Essays and Addresses*don't think that the military will withdraw from the Occupied Territories, but they will withdraw from the streets, and that will be a big liberation for the people in itself.' *I do not myself believe that Israel is interested in peace. Do you?* 'Israel left to itself does not seek peace. The logic of Zionism is expansionist. The Jews will need more room than is available to them. They will need to expand.' *Do you mean that they have designs beyond the Occupied Territories?* 'Yes, including Jordan, and other adjoining countries. The Arabs, on their part, harbour resentment towards the Israelis for the damage done them. So we have two conflicting ideologies: Jewish expansionism and Arab revenge. The Israelis have real reason to fear.' *On what basis, then, are you hopeful for peace?* 'There have been so many words, and so many hopes raised that something must come out of it. Ultimately it is the Americans who can impose on a reluctant Israel the need to instigate peace. The future will depend on the magnanimity of the terms for peace.'

These two snapshots of church life in Palestine indicate the backdrop for theological reflection and church life. The liturgy in Beit Sahour had more obvious links with the Christian celebration of Good Friday/Easter Sunday than our normal parish Masses have. The church leader's spontaneous answer to the question of the state of the church could not exclude the socio-politico-military context of Palestinian life.

The Oxford Dictionary defines Zionism as 'a movement aiming at the re-establishment of the Jewish nation in Palestine 1896'. Put in these terms it could be considered to have been a harmless restoration of something from the past, like the repair of antique furniture. The definition hides the reality that the re-establishment of the Jewish nation as a state in Palestine was achieved by the destruction of another people, the Palestinians.

At the heart of contemporary liberation theologies is the urge to improve the lot of the oppressed. Two questions spring to mind immediately: who are the oppressed, and how does one go about improving their lot? While most of the excitement of liberation theology comes from South America, and reflects a fundamental concern with issues of economic poverty, it must be conceded that the Good News of Jesus Christ is much wider in its scope. All oppression inhibits the capacity of a society, and an individual, to realise its potential.

One might expect to find a thriving liberation theology in the land where Jesus delivered his message of freedom. Palestine has a long line of liberation theologians, from Moses to Jesus. The circumstances of the indigenous Christian communities are ripe for a theological reflection on life under military occupation within the Occupied Territories, and on life as third-, fourth- or fifth-class citizens of the Jewish State of Israel.

The fundamental problem of the Palestinians is the price they have had to pay, and continue to pay for the encroachment on their land by Zionists from the diaspora. The creation of the State of Israel was not brought about without the destruction of some four hundred Arab villages, and the exodus, and expulsion, of more than 700,000 Arab inhabitants. At least a further 300,000 left Palestine as a result of the 1967 Six Day War. There can be no question of a *just* solution to the problem unless these refugees are allowed to return to their former homes, or are adequately compensated in accordance with international law. There can, of course, be a pragmatic solution, based on compromise by the parties concerned.

SLAVERY AND INJUSTICE

A number of the practitioners of Palestinian liberation theology are well known in the West, for example, Fr Elias Chacour, Canon Naim Ateek, and Revd Audeh Rantisi. Each of them has written a book on the subject.[1] Their theological reflections are distinctive in that they are quarried out of the sad memory of expulsion from their own homes and land, and the ongoing tragedy of living under occupation or oppression. Together with other colleagues they have established a Committee of Palestinian Liberation Theology. They held their First International Symposium at Tantur Ecumenical Institute, near Bethlehem, 10-17 March 1990, and the papers have since been published.[2]

One of the results of the *intifada* has been an increased politicisation of the Christian churches in the Holy Land. To this can be coupled a growing awareness of the situation of the Palestinians in the churches in the West. Many Christians in the West have seen enough for themselves to be very distressed by what is happening in the Holy Land. Palestinian Christians like to remind visitors that the Arabic word *intifada* suggests more than 'uprising'. They like to quote the saying of Jesus as recorded in Matthew 10: 14, *unfu'l-gubara en arjulikum* ('Shake the dust from your feet'). *Unfudu* means 'shake off, 'recover, recuperate, jump to one's feet'. On the reality of life under the occupation an Arab Christian priest says, 'Occupation is always a corrupting situation both for occupier and occupied. A wooden cage or a golden cage is still a cage.'[3]

Canon Naim Ateek's work is written in the tradition of Western theological reflection. He discerns two major issues in Palestinian

[1] Elias Chacour, 1985. *Blood Brothers*. Eastbourne: Kingsway. Naim Stifan Ateek, 1989. *Justice and Only Justice. A Palestinian Theology of Liberation*. New York, Maryknoll: Orbis. Audeh Rantisi, 1990. *Blessed are the Peacemakers. The Story of a Palestinian Christian*. Guildford: Eagle.
[2] *Faith and the Intifada. Palestinian Christian Voices,* ed. N S Ateek, M H Ellis, and R R Ruether, New York: Marylenoll (Orbis Books) 1992.
[3] *Impressions of Intifada. Report of a British Council of Churches Delegation to Israel and the Occupied Territories*, March 1989, p.2.

liberation perspectives, justice and the Bible. His reflections on the Bible are striking. Whereas one looks to the Bible for strength and liberation, it is being used by some Christians and Jews in a way which offers Palestinians slavery rather than freedom, injustice rather than justice, and death to their national and political life (p. 75). Since the establishment of the State of Israel, which was

> a seismic tremor of enormous magnitude that has shaken the very foundation of their beliefs ... the Old Testament has generally fallen into disuse among both clergy and laity, and the Church has been unable to come to terms with its ambiguities, questions, and paradoxes—especially with its direct application to the twentieth-century events in Palestine. The fundamental question of many Christians, whether uttered or not, is: 'How can the Old Testament be the Word of God in light of the Palestinian Christians' experience with its use to support Zionism?' (pp. 77-8).

Ateek searches for a hermeneutic of the Bible that will be sound both biblically and theologically, and finds it in the person of Jesus Christ. Palestinian Christians should begin with him, go backwards to the Old Testament, and forward to the New Testament and beyond (p. 80). If a passage fits in with what one knows of God through Christ, it is valid and authoritative. If it does not fit, it is invalid (p. 82).

Ateek protests against the use of the Exodus account as a paradigm for the establishment of the State of Israel. He regards the story of Naboth's vineyard (1 Kgs 2:1) as more promising, in that it demonstrates God's unwavering concern for justice. However, Ateek does not wish on the Israelis a retribution similar to that meted out to Ahab and Jezebel. He has recourse also to the story of the prophecy of Micaiah Ben Inilah, which did not flinch from speaking an unpopular truth to King Ahab (1 Kings 22). The third example of biblical texts suitable for Palestinian liberation is contained in Psalms 42 and 43, laments of exiles longing to return home.

Ateek sketches the biblical tension between the portrayal of God as nationalist and universalist. He traces the development of the nationalistic/exclusivist perspective of the early prophets (Joshua, Judges, 1 and 2 Samuel, and 1 and 2 Kings), notes the concentration on the Torah in the Pentateuch, and later in the tradition of the Pharisees, and draws attention to the greater emphasis on the universalism of God as detected in the later Prophets, and more especially in Jonah. He sees this third strand raised to a new intensity in the universalism of Jesus and the New Testament.

RETROGRESSION

He sees in the emergence of the Zionist movement in the twentieth century a retrogression of the Jewish community into its distant past, a period marked by its most elementary and primitive forms of the concept of God. 'Zionism has succeeded in re-animating the nationalist tradition within Judaism. Its inspiration has been drawn not from the profound thoughts of the Hebrew Scriptures, but from those portions that betray a narrow and exclusive concept of a tribal god' (p. 101). The universalist outlook of ethical Judaism has been swamped by the resurgence of a racially exclusive concept of a people and their god (p. 102).

He appeals to Christian pilgrims to meet the *living stones* of the land-the Christians.

> To visit the holy sites is a very moving experience for many; meeting the 'holy' people can be a very rewarding and enriching experience for both ... indigenous Christians who are privileged to live in Israel-Palestine today have a responsibility to Christian pilgrims from all over the world— to make their pilgrimage a revitalising experience of their faith. Their responsibility and privilege is to be host to their brothers and sisters from abroad (p.114).

He writes as a pastor, not as a politician. He accepts the existence of the State of Israel in his Palestine, not as of right, but as of need, 'since the elimination of Israel would mean greater injustice to millions of innocent people who know no home except Israel' (p. 164). Any genuine solution, he insists, must pass the test of two sayings of Jesus: 'So whatever you wish that men should do to you, do so to them; for this is the law and the prophets' (Matt 7:12), and, 'You shall love your neighbour as yourself (Mk 12:3 1). His solution moves out from the major premise: Palestine is a country for both the Jews and the Palestinians. Although the ideal would be the creation of one united democratic state for all Palestinians and Jews, he concedes that the existence of the Jewish State is a requirement for Jews. The minor premise is the creation of a Palestinian State, alongside the State of Israel in the West Bank and Gaza, in which all inhabitants would live as first-class citizens. Ateek insists that the security and well-being of Israel demands the creation of a Palestinian State. With the two states living side by side the way would be open to fostering the patient work of reconciliation.

THEOLOGY IN ACTION

Ateek does not look for justice, but only for an accommodation with the political and social realities, which have sprung from the fundamental injustice done to the Palestinians. He ought to be more demanding, since it is the task of a Christian theologian to suggest what *ought* to be, rather than what can come about through the efforts of politicians.

I asked Canon Ateek about the task of Palestinian liberation theology.

> There are two levels to work on, the internal and the external. We ask ourselves what we can do to help our own people by way of liberation. We are agreed that one of the things we can do is to conduct workshops. We take a theme, and develop it in a day conference, with one or two papers. We have discussion groups and allow people to do theology. We have done this successfully on a number of occasions, both in Jerusalem and Galilee. We have requests now to hold workshops in several places. Our problem is to respond to the need. Another area is more long-term, where a number of people commit themselves to long-term study, in which we will work more deeply.
> We have also completed a training course for speakers. There are so many groups coming to the country, but only a few of us who speak. Now we have twenty two young people, who are brilliant, with good personalities, almost all university graduates, with good English, some German and French. We train them for two months. They are already in operation, speaking to groups. We are in touch with travel agents. We are trying to get in touch with tour groups outside the country to tell them that this ministry is available. We speak to Christian groups, about the situation; about the Christian community.

Other activities include working with the Christian schools, and availing of visits from theologians from abroad.[4] They hope to produce a newsletter, and do some writing in Arabic. It is their hope that once a year they will bring a group of between ten and twenty theologians for a symposium, to share with, learn from, and teach. 'We want to expose them to who we are, to what is happening here. They can share their experience, and we ours. We can check out our theology with them. We will spend some days in reflection, and do some visiting of people, going to Gaza, and so on.'

They are particularly interested in theologians from South Africa. 'They have a situation similar to us, but they are ahead of us in theology.' Serious thought is also being given to theologians from the European community, and the USA. They, too, must see the oppression of the Palestinians for themselves. 'We are trying to rediscover the liberation that Christ has given us-reclaim it, re-use it. *Lahut Al-Quds* ("Jerusalem Theology") would be a beautiful name!'

Is there any way of including Islam in the discussion? 'It will come, but it hasn't come yet.'

UNIQUE FEATURES

Palestinian liberation theologians have to contend with a number of very sensitive issues. Firstly, they are all victims of oppression. Together with their families they have lost their homes, and their natural place in their own society. One born in Lydda, for example, suffered expulsion to the West Bank in 1948.

Subsequently, he has suffered twenty-six years of brutal Israeli oppression in the Occupied Territories.

Secondly, it appears that some Christians see in the establishment of the State of Israel in 1948 the fulfilment of God's promises to the Children of Israel. While in the Hebrew Scriptures, the Testament revered, albeit variously, by both Jews and Christians, Palestinian Christians discover some strong strands of liberation of the oppressed, they find also what some take as God's approval for their lot. The people of Israel are

---

[4] I had the honour of addressing the group in Jerusalem in August 1992, on the subject of *Jesus in the Synagogue of Nazareth (Luke 4:16-30).*

God's chosen ones, they learn, and the land of Israel is given to them as God's gift! For religious people there is no greater vindication of political fortune than divine authentication. What could be considered immoral, or unethical about God restoring his land to the people he chose of old? Does a Palestinian theology of liberation, then, not run in the face of the biblical witness to God's choice?

Thirdly, the attitude of Christians throughout the world to the fate of the Palestinians, including Palestinian Christians, is ambivalent. Fundamentalist Christians share with fundamentalist Jews some views about the resettlement of Jews in Palestine as a stage preliminary to the coming of the Messiah's End-Time Kingdom, for Jews, or the Second Coming, as awaited by Christians. Proponents of biblical fundamentalism read the Pentateuch as providing the guarantee of God's unconditional gift of the land to the Israelites, without any regard to those who were living in the land already.

Fourthly, even when there is abundant evidence of Israeli oppression, there is a deep unease within Western Christian circles about even the most tame criticism of Israeli policies. It is as if the horror of the Nazi Holocaust of Jews sanctions the oppression of an innocent third party. The pro-Zionist lobbies in the West have been very successful in ensuring that the guilt felt by western Christians in the wake of the Holocaust would be paid for by an uncritical support of Israel. Professor Arnold Toynbee observes: 'Right and wrong are the same in Palestine as anywhere else. What is peculiar about the Palestine conflict is that the world has listened to the party that committed the offence and has turned a deaf ear to the victims.'[5]

Fifthly, in western circles the revulsion which one expects to surface at any form of wicked behaviour is muted in the case of the State of Israel. It is one of the great anomalies of recent church history that while Christians throughout the world have engaged energetically in favour of the oppressed in all kinds of areas, there has been almost total silence on the state terrorism of Israel, and its persistent abuse of human rights. For many liberal Jews also, who are active in all kinds of issues of human rights, Israel and the Occupied Territories are no-go areas for moral concern.

---

[5] Quoted in Kayyali, Introduction, p. 5 of *Zionism, Imperialism and Racism,* ed. Abdul Wahhab Al Kayyali, London: Croom Helm, 1979.

Sixthly, some influential members of organisations committed to the noble ideal of Jewish-Christian dialogue remain silent on the oppression of the Palestinians, in spite of the presence of overwhelming, embarrassing evidence. They create a climate in which good relations between Jews and Christians appear to exact a condoning, by silence, of Israeli brutality. The public stance of some of their officers (letters to the press, and so on) scandalise most people of goodwill, and are of no little embarrassment to many Christians and Jews. Silence in the face of contemporary violations of human dignity is unworthy of adherents of any worthwhile religion. It should not be tolerated by people concerned with the integrity of Judaism and Christianity, and with the relations between their believers. If we allow others to suffer, and even be killed without protesting, we become 'accomplices by omission'.

One notices a shift in the language of the almost professional defenders of the State of Israel. Until recently, anyone daring to criticise the gross abuses of civilised behaviour by those acting in the name of the State of Israel was branded as anti-Semitic, and in the case of Jewish critics, as self-hating Jews. *Balance,* and the lack of it, has taken over in the discourse as the new offence.

Virtually any attempt to provide a forum for the exposition of the sad plight of the Palestinians is countered by the accusation of being unbalanced. When this attempted censorship is carried out by groups alleging to be acting in the interests of ecumenical dialogue, one must protest at the disregard for the claims of truth, justice and peace. Honest Jewish-Christian dialogue must confront the major, contemporary ethical question, namely, the morality of the behaviour of the State of Israel, and its responsibilities towards the Palestinian people. Protestors against the virtual annihilation of Palestinian society must stand in the face of the cheap jibes, abuse, and the predictable, organised intimidation of such pro-Israeli lobbies.

THE PROMISED LAND

The way in which the people of Israel settled in the land of Canaan is a matter of considerable scholastic interest, and of great contemporary relevance. It has implications for our understanding of God, and his relation to the people of Israel, to non-Israelites such as the Canaanites, and by extension to all other peoples.

On moral grounds, any association of God with barbarism must be looked at with care. Religious people in particular ought to question whether God's ways are any different from those of colonisers. When there is a fundamental contradiction between what some claim to be God's will and ordinary civilised, decent behaviour, the apologists for God had better question what kind of a monster they consider their God to be. Is God a chauvinist-a militaristic and nationalistic xenophobe?

There is much support in the Hebrew Scriptures for the view that the land of Israel was promised by God to Abraham and his descendants, and that their possession of it was in conformity with God's will (for example Gen 12:6f.). Subsequently, the promise is made to Isaac also (Gen 263f.), who in his turn wished it on his son Jacob (Gen 28:4). While Jacob was asleep near Haran, and dreaming of the ladder, he heard the similar promise of the land (Gen 28:13-15). At this point, if not before, one is encouraged to enquire into the historical value of these reports. Only the most naive in matters of literary criticism, or the most cynical in political matters would take these one-sided accounts at face value.

One readily understands the significance of having the divine approval for possession of the land, even before the people became a nation. Their new fortune was not the result of the chance opportunities of international changes, but emanated from the will of God himself. The conquest of Canaan, then, was in conformity with the divine will. It had come directly as a gift from God to Abraham.

In broad terms, the Israelites controlled their own territory from 1200 until 587, and from 165-63 BCE, and only again since 1948 with the founding of the State of Israel. During the other years it was occupied by Babylonians (586-538), Persians (538-323), Hellenists (323-165), Romans (63 BCE-324 CE), Byzantines (CE 324-640), Early Arabs (640-1009), European Crusaders (1009-1291), Mamluks (1250-1517), Ottoman Turks (1517-1918), and British Mandate (1918-1948). Of necessity, therefore, the religion of the Jews had every opportunity to express itself in the changing circumstances of political life in Palestine itself, and in the diaspora. Plainly, any suggestion that the establishment of the State of Israel in 1948 restores the *status quo* before the defeat of the revolt against the Romans in 66-70 CE is a simplistic distortion of complex political realities. Any suggestion that diaspora Judaisms were shot through with a longing for the day when they would *return to Zion* in the sense outlined by the ideologues of Zionism is a mixture of the religiously romantic and the politically cynical. And such cocktails are lethal.

Nevertheless, Moses Hess (1812-75) in his *Rome and Jerusalem* argued that Jewish nationhood provided the setting for the realisation of Judaism's ethical ideals.

The economic and social conditions of the diaspora made impossible the Jewish task of establishing a model society and of being a light to the nations. A Jewish homeland in Palestine would provide the context in which Jewish life and ethics would flourish, and would serve as a model for the oppressed peoples of Asia and Africa.

A UNIQUE RELATIONSHIP

The land of God's promise is one of the most pervasive doctrines of the Hebrew Scriptures, and is fundamental to Zionism. While the question of Jewish identity is an ongoing one ('Who is a Jew?'), there is virtually no questioning concerning the promise of the land. Settlement in the land, therefore, becomes an act of piety, which overrides other considerations, such as the human rights of the indigenous people, and the civilised behaviour of those entering.

In Martin Buber's terms, 'The union of people and land is intended to contribute to the perfecting of the world in order to become the Kingdom of God'.[6]

Whereas other nations who dispossessed indigenous people can legitimately be accused of robbery,

> their charge against Israel is totally unjust for it acted under authority and in the confident knowledge of its authorisation ... no other people has ever heard and accepted the command from heaven as did the people of Israel ... So long as it sincerely carried out the command it was in the right and is in the right in so far as it still carries it out. Its unique relationship to its

---

[6] *On Zion: The History of an Idea,* 1973. New York: Schocken Books, p. 47.

land must be seen in this light ... Where a command and a faith
are present,—in certain historical situations conquest need not
be robbery (Buber 1973: 146).

The romantic view of the land as holy is reflected also in an
essay by Andre Neher, one of the leading Jewish thinkers of this century.[7]
Palestine holds the key to Jewish existence. But the elevated spiritual and
moral tenets of the Torah must be obeyed. 'Otherwise, this land will
vomit him (Israel) forth, as it previously vomited the Canaanites, to whom
God had confided it in a moment of hasty imprudence' (p.20). Neher
writes of a 'geo-theology' and its charm (p.22). He subscribes to the
view that *aliyah* (going up to Israel) will foreshorten the coming of the
messiah (p.23). The state of Israel is the agent of mass reconciliation: of
Jews, Christians and Muslims; of the sacred and the profane; and of Jews
who differ in the immediacy of their messianic expectations. As is typical
of the discourse that permeates much Jewish-Christian dialogue, there is
no discussion of the moral issues raised by the establishment of the State
of Israel, nothing of the tragedy of those dispossessed, expelled, murdered,
or permanently exiled. Christians, too, are expected to recognise that
Palestine belongs to the Jews by virtue of the Bible, the divinely established
title-deed. Walter Brueggemann writes:

> The understanding of land we have discerned in the Bible is
> never just about land, never only land possessed and managed.
> It is always a land of gift and promise, a gift given when it
> could never be taken or grasped or seized, a promise by the
> Promiser who stands outside history but has been found faithful
> in history.[8]

THE DREAM AND THE REALITY

The rhetoric of this kind of sacral discourse is punctured by the sad
reality of its political realisation. Of necessity, the establishment of a
Zionist state involved the invasion of a country, the eviction of the majority

---

[7] 'The Land as Locus of the Sacred,' in D Burrell and Y Landau, 1992. *Voices from Jerusalem.
Jews and Christians Reflect on the Holy Land*. New York: Paulist, pp. 18-29.
[8] W Brueggemann, 1977. *The Land*. Philadelphia: Fortress, p. 19 1.

of its inhabitants, and the continual use of force and terrorism, culminating in a series of wars and military occupations. Since its foundation, Israel has been a major player in the wars of 1948, 1956, 1967, 1973 and 1982. In terms of approval, few countries have incurred the wrath of the international community more than Israel has. The degrading of the Palestinian culture, the existence of the Palestinian diaspora, the refugee camps, the litany of atrocities, of which the invasion of Lebanon ranks as high as any, combine to raise the question of the success of the dream of nineteenth century Jewish nationalists.

So great is the disjuncture between the ideal and practice that the Jewish theologian, Professor Marc Ellis suspects that Judaism and statehood may be incompatible.

> The strain of keeping religious values and statehood in harmony is clearly increasing and with no resolution in sight. ... Judaism will continue much as Christianity continued after Constantine, as a religion that legitimates empire and the violence which comes with empire.[9] ... What has been touted as our finest moment is today to be remembered with shame ... because what we have done historically and what we are doing today betrays the suffering and struggle which gave birth to us, guided us, and for some moments at least helped give light to the world.

The following is a strident assessment of the achievement of Zionism from the perspective of the dispossessed.

> Inasmuch as Israel is a regression to the idea of religion as a basis of a nation state, it is an anachronism. Inasmuch as it is an alien western invasion of Arab land, it is another crusade doomed to failure. Inasmuch as it is a colonial racist state, it is an enemy of the spirit of the age of liberation and equality ... Inasmuch as it is naturally allied to the Imperialist powers in their battle against Arab rights and the Arab future, it will collapse with the defeat of imperialism in the Arab homeland as it was defeated elsewhere. The verdict of history is clear: there is no

---

[9] M Ellis, 1990. 'On the 8th Anniversary of Sabra and Shatila: Jewish Progressives and Complicity in the Oppression of the Palestinian Peole,' in 'The Role of American Religious Leaders in the Middle East Peace Process,'*American-Arab Affairs* no.34 (Fall): 67-77, pp.73f.

place in the coming century for racism, zionism, and imperialism. The peoples of the third world shall assert their rights and liberate themselves, thus ridding all societies of the burden of inequality and oppression.[10]

INVOLVEMENT IN A NEW ORDER

One of the major achievements of the challenge which liberation theologies have offered to the western dominated theology is its insistence that authentic theological reflection cannot be divorced from the social and political realities of life. It is only when theology involves itself with the realities of the conditions of people, and particularly those in oppression that it can be seen to offer a new order. However, liberation rhetoric is not sufficient. Liberation requires great people who can elevate into concrete political programmes the ideals of liberation theologies.

In an ideal world those who contribute to liberation theologies should be as skilled in the discipline of social analysis as they are in theological rhetoric. Specialisation in human learning has the adverse effect of reducing the number of those with equal skills in diverse areas. The rare being who is academically competent in biblical exegesis, theology and even economics is not likely also to have the capacity to elevate admirable ideological insights into macroplans for national and even international economies.

The Christian Palestinian voice is only one of several voices which cry out under oppression in the Holy Land. It is part of the larger Palestinian protest. By and large, it is firmly in conformity with the aspiration of most Palestinians for national independence in a democratic, secular State of Palestine.[11] It works towards that end in the context of Israeli intransigence, and the alternative solutions proposed by Hamas and Islamic Jihad. Most important of all, the struggle for Palestinian justice and liberation depends for its success on the readiness of the United

---

[10] Abdul Wahhab Al Kayyali, 1979. *Zionism, Imperialism and Racism*, ed. Abdul Wahhab Al Kayyali, London: Croom Helm, pp. 9-26, p. 24.

[11] The official delegation of Christians from the Holy Land, meeting in Cumberland Lodge, Pentecost 1993, declared, 'We share the aspirations of the Palestinian people for an end to occupation and for national independence. We therefore advocate and support a just and lasting peace in the region.'

States of America to forego its virtually unqualified support for, and financing of, Israeli oppression, in the interests of its own foreign policy. Dwarfed by such political giants, Palestinian liberation theology may not succeed in doing much more than explicating a moral ideal, and giving its people a dignity in their suffering.

Good Friday invites Palestinian Christians, and others to grapple with the perplexity of apparent disaster. Its liturgy invites theoreticians, and liberation theologians to face into the reality of dreams which have become nightmares, of visions which have never come off the drawing-board. Christians are invited to die with Christ, to enter the tomb with the spirit-less corpse of Jesus. As they enter the tomb with Jesus they bring 'our body's labour, our spirit's grief, our selfish hearts, our failing faith, our daily toil, the plants in our heart's poor soil, all that we start and spoil, each hopeful dream, the chances we have missed, the graces we resist' (Kevin Nichols). At the heart of the Christian Gospel is the reality of the Cross. It is a paradox. At the level of phenomena it depicts failure. But seen in the light of faith in the Crucified God it enfleshes victory.

The gospel of Christian faith, hope and love must stand above the misery of the plight of the Palestinians, and of others who suffer at the hands of powerful oppressors. The pervasiveness and ubiquity of evil in the world tempts one to abandon the struggle to continue to bring the Kingdom about, and leave things to God to sort out at the end of time. This cannot be a legitimate Christian option. Alone, or even with God on one's side, all cannot be achieved on this side of the eschatological Day of the Lord. But to do nothing is not an acceptable alternative. The Christian Church, in Palestine and abroad, in collaboration with different groups, should seek always to promote the growth of the Kingdom in an energetic and humble way. Its message is fundamentally Good News which brings peace and joy. It must be striven for in the midst of the reality of human life in all its complexity, at the basic level of personal, interpersonal and social relations of all kinds. And even while grappling with it, Christians realise that God's Kingdom and Good News for the oppressed will never be enacted fully in history. Nevertheless, there is a certain peace and fulfilment in seeing what can be achieved, and in submitting to the constant call to conversion to goodness.

THE VATICAN-ISRAEL
FUNDAMENTAL AGREEMENT

The 1993 Vatican-Israel agreement prompted Michael to challenge the assertion that
this represented a milestone in Jewish-Catholic relations
(Living Stones Magazine, 1994).

The signing of the Fundamental Agreement between the Vatican and the State of Israel on 30 December 1993, like many agreed statements before it, is seen very differently from the perspectives of the two participants. As he signed the agreement on behalf of the State of Israel, Dr Yossi Beilin, the Deputy Foreign Minister, invoked 'thousands of years of history, full of hatred, fear and ignorance—and a few islands of understanding, cooperation and dialogue ... Behind the agreement there are very few years of light and too many years of darkness.'

By way of contrast, the remarks of Mgr Claudio Maria Celli, the Holy See's Under-Secretary for Foreign Relations, were more downbeat: 'The signing of the agreement, while certainly marking an important historical event, must also be acknowledged to have a fundamental religious and spiritual significance, not only for the Holy See and the State of Israel, but for millions of people throughout the world.' *The Guardian* journalist at the ceremony judged Mgr Celli to have deflected awkward questions with typical clerical waffle.

According to Chief Rabbi Jonathan Sacks the agreement 'counts as one of the great interfaith achievements of the century' (*The Daily Telegraph*, 31 December 1993, 'Sacred and Profane', p. 21). He points out that while many saw in Vatican II's *Nostra Aetate* (1965) the beginning of a new era, that document had said nothing of the State of Israel, whose creation, in his view, was 'the most significant development in Jewish life since the Holocaust'.

The Chief Rabbi hints that it was mainly because of traces of ancient theological prejudices that the Vatican has withheld diplomatic recognition up to now, rather than any concern about Israel's disputed borders, the status of Jerusalem, Palestinian refugees, and the position of the Church in Arab lands. 'Homelessness, the Church had taught, was the divine judgement against Jews for not becoming Christians. Therefore a Jewish homecoming was impossible.'

On this matter the Chief Rabbi is off target. Unless one is prepared *a priori* to disbelieve anything coming from the Vatican, there is an abundance of formidable evidence pointing to quite different reasons. From the foundation of the State of Israel the Vatican has withheld formal diplomatic recognition. To ascribe this reluctance to long-abandoned Catholic bigotries is to ignore a whole range of factors which have influenced the Catholic Church. Not least of these is the lack of fulfilment of the other half of UN Resolution 181, adopted on 29 November 1947, which urged a two-state solution, a Jewish state, and an Arab state, with Jerusalem governed by a Special International Regime. Moreover, the failure of the State of Israel to comply with UN Resolution 242, requiring withdrawal from territory occupied in the 1967 War, added to the weight of difficulties of the Vatican, making it impossible for it to establish full diplomatic relations.

The Vatican's withholding of diplomatic recognition of Israel respected its dissatisfaction with the prevailing political climate: the absence of a solution to the problem of Palestinian refugees, and Israel's general disdain for the will of the international community reflected in its non-compliance with Resolutions 465 (concerning its 'flagrant violation of the fourth Geneva convention' and its settlement of the occupied territories etc.).

Rabbi Sacks quotes Pius X's reply to Herzl's exposition of his dream of a Jewish State, 'The Jews have not recognized our Lord, therefore we cannot recognize the Jewish people.' The Chief Rabbi goes on, 'Such sentiments were surely untenable after Auschwitz. How could the Vatican recognize Jewry without including its most powerful collective expression, its state?' Of course, the reported sentiments of Pius X, not to recognize the Jewish people, are theologically indefensible, either before or after Auschwitz—indeed, they are absurd. There has been quite a lot of change within the Catholic Church since Pius X's time. However, recognizing the most powerful collective expression of Jewry, its state, is a less than sanguine enterprise. To grant diplomatic recognition to the State of Israel might be considered by many to accord ethical, and even religious legitimacy to the underside of the establishment of the State of Israel, the destruction of another people, the Palestinians. Moreover, there is the very sensitive question of timing.

The Chief Rabbi's comments do not show any sensitivity to the innocent people who have paid the price for the most significant development in Jewish life since the Holocaust. Surely one must experience some moral perturbation when one reviews the conditions under which the State of Israel was established, and is maintained. The consistency with which the State of Israel is excused from having to conform to decent behaviour is one of the great eccentricities of 20th-century political ethics.

JEWRY, ZIONISM AND THE VATICAN

The relations between the Holy See and the State of Israel are not to be understood as identical with those between two faiths, Catholicism and Judaism. This appears to be seen more clearly on the Vatican side than on that of the State of Israel. Relations between the Catholic Church and the representatives of Zionism, prior to the establishment of the State of Israel in 1948 and with the State of Israel itself since then, reflect the changing, relevant political circumstances which obtained throughout the period. The wider international, as well as religious context has seen many fundamental changes since the advent of Zionism, and its hopes for the establishment of a Jewish homeland or state in the late 19th century, and the realization of that ideal in the establishment of the State of Israel in 1948.

Many people, including numerous Jews who keep alive the Hebrew prophetic concern for justice, see in the emergence of the Zionist movement in the 19th and 20th centuries a retrogression of Jewry into that part of its past, which is marked by its most elementary and primitive forms of the concept of God. The biblical inspiration for the establishment of the State of Israel has been drawn from those portions of the Hebrew Scriptures that betray a narrow and exclusive concept of a tribal, xenophobic and militaristic god, rather than from those which highlight the universalist outlook which is characteristic of a more progressive, ethical Judaism.

During the Ottoman period the primary interest of the Vatican was in the Christian Holy Places, the sites and shrines associated particularly with Christian origins. The Turks had proved to be very even-handed in their administration of the Holy Land. In line with the growth of Western interest in the region during the period of decline of the Ottoman empire the Vatican expanded its interest in the region. From the beginning, Christians were among the staunchest Arab opponents of Zionism, and were to the fore in nascent Arab nationalism. Prior to the Balfour Declaration of 1917 the major concern of the Vatican focussed on the likely fate of the Holy Places in the custody of the synagogue.

The aftermath of the First World War brought great international change. Reflecting the new order, the Holy See began to pay more attention to the interests of the Christian community in the Holy Land, which was overwhelmingly Arab (80 percent in the 1931 British Census of Palestine). Interest in the affairs of Arab Christians inevitably led to concern for the wider Arab nationalist community.

On 6 March 1922, the Vatican Secretary of State, Cardinal Gasparri, severely criticized the draft British Mandate for Palestine, which Lord Balfour had presented to the League of Nations on 7 December 1920. He argued that those articles which were designed to implement the Balfour Declaration were incompatible with the Covenant of the League of Nations. The British plan, in his judgement, would establish 'an absolute economic, administrative, and political preponderance of Jews over other nationalities,' and would act as 'the instrument for subordinating native populations, to the advantage of another nationality' (quoted with reference in A Kreutz, 1992. 'The Vatican and the Palestinians: A Historical Overview'. *Islamochristiana* 18: 109-125, p. 115). One can see here the emergence of a concern for the rights of the Palestinians in the land.

It is equally clear, however, that the Vatican had little enthusiasm for an Arab government in the area, which it predicted would be unreliable and weak. The Vatican was happy to support the social and economic interests of the Palestinians, but not the implications of Palestinian self-determination. As late as January 1948, Mgr G Montini (the future Paul VI, then the Under Secretary for Ordinary Affairs) told the British Minister to the Vatican that the Holy See preferred that 'a third power, neither Jew nor Arab ... have control of the Holy Land' (Perowne [Rome] to Burrows, Jan 19, 1948—FO 371/68500, quoted in Kreutz, p. 116).

The Holocaust provided a major change in the Vatican's stance. Such was the international support for Zionism in the wake of the virtual annihilation of mainland European Jewry that it was virtually impossible for the Vatican to challenge Zionism publicly. In particular, it would not have been wise for it to offend the USA in its support, since it needed its alliance in the face of Soviet expansionism.

The establishment of the State of Israel on 79 percent of British Mandate Palestine, and the expulsion and displacement of 714,000 Palestinian Arabs, including some 50,000 Christians, 35 percent of all Christians who lived in Palestine prior to 15 May 1948, while acknowledged to be a disaster, did not induce the Vatican to make any diplomatic representations. In his Encyclical Letter, *In Multiplicibus* of October 1948, Pope Pius XII only expressed his anguish at the general conditions of refugees, and in that which followed it six months later, *Redemptoris Nostri*, he was no more specific. The two do not go beyond the expression of predictable, broad moral and religious principles, with no explicit political implications. The Roman Catholic institutions throughout the world, however, were to the fore in answering the Pope's appeal for assistance.

Mgr Thomas McMahon, the Vatican envoy, insisted in several meetings with Israeli and American officials that the return of the Christian exiles was 'basic to an Israeli-Church rapprochement' (Kreutz, p. 117). Nevertheless, the whole Palestinian issue was not mentioned publicly for the next twenty years.

POST VATICAN II

Vatican II itself opened the Catholic Church to the world in an unprecedented way. In the spirit of the Council, the Church began to abandon its citadel character, and to relate in a more modest way towards others, both in the Church and the World. There was a new respect for diversity of religion, and a coming to terms with the post-colonial, so-called Third World.

Vatican II's Declaration on Religious Freedom, *Nostra Aetate* reflected the new climate of respect for the great religions of the world, and provided a stimulus to better relations between Christianity and other religions, including, of course, Judaism. Parallel with this was the growing sense of the relationship between the gospel and justice and peace. The Vatican's growing sensitivities to justice and peace were to be seen in a range of documents (see the encyclicals of John XXIII, *Mater et Magistra, Pacem in Terris*, of Paul VI, *Populorum Progressio, Evangelii Nuntiandi*, and more recently of John Paul II, *Redemptoris Hominis*, and *Laborem Exercens*). Translated to the Middle East, there were two, somewhat conflicting tendencies developing, namely, a greater respect for the Jews, and a growing sympathy for the plight of the Palestinians.

POPE PAUL VI

A number of significant factors influenced future developments. The victory of Israel in the Six-Day War of June 1967 imposed a new sense of the reality and power of the Jewish state. Contacts between Jews and Catholics increased. Pope Paul VI stated his concern at the decrease in the numbers of Christians in the Holy Land. If their presence in the Holy Land were to 'cease, the shrines would be without the warmth of the living witness of the Holy Places of Jerusalem and the Holy Land would become like a museum' (Apostolic Exhortation, 'Concerning the increased needs of the Church in the Holy Land', 1974).

In addressing Israeli Jews on 22 December 1975, he said,

> Although we are conscious of the still very recent tragedies which led the Jewish people to search for safe protection in a state of its own, sovereign and independent, and in fact precisely because we are aware of this, we would like to ask the sons of this people to recognize the rights and legitimate aspirations of another people, which have also suffered for a long time, the Palestinian people' (*Acta Apostolicae Sedis*, Jan–Mar 1976, p. 134).

This was the first time that any Pope had recognized the rights and legitimate aspirations of the Jews to a sovereign and independent state of its own. The other side of the coin lay in his appeal to the victors to recognize the corresponding rights of the vanquished.

POPE JOHN PAUL II

By 1983 Mgr W Murphy, Under-Secretary of the Pontifical Commission for Justice and Peace acknowledged that the Vatican 'recognizes the factual existence of Israel, its right to exist, its right to secure borders, and other rights that a sovereign nation possesses.' Pope John Paul II welcomed

Shimon Peres, the Israeli Prime Minister, to the Vatican on 19 February 1985. His visit to the Roman synagogue on 25 June 1986 marked another stage in the growing cordiality between the two bodies.

After the Peres' visit, the Vatican spokesman referred to divergencies on essential problems, which included the status of Jerusalem, the sovereignty of Lebanon over all its territory, and the lot of the Palestinian people. According to Fr Giovanni Caprile ('La Santa Sede e lo Stato d'Israele', in *La Civilta Cattolica*, 16 February 1991, pp. 357-8) the problems were: a just solution to the Palestinian problem, and the establishment of a Palestinian homeland; an internationally guaranteed special status for Jerusalem, with access to, and equality for Christians, Jews and Muslims, making Jerusalem a real centre of spiritual and fraternal development; and, finally, an improvement in the legal rights and social situations of the Christian communities living under Israeli control.

The appeal for recognition of the rights of both peoples has been a constant call of Pope John Paul II. The most comprehensive expression of this is contained in his communique released to the press after the visit of Yassir Arafat to the Pope on 15 September 1982 (*La Documentation Catholique* 73, 17 October, pp. 921 and 947). In his Apostolic Letter, *Redemptionis Anno* of April 1984, he said,

> The Palestinian people who find their historical roots in that land and who for decades have been dispersed, have the natural right in justice to find once more a homeland and to be able to live in peace and tranquillity with the other peoples of the area (Secretariatus pro non-Christianis, Bulletin 57 [1984], XIX [3], p. 254).

During his visit to Austria in June 1988, the Pope called again for equality for Israeli Jews and Palestinians, and pointed out that full diplomatic relations between the Holy See and Israel are 'dependent on a solution to the Palestinian Question and the international status of Jerusalem.' The Palestinians, he went on, have a right to a homeland, 'like every other nation, according to international law.'

In his Easter Message of 1991 John Paul II said, 'Lend an ear, humanity of our time, to the long ignored aspirations of oppressed peoples such as the Palestinians, the Lebanese, the Kurds, who claim the right to exist with dignity, justice and freedom.'

CONCLUSION

Several factors have influenced the Vatican in its assessment of the region. The Catholic Church world-wide has become more aware of its mission to be the Church of the Poor. Liberation from social and political oppression has become more and more an integral part of the Church's good news. The Church is also becoming involved in a new dialogue with Islam, which could not but intensify the interest of these two Abrahamic religions in Jerusalem. Israel, meanwhile, remains the most potent military force in the region, with the USA as its powerful ally.

In the course of this century the attitude of the Vatican to the Holy Land has changed profoundly, in line with the momentous changes which have taken place in the Middle East and in its own perception of its role in the world. Contemporary theology, with its recovery of the sense of the Church as the People of God would never allow its interests in the people of the region to be swallowed up by a parochial interest in the religious museum pieces of the past. The Church is a building composed of living stones.

But concern for the Christian communities of the Holy Land could never have exhausted the Catholic Church's interest in a region which had by now become a focus of global interest. The Middle East had become a potential flash-point of conflict between the great powers. More than the future of a Jewish homeland, or the recovery of the dignity of a downtrodden people, the Palestinians, was at stake. Future regional, and even world peace would depend on the establishment of a lasting peace in the region.

The Vatican has its own reasons for establishing diplomatic relations with all kinds of regimes. These owe at least as much to the pragmatism of *Realpolitik* as to the high moral ideals associated with Jesus, the Jew it most reveres. The declaration can be seen primarily as the mutual recognition by one body of the other, with each of the two parties looking to its own interests. It would be a moral scandal if the agreement were, or were even considered to be an approval by a religious body of the legitimacy of the barbarisms associated with the establishment of the State of Israel, its expulsion of up to a million Palestinians, its persistent violation of international laws and conventions, and its failure to deal justly with the Palestinians.

If the Vatican chooses to take advantage of this new relationship to use its good offices to promote peace and justice in the region so much the better. One hopes that the agreement may contribute towards some form of restitution for the injustices done to the Palestinians, and towards a sensible peace in the region. If the members of the Catholic Church consider that the Church has much to do to atone for its brutality towards Jews in the past, let them argue for it to be done graciously, and at the Church's own expense. Present-day Palestinians, as the innocent third party, should not have to continue to pay the price for the sins of others.

CLINTON'S BIBLE, GOLDSTEIN'S HERMENEUTICS AND RABIN'S METAL DETECTORS

This article published, in The Middle East International *in 1994, challenges the idea that the Exodus story provides an unambiguous inspiration for political liberation movements.*

God occupies the high moral ground even in societies in which there is little more than lip-service paid to him. Nothing compares with having him on one's side. On the White House lawn on September 13 1993, President Clinton introduced the leaders of Israel and the Palestinians, saying that both people pledged themselves to a shared future, *shaped by the values of the Torah, the Koran, and the Bible.* Both President Clinton's and Premier Rabin's speeches referred to the Bible, while Chairman Arafat began his with the traditional Muslim invocation of the one God. The Bible is a significant source-book in the so-called, but confused concept of *the Judaeo-Christian tradition*, while Muslims look to the Koran for divine guidance.

President Clinton, fearing that his speech required more work, had been unable to sleep on the night before the signing. He woke at 3.00 a.m., and reached for his Bible. He reread the entire Book of Joshua and portions of the New Testament. The *Washington Post* report does not reveal whether the President was able to sleep after the blood-curling lection from Joshua, nor, if so, whether he suffered any violent dreams! In any case, his mode of address later in the day was a mixture of bible-based exhortation in the Baptist tradition, and shrewd political manoeuvring. As if to consolidate the US's self-portrayal as an honest broker, the biblical imagery of his speech was supplemented by a quotation from the Koran.

The Hebron massacre of 25 February made the Arafat-Rabin handshake, and the high hopes of the September declaration look like romanticized memories. Britain's Chief Rabbi, Jonathan Sacks expressed shock and grief at the massacre: 'Violence is evil. Violence committed in the name of God is doubly evil. Violence against those engaged in worshipping God is unspeakably evil.' Rabin told the Knesset that Baruch Goldstein and his followers were a foreign implant and an errant weed. 'Sensible Judaism,' he declared, 'spits you out. You are a shame on Zionism and an embarrassment to Judaism.' Fine words—but what about much of the Book of Deuteronomy, the Book of Joshua, and, in particular, the Book of Esther, the prescribed biblical reading for the Jewish Feast of Purim?

The five-man enquiry into the Hebron massacre has concluded that Dr Goldstein acted alone, and its 338-page report exonerates the Israeli government and army command of any responsibility for the murder of the Palestinian worshippers in the mosque. It concedes that security was lax—five soldiers, three of whom had overslept, had failed to turn up for duty—but there was no question of any collusion between settlers and the army. Perhaps the army will discipline them, perhaps not. In any case, the biblicism of the settlers will go unchecked, and Rabin promises to install metal detectors to prevent arms being brought into mosques in future.

Contrary to the initial reports, Dr Goldstein was no ordinary man whose mental state the tensions of the area had triggered into a moment of insanity. He was steeped in the Bible, and would have surpassed even President Clinton in having his mind *shaped by the values of the Torah*. It is highly likely that his bedtime reading for the feast of Purim, which occurred on that fateful day, was from the Book of Esther, the biblical text which celebrates the fight-back of Jews.

We learn from that book that King Ahasuerus (a Latin-English transcription of the Hebrew form of the Persian King, known in Greek as Xerxes), too, could not sleep on the eve of Queen Esther's banquet, and called for the annals to be brought and read to him. Xerxes' nocturnal reading led to a bad outcome for Haman, the enemy of the Jews, and, subsequently, for many more of their enemies, near and far. Goldstein would have read how, with regal and unchallengable divine approval, the Jews could avenge their enemies on the appropriate date (subsequently in the story, the Feast of Purim). Details follow in chapter 9: 'The Jews struck down all their enemies with the sword ... five hundred men in the citadel of Susa alone,' and that, on hearing the good news, Queen Esther asked the king for an extension of his decree for the morrow also. On the fourteenth day of the month of Adar the Jews killed three hundred men in the city. It is a small mercy that the avenging Jews of the Book of Esther took a day off on the fifteenth day of the month.

Goldstein would have read that things were even worse outside Susa. On the thirteenth day of the month the Jews slaughtered seventy-five thousand (although the Greek version of the text gives the more modest figure of fifteen thousand). Mercifully, the Jews of the province rested and feasted on the fourteenth day. Xerxes ordered for the fourteenth and fifteenth days of the month of Adar an annual commemoration of the days on which Jews had rid themselves of their enemies, had had their sorrow turned into gladness and mourning into a holiday. Jews were to exchange presents and give gifts to the poor.

Goldstein's biblical hermeneutics, alas, went further, and authorized a one-man re-enactment of the legendary slaughter, apparently sanctioned by God's word. It is no wonder, then, that Rabbi Yaacov Perrin, one of the religious leaders in Goldstein's settlement in Kiryat Arba, eulogizing him at his funeral, declared, 'One million Arabs are not worth a Jewish fingernail,' and another mourner declared Goldstein to be 'the greatest Jew alive.' Some of the more dubious *values of the Torah*, and the books of Joshua and Esther, had come back to haunt the civilized world, and, in his own circle of like-minded biblical interpretation, Goldstein was on the verge of canonization. However, he is not alone in a literalist interpretation of the Bible. Such literalism has justified the butchering of people in the Crusades and in North America in the past, supports the expulsion and humiliation of Palestinians in the present, and has given the divine approval for various other dehumanizing regimes elsewhere.

The Bible poses a fundamental moral problem for anyone who takes it at face value. There is no shortage of post-biblical texts, within both Judaism and Christianity, which point to its alleged divine origins. Goldstein would surely have known his Mishnah, which in its tract, Sanhedrin, states that all Israelites have a share in the world to come except '... those who assert that the Torah is not from heaven' (*mSanh.* 10:1). The Torah, in a crude interpretation, must be accepted in its totality, and in all its parts.

The Torah, however, is fundamentally rooted in the escape from Egypt of the Hebrew slaves, who entered and occupied a land which was already occupied by others. The occupation of another people's land realistically demands systematic pillage and killing. What distinguishes the biblical account of this activity is that it is presented as having not only divine approval, but as happening at the command of the divinity.

In the traditions in the Book of Joshua, in particular, the Israelites killed and butchered in conformity with the directives of God. This presentation of God as a monster gloating over the destruction of others must be rejected out of hand by anyone who presumes that the conduct of an ethical God, at the very least, will not fall lower than that of ordinary secular decency.

Encounter with the contemporary political realities of the Holy Land raises important questions for students of the Bible. The commandment that, 'You shall destroy all the peoples that the Lord your God will give over to you, your eye shall not pity them' (Deut 7.16), and the statement that, 'The Lord your God will clear away these nations before you little by little, ... and you shall make their name perish from under heaven' (Deut 7.22-24), are seen in a new light, when one meets the Palestinians, the modern counterparts of the Hittites, the Girgashites, the Amorites, the Canaanites, the Perizzites, the Hivites, and the Jebusites. In our society such biblical sentiments, rightly, would be regarded as an incitement to racial hatred. On moral grounds, one is forced to question whether the Torah continues to provide the figment of divine legitimacy for the occupation of other people's land, and their virtual annihilation. By any reasonable standards, the first five books of the Hebrew Bible are seen to contain racist and xenophobic sentiments. They promote an attitude of ethnocentricity, which appears to receive the highest possible legitimacy in the form of divine approval.

Contemporary liberation theologies, like all theologies, look to the Bible for their underpinning. It is not difficult to discern within the Hebrew Bible a whole range of themes which fit the concept of liberation very comfortably (e.g., liberation from oppression in Egypt, Babylon, etc.). However, does God, who is on the side of the oppressed Israelites, and who frees them from Egypt, remain on their side when they become the oppressor? If the Bible is looked to as providing a theological basis for Liberation Theology elsewhere, the sad reality is that in its place of origin it has become an equally well-founded basis for a Theology of Oppression.

Anyone with moral sensitivities, and concern for the dignity of other peoples, must reject the kind of biblicism which sees the core of biblical revelation to be frozen in the primitive concepts of Chosen People and Promised Land. The biblical claim of the divine gift of land is integrally linked with the claim of divine approval for the barbarous extermination of the indigenous people (see, e.g., Deut 20.16-18). It would be a far more ethical hermeneutical stance to recognise in the biblical legend the *attribution* to God of His approval for the *de facto* Israelite possession of the land, and the extermination of the inhabitants, whose presence was an obstacle to the accomplishments of that command.

Neither the Book of Joshua, nor the Book of Esther is the best distraction for a person transfixed between wakefulness and sleep. They should not be accorded a favoured place in the search for moral exhortation. Hotel managers may need to censor their Gideon Bibles, lest their clients be driven to appalling behaviour in the wake of sleepless nights, spent reading the more racist, xenophobic and militaristic elements within the biblical text.

President Clinton may well have had the Hebrew prophetic tradition in mind as he appealed to the Bible. For many religious Jews, however, the noble traditions of the Hebrew prophets, which are the favourites of Christians, are of secondary importance when compared with the Torah. For a particular religious mind-set, the God as revealed in the Torah is beyond the possibility of any moral reproach, even those derived from other parts of the Bible.

Since there is little hope, therefore, that the modest moral exhortations of the *Fourth Geneva Convention* could ever displace the divinely-sanctioned, and often divinely-mandated decrees of some of the traditions of the Torah, we can only hope that Premier Rabin's metal detectors will be in place before the next Feast of Purim.

A LAND FLOWING WITH MILK, HONEY AND PEOPLE

This lecture, given at Cambridge in 1997, developed the ethical critique of the Exodus and Conquest narratives, attacking the 'orientalism' of respected Old Testament scholars.

I am very grateful to the Von Hügel Institute and the Catholic Biblical Association of Great Britain for inviting me, and honoured to deliver the third Lattey Lecture. My two previous visits to this lecture hall were to attend the first Lattey Lecture in 1993, and the second one in 1995. While I sat reverentially in the audience after Professor Raymond E Brown had delivered his lecture on the Passion Narratives of the gospels, in the course of proposing a vote of thanks to Professor Norbert Lohfink I presumed to interact with what he had said. He had interpreted the laws of Deuteronomy in terms of defining a utopian society in which there would be no poor.[1] Naturally I found the prospect inviting, and was pleased to reflect upon 'Mount Zion as the place where they (the nations) can learn how a better society functions'. I was attracted by his invitation to join those 'who take the Bible seriously' in constructing a 'city set on a hill', a society in which there would be no poor.[2] However, I balked somewhat at his benevolent assessment that the Book of Deuteronomy 'announces a utopia'. Moreover, despite his erudite discussion of the semantic field of 'poverty', I was not of a mind to share his enthusiasm for the Book of Exodus, which, in his words, describes only the delivery from Egypt of a marginalised and exploited group, without any reference to what was to follow. At the time I was coming towards the end of a long period of academic endeavour, stretching back at least to the early 1980s, in which I wrestled with my perception that

---

[1] Lohfink, Norbert, 'The Laws of Deuteronomy. A Utopian Project for a World without any Poor?' (St Edmund's College, Cambridge: Von Hügel Institute, 1996), published also as, 'The Laws of Deuteronomy. A Utopian Project for a World without any Poor' (without the question mark in the title), in *Scripture Bulletin* 26 (1996): 2-19.

[2] But see Lohfink's discussion as he contrasts the utopia of Deut 15.4 and Acts 4.33-35 with the realism of Mark 14.7 and Deut 15.11 (pp. 3-4, or pp. 4-5 in *Scripture Bulletin*).

the land traditions of the Bible were inherently oppressive, and morally reprehensible narratives.[3]

Not only did these traditions—of promises of land to Abraham and his descendants, and the consummation of the promise through the military achievements narrated in the Books of Joshua and Judges—have the capacity to infuse exploitative tendencies in their readers, but my research was confirming how in practice that biblical paradigm had fuelled virtually every form of militant colonialism emanating out of Europe. The traditions of Deuteronomy had provided intellectual and moral authority for the Iberian devastation of 'Latin America' in the late mediaeval period, for the Afrikaner exploitation of non-whites in southern Africa right up to this decade, and was continuing to do so today for Zionists in their ongoing exspoliation of the Arabs of Palestine.

In the narrative of the Book of Deuteronomy, after the King of Heshbon refused passage to the Israelites, Yahweh gave him over to them, and they captured and utterly destroyed all the cities, killing all the men, women, and children (Deut 2.33-34). The fate of the King of Bashan was no better (Deut 3.3). After the *Shema* ('Hear, O Israel'), the great summons to worship the one God, which even in these secular times awakens the population of Israel on *Qol Israel* (the Voice of Israel) radio, we learn how the invaders are to behave religiously after they have dispossessed the indigenous population:

> And when the Lord your God brings you into the land which he swore to your fathers ... to give you, with great and goodly cities, which you did not build, and houses full of all good things ... take heed lest you forget the Lord...lest he...destroy you from off the face of the earth (Deut 6.10-15; see also 6.18-19).

Yahweh's vital role in the conquest is emphasised:

> When Yahweh your God brings you into the land that you are about to enter and occupy, and he clears away many nations before you—the Hittites, the Girgashites, the Amorites, the Canaanites, the Perizzites, the Hivites ... and when Yahweh your God gives them over to you and you defeat them, then you

---

[3] My 'The Bible as Instrument of Oppression' had already been published in *Scripture Bulletin* 25 (1995): 2-14, and my *The Bible and Colonialism. A Moral Critique* (Sheffield: Sheffield Academic Press, 1997) was well underway.

must utterly destroy them. Make no covenant with them and
show them no mercy...Break down their altars, smash their pillars,
hew down their sacred poles, and burn their idols with fire.
For you are a people holy to Yahweh your God; Yahweh your
God has chosen you out of all the peoples on earth to be his
people, his treasured possession (Deut 7.1-11; see also 9.1-5;
11.8-9, 23, 31-32).

In the rules for the conduct of war, when a besieged town
surrenders, all its inhabitants shall serve at forced labour; if not, the Israelites
shall kill all its males, and take as booty the women, the children, livestock,
and everything else in the town (Deut 20.11-14). The narrative presents
'ethnic cleansing' as not only legitimate, but as required by the divinity:

'But as for the towns of these peoples that Yahweh your God
is giving you as an inheritance, you must not let anything that
breathes remain alive. You shall annihilate them—the Hittites
and the Amorites, the Canaanites and the Perizzites, the Hivites
and the Jebusites—just as Yahweh your God has commanded,
so that they may not teach you to do all the abhorrent things
that they do for their gods, and you thus sin against Yahweh
your God' (Deut 20.16-18).

Mercifully, in a gesture of ecological indulgence, the fruit-bearing
trees are to be spared, as is a captive 'beautiful woman whom you desire
and want to marry' (Deut 21.11). Much of the remainder of the book
deals with the Last Will and Testament of Moses, and his commissioning
of Joshua, who would lead the people across the Jordan (Deut 31.3-6),
and the book ends with Moses' sight of the promised land before he dies
(Deut 34.1-3). Although Moses was unequalled in his deeds, he left a
worthy successor, Joshua, who, after Moses had lain his hands on him,
was full of the spirit of wisdom (Deut 34.4-12).

Having had my moral being sensitised by Deuteronomy's
mandate to commit genocide, I invited Professor Lohfink to consider
whether the utopian society which he detected in the book was possible
only after the invading Israelites had wiped out the indigenous inhabitants
of the promised land. Alas, the Order of Service at the Lattey Lecture on
that occasion left the last word with me, the proposer of the vote of
thanks. And today, I am given a second word.

Professor Lohfink is not alone in his high esteem for the Book of Deuteronomy. Commentators conventionally assess it to be a theological book *par excellence*, and the focal point of the religious history of the Old Testament. Typically one reads that its central theme is a call to the service of the one God by an elect people centred around one sanctuary, by obeying the *Torah* in the land which God has promised. It is pointed out that the central issue in its theology is the belief in the one God, with 'Yahweh' occurring no less than 561 times in the book. However, one ought not to fail to notice that while it stresses the chosenness of Israel, the narrative requires the genocide of the indigenous population of Canaan.

YAHWEH AND ETHNIC CLEANSING

The Exodus narrative—that cherished biblical charter of liberation, invoked with such enthusiasm by Christians gathered at the Easter Fire in celebration of the Paschal Mystery, and looked to by all theologies of liberation as their ideological foundation document—does indeed portray Yahweh as having compassion on the misery of his people, and as willing to deliver them from the Egyptians, and bring to a land flowing with milk and honey (Exod 3.7-8). But even though the reading of Exod 3, both in the Christian liturgy and in the classical texts of liberation theologies halts abruptly in the middle of v. 8 at the description of the land as one 'flowing with milk and honey', the biblical text itself continues, 'to the country of the Canaanites, the Hittites, the Amorites, the Perizzites, the Hivites, and the Jebusites'.[4] Manifestly, while the promised land of the narrative indeed flowed with milk and honey, it had no lack of indigenous peoples.

The hero of the Book of Joshua is presented as the divinely-chosen successor of Moses, who is destined to complete his work (Josh 1). The first part (2.1-12.24) describes in epic style the conquest of the land, concentrating on the capture of a few key cities, and their fate in accordance with the laws of the Holy War. After its wall had collapsed, all

---

[4] See my discussion of the liturgical censoring of the Word of God, and of the ambivalence of the Exodus paradigm in *The Bible and Colonialism* (pp. 273-84). As one of many examples from liberation theology, the title page of Esther and Mortimer Arias' study, *The Cry of My People. Out of Captivity in Latin America* (New York: Friendship Press, 1980) reproduces Exod 3.7-8, but ends with, 'a land of milk and honey ...'

the men and women (excepting Rahab's family), oxen, sheep, and donkeys of Jericho were slaughtered, and Joshua pronounced a curse on anyone who would try to rebuild the city (Josh 6.21-27). The marauding party moved on to Ai at Yahweh's command, to do to it what was done to Jericho: not one of the twelve thousand inhabitants survived or escaped, and Joshua burned it, and made it forever a heap of ruins (Josh 8.2, 19-29). The liturgical *Te Deum* and reading of the Law followed in style, with one choir on Mount Gerizim and the other on Mount Ebal (Josh 8.30-35). The ravaging troops of Joshua were to be met with a concerted defence of the Hittites, the Amorites, the Canaanites, the Perizzites, the Hivites, and the Jebusites (Josh 9.1-2). Even when the Gibeonites were to be spared, to become 'hewers of wood and drawers of water for all the congregation', the Israelite elders complained at the lapse in fidelity to the mandate to destroy all the inhabitants of the land (Josh 9.21-27).

Chapter 10 describes the campaign in the south, and chapter 11 that in the north, in each case ensuring the rigorous enforcement of the ban (*herem*). After the retreat of the coalition of the five kings (of Jerusalem, Hebron, Jarmuth, Lachish and Eglon) who had attacked Gibeon, 'Yahweh threw down huge stones from heaven on them ...; there were more who died because of the hailstones than the Israelites killed with the sword.' In another gesture of divine collaboration, Yahweh granted the prayer of Joshua, making the sun and moon stand still at Gibeon, lest the darkness of the night inhibit the Israelites in taking vengeance on their enemies (Josh 10.10-13). To bring the day's work to a satisfactory close, Joshua pursued the five kings who were hiding in the cave at Makkedah, put them to death, and hung them on five trees until evening. At sunset he commanded that their bodies be thrown into the cave, which would be closed by large stones. The author adds a contemporary note that they remain there 'to this very day' (Josh 10.16-27). In conformity with the rules of the Holy War, Joshua took Makkedah and utterly destroyed every person in it (Josh 10.28). A similar fate befell Libnah, Lachish, Eglon, Hebron, and Debir (Josh 10.29-39). The author summarises Joshua's destruction of everything that breathed, from Kadesh-barnea to Gaza, and so on, as Yahweh commanded (Josh 10. 40-43). Chapter 11 describes the northern campaign, with the literary account showing signs of a conscious parallel with chapter 10. Israel left no one remaining: Joshua took all the land, utterly destroying its inhabitants (Josh 11.1-23). The whole achievement is summed up: Yahweh gave to Israel all the land that he swore to their ancestors he would give them (Josh 21.43-45).

The picture in the Book of Judges is considerably different from that recorded in the Book of Joshua. Whereas the Book of Joshua gives details of the conquest in a series of 'punctiliar', efficient military activities, the Book of Judges sees it as a more complex and gradual phenomenon, punctuated by partial success and failure.

Given the foundational significance of the alleged events of the conquest and settlement of the promised land, there is a notable lack of evidence for the popularity of these traditions prior to the period of the Babylonian exile: with the exception of their importance in Genesis to Judges, the conquest and settlement traditions occupy an insignificant place within the Bible. But, however late the traditions, the narratives themselves pose moral problems. Moreover, the legendary achievements of Yahweh through Moses, Aaron, and Joshua are kept before the Israelites, even in their prayers:

> You brought a vine out of Egypt; you drove out the nations
> and planted it (Ps 80.8; see also Pss 78.54-55; 105.44).[5]

Two recent events shocked Israelis into a new level of understanding of the extent of the religious dimension within Israeli politics, and underline dramatically the power of the land traditions of the Bible to influence political behaviour: medical doctor Baruch Goldstein's massacre of twenty nine worshippers in the Ibrahimi Mosque in Hebron (25 February 1994), and the assassination of Prime Minister

---

[5] On a contemporary note, the attempt by Israeli settler terrorists to blow up Jerusalem's Dome of the Rock in 1984 caused widespread panic in Israel. The newspapers published a picture of the second person to be sentenced (to ten years imprisonment), wearing a full, dark beard, a knitted kippa, and with tzitziot hanging under his shirt—the typical dress of the (religious) settler *Gush Emunim* movement. The newspaper reported that he had the Book of Psalms in his hand as the judge read out his 11-page verdict (see my 'Israel: Library, Land and Peoples', *Scripture Bulletin* 15[1984]: 6-11, p. 8).

[6] Dr Goldstein was steeped in the Bible and, on that fateful feast of Purim in particular, in the Book of Esther, the biblical legend celebrating the fight-back of Jews, which is interwoven into the prayers for the feast. Goldstein's burial-place in his settlement (Kiryat Arba) has the character of a combination of a national garden of remembrance and a shrine. Admirers kiss his tomb, and pray over the grave of 'the upright, martyr'. On the occasion of the *bar mitzvah* of Goldstein's son, Kiryat Arba's chief Rabbi, Dov Lior, addressed him: 'Ya'akov Yair, follow in your father's footsteps. He was righteous and a great hero' (*Jerusalem Report* 12 December 1996, p. 10).

Rabin (4 November 1995). Dr Goldstein was a graduate of the most prestigious yeshiva in the USA,[6] and Rabin's murderer, Yigal Amir, the son of an orthodox rabbi, is a religious Jew, and was a student in the Institute for Advanced *Torah* Studies in Bar-Ilan University. Amir claimed to be acting in God's name. Among the books found in his room was one lauding Goldstein (*Jewish Chronicle*, 10 November 1995, p. 3). In the first hearing of his case, he explained that he derived his motivation from *halakhah*.[7] Although the activities of Goldstein and Amir evoked widespread revulsion in Israel and among Jews world-wide, there was considerable support for them from within the most zealous and uncompromising wing of religious Zionism. In fact, the secular left laid the collective blame for the assassination firmly at the feet of the religious nationalist camp. If the zealotry of the religious nationalist movement offends the liberal views to which Western society has become accustomed, it is in strict conformity with the ideals of certain traditions in the Bible, and in sympathy with the demands of a popular religious Zionist soteriology which derived from these biblical traditions.

Christians also use these texts, if somewhat more sparingly in their liturgies. Indeed, according to a report in the *Washington Post*, President Clinton had not been able to sleep on the night before the signing of the Declaration of Principles on the White House Lawn on 13 September 1993. Fearing that his speech required more work, he woke at 3.00 a.m., and reread the entire Book of Joshua and portions of the New Testament. On the day itself, the President introduced Prime Minister Rabin and President Arafat, and announced to the world that both peoples pledged themselves to a shared future, 'shaped by the values of the *Torah*, the Koran, and the Bible'. President Clinton's mode of address was a mixture of Bible-based exhortation in the Baptist tradition, and shrewd political manoeuvring. The late Premier Rabin's speech also referred to the Bible. One might reasonably question whether *the values of the Torah, the Koran, and the Bible* can be relied upon to promote justice and peace, and underpin the imperatives of human rights.

---

[7] Moreover, a certain Avigdor Eskin was convicted in May 1997 of violating the Prevention of Terrorism Act by putting a curse on Rabin a month before he was assassinated. Besides, a number of American rabbis, e.g., Moshe Tendler of Monsey, New York, and Abraham Hecht of Brooklyn, had stressed that not an inch of occupied land could be surrendered (sic!), and Hecht added that any Jewish leader who would give back land should be killed (see Hertzberg, Arthur, 'The End of the Dream of the Undivided Land of Israel', in *Journal of Palestine Studies* 25[1996]: 35–45, p. 37).

THE MORAL PROBLEM

G E M de Ste Croix, the greatest authority on the history of class politics in the ancient world, notes the unprecedented character of the biblical traditions of divinely mandated ferocity:

> I can say that I know of only one people which felt able to assert that it actually had a divine command to exterminate whole populations among those it conquered; namely, Israel. Nowadays Christians, as well as Jews, seldom care to dwell on the merciless ferocity of Yahweh, as revealed not by hostile sources but by the very literature they themselves regard as sacred. Indeed, they continue as a rule to forget the very existence of this incriminating material ... There is little in pagan literature quite as morally revolting as the stories of the massacres allegedly carried out at Jericho, Ai, and Hazor, and of the Amorites and Amalekites, all not merely countenanced by Yahweh but strictly ordained by him ... The Greek and Roman gods could be cruel enough, in the traditions preserved by their worshippers, but at least their devotees did not seek to represent them as prescribing genocide.[8]

The moral problem of these biblical traditions is exacerbated by the fact that they enjoy unique authority within both Synagogue and Church. In the estimation of Jews, the *Torah* emanates from heaven, and a punctilious observance of its laws is the supreme religious duty.[9] The

[8] De Ste Croix, G E M, *The Class Struggle in and Ancient Greek World from the Archaic Age to the Arab Conquests* (London: Duckworth, 1981), pp. 331-32. De Ste Croix adds, 'Few narratives are more blood-curdling than that of the Prophet Samuel 'hewing Agag [king of the Amalekites] in pieces before Yahweh in Gilgal' (1 Sam 15.32-33)' (p. 332).

[9] See Schürer, E, *The History of the Jewish People in the Age of Jesus Christ (175 B.C.-A.D. 135)*, vol. II, revised and ed. by G Vermes, *et al.* (Edinburgh: T&T Clark, 1979) p. 314. That the *Torah* is from heaven is the touchstone of Jewish Orthodoxy to this day, and polarises the United Synagogue and the Masorti movement in contemporary British Jewry. In an article in the Orthodox *Jewish Tribune* (January, 1995—reproduced in *Jewish Chronicle*, 20 January), Chief Rabbi Jonathan Sacks claimed, 'An individual who does not believe in *Torah min haShamayim* (i.e., that the Torah is from heaven) has severed his links with the faith of his ancestors.' Even more recently (14 November 1997), *Jewish Chronicle* advertised a lecture, 'Is the Torah True? Why I believe Torah is from Heaven,' by Rabbi Shlomo Riskin, Chief Rabbi of (the illegal settlement of) Efrat, and Dean of Ohr Torah Institutions. During the invasion of Lebanon in 1982, the same Riskin, following the army to study the Talmud with the troops, was deeply impressed that the soldiers, when resting from battle,

Torah, in such an interpretation, must be accepted in its totality, and in all its parts. The Bible enjoys a corresponding authority in the Church as the Word of God. Nevertheless, the first six books of the Hebrew Bible, when judged by the standards of ethics and human rights to which our society has become accustomed, reflect some ethnocentric, racist and xenophobic sentiments, which receive the highest possible legitimacy, namely divine approval. Were it not for their religious provenance, they would be regarded as incitements to racial hatred, destined to precipitate acts of genocide. Academic and religious tradents of these narratives cannot evade some responsibility for the evils that are perpetrated in conformity with the values contained in them, in particular in ascribing to the divine will the occupation of other people's land, and the very annihilation of the indigenous population.

Manifestly, these narratives pose a fundamental moral problem for anyone who takes them at face value, and it appears that most people view them as records of what actually happened: the Hebrew slaves who left Egypt invaded a land already occupied, and, in obedience to the divine command, systematically killed and pillaged. What most distinguishes the biblical account of Joshua's *Blitzkrieg* is that it is presented as having not only the approval of, but as being mandated by the divinity. This portrayal of God as requiring the destruction of others as an act of piety poses problems for anyone who presumes that the conduct of an ethical God will not fall lower than decent, secular behaviour.

Suspicious of the possible impact of these narratives on the formation of conscience, the Israeli socio-psychologist, Georges Tamarin, surveyed the presence of prejudices in the ideology of Israeli youth. He was particularly anxious to evaluate the degree to which an uncritical teaching of notions of the 'chosen people', the superiority of monotheistic religion, and the study of acts of genocide carried out by biblical heroes contributed to the development of prejudice. He chose the Book of Joshua, in particular the genocides at Jericho and Makkedah, because of that book's special position in the Israeli educational system, both as national history and as one of the cornerstones of Israel's national mythology. He asked two questions: 1. 'Do you think Joshua and the

---

spent long hours discussing whether it would be right to pick Lebanese cherries (see Bermant, Chaim, 'Rabbi's Blinkers and Professor's Vision', in *Jewish Chronicle*, 26 August 1994, p. 21).

Israelites acted rightly or not? Explain why you think as you do; 2. Suppose that the Israeli Army conquers an Arab village in battle. Do you think it would be good or bad to act towards the inhabitants as Joshua did towards the people of Jericho and Makkedah? Explain why. Only 26 percent of the respondents disapproved of Joshua's behaviour, while 62 percent would disapprove of genocide carried out by the Israeli Army. The figures were quite different when Tamarin substituted a 'Chinese version' of the Book of Joshua, with 'General Lin' committing a god-inspired genocide. Seventy-five per cent of the respondents totally disapproved of General Lin's genocide. Tamarin concluded that,

> The uncritical teaching of the Bible—to students too young—even if not taught explicitly as a sacred text, but as national history or in a quasi-neutral atmosphere concerning the real or mythological character of its content, no doubt profoundly affects the genesis of prejudices...even among non-religious students, in accentuating the negative-hostile character of the strangers.[10]

His findings were a severe indictment of the Israeli educational system. His research brought him unsought and unexpected notoriety and led to his losing his professorship in Tel Aviv University. In a letter to the senate he wrote that while embarking on his scholarly investigation he had never dreamt that he would become the last victim of Joshua's conquest of Jericho (p. 190).

Two Peoples, One Land

Unlike Arthur C Balfour, the promulgator of the *Balfour Declaration* by which one nation solemnly promised to a second nation the country of a third,[11] Italy's King Victor Emmanuel III did not prevaricate on the problem of giving a land that was already inhabited to a people desirous

---

[10] Tamarin, Georges R, 'The influence of ethnic and religious prejudice on moral judgement', in Tamarin, Georges R (ed. Johan Niezing). *The Israeli Dilemma. Essays on a Warfare State* (Rotterdam: Rotterdam University Press, 1973 [original 1963]), 183-90 (p. 189).

[11] Koestler, Arthur, *Promise and Fulfilment. Palestine 1917-1949* (London: Macmillan, 1949), 4.

of one, as he indicated in his response to Theodor Herzl's proposal in 1904 to establish a Jewish state in Tripoli. The King responded, '*Ma è ancora casa di altri*' ('But it is already the home of other people').[12] It is the existence of indigenous peoples already in the land that holds in relief the moral problematic of the biblical narratives of the promise, gift, and acquisition of the promised land. We in the West—and, strangely, even liberation theologians throughout the post-colonial world—read the biblical accounts with the eyes of the liberated Israelite slaves as they set about the construction of their utopia in the land flowing with milk and honey.

My argument is that the biblical narratives which deal with the promise and gift of land are potentially corrupting in themselves, and have in fact contributed to war crimes and crimes against humanity in virtually every colonised region, by providing allegedly divine legitimation for Western colonisers in their zeal to implant 'outposts of progress' in 'the heart of darkness'. The ongoing identification in subsequent history with the warring scenes of the Hebrew Bible is a burden the biblical tradition must bear. The fact that the particular violence of the Hebrew Scriptures has inspired violence, and has served as a model of, and for persecution, subjugation, and extermination for millennia beyond its own reality makes investigation of these traditions a critical task.[13] Nevertheless, the ethnocentric, xenophobic and militaristic character of the biblical narratives of Israelite origins is treated in conventional biblical scholarship as if it were above any questioning on moral grounds, even by criteria derived from other parts of the Bible. Most commentators are uninfluenced by considerations of human rights, when these conflict with a naive reading of the sacred text, and appear to be unperturbed by the text's advocacy of plunder, murder, and the exploitation of indigenous peoples, all under the guise of fidelity to the eternal validity of the covenant of Sinai.[14]

---

[12] Herzl, Theodor, *Zionistiches Tagebuch 1899-1904* (Vol III [1985], ed. Johannes Wachten *et al.*, Berlin: Propylaen Verlag), 653.

[13] See Niditch, Susan, *War in the Hebrew Bible. A Study of the Ethics of Violence* (Oxford: Oxford University Press, 1993), 4.

[14] See my *The Bible and Colonialism*, 253-60.

'ORIENTALISM' AND BIBLICAL STUDIES

Alas, the discipline of biblical studies over the last hundred years has reflected the Eurocentric perspectives of virtually all Western historiography, and has contributed significantly to the exspoliation of native peoples, most recently of the Arabs of Palestine. The benevolent interpretation of biblical traditions which advocate atrocities and war crimes has given solace and comfort to those bent on the exploitation of native peoples. The Bishop of Salisbury had no hesitation in informing members of the Palestine Exploration Fund in 1903, that, 'Nothing ... that has been discovered makes us feel any regret at the suppression of Canaanite civilisation by Israelite civilisation ... The Bible has not misrepresented at all the abomination of Canaanite culture which was superseded by the Israelite culture.' One wonders what evidence can be adduced for this claim, apart from that provided by the biblical narrative? The Dean of Westminster could refer to 'that singular union of craft, ignorance and stupidity, which can only be found in Orientals', and C R Conder could describe the native peasantry of Palestine as 'brutally ignorant, fanatical, and above all, inveterate liars'. Sir Flinders Petrie described the Arab as 'disgustingly incapable as most other savages, and no more worth romancing about than Red Indians or Maoris.'[15]

Even though the biblical paradigm has been used to sanction the British conquest of North America, Ireland and Australia, the Dutch conquest of southern Africa, and the Zionist conquest of Palestine, discussion among biblical scholars on the Israelite settlement in Canaan is distinguished by its indifference to the indigenous inhabitants of the region. This absence of concern for 'the natives' reflects the deeply ingrained Eurocentric, colonialist prejudice which characterises virtually all historiography, as well as the discipline of biblical studies itself.[16] Biblical commentators are unperturbed that the behaviour of the God of the land traditions of the biblical narrative does not conform with even the minimum conditions for waging war as laid down by the Fourth Geneva

---

[15] Cited in Said, Edward W, *The Question of Palestine* (London: Vintage, 1992 [new edition]), 79–80.

[16] See Whitelam, Keith W, *The Invention of Ancient Israel. The Silencing of Palestinian History* (London and New York: Routledge, 1996) *passim*, and 'Western Scholarship and the Silencing of Palestinian History', in Prior, Michael, ed.., *Western Scholarship and the History of Palestine* (London: Melisende [Fox Communications and Publications], 1998), 9–21.

Convention.[17] Indeed, only a decade after the full horrors of the Nazi ethnic cleansing had been revealed, William Foxwell Albright, the doyen of biblical archaeologists this century, had no qualms about the plunder attendant upon Joshua's enterprise, which he understood in a largely historically reliable way:

> From the impartial standpoint of a philosopher of history, it often seems necessary that a people of markedly inferior type should vanish before a people of superior potentialities, since there is a point beyond which racial mixture cannot go without disaster...Thus the Canaanites, with their orgiastic nature worship, their cult of fertility in the form of serpent symbols and sensuous nudity, and their gross mythology, were replaced by Israel, with its pastoral simplicity and purity of life, its lofty monotheism, and its severe code of ethics.[18]

Prior to Keith Whitelam's critique,[19] no commentator had drawn attention to Albright's undisguised racist attitudes, which were typical of virtually every Western colonial enterprise which predicated that the 'superior' peoples of the West had the right to exploit, and in some cases exterminate the 'natives'. Reflecting these conventional values, Albright also judged that through Zionism Jews would bring to the Near East all the benefits of European civilisation.[20] Albright's support for political Zionism was all the greater after Hitler had brought all the benefits of Nazi culture to Eastern Europe and elsewhere. In a similar vein, George E Wright, another distinguished American biblical scholar, justifies the

---

[17] Even Gerd Lüdemann's strident denunciation of Deuteronomy's 'utopia of violence' is diluted by virtually restricting its evil effects to Ezra and Nehemiah's prohibition of miscegenation (*The Unholy in Holy Scripture. The Dark Side of the Bible*, translated and with an Appendix by John Bowden, London: SCM, 1997, 73-75). He might have noted that the mindset of the Book of Deuteronomy, with its emphasis on chosenness and its disparagement of the Other, in fact played a critical supporting role in virtually every form of colonialism emanating out of Europe. This is particularly true in our own day of the Zionist colonisation of Palestine, which despite its being despised by virtually all religious Jews at the beginning, now proceeds with their blessing, and that of both mainstream and evangelical Western Christian Churches and their theologies.
[18] Albright. William F, *From the Stone Age to Christianity: Monotheism and the Historical Process* (New York: Doubleday, 1957), 280-81.
[19] *The Invention of Ancient Israel*, 88.
[20] 'Why the Near East needs the Jews', *New Palestine* 32 (1942): 12-13.

genocide of the narrative of Joshua in terms of the inferiority of the indigenous culture.[21]

The exegetical skills of W D Davies were displayed in a range of seminal studies on the land traditions of the Bible, easily the most significant in the field.[22] However, they too are not models of objectivity. His 1974 study was written at the request of friends in Jerusalem, who just before the war in June 1967, urged his support for the cause of Israel (1982: xiii). His second work was written under the direct impact of that war: 'Here I have concentrated on what in my judgement must be the beginning for an understanding of this conflict: the sympathetic attempt to comprehend the Jewish tradition' (1982: xiii-xiv). Its updated version was written because of the mounting need to understand the theme in the light of events in the Middle East, culminating in the Gulf War and its aftermath (1991: xiii). While Davies considers the topic of the land from virtually every conceivable perspective in his 1974 and 1982 works, little attention is given to broadly moral and human rights' issues. He takes the establishment of the State of Israel in his stride. Only the post-1967 occupation is a problem. The colonial plunder associated with the foundation of the state is above reproach, and appears to enjoy the same allegedly divinely sanctioned legitimacy and mandate as the Joshua-led encroachment on the land. Davies excluded from his concern, 'What happens when the understanding of the Promised Land in Judaism conflicts with the claims of the traditions and occupancy of its other peoples'. He excuses himself by saying that to engage that issue would demand another volume (1991: xv), without indicating his intention of embarking upon such an enterprise. Similarly, at the end of his 1981 article (p. 96), he claimed that it was impossible to discuss that issue. One wonders whether Davies would be equally sanguine had white, Anglo-

---

[21] Wright, George E, in Wright G E and R H Fuller, eds., *The Book of the Acts of God: Christian Scholarship Interprets the Bible* (London: Duckworth, 1960), 109.

[22] *The Gospel and the Land. Early Christianity and Jewish Territorial Doctrine* (Berkeley: University of California Press, 1974); 'The Territorial Dimensions of Judaism', in Dikran Y Hadidian ed., *Intergerini Parietis Septum (Eph. 2:14). Essays Presented to Markus Barth on his Sixty-fifth Birthday* (Pittsburgh: The Pickwick Press, 1981), pp. 61-96; *The Territorial Dimensions of Judaism* (Berkeley: University of California Press, 1982); 'The 'Land' in the Pre-Exilic and Early Post-Exilic Prophets', in Butler, J T, E W Conrad, and B C Ollenburger (eds.), *Understanding the Word.* JSOTSS 37 (Sheffield: JSOT Press, 1985), pp. 247-62; and *The Territorial Dimensions of Judaism. With a Symposium and Further Reflections* (Minneapolis: Fortress, 1991).

Saxon Protestants, or even white Catholics of European provenance been among the displaced people who paid the price for the enactment of the divine mandate of Zionism. Davies shows no concern for the fundamental injustice done to the Palestinian Arabs by the encroachment on their land by Zionists. Despite the foundational plunder of 1948, Davies writes as if there were now a moral equivalence between the dispossessed Palestinians and the dispossessor Zionists. The rights of the victim and the rapist are finely balanced.

Against the background of even some knowledge of the consequences of colonisation for indigenous populations, biblical scholarship has been modest in its concern for the moral dimension of the problematic. Since virtually all of the scholarship has been done since the establishment of the State of Israel in 1948, and most of it since 1967, the achievement of biblical scholarship, when judged by its concern for the indigenous people, and the values enshrined in international law and conventions on human rights, is not impressive. The support which these activities have acquired from theological and exegetical assertions from within academic and religious circles, Jewish and Christian, is not a legacy which I am proud to bequeath to the next generation of exegetes and religious. Such support in my generation will elicit condemnation and repudiation from future generations, in a manner corresponding to the way other forms of theocratic colonialisms have been rejected. Ultimately, and probably soon, other traditions within Judaism and Christianity will achieve enough support to ensure that Judaism will not be condemned forever to those forms of theocratic imperialism which receive support from only the more disreputable traditions of the Bible, and from those forms of Jewish and Christian eschatology which are scandalous to even secular humankind.

READING THE BIBLE WITH THE EYES OF THE CANAANITES

Liberation theologians from virtually every region have appropriated the Exodus story in their long and tortuous struggle against colonialism, imperialism and dictatorship. Readers of the biblical narrative are easily impressed and consoled by that story's capacity to lift the spirits of the oppressed. However, one's perspective on the Exodus story takes on a different complexion when read 'with the eyes of the Canaanites', that

175

is, with the eyes of any of several different cultures, which have been victims of a colonialism fired by religious imperialism, whether of the Indians in North or Latin America, the Maoris in New Zealand, the Aborigines in Australia, the Khoikhoi and San in southern Africa, or, the Palestinians in Palestine.

Does not a consistent reading of the biblical text require the liberating God of the Exodus to become the oppressive God of the occupation of Canaan? The problem is held in sharp relief in the comment of a North American Indian:

> The obvious characters for Native Americans to identify with
> are the Canaanites, the people who already lived in the promised
> land ... I read the Exodus stories with Canaanite eyes.[23]

The black people of South Africa, too, recognise the central position which the Bible occupied in their colonisation, national oppression and exploitation. Paradoxically, as converts to Christianity, the religion of their conquerors, they embraced the Bible, the text book of their exploitation. However, accordingly as they encounter the Bible being used in support of unjust causes they realise that the book itself is a serious problem for people in search of freedom. Many young South African blacks consider the Bible to be an oppressive document by its very nature and its very core, and even call for its displacement.

Many theologians sensitive to issues of human rights, especially those whose traditions depend heavily on the Bible face a dilemma. While they revere the sacred text, they see how it has been used as an instrument of oppression. They seek refuge in the view that it is the mis-use of the Bible, rather than the text of the Bible itself which is the problem. The blame is shifted from the non-problematic biblical text to the perverse predispositions of the biblical interpreter. This 'solution' evades the problem. Examples from the past and the present indicate the pervasiveness, the persistence and the moral seriousness of the question. Several traditions within the Bible lend themselves to oppressive interpretations and applications, precisely because of their inherently oppressive nature.

---

[23] Warrior, Robert Allen, 'A North American Perspective: Canaanites, Cowboys, and Indians', in Sugirtharajah, R S, ed., *Voices from the Margin: Interpreting the Bible in the Third World* (London: SPCK, 1991), 287-95 (p. 289).

Reflecting the Black experience in South Africa, Takatso Mofokeng goes to the heart of the matter. Black people of South Africa point to the central position which the Bible occupied in the ongoing process of colonisation, national oppression and exploitation. Paradoxically, having been converted to the religion of the conquerors, they accepted their Bible, the ideological instrument of their colonisation, oppression and exploitation. When Black Christians hear the Bible being quoted in support of reactionary causes they realise that the Bible itself is a serious problem for people who want to be free.[24]

When Pope John-Paul II made his first visit to Peru, he received an open letter from various indigenous movements:

> John–Paul II, we, Andean and American Indians, have decided to take advantage of your visit to return to you your Bible, since in five centuries it has not given us love, peace or justice. Please take back your Bible and give it back to our oppressors, because they need its moral teachings more than we do. Ever since the arrival of Christopher Columbus a culture, a language, religion and values which belong to Europe have been imposed on Latin America by force. The Bible came to us as part of the imposed colonial transformation. It was the ideological weapon of this colonialist assault. The Spanish sword which attacked and murdered the bodies of Indians by day and night became the cross which attacked the Indian soul.[25]

The Palestinian liberation theologian, Canon Naim Ateek, also poses the problematic in a striking fashion, since in his region, above all others, the applicability of the Exodus paradigm appears most natural.

> Before the creation of the State (of Israel), the Old Testament was considered to be an essential part of Christian Scripture, pointing and witnessing to Jesus. Since the creation of the State, some Jewish and Christian interpreters have read the Old Testament largely as a Zionist text to such an extent that it

---

[24] Mofokeng, Takatso A, 'Black Christians, the Bible and Liberation', in *Journal of Black Theology* 2 (1988): 34-37.

[25] In Richard, Pablo, '1492: The Violence of God and the Future of Christianity', in Boff, Leonardo and Virgil Elizondo, ed. *1492-1992 The Voice of the Victims. Concilium* 1990(6) (London: SCM; Philadelphia: Trinity Press International), 59-67 (pp. 64-65).

has become almost repugnant to Palestinian Christians...The fundamental question of many Christians, whether uttered or not, is: 'How can the Old Testament be the Word of God in the light of the Palestinian Christians' experience with its use to support Zionism?'[26]

I respectfully suggest that it is high time that we biblical scholars, Church people, and Western intellectuals read the biblical narratives we have discussed here with the eyes of the Canaanites. A Lattey Lecture is an appropriate context in which to make such a proposal, since the Lattey Lecture series promotes examination of the Bible from the perspective of justice, and with an eye to the real questions of contemporary society. It is seemly to do so also under the aegis of the Von Hügel Institute, a distinctive feature of whose work is 'the attempt to conduct its research from the perspective of the under-privileged.' It is, perhaps, also fitting that the task be undertaken here by a disciple of St Vincent de Paul, whose interpretation of the Scriptures was significantly influenced by his encounter with the marginalised, whom he described as 'our lords and masters', and to whose needs he attended indefatigably.

---

[26] Ateek, Naim Stifan, 'A Palestinian Perspective: The Bible and Liberation', in Sugirtharajah, R S, ed., *Voices from the Margin: Interpreting the Bible in the Third World* (London: SPCK, 1991), pp. 280-86 (p. 283).

SETTLING FOR GOD

In this 1997 article for The Middle East International *Michael traces the conversion of much of the religion of Judaism into Zionist political ideology.*

Israel's pre-emptive strike against Egypt, under the pretext of the imminence of Arab aggression which 'threatened the very existence of the state', initiated the war of 5-11 June 1967. Israel, of course, was under no significant threat, let alone in mortal danger. Its real intent was to reap the fruits of victory which the war would bring, thereby fulfilling one of the major goals of the state since its foundation in 1948. On the eve of the war, Cabinet Minister Yigal Allon insisted that Israel must set as one of its central aims 'the territorial fulfilment of the Land of Israel'. Israel's victory resulted in the conquest of the West Bank (including East Jerusalem) from Jordan, the Golan Heights from Syria, and Gaza and the Sinai from Egypt. No wonder it is a watershed in modern Jewish life.

As a student of theology I rushed to the TV on each of the six evenings of the war and watched enthusiastically the comprehensive victory of tiny Israel over its rapacious Arab predators. Israeli propaganda was totally convincing. TV, newspaper and magazine pictures of the liberation of the Old City of Jerusalem in particular resonated with my studies of Israelite history. Moreover, billboards in London assured readers that those who trusted in biblical prophecy would not be surprised by Israel's victory. It was exciting to be reliving biblical history.

Since 1967 the rhetoric of Zionism has been transposed from a secular aspiration to create a state for Jews to the apocalyptic one of redeeming *Eretz Yisrael*. However, like the first wave of Zionist conquest in 1948, the period since 1967 has been a catastrophe for the indigenous population. The establishment of a Jewish state in 1948 involved the eviction of the majority of the Palestinians, and the destruction of most of their villages. The occupation has brought more problems. The extension of the Zionist dream into the religious realm continues to involve the daily humiliation of the indigenous people. But, in the view of religious

Jewish Zionists, and not a few foreign Christians, this is a small price to pay for the benefits of messianic redemption—especially when someone else is paying.

THE CONQUEST OF 'BIBLICAL ISRAEL'

Israel's long-term territorial intentions were signalled by making 4,000 Palestinians homeless in the ancient Maghrebi Quarter, to make way for the plaza in front of the Wailing Wall, and by extending the boundaries of East Jerusalem within days of the occupation. There was virtual unanimity in the emergency session of the UN General Assembly that Israel should withdraw to the borders of 4 June. The Security Council passed Resolution 242, emphasizing 'the inadmissibility of the acquisition of territory by war,' and called for the 'withdrawal of Israeli armed forces from territories occupied in the recent conflict.'

My first visit to the Holy Land in 1972, albeit one enquiring exclusively into the archaeological remains of ancient civilizations, offered the first challenge to my entirely favourable predispositions towards Israel. I was disturbed by the ubiquitous signs of the oppression of the Arabs, whom later I learnt to call Palestinians. My next visit was in 1981 to Bir Zeit University. Because the campus was closed by the military just before our arrival, our hosts put a bus at our disposal, and equal numbers of Bir Zeit and our students constituted a university on wheels. The experience was an eye-opener. I saw at first hand the creeping Jewish settlement of the West Bank. For the first time, I began to question the prevailing view that the Israeli occupation was for security reasons, and my year-long stay in the *Ecole Biblique* in Jerusalem in 1983-84 convinced me that it was for expansion towards the achievement of Greater Israel. It took some time, further visits and intensive study to give my experience an ideological framework. In surveying the 30 year-old occupation, I am struck by the coalition between secular Zionism and the dictates of a particular form of Jewish eschatology which has sustained it.

FROM OCCUPATION TO UNIVERSAL REDEMPTION

Religious Zionists saw the war of 1967 as a turning point in the tortuous process of Messianic redemption, and since then religious values have renewed the ideological drive and pioneering zeal of a Zionism that had become 'routinized'. Without appeal to religious values, Greater Israel would be little different from the fruits of old fashioned colonial plunder. But clothed in the pure garment of religious rectitude, religious Zionism could appeal to its divine provenance and be fuelled by eschatological fervour. Its theological underpinning was provided by father and son Kook, and the *Merkaz HaRav*, the centre for the training of rabbis established by the elder Kook in 1921.

By the time Rabbi Avraham Yitzhak Kook (1865-1935) immigrated to Palestine in 1904, Orthodox Jewry was vehemently opposed to Zionism. They rejected it because of its secular inspiration and values, and regarded Zionists as heretics and sinners who presumed to usher in the messianic era without waiting for God. Rav Kook's teachings integrated the traditional, passive religious longing for the land with the modern, secular, active Zionism, giving birth to a comprehensive religious-nationalist ideology. The Rav saw secular Zionism as an instrument of God to further the messianic redemption and restoration not only of Jews, but of all humanity. He was convinced that God was leading Jews, whether secular or religious to return to the Holy Land, after which the nation would return to its faith. God was bringing about redemption through the 'divinely inspired' Balfour Declaration that 'mirrored the Dawn of Salvation'.

In Rav Kook's view, the divine energy was at its strongest in the creative pioneers of the secular Zionist revolution who were agents of God, even while professing atheism. If their utopian secularism was heretical in the minds of the Orthodox establishment, for him it represented the source of renewal. Practical activities were inseparable from spiritual aspirations, and social activity as well as mysticism had religious meaning: stirrings 'down below' were a necessary preamble to evoking messianic grace 'from above'.

If Rav Kook's metamorphosis of secular Zionism into a full-blown practical and eschatological mysticism was virtually unknown during his lifetime, his writings, selectively mediated by his son, and especially his founding of the centre have proven to be critical in the renaissance of religio-political Zionism up to the present. It was only after his death that he became a cult hero and an idolized spiritual guide in the 1970s after the settler movement, *Gush Emunim*, claimed him as its forefather, and devoted itself to carrying out his legacy, under the authoritative guidance of his only son. Rabbi Zvi Yehuda Kook produced doctored versions of his father's writings, reducing them to collections of articles that distilled Judaism into Zionism by means of messianism. One such collection, *Orot* (Lights) was the 'red book' of the *Gush Emunim* cadres.

The link between the two Kooks is the key to understanding *Gush Emunim*: the father is known mostly through the son, and the son inherited the aurora of the father. While the father's view that the messianic era had begun was not taken seriously in his own day, his son now supported it with a programme of messianic political activism. He saw in the rebirth of the Jewish state the first step towards the coming of the Messiah. All its institutions were means to a messianic end: its government and army were *Kadosh* (Holy).

In the wake of the June war, nobody was more prepared to build on what they believed God had handed them than a group of rabbis who had come under the son's influence in the centre. They included Moshe Levinger, Haim Druckman, Eliezer Waldman, Ya'akov Ariel, Shlomo Aviner, Avraham Shapira and others who were to become household names in Israel over the next thirty years. For them, the biblical texts were no mere literary heritage, but constituted a living title-deed. Every advance of the army recalled the promise, 'Every place on which you set foot shall be yours,' anticipating some future time when 'Your territory shall extend from the wilderness to the Lebanon and from the River, the river Euphrates, to the Western Sea' (Deut 11.24).

On the final day of the war some of these rabbis carried their mentor to the Western Wall, where Rav Kook declared, 'We announce to all of Israel, and to all of the world that by a divine command we have returned to our home, to our holy city. From this day forth, we shall never budge from here.' Since the dimensions of *Eretz Yisrael* were those of Genesis 15, rather than of pre-1967 Israel, Jews were obliged to fulfil the 'commandment of conquest', by settling in the whole land and defending Jewish sovereignty over it.

Since such settlement had redemptive and messianic meaning, and would mark a Jewish renaissance, the indigenous population could be pushed aside. It was a sacred activity, and those engaged in such a holy enterprise had 'souls equal to the most righteous Jew'. The first settlements were founded by young rabbi graduates of the centre. Under their influence, the superficial nationalism of secular Zionism was giving way to a religious Zionism, issuing in the popular slogan, 'There is no

Zionism without Judaism, and no Judaism without Zionism.' The settlements dotting the landscape of the West Bank in every direction are a testimony to the success of their enterprise. In addition to being a violation of international law and of the rights of the indigenes, they are a major obstacle to peace in the region.

MESSIANIC SALVATION AND THE PALESTINIANS

For the indigenous inhabitants of the region, participation in the universal redemption associated with 'Kookist' settlement of the land is somewhat down the line towards the eschaton. The example of Joshua's divine mission is eternally true: the Palestinians are *Gerim* (non-Jewish residents) who according to the Torah are to be treated with tolerance and respect, but not more. More seriously, they are perceived to be an obstacle to the redemptive process. Since the universal principle of self-determination is no match for God's mandate, it does not apply in *Eretz Yisrael*. Hence, talk of human rights and demands for national self-determination are meaningless. Palestinians have three choices: to acknowledge the legitimacy of 'Kookist' Zionism and receive full civil rights; to obey the laws of the state without formal recognition of Zionism, and be granted the rights of resident aliens; or, to accept incentives—including the inducement of force—and emigrate.

Altogether, the two stages of Zionist achievement cast a dark cloud over the aspirations of the ethnocentric dream of 19th-century Jewish nationalist colonialists. Although vehemently opposed to its programme from the beginning, no body now is more supportive of its achievement in establishing the State of Israel and expanding its territory than the religious establishment. The secular movement of Zionism, whose tenets diverged fundamentally from rabbinic eschatology has been transposed into an ideology which the majority of religious Jews regard as of divine origin. We are witnessing a process of resacralization, whereby the irreligious programme of secular, nationalist salvation has been endowed with the mythology of traditional Jewish soteriology.

The major ideological support for Zionist imperialism and the principal obstacle to treating the indigenous people with respect come from religious circles for whom the biblical narratives of land, understood in a fundamentalist fashion, are normative. This was seen at its starkest in the assassination of Premier Rabin by a religious zealot acting in God's name, but his action was merely the tip of the iceberg of Orthodox opposition to 'territorial compromise'. The cultural Zionist, Ahad Ha'am, saw dark clouds in the future: as early as 1913, the behaviour of Zionists towards the Palestinians made him fear for the future if Jews ever came to power. In a letter to a settler in Palestine, he wrote 'If this be the "Messiah": I do not wish to see his coming.'

THE BIBLE AS INSTRUMENT
OF OPPRESSION

This major article, published in Scripture Bulletin *in 1995, sets out the argument to be developed in his influential* The Bible and Colonialism *in 1997.*

On 13 September 1993, President Clinton introduced the leaders of Israel and the Palestinians on the White House lawn, saying that both people pledged themselves to a shared future, shaped by the values of the Torah, the Qur'an, and the Bible. The president, fearing that his speech required more work, had been unable to sleep on the night before the signing. He woke at 3.00 a.m., and reached for his Bible. He reread the entire Book of Joshua and portions of the New Testament. The *Washington Post* report does not reveal whether the president was able to sleep after the blood-curling lection from Joshua, nor, if so, whether he suffered any violent dreams! In any case, his mode of address later in the day was a mixture of Bible-based exhortation in the Baptist tradition, and shrewd political manoeuvring. As if to consolidate the US's self-portrayal as an honest broker, the biblical imagery of his speech was supplemented by a quotation from the Qur'an. Premier Rabin's speech also referred to the Bible, while Chairman Arafat began his with the traditional Muslim invocation of the one God. In the light of history one must question whether the values of the Torah, the Qur'an, and the Bible can be relied upon to promote justice and peace, and underpin the imperatives of human rights.

I argue here that the Bible, commonly looked to as the supreme source-book of liberation, can function as a charter for oppression, and support the argument by a consideration of the application of the biblical paradigm in the past and the present. There is a saying in South Africa, 'When the white man came to our country he had the Bible and we had the land. The white man said to us, "Let us pray". After the prayer, the white man had the land and we had the Bible.' The black people of South Africa recognize the central position which the Bible occupied in the process of their colonization, national oppression and exploitation. Paradoxically, as converts to Christianity, the religion of their conquerors, they embraced the Bible, the textbook of their exploitation. However, accordingly as they encounter the Bible being used in support of unjust causes they realise that the book itself is a serious problem for people in search of freedom. Many young South African blacks consider the Bible to be an oppressive document by its very nature and its very core, and even call for its displacement. In the northern hemisphere, a North American Indian exegete remarks that, 'The obvious characters for Native Americans to identify with are the Canaanites, the people who already lived in the promised land ... I read the Exodus stories with Canaanite eyes' (Sugirtharajah, ed. 1991: 289).

Many theologians sensitive to issues of human rights, especially those whose traditions depend heavily on the Bible face a dilemma. While they revere the sacred text, they see how it has been used as an instrument of oppression. They seek refuge in the view that it is the misuse of the Bible, rather than the text of the Bible itself which is the problem. The blame is shifted from the non-problematic biblical text to the perverse predispositions of the biblical interpreter. This 'solution' evades the problem. Two examples from the past and one from the present indicate the pervasiveness, the persistence and the moral seriousness of the question. They are from three different regions, from three different traditions of biblical hermeneutics, and highlight some of the moral problems at the heart of the Bible itself. It will be seen that several traditions within the Bible lend themselves to oppressive interpretations and applications, precisely because of their inherent oppressive nature.

SOUTH AMERICA

Medieval Christian theologians shared a common conception with Israelite theologians, involving a radical sacralization of the state, and all its institutions, including its land. Both claimed that land was the gift of God, for the Israelites in their time, and later for the Spanish and Portuguese in the New World. God's possession of the land was not considered to have derived solely from the assertion that he had created everything. It also included his political sovereignty over the territories of the earth (Lamadrid 1981: 329). For the Israelites the land comes from God (e.g., Lev 25.23—see Brueggemann 1977, Davies 1974, 1981, 1982, 1991, von Waldow 1974). That the land is the inheritance of Israel is a fundamental thrust in Deuteronomy (e.g., Deut 8.17f; 9.6). The sanctity and purity of the land spring logically from these views. One reads of land separated and consecrated to God. Because of their impurity God vomited the defiling inhabitants out of the land (see Lev 18.24-27). The prophets are at one in condemning the profanation of the land by the people (Isa 5.1-7; Hos 1-3).

The Israelite king ruled in virtue of the grace of God, and all the institutions of the state, therefore, derived from the divine authority. In a corresponding way, in the medieval period the Pope, as the Vicar of Christ, had total power in heaven and earth. As in the Old Testament period, religion invaded every facet of life in the Middle Ages. The majority of theologians and jurists considered the Pope to be sovereign of all the earth. That he crowned the kings confirmed the subordination of the temporal to the spiritual, the empire to the Papacy, in much the same way as earth is subject to heaven.

The papal Bull, *Inter cetera divina*, of Pope Alexander VI (1493), which divided the New World between Spain and Portugal, provides an insight into the dominant medieval theology of land. The Pope was the Lord of the Earth (*Papa dominus orbis*), in virtue of his being considered the Vicar of Christ, who confided to him all power, in heaven and on earth. The *Tractado de Alcoçoba* ceded to Portugal all the discovered territories, these being considered to be at the disposal of Alexander VI. The catholic kings were authorized to engage in a holy war, which would implant the true faith in the regions of the infidel. The major justification for holy war of the *Decreto de Graciano* derived from the Old Testament, with Joshua, the Judges, Saul, David, etc., reflecting the divine mandate to wage a holy war to conquer the promised land. Doubts about belligerent aggression were assuaged by Augustine's claim that, 'Without a doubt, a war ordained by God is just,' since there can be no evil in God.

Juan Mair's *Sentencias* (1510) was the first to tackle theologically the problem of the conquest of the land of the infidels. Although he treated the subject in general terms, he referred to the Spanish conquest of the American Indians by way of example. The first justification for confiscating land already inhabited, and subjugating the indigenous population was missionary: Christians may take to arms with the aim of preaching the Gospel. Moreover, since, in line with the theory of Aristotle, barbarians are slaves to naturalism, subjecting them to the rule of Christian principles was justifiable. The theology of Genessi Sepulvedae is representative of the justification of war against the Indians as a prerequisite for their future evangelization, citing various passages from Deuteronomy and Leviticus, detailing the violent expulsion of the Canaanites from their land, and their replacement by Israelites, at the behest of God. He held that the preaching of the Gospel would not be possible before the people were subjected politically to the Christians, and that the pagan barbarism of the Indians was such as to make them fit to be no more than slaves.

There were, however, some dissenting voices. In rejecting such a justification for the Spanish destruction of the Indians Francisco de Vitoria (1538-39) represented a radical reaction against the theocratic imperialism of the medieval period (p. 702). He argued against the subjugation of the Indians, and was energetic in defence of their freedom and rights. He had a more nuanced approach—only if the Indians offered resistance to the rights of the Spanish to do commerce, etc., could they be engaged in justifiable war. But in general, for Christian theologians in the medieval period, the Indians' unbelief, abominations and crimes against nature justified the occupation of their lands. Justification for violence was based on the conquest of Canaan by the Israelites.

The majority of the medieval theologians, in espousing theocratic imperialism and supporting the notion of holy war, bypassed the higher tendencies reflected in much of the Hebrew prophetic tradition, and the altogether pacifist tendencies within the New Testament. They settled for a regression to those traditions within the Old Testament which glorify war as an instrument of divine justice, thereby doing a serious injustice to the spirit of the Gospel in ignoring its detachment from the concept of territoriality so prominent in the Torah.

SOUTH AFRICA

The majority of South African Dutch Reformed theologians in the period 1930-60, during which the policy of apartheid was invented, formulated and defended, underpinned it by recourse to the Book of Deuteronomy (Deist 1994). Deist shows convincingly that the readers' own epoch and vested interests are critical to the interpretation of the biblical text. The readers in this case were the Afrikaners, who for centuries from having been independent farmers and landowners with a culture of their own suddenly became urban day labourers and found themselves in a foreign culture and at the bottom of the social ladder. The influx of black people into the cities, competing for unskilled, low-cost jobs exacerbated the problem for the Afrikaans-speaking people, who felt threatened by the advance of the black people, and began to insist that the principle of *geen gelykstelling* (no equalization) between blacks and whites be applied (see Deist 1986).

The notion of *no equalization* came from the Boers' perception that, as they embarked on the Great Trek from the Cape Colony to the Orange Free State and Transvaal (1838), they were the chosen people, rescued from Egypt (British oppression), on their way to the Promised Land. This is reflected in the names on the way: Bethlehem, Jordan River, Jericho, Nylstroom (River Nile). The Bible served as the Boers' source of self-interpretation and indicated their future. They regarded the indigenous black people among whom they now found themselves as the 'Canaanites' who served foreign gods and with whom 'Israel' should not intermarry. Already in 1858 this resulted in a clause in the constitution of the *Zuid-Afrikaanse Republiek* stating that the people did not want equalization (*gelykstelling*) of black and white, neither in the church nor in the state (Deist 1994: 16).

The spontaneous, though naive identification with Israel can be seen in the parallel Kritzinger drew in a sermon on the occasion of the commemoration of the Day of the Covenant (16 December—see Deist 1994):

Israel	*Afrikaners*
Went from Palestine to Egypt	Went from Europe to Africa
Suffered under foreign rulers	Suffered under British rule
Escaped from Egypt to Canaan	Escaped from the Cape Colony to the north
Considered the nations as numerous and strong	Considered black people as numerous and strong
Miraculously received a new land	Miraculously received a new land
Made a covenant with God	Made a covenant with God
Erected memorial stones	Erected the Cilliers memorial church
Fathers recounted their history to posterity	Fathers recounted their history to posterity

The Afrikaans speakers developed their own brand of Calvinism, which emerged from the soil and their own history. 'Boer Calvinism', a term coined by the Calvinists themselves, was based on the plain sense of the Bible, uninfluenced by any critical handling of the text (Deist 1994: 18f.). In particular, it invoked a naive realist reading of Deuteronomy and played an enormous role in the establishment of the policy of apartheid. Sermons and official publications of the Dutch Reformed Church kept reminding their Bible readers of the *kairos*, the moment when, like Moses, they were on the verge of a new era, which came to mean a white South Africa for their children. But the Afrikaners saw their situation as vulnerable, corresponding to that of the introduction to Deuteronomy (see Stuhlman 1990: 626).

Like Moses, the Dutch Reformed Church leadership saw that their only chance of survival in this hostile world lay in strictly keeping to God's commandments. The naive reading of the book of Deuteronomy played an enormous role in the establishment of the policy of apartheid (Deist 1994: 22). Deuteronomy has a divinely instituted division of nations, and a special, pre-ordained and unbreakable bond between Yahweh and Israel (14.2), which made it different from the nations (4.37f; 7.7f.; 10.14f.). If God had divided the nations, no one had the right to unite them! Deuteronomy was appealed to as promoting the unity of the Afrikaners, on the one hand, and their separation from the black peoples, on the other. The policy of apartheid in church and state was justified theologically by the reformed principle of separate, independent groups within the kingdom (of God). Apartheid, having been instituted by the great Creator himself must be defended by the Afrikaner people and the Church of the Boers, especially against modern liberalism's policy of equalization (Deist 1994: 23). The separation of peoples is based on Scripture, equality of the races is a human construct.

The social polarity in Deuteronomy is between 'brother' and 'foreigner' in the same geographical area (see Eilberg-Schwartz 1986/7; Smick 1989). Whereas it is forbidden for a 'brother' to eat something that died, it may be given to a 'foreigner' (Deut 14.21; cf., however, Lev 17.15). Special provision is made for the poor *Israelite* (Deut 15.7-15), and while interest on loans may be extracted from foreigners, this may not happen with brothers (Deut 15.3; 23.19f.). Stuhlman correctly notes that the author of Deuteronomy attempted to produce a programme in which the integrity of Israel's inner boundaries is (re)established and clarified in order to protect insiders from potentially harmful outsiders, especially indigenous outsiders (Deist 1994: 24f.; see also, Deist 1987, McBride 1987, Nicholson 1991). Deist notes, 'Given their own tradition, self-understanding and socio-economic position Afrikaans-speaking theologians easily identified with these sentiments' (1994: 25).

Deuteronomy's prohibition of mixing with the indigenous people (7.3f.—see Cohen 1983, Dion 1985, O'Connell 1992) provided the scriptural basis for the South African immorality act prohibiting mixed marriages—the Afrikaners had to be kept pure. The authors of Deuteronomy also justified the Afrikaner seizure of the land. Just as the Israelites were a minority, who through the help of God acquired possession of the land (4.4-6, 32-34, 37-38; 7.17-18; 9.1-3), so too the South African Calvinists regarded their possession of the land as divinely ordained. Like the authors of Deuteronomy, the South African Calvinists were quite insensitive to the fact that the land had already been inhabited. The occupation of the land was to be celebrated, rather than questioned along ordinary historical lines.

PALESTINE

Religious and theological comment on contemporary developments in the region is substantial, but that reflecting a moral sensitivity to the underside of the establishment of the Jewish State of Israel, namely the disruption of the indigenous Arab population of Palestine is modest. Biblically- and theologically-based discussion concerning this region, until very recently at least, is singularly deficient in its interest in those issues with which human rights and humanitarian bodies concern themselves. This is not only surprising but alarming, since biblical scholars and theologians in virtually every other arena inform their discussions with a sensitivity to the victims of oppression.

Until recently both Jewish and Christian scholars of the Bible have neglected the theme of the Land. While we may never explain the reasons for the relative academic silence in the past, the reasons for the recent interest are not difficult to discover. However, when one moves on to a moral consideration of modern events in Palestine one trespasses on a virtual academic no-go area. The view that the Bible provides the title-deed for the establishment of the modern state of Israel, and for its expansionist policies since 1948 is so pervasive, in both Christian Zionist and Jewish Zionist circles, that the very attempt to discuss the issue is sure to encounter opposition.

When President Carter shocked fundamentalists and charismatics with his concern for human rights, and used the words 'Palestinian homeland' in a speech in March 1977, full-page advertisements, signed by prominent evangelicals, appeared throughout the USA, e.g., 'The time has come for evangelicals to affirm their belief in biblical prophecy and Israel's divine right to the Holy Land' ('Evangelicals' Concern for Israel', paid advertisement, the *Christian Science Monitor*, 3 November 1977). With the US Protestant churches beginning to support third world countries, and giving the impression of supporting the PLO, the pro-Israeli lobby targeted the evangelicals, who had fifty-to-sixty million Americans, and a lot of money. Jerry Falwell was a confidant of Begin, and televangelist Pat Robertson charted the Israeli invasion of Lebanon, begun on 6 June 1982, with daily reports on CBN, interpreting the events according to the end time fulfilment of biblical prophecy. Israel's attack, he said, was a modern Joshua event. He urged American viewers to phone President Reagan immediately, offering encouragement to Israel's war (O'Neill and Wagner 1993). Meanwhile, back with the action, Rabbi Schlomo Riskin followed the army to study the Talmud with the troops. He was deeply impressed by the fact that the soldiers, when resting from battle, spent long hours discussing whether it would have been right to pick Lebanese cherries (see Bermant 1994 for a moral critique).

Military barbarism, such as the Israeli invasion of Lebanon in 1982, is viewed rather more tolerantly than that of a man in full view of his victims. When the Jewish settler, Dr Baruch Goldstein, a graduate of the most prestigious yeshiva in the US, appeared at the Hebron mosque of Abraham on 25 February, 1994, and massacred twenty-nine worshippers, there was a sense of widespread revulsion, even from circles silent on the devastation caused in Israel's aggressive incursion into Lebanon.

Britain's Chief Rabbi, Jonathan Sacks expressed shock and grief at the massacre: 'Violence is evil. Violence committed in the name of God is doubly evil. Violence against those engaged in worshipping God is unspeakably evil.' Premier Rabin told the Knesset that Baruch Goldstein and his followers were a foreign implant and an errant weed. 'Sensible Judaism', he declared, 'spits you out. You are a shame on Zionism and an embarrassment to Judaism.' People with sensitivity to questions of human rights and decency readily agree, but one asks, what distinguishes this kind of behaviour from that presented as divinely mandated in some of the traditions of the Old Testament? Bible readers may wonder to what extent the Book of Deuteronomy, the Book of Joshua, and, in particular, the Book of Esther, the biblical reading for the Jewish Feast of Purim, may have contributed to the world view of Dr Goldstein. The official enquiry into the Hebron massacre concluded that Goldstein acted alone, and while it concedes that security was lax, it leaves a particularly loathsome form of applied biblical hermeneutics unchecked. Prime Minister Rabin promised to install metal detectors to prevent arms being brought into mosques in future.

Dr Goldstein was no ordinary man whose mental state the tensions of the area had triggered into a moment of insanity. He was steeped in the Bible, and would have surpassed even President Clinton in having his mind shaped by the values of the Torah. It is highly likely that he absorbed thoroughly the legendary Book of Esther, the biblical text which celebrates the fight-back of Jews, and the reading of which was prescribed for the feast of Purim, which occurred on that fateful day.

He learned from the Book of Esther that King Ahasuerus also suffered from nocturnal restlessness—he could not sleep on the eve of Queen Esther's banquet, and called for the annals to be brought and read to him. Xerxes' reading issued in a personal catastrophe for Haman, the enemy of the Jews, and, subsequently, for many more of their enemies, near and far. He would have read how, with regal and unchallengable divine approval, 'The Jews struck down all their enemies with the sword ... five hundred men in the citadel of Susa alone,' and that, on hearing the good news, Queen Esther asked King Ahasuerus for an extension of his decree for the morrow also. On the fourteenth day of the month of Adar the Jews killed three hundred men in the city. It is a small mercy that the avenging Jews of the Book of Esther took a day off on the fifteenth day of the month (chapter 9). Goldstein would have read that things were even worse outside Susa. On the thirteenth day of the month the Jews slaughtered seventy-five thousand (although the Greek version of the text gives the more modest figure of fifteen thousand). Mercifully, the Jews of the province rested and feasted on the fourteenth day. Xerxes ordered for the fourteenth and fifteenth days of the month of Adar an annual commemoration (the Feast of Purim) of the days on which Jews had rid themselves of their enemies, had had their sorrow turned into gladness and mourning into a holiday. Jews were to exchange presents and give gifts to the poor.

Goldstein's biblical hermeneutics, alas, went further, and authorized a one-man re-enactment of the legendary slaughter, apparently sanctioned by God's word, right on the Feast of Purim. His actions were not without support, particularly from some branches of political Zionists who lean heavily on a literalist reading of the biblical text. Many Jewish religious settlers, and their Torah-based ideologists, do not distinguish between the literary genre of legend and that of historical writing, and are not influenced by hermeneutical considerations which derive from the generally accepted findings of biblical criticism over the last few centuries. Rabbi Yaacov Perrin, one of the religious leaders in Goldstein's settlement in Kiryat Arba, eulogizing him at his funeral, declared, 'One million Arabs are not worth a Jewish fingernail,' and another mourner declared Goldstein to be 'the greatest Jew alive.' Some of the more dubious values of the Torah, and the books of Joshua and Esther, had come back to haunt the civilized world, and, in his own circle of like-minded biblical interpretation, Goldstein was held in high regard.

While Goldstein's action is unique in the long list of barbarisms perpetrated recently in the region, there is, especially in Christian circles, abundant evidence for appeal to sacred writings to justify inhumane behaviour—my academic competence requires me to leave to others the urgent task of discussing the morality of the atrocities which are presented as deriving from a literalist exegesis of Islamic texts. With respect to biblical hermeneutics, Dr Goldstein, alas, is merely the tip of the iceberg of literalism, which justifies the most blatantly indecent acts on the basis of the alleged divine mandate. Constant exposure to a literalist interpretation of the Torah, whether in the curriculum of Israeli schools (see the *Tamarin Affair*, and Tamarin 1973), or through some of the many schools of biblical and talmudic learning, avoids with difficulty descent into attitudes of racism, xenophobia and militarism (e.g., those associated with the former Chief Rabbi of Palestine, Avraham Yitzhak Kook, and his son, Rabbi Zvi Yehuda Kook, and their spiritual offspring in the settler *Gush Emunim* movement—see Newman, ed. 1985).

The Bible poses a fundamental moral problem for anyone who takes it at face value. There is no shortage of post-biblical texts which point to its alleged divine origins—*Torah min haShamayim*. Goldstein's hermeneutical tradition would have assured him that, 'Whoever says that the whole Torah is from heaven except this verse, for God did not utter it, but Moses from his own mouth, he is one (of whom it is written) "For he has despised the word of God" (Num 15.31)' (bSanh. 99a), and that all Israelites have a share in the world to come except '... those who assert that the Torah is not from heaven' (*mSanh.* 10.1). The Torah, in such a crude interpretation, must be accepted in its totality, and in all its parts.

The Torah, however, is fundamentally rooted in the escape from Egypt of the Hebrew slaves, who entered and occupied a land which was already occupied by others. The occupation of another people's land, as we are reminded constantly, demands systematic pillage and killing. What distinguishes the biblical accounts of this activity, whether through the *Blitzkrieg* mode represented in the legend of the Book of Joshua, or through the more gradual gaining of control as reflected in the Book of Judges, is that it is presented as having not only divine approval, but as being mandated by the divinity. In the traditions in the Book of Joshua, in particular, the Israelites killed and butchered in conformity with the directives of God. This presentation of God as gloating over the destruction of others must be rejected out of hand by anyone who presumes that the conduct of an ethical God, at the very least, will not fall lower than ordinary secular decent behaviour. Nevertheless, even theologians, in their appeal to the Old Testament title to land, systematically ignore both the humanistic concerns of international human rights and the more noble traditions of theology itself.

Encounter with such examples of applied biblical hermeneutics as discussed above raises important questions for students of the Bible. The commandment that, 'You shall destroy all the peoples that the Lord your God will give over to you, your eye shall not pity them' (Deut 7.16), and the statement that, 'The Lord your God will clear away these nations before you little by little, ... and you shall make their name perish from under heaven' (Deut 7.22-24), are seen in a new light, when one reads the history of colonialism in South America, or reflects upon the

195

inhumanity associated with apartheid, or meets the Palestinians. South American Indians, South African Blacks and Palestinians are modern counterparts of the Hittites, the Girgashites, the Amorites, the Canaanites, the Perizzites, the Hivites, and the Jebusites. In our society such biblical sentiments, rightly, would be regarded as an incitement to racial hatred. On moral grounds, one is forced to question whether the Torah continues to provide divine legitimacy for the occupation of other people's land, and their virtual annihilation. By any standards of ethics and human rights, the first six books of the Hebrew Bible are seen to reflect some racist and xenophobic sentiments, promoting an attitude of ethnocentricity, which appears to receive the highest possible legitimacy in the form of divine approval.

Contemporary liberation theologies, like all theologies, look to the Bible for their underpinning. It is not difficult to discern within the Hebrew Bible a whole range of themes which fit the concept of liberation very comfortably (e.g., liberation from oppression in Egypt, Babylon, etc.). However, does not a consistent reading of the biblical text require the liberating God of the Exodus to become the oppressive God of the occupation of Canaan?

WAYS FORWARD

There are major errors involved in a naive interpretation of the Bible. Every effort must be made to rescue it from being a blunt instrument in the oppression of one people by another. A major problem with much of the Old Testament, especially the first four books, is its portrayal of God as, what many modern people would regard as a racist, militaristic xenophobe, whose views would not be tolerated in any modern Western democracy. Anyone with moral sensitivities, and concern for the dignity of other peoples, must question the kind of biblicism which sees the core of biblical revelation frozen in the concepts of Chosen People and Promised Land, when the application of such views can have such morally questionable outcomes as discussed above. The biblical claim of the divine gift of land is integrally linked with the claim of divine approval for the extermination of the indigenous people (see, e.g., Deut 20.16-18). A more ethical hermeneutical stance requires one to recognise in the biblical legend the attribution to God of His approval of the *de facto* Israelite possession of the land, and the extermination of the inhabitants, or, taking account of the date of the final redaction of the traditions, the *de spe* re-possession of the land aspired to during the period of the Babylonian captivity

Much popular engagement with the Bible, and especially that on the question of land, settles for a synchronic reading of the text, which does not consider its literary evolution. Although it is not generally acknowledged, there is virtually always an unstated assumption that the literary genre of the biblical treatment of the origins of Israel in the land of Canaan is history, even though this view runs in the face of all serious scholarly comment. In addition, one notes a lack of differentiation, in discussion of the theme of land, between the different stages in the life of the Israelites, e.g., before the occupation of Canaan, during the period of the monarchy, and before, during and after exile. There is also the unspoken assumption in most cases that one is dealing with a homogeneous people of Israel, ethnically, culturally and religiously one at all periods. More seriously still, the biblical attitudes towards the land are treated, even by those scholars who have written at length on the subject (e.g., Davies, Brueggemann, Orlinsky), as if they were above any questioning on moral grounds, even by criteria derived from other parts of the Bible. Uniquely in the matter of biblical attitudes to land, no value judgement is made upon the biblical text, and the mind-set of the biblical writers is assumed to be free of moral reproach. There is often the unspoken assumption that the attitudes to land portrayed at one period have an automatic currency for quite a different one. In particular, there is the undeclared assumption that the attitudes to land portrayed at any one biblical period automatically transfer to that specific form of theology of land which one encounters in medieval theology, or Boer Calvinism, or political Zionism. In order to ensure the academic integrity of the discourse each of these limitations must be addressed, but detailed treatment will have to be postponed. The task is daunting, but becomes a moral imperative when one realizes that the investigation is sensitive to moral issues, and reflects a certain compassion for the victims of oppression.

Any ancient book, including the Bible, presents problems of interpretation for a modern reader. All authors, even those to whom one might wish to ascribe divine inspiration, write from within their own world-view. The language and thought-patterns they use are circumscribed by their cosmological, anthropological and theological perspectives, and very often reflect a quite specific social and political context, for example, of persecution by an enemy. An author's spirit of blood-thirsty retribution is understandable in such circumstances, but cannot be squared with the universalism which runs through most of the New Testament. There is a major question of whether God conforms to even the minimal morality which nation states commit themselves to today. When readers of the Bible settle for those portions of its traditions which portray God as a militaristic and xenophobic ethnicist, the omnipotent, merciful, and universal God, as revealed in Jesus Christ is presented as not being able to live up to even the minimum moral ideals of the UN Declarations on Human Rights, or the prescriptions of the Fourth Geneva Convention which govern belligerent occupation.

Many ingenuous commentators do not respect the genre of the biblical text, and, more seriously, are seldom influenced by considerations of human rights, when these conflict with a naive reading of the sacred text. Surely, religious people ought to be concerned about the biblical paradigm proffered in justification of such indecent deeds as the occupation of other people's land, murder, and the exploitation of indigenous peoples, all under the guise of fidelity to the eternal validity of the Sinaitic covenant. A God who insists on the destruction of people as an act of devotion to Him is one from whom most decent people will recoil. Religious supporters of militant Zionism must question whether the ideals of Judaism are best served by emphasizing those portions of their tradition which betray a narrow and exclusivist concept of a tribal god. South African Calvinists have an opportunity for repudiation of, and repentance for their use of the biblical legend to justify their abuse of the human rights of the blacks and coloureds. The most that can be done for the medieval Spanish and Portuguese colonialists is for us to pray God's forgiveness for them, and for those who provided a theological rationale for their evil deeds. Those charged with the responsibility of engaging in biblical exegesis have the most serious obligations.

One hopes that the tragic histories alluded to above will encourage biblical scholars, theologians and religious leaders to acknowledge the profound influence which their hermeneutical presuppositions and epistemological choices impose on the biblical texts. The application of the Bible in defence of Spanish and Portuguese colonialism, South African apartheid, and political Zionism has been a disaster, leading to the suffering and humiliation of millions of people, and to the loss of respect for the Bible as having something significant to contribute to humanity.

Pace Deist (1994: 28f.) and others, it is not sufficient to attribute the ill effects of the application of the Bible to the inadequacies reflected in the predispositions of the readers of the Bible. The moral problem stems from the nature of some of the material of the Bible itself. Neither the Book of Joshua, nor the Book of Esther is the best distraction for a person transfixed between wakefulness and sleep. Such tracts should not be accorded a favoured place in the search for moral exhortation. Hotel managers may need to censor their Gideon Bibles, lest their clients be driven to appalling behaviour in the wake of sleepless nights, spent reading some of the more racist, xenophobic and militaristic elements within the biblical text.

REFERENCES

Bermant, C. 1994. 'Rabbi's blinkers and professor's vision'. *Jewish Chronicle*, 26 August, 21.
Brueggemann, W. 1977. *The Land. Place as Gift, Promise, and Challenge in Biblical Faith.* (Overtures to Biblical Theology). Philadelphia: Fortress.
Cohen, S J D. 1983. 'From the Bible to Talmud: the prohibition of intermarriage'. *Hebrew Annual Review* 7: 23-39.
Davies, W D. 1974. *The Gospel and the Land. Early Christianity and Jewish Territorial Doctrine.* Berkeley: University of California Press.
_____ 1981. 'The Territorial Dimensions of Judaism', in *Intergerini Parietis Septum (Eph. 2:14. Essays Presented to Markus Barth on his sixty-fifth birthday*, ed. Dikran Y Hadidian. Pittsburgh: The Pickwick Press, pp. 61-96.
_____ 1982. *The Territorial Dimensions of Judaism.* Berkeley: University of California Press.
_____ 1991. *The Territorial Dimensions of Judaism. With a Symposium and Further Reflections.* Minneapolis: Fortress.
Deist, F E. 1986. 'Aufstieg und Niedergang der Apartheid', in *Politische Studien* (Sonderheft 2), 19-30.
_____ 1987. *Revolution and reinterpretation. Chapters from the history of Israel*, ed. F E Deist and J H le Roux. Cape Town. 91-97.
_____ 1994. 'The Dangers of Deuteronomy: A Page from the Reception History of the Book'. Martínez, F García, *et al.*, eds. 1994, 13-29.
Dion, P E. 1985. 'Deuteronomy and the gentile world: a study in biblical theology'. *Toronto Journal of Theology* 1: 200-221.
Eilberg-Schwartz, H. 1986/7. 'Creation and Classification in Judaism: From Priestly to rabbinic conceptions'. *History of Religions* 26: 357-381.

Fiorenza, E Schüssler. 1988. 'The ethics of biblical interpretation decentring Biblical scholarship'. *JBL* 107: 3-17.

Fowl, S E. 1990. 'The ethics of interpretation, or what's left after the elimination of meaning', in *The Bible in three Dimensions*, ed. D J A Clines (*JSOTS* 87) Sheffield, 379-398.

Lamadrid, A G. 1981. 'Canaán y América. La Biblia y la Teologia medieval ante la Conquista de la Tierra'. *Escritos de Biblia y Oriente*. Bibliotheca Salmanticensis Estudios 38. Salamanca-Jerusalén: Universidad Pontificia, 329-346.

McBride, S D. 1987. 'Polity of the Covenant People: the Book of Deuteronomy'. *Interpretation*: 41: 229-244.

Mair, Juan. 1510. *Libro II de las Sentencias*. Paris.

Martínez, F García, A Hilhorst, J T A G M. van Ruiten, and AS. van der Woude, eds. 1994. *Studies in Deuteronomy. In Honour of C.J. Labuschagne on the Occasion of his 65th Birthday*. Leiden/New York/Köln: E J Brill.

Newman, D, ed. 1985. *The Impact of Gush Emunim. Political Settlement in the West Bank*. London and Sydney: Crook Helm.

Nicholson, E. 1991. 'Deuteronomy's Vision of Israel'. *Storia e Tradizioni di Israele. Scritti in onore di J Alberto Soggin*, ed. D Garrone and F Israel. Brescia, 191-203.

O'Connell, R H. 1992. 'Deuteronomy vii, 1-26: asymmetric concentricity and the rhetoric of the conquest'. *Vetus Testamentum* 42: 248-265.

O'Neill and D Wagner. 1993. *Peace or Armageddon? The Unfolding Drama of the Middle East Peace Accord*. Grand Rapids: Zondervan Publishing House.

Orlinsky, Harry M. 1985. 'The Biblical Concept of the Land of Israel: Cornerstone of the Covenant between God and Israel'. *Eretz-Israel* 18: 43-55.

Sepulvedae, Genessi. *Democrates alter sive de iustis belli causis apud indios*, ed. crítica con versión castellana por R. Losada. Madrid 1951.

Smick, E B. 1989. 'Old Testament cross-culturation: Paradigmatic or enigmatic?', *Journal of the Evangelical Theological Society* 32: 3-16.

Stuhlman, L. 1990. 'Encroachment in Deuteronomy: An Analysis of the Social World of the D Code'. *JBL* 109: 613-632.

Sugirtharajah, R S. ed. 1991. *Voices from the Margin: Interpreting the Bible in the Third World*. London: SPCK.

Tamarin, G. 1973. *The Israeli Dilemma: Essays on a Warfare State*. Rotterdam.

Vitoria, Francisco de. 1538-39. *De indis recenter inventis relectio prior (1538-39)*, ed. crítica con traductión castellana por T. Urdánoz, Obras de Francisco de Vitoria. Relecciones Teológicas. Madrid 1960: 541-726.

von Waldow, Hans Eberhard. 1974. 'Israel and her Land: Some Theological Considerations', in *A Light unto my Path*, ed. H N Bream, R D Heim, C A Moore, Philadelphia: Temple University Press, 493-508.

ZIONIST ETHNIC CLEANSING: THE FULFILMENT OF BIBLICAL PROPHECY?

*In this article Michael reflects on the impact of events on his understanding of the Bible and of the State of Israel (*Epworth Review, 2000*).*

In the light of the unique theological claims that are made for the State of Israel it is appropriate to reflect on it from a theological and religious perspective. In the first instance, the Bible is alleged to be the 'Jews' sacrosanct title-deed to Palestine'. Moreover, the existence of the state attracts a unique vocabulary of approval by (religious) Jews and Christians. Indeed, some associate it with the fulfilment of biblical prophecy, while the more fundamentalist Christian Evangelical wing frequently links it with the end-time. Since it is not possible here to review all the relevant matters of the discourse, I confine myself to a consideration of the moral problem which the underside of the creation of the state poses, and the challenge that that offers to a moral exegesis of the Bible.

Whereas the establishment of the State of Israel has been viewed favourably by many in the West, in the perspective of those who have paid the price for the prize of Zionism it has been a disaster. The Palestinian *Nakba* (catastrophe) of 1948-49 resulted in the country being conquered by a foreign minority, and being emptied almost entirely of its indigenous people, followed by the destruction of the majority of their villages, to ensure they could not return. The expulsion of the inhabitants of Kosovo, and the ruin of their houses and villages behind them offers a contemporary analogy. Nevertheless, not infrequently the Zionist conquest, unlike that of the Serbs, is hailed as a victory for freedom and civilised values, and in some religious circles as a miraculous act of God. Moreover, the foreseen and planned forcible displacement of an indigenous Arab population of Palestine from its homeland continues to be supported from abroad, financially, politically, and even theologically. Frequently, the extent of the *Nakba* is suppressed, denied, or simply ignored.

Since much of my postgraduate biblical studies was done in the land of the Bible it would scarcely have been possible for me to ignore the social and political context in which I carried out my mainly historical critical research. As will become clear, it took me some time to realise that there was an alleged link between the Bible and the modern history of the region. Since personal experience usually precedes reflection and analysis an autobiographical perspective is instructive.

Halfway through my four years of undergraduate theology the Israeli-Arab war broke out on 5 June 1967, arousing my first interest in the region. Although not matching the nintendo-like portrayal of war pioneered during the Gulf War of 1991 the television pictures, reports and comment portrayed a classic David versus Goliath conflict, with diminutive, innocent Israel repulsing its rapacious Arab predators. The comprehensive victory of Israel over several Arab states, conquering East Jerusalem, the West Bank, the Golan Heights, Gaza, and Sinai, all in six days, produced surges of delight in me. My day time study of ancient Israelite history provided an intriguing backdrop to the nightly reports of the modern State of Israel engaged in war.

Later that summer, billboards in London, quoting the Hebrew prophets, assured readers that those who trusted in biblical prophecy would not be surprised by Israel's victory. I was taken aback that some people related contemporary events to Hebrew prophecies, especially in the light of the insistence of historical critical scholarship—the prevailing methodology of my school of exegesis—that biblical prophecy concerned the period of the *prophet*: the prophets were 'forth-tellers' for God, rather than foretellers of future events. I was intrigued that others thought differently.

I was to learn much later that the 1967 war inaugurated a new phase in the Zionist conquest of Mandated Palestine, one which brought theological assertions and biblical interpretations to the very heart of the ideology which propelled the Israeli conquest, and set the pattern of Jewish settlement in the Occupied Territories. After two more years of theology and three years of postgraduate biblical studies, I made my first visit to Israel-Palestine in Easter 1972 with an international party of postgraduate biblical scholars.

SEEING AND BELIEVING

Although the visit enquired exclusively into the archaeological remains of ancient civilisations, it offered the first challenge to my totally favourable dispositions towards Israel. I was disturbed by the obvious *apartheid* nature of Israeli–Arab society, and by the oppression of the Arabs of the Occupied Territories. During my second visit (1981) I began to see from the inside the reality of land expropriation, the increasing settlement of Jews in the West Bank, and the quotidian sufferings of its Palestinian inhabitants. Yet, I had no doubt that Israel's occupancy was justified in terms of its security needs, a position I began to question only during the course of my sabbatical year in Jerusalem (1983-84). Prior to that period I had never even given thought to the possibility that the oppression of the Palestinians, and the aggressive programme of Jewish settlement on their land, might in some way be related to the biblical narrative.

Even though I was researching on the Pauline Epistles, one dramatic incident in particular forced me to reflect on the broader political context of my location, and alerted me to its religious dimension. The first news item on the Voice of Israel radio one morning reported that during the night a Jewish terrorist group had been caught in the act of attempting to blow up the Dome of the Rock and the Al-Aqsa Mosque on the Haram al-Sharif (the Temple Mount), only a few hundred metres south of my residence in the serene cloisters of the *École Biblique*. For fifty days the identity of the terrorists was kept private, but, later, newspapers published a picture of one of those convicted of the offence wearing the typical dress of the Jewish settler movement, *Gush Emunim*. He had the Book of Psalms in his hand as the judge read out the verdict.[1] That an attempted act of such enormous international and inter-faith significance, frustrated only by a whisker, derived from religious motivation was quite shocking. However, it was not the only act of Jewish terrorist activity during that year. Moreover, the name of the Rabbi Meir Kahane was seldom off the headlines.

After the massacre of Israeli athletes in the 1972 Munich Olympic Games, Kahane openly promoted 'Jewish counter-terror', and founded *Kach*. He approved of the armed attacks on the West Bank Arab mayors in 1980, and of the killing of students at Hebron's Islamic University. Moreover, in 1984, *Terror Against Terror*, the suspected armed wing of *Kach*, was formed and was responsible for several acts of terrorism against non-Jews. For Kahane, God's Torah, rather than human democracy, was the basis of Israel. Zionism and Western democracy were irreconcilable,

---

[1] See my 'Israel: Library, Land and Peoples', *Scripture Bulletin* 15(1984): 6-11, 8.

and secular Judaism was but atheism wrapped in a prayer shawl. The Torah provided the only reason to live in an otherwise miserable land. Since God had delivered the Jews from slavery in Egypt, gave them the Promised Land, and commanded Jews to live there, all Jews should leave the diaspora and settle in the land, whose borders the Torah establishes: 'minimally, from El Arish, northern Sinai, including Yamit, part of the east bank of the Jordan, part of Lebanon and certain parts of Syria, and part of Iraq, to the Tigris river'.[2]

Kahane, elected to the Knesset in July 1984, considered that Zionism accelerated the coming of the Messiah, and that the creation of the state marked the beginning of the messianic era. Such considerations overrode any concern for the indigenes, who should be deported, a position which, he claimed, was supported by all the rabbis, albeit only in private. Kahane would applaud anyone who blew up the two mosques on 'the Temple Mount'.[3] His association of the State of Israel with the events of the Messianic end-time resonated sympathetically with the increasingly popular teleology of the religious–ultranationalist camp. Kahane's brazenly violent methods and offensive language confounded the political establishment, which had long forgotten the methods by which it had reaped its bounty in 1948-49. *Kach* was banned from the elections in 1988, and found its place on the 'lunatic' fringe of Israeli society. However, there were more subtle, and less embarrassing ways of arriving at a not altogether dissimilar goal: a state cleansed of non-Jews, preferably of a theocratic variety based on the Torah.

Gush Emunim (Bloc of the Faithful) was founded in February 1974 in the wake of the trauma of the *Yom Kippur* War of 1973 as an extra-parliamentary movement to promote Jewish settlement in the Occupied Territories. Religious zealotry was at the heart of the new movement. Typically *Gush Emunim* settlers first established maximalist 'facts on the ground' illegally, after which they negotiated with the authorities, and arrived at a compromise of a withdrawal from the maximalist position. Thus at a stroke, an 'illegal' settlement was legitimised, and afterwards received the government's blessing and financial support. Settlement was facilitated also by the arrangement (*hesder*) whereby

---

[2] In Mergui, Raphael and Philippe Simonnot (1987) *Israel's Ayatollahs. Meir Kahane and the Far Right in Israel,* London, Saqi Books, 38-40, 54-55.

[3] Mergui and Simonnot, 43-48, 85-86.

religious Jews could continue their *yeshiva* ('seminary') studies while serving in the army. By the 1980s, many graduates of the *hesder yeshiva* system had joined the officer corps and the elite units of the army, and considered themselves to be the true heirs of Zionism.

From the beginning, *Gush Emunim* was guided by the teachings of the late Rabbi Avraham Yitzhak Kook, the first Ashkenazi Chief Rabbi of Palestine (1921-35). and those of his son, Rabbi Zvi Yehuda Kook, who became its major spiritual leader until his death in 1982. The elder Kook was the key figure in accommodating the ideology of secular Zionism to classical Orthodoxy—putting the new wine of activist, secular and political Zionism into the old bottles of Orthodox Judaism. His teachings integrated traditional, passive religious longing for the land with the modern, secular and aggressively active praxis of Zionism, giving birth to a comprehensive religious-nationalist Zionism. He saw secular Zionism as an instrument of God to further the messianic redemption and restoration not only of Jews, but of all humanity.

Gush Emunim saw itself as an agent for the general renewal of Zionism, which after the establishment of the state had substituted materialistic achievement for the national goal and mission. It determined to advance national messianic redemption as mandated by the *Torah* by Jewish settlement of 'Judea and Samaria', as an antidote to the materialism and permissiveness which had swept the country. It injected a strong political and violent element into religious Zionism. It enjoyed cordial relations with the different Israeli governments until 'the virus of peace' and talk of 'territorial compromise' began to enter Israeli political rhetoric.

Settling 'Judea and Samaria' prepared the way for the Messiah and was as sacred a duty as observing the Sabbath. The dozens of communities on the hills of 'Judea and Samaria' grew out of the insistence that settlement was a straightforward commandant of the *Torah* which constituted Jewish 'title deeds'. Considering the land to belong to the Jews by Divine command the *Gush* cared little about the indigenous population, whose human rights and aspirations to national self-determination were no match for the divine imperative. The Palestinians were illegitimate tenants and a threat to the redemptive process. The ideology of the *Gush*—which I was to study only much later—was only the tip of an iceberg of a broader religious subculture, which has redefined in religious terms some of the pioneering values of secular Zionism at a time when it had lost much of its vision. Settlement was a natural complement to *Torah*, and each new settlement was a witness to God's choice of the People of Israel, to the truth of *Torah*, and to the word of God and his prophets:

> The land that was desolate shall be tilled, instead of being the desolation that it was in the sight of all who passed by. And they will say, 'This land that was desolate has become like the garden of Eden; and the waste and desolate and ruined towns are now inhabited and fortified.' Then the nations that are left all around you shall know that I, YHWH, have rebuilt the ruined places, and replanted that which was desolate; I, YHWH, have spoken, and I will do it (Ezek 36.34-36).

The activities of the religious-ultranationalist camp raised for me questions about the role of the biblical narrative of the promise and possession of land in the expansionist activity of the Jewish settlers. I was beginning to suspect also that the Israeli occupation was in fact an expansion towards the achievement of 'Greater Israel'. I can date to 1984 also my unease with the biblical narrative which mandated the genocide of the indigenous inhabitants of 'Canaan'. At a time when it was customary to look to selected portions of the Bible as a source for constructing a theology of liberation, I was becoming aware that the Jewish settlers not far from where I lived were engaging in a praxis of a theology of oppression on the basis of other biblical traditions, particularly those relating to 'Israelite origins' and the traditions that demanded the destruction of indigenous peoples.

Further extended study visits in the 1980s and throughout the 1990s, culminating in my tenure as Visiting Professor in Bethlehem University and Scholar-in-Residence in Tantur Ecumenical Institute, Jerusalem (1996-97) provided a lively context for ongoing reflection on the Bible. As is well known, the biblical narrative was also at the core of the motivation for the assassination of Premier Rabin, and is the major plank for the opposition of virtually the entire Orthodox Jewish camp to the 'peace process'.

ZIONISM, THE BIBLE AND TERRORISM

The view that the Bible provides the title-deed for the establishment of the State of Israel,[4] and for its policies since 1948 is so pervasive, not only in Jewish and Christian Zionist circles and in much Christian ecclesial and theological opinion, but even within mainstream Christian theology and university biblical studies, that, until recently, the very attempt to raise the issue was sure to elicit opposition. The disfavour usually took the form of personal abuse, and the intimidation of publishers.

Yet the moral issue must be raised, both out of respect for the truthfulness of history and for the dire consequences of a naive reading of the biblical material concerning land. It was with some surprise that I learned that these biblical narratives have provided alleged legitimacy for virtually all forms of colonialism emanating out of Europe, clothing naked, exploitative imperialism in religious garments.[5] The symbiotic relationship between political and religious motivation for colonialism is most focused in the case of Zionism. If other peoples could adapt the biblical paradigm of conquest and plunder to underpin their claim to analogous 'rights', the rights of Jews appear to have canonical and unique status, and are supported enthusiastically in the West. Indeed, in some Christian and Jewish circles Zionism is viewed as the instrument of God promoting the ingathering of Jews; hence, anyone opposing Zionism opposes God himself.

Support for the 'Restoration of Jews' to Palestine in some Western Christian circles antedated the political Zionism of Theodor Herzl (1860–1904), and can be traced back to views which surfaced at the Reformation. These depended on a literalist interpretation of some of the biblical traditions, and were held zealously in some Christian circles, especially

---

[4] Ben-Gurion claimed that the Bible is the 'Jews' sacrosanct title-deed to Palestine...with a genealogy of 3,500 years' (*The Rebirth and Destiny of Israel*, Philosophical Library, New York, 1954, 100). In the choice of names for some of their settlements, the early Zionists pioneers evoked the Bible: *Rosh Pinna* (The Head of the Corner, Ps 118.22) *Rishon le-Zion* (First for Zion, Isa 41.27), *Nahalal* (Josh 19.15; 21.35), *She'ar Yashuv* (A Remnant shall return, Isa 10.21), *Revivim* (Dew Drops, Ps 65.11), *Petah Tikva*, etc.

[5] I have illustrated the thesis by recourse to three examples: the Catholic Iberian devastation of Latin America, Calvinist Afrikaner exploitation of the blacks of South Africa, and Zionist Jews' exspoliation of Palestinian Arabs: see my *The Bible and Colonialism. A Moral Critique*, Sheffield Academic Press, Sheffield, 1997.

those of a dispensationalist viewpoint.[6] Ironically throughout the Reformation period, and up to the emergence of political Zionism in the 1890s, Jews themselves viewed the biblical texts promoting a culture of Restoration as requiring divine, rather than political intervention. The Orthodox Jewish establishment continued to hold to the traditional position for several more decades, while Reform Judaism rejected the notion that Jews constituted a nation, and any special attachment to Palestine.[7] Nevertheless, the ground had been laid in Reformed Europe, and later yielded a steady stream of supporting literature.

Despite the shifting claims to the contrary and the protestations that Zionism was from the beginning a secular, and even anti-religious enterprise, the Bible is a *sine qua non* for the provision of alleged moral legitimacy. The Zionist claim 'to return' and expel 'the Canaanites' rests with the Bible, since there is no other convincing moral ground to support it. The expulsion of an indigenous people and their replacement by invading settlers is not a programme that commands moral approval in our day, as witnessed by the widespread abhorrence at the expulsion of the Kosovars and the destruction of their villages. However, a straightforward reading of the biblical narrative of 'Israelite origins' offers an example showing that an earlier, analogous Israelite enterprise had not only alleged divine support, but was in fulfilment of the alleged express command of God. The Bible read at face value, then, provides not only a moral framework which transposes Jewish claims into a divinely sanctioned legitimacy, but postulates the taking possession of the Promised Land and the forcible expulsion of the indigenous population as the fulfilment of a biblical mandate. Without the Bible Zionism would be a discourse exclusively in the conquest mode, as against a moral one. While some religious Jews are embarrassed by the obvious conflict between the Bible's mandate and decent human behaviour, most of even them do little more than bear guilt for their prudent silence.[8]

---

[6] See Sharif, Regina S., *Non-Jewish Zionism. Its Roots in Western History*, Zed Press, London, 1983 for details from the past.

[7] For a discussion of the *volte face* with respect to Zionism of both the Jewish Orthodox and Reform establishment see my *Zionism and the State of Israel: A Moral Inquiry*, London, Routledge, 1999, 69-81.

[8] But see my treatment of Jewish critiques of Zionism in *Zionism and the State of Israel*, 225-51.

Although Zionism was a secular ideology and enterprise from the beginning, and was bitterly opposed by the religious establishment, some of its proponents, when it suited their purposes, could point to the Bible in support of its achievement. In particular, the narratives of the promise of land to Abraham and his descendants and the execution of the promise in the conquest as narrated in the Book of Joshua were available. Although apologists for Zionism appeal to a number of other factors also (endemic antisemitism in Europe, the *Shoah*, etc.) the appeal to the Bible is the most convincing to the Western world, since its witness can be skilfully deployed to argue that the Zionist conquest is merely restoring the land to the Jews in accordance with the clear intentions of the God of the Christians as well as of the Jews.

Successive Israeli governments have been quick to latch on to Zionist Christian circles whose ideology derives from an unique, literalist interpretation of apocalyptic and prophetic biblical texts. In line with the precedent of courting the support of Christian evangelicals established by Premiers Begin, Shamir and Rabin, in his January 1998 visit to Washington Prime Minister Netanyahu attended a reception hosted by Christian Evangelicals. Afterwards, Rev Jerry Falwell pledged that he and the Southern Baptists would mobilise '200,000 evangelical pastors ... to go into their pulpits and use their influence in support of the State of Israel and the Prime Minister' (Martin Sieff, *Jewish Chronicle*, 30 January 1998, p. 3).

The influence of the biblical narrative in the secular intentions of Zionism is reflected even in the 'father of Zionism', the religiously indifferent Theodor Herzl. It was the testimony of the Bible above all which allowed him in *Der Judenstaat* (1896) to insist that Jews worldwide constituted one people and a *distinctive nationality* (pp. 76-79), whose problem could be solved only through the *restoration* of the Jewish state (p. 69).[9] He insisted that 'Palestine is our ever-memorable historic home', and that its very name 'would attract our people with a force of marvellous potency' (p. 96). Herzl ended his pamphlet by promising that 'a wondrous

---

[9] The page numbers refer to *The Jewish State*, Dover Edition, New York, 1988, a translation of Herzl's *Der Judenstaat. Versuch einer Modernen Lösung der Judenfrage*, M. Breitenstein's Verlags-Buchhandlung, Leipzig und Wien, 1896. The English translation by Sylvie d'Avigdor (*A Jewish State*, and in 1946, *The Jewish State*) was first published by the American Zionist Emergency Council. *Der Judenstaat* might be translated more appropriately by 'The State for Jews', to distinguished it from the implications of a Jewish state (*Jüdischer Staat*).

generation of Jews will spring into existence. The Maccabeans will rise again.' Furthermore, fearing that the option of Jews settling in Uganda, discussed at length at the Sixth Zionist Congress at Basle (22-28 August 1903), might split the Zionist movement, Herzl emphasised that Uganda would only be a staging post to the ultimate goal of Palestine, and lifting his right hand, he cried out, '*Im Yeshkakhekh Yerushalayim...*' ('If I forget you, O Jerusalem, may my right hand wither'), quoting Ps 137.5.[10]

Although not widely acknowledged, the British clergyman, William Hechler, played a critical role in assisting Herzl's Zionist plans.[11] Already in 1882 Hechler had argued in a pamphlet (*Die bevorstehende Rückkehr der Juden nach Palästina*) for the restoration of Jews to their ancestral land, in fulfilment of the Hebrew prophets. Soon after the publication of *Der Judenstaat* he presented himself in Herzl's study in Vienna, promising his help. Relying on his good reputation with the Grand Duke of Baden—he had been a tutor to his children—Hechler arranged Herzl's meeting with him, and later in Jerusalem with the Grand Duke's uncle, Kaiser Wilhelm II. As he made clear in a letter to the Grand Duke (26 March 1896)—in which he also promised to send three copies of Herzl's pamphlet—Hechler saw a clear correspondence between *Der Judenstaat* and the Hebrew prophetic tradition of Jewish restoration. Indeed, in a letter to a colleague in Jerusalem in 1898 he wrote,

> We are now entering, thanks to the Zionist Movement, into
> Israel's Messianic age. Thus, it is not a matter these days of
> opening all the doors of your churches to the Jews, but rather
> of opening the gates of their homeland, and of sustaining them
> in their work of clearing the land, and irrigating it, and bringing
> water to it. All of this ... is messianic work; all of this the breath
> of the Holy Spirit announces. But, first, the dry bones must
> come to life, and draw together.[12]

Earlier, while discussing Leo Pinsker's *Autoemancipation* with the author, Hechler, arguing against Pinsker's toleration of a Jewish homeland other than in Palestine, took out his Bible and pointed to passages in

---

[10] Laqueur, Walter, *History of Zionism*, Holt, Rinehart and Winston, New York, 1972, 129.

[11] See Merkley, Paul C., *The Politics of Christian Zionism 1891-1948*, Frank Cass, London/ Portland OR, 1998, 3-34.

[12] In Merkley, 15-16.

Amos, Jeremiah, Isaiah, and elsewhere, making clear God's plan to bring the diaspora to Jerusalem.

Moreover, Herzl records that on the train returning to Vienna after meeting the Grand Duke of Baden, Hechler unfolded his maps of Palestine, and instructed him for hours on end that the northern frontier of the Jewish state should be the mountains facing Cappadocia, and the southern, the Suez Canal. 'The slogan to be circulated: The Palestine of David and Solomon'. Hechler was so attached to a literalist reading of the Bible that he was confident that archaeologists would find on Mount Nebo the manuscripts of the five books of Moses, written in his own hand, and hidden away in the Ark. The discovery would prove how deranged were the theologians who said that Moses wrote nothing. Such was the respect for Hechler's friendship with Herzl that he was the last person, outside of Herzl's immediate family, to visit him on 2 July 1904, the eve of his death.[13] On the day of Herzl's burial, Israel Zangwill, the Anglo-Jewish writer and propagandist, compared him with Moses, who had been given only a sight of the Promised Land. But all was not lost, since, after Moses, Herzl 'has laid his hands upon the head of more than one Joshua, and filled them with the spirit of his wisdom to carry on his work'.[14] The exploits of Joshua would be appealed to again.

On the fundamentalist wing, USA Televangelist Pat Robertson considered Israel's 1982 merciless invasion of Lebanon to be a modern Joshua event, and urged American viewers to phone President Reagan offering encouragement to Israel's war. Joshua featured again on 13 September 1993 when, according to a report in the *Washington Post* (14 September, A1), President Bill Clinton awoke at 3.00 a.m., reread the Book of Joshua, and resumed work on his speech. At the famous signing of the Declaration of Principles he introduced Prime Minister Rabin and President Arafat on the White House lawn, announcing to the world that both people pledged themselves to a shared future, 'shaped by the values of the Torah, the Koran, and the Bible'. President Clinton's address was a mixture of Bible-based exhortation in the Baptist tradition, and shrewd political manoeuvring. The late Premier Rabin's speech also referred to the Bible. In the light of the history of reception of these

---

[13] In Merkley, 16, 22, 31.
[14] Zangwill, Israel, *Speeches, Articles and Letters of Israel Zangwill, Selected and Edited by Maurice Simon*, Soncino Press, London, 1937, 131-32.

texts one must question whether one can rely on 'the values of the Torah, the Koran, and the Bible' to promote justice and peace, and underpin the imperatives of human and national rights.

While appeal to the Bible as providing moral legitimation for the establishment of the State of Israel is common two observations are in order. Firstly, it refers mainly to those traditions which portray Yahweh as, what many modern people would regard as a racist, militaristic xenophobe, whose views would not be tolerated in any modern democracy. Secondly, the ideologues of Zionism were much more influenced by nineteenth century European colonialist attitudes. In the vision of the First Zionist Congress (29-31 August 1897), the Zionist project would 'advance the interests of civilisation, by establishing a cultural station, on the shortest road to Asia'.[15] Herzl himself presented the proposed state for Jews as 'a portion of the rampart of Europe against Asia, an outpost of civilisation (*Kultur*) opposed to barbarism'.[16] Elsewhere he reflects the world-view of European racist superiority. He assured the Grand Duke of Baden that Jews returning to their 'historic fatherland' would do so as representatives of Western civilisation, bringing 'cleanliness, order and the well-established customs of the Occident to this plague-ridden, blighted corner of the Orient'.[17] In Joseph Conrad's terms, Herzl's Jewish State would be an 'outpost of progress' in 'the heart of darkness'.

Alas, the discipline of biblical studies over the last hundred years also has not been free of stereotypical Eurocentric colonialist attitudes. To give only one of many examples, William Foxwell Albright, a decade after the full horrors of the Nazi genocidal activity were revealed, had no qualms about the plunder attendant upon Joshua's enterprise, which he understood in a largely literalist fashion:

---

[15] (1911) *Protokoll des I. Zionistenkongresses in Basel vom 29. bis 31. August 1897,* Prag: Selbstverlag—Druck von Richard Brandeis in Prag, 15.

[16] *The Jewish State,* 96.

[17] *The Complete Diaries,* Vol I: 343. Herzl began his Diaries in 1895, and continued until shortly before his death. Seven volumes of the Letters and Diaries have been published, Vols I-III edited by Johannes Wachten *et al.*(1983-85), and Vols IV-VII by Barbara Schäfer (1990-96). Raphael Patai edited an English translation of the diaries in five volumes. In general, I quote from Patai's edition (rendered Herzl 1960), which I have checked against the original in Wachten and Schäfer. Where I judge it to be important, I give the original German (or other language) from the latter (rendered Herzl 1983-96). I indicate the volume number of the English translation by 1,2, etc., and the German ones by I, II, etc.

From the impartial standpoint of a philosopher of history, it often seems necessary that a people of markedly inferior type should vanish before a people of superior potentialities, since there is a point beyond which racial mixture cannot go without disaster ... Thus the Canaanites, with their orgiastic nature worship, their cult of fertility in the form of serpent symbols and sensuous nudity, and their gross mythology, were replaced by Israel, with its pastoral simplicity and purity of life, its lofty monotheism, and its severe code of ethics.[18]

Moreover, the treatment of the theme of the promise and conquest of the Promised Land in recent Western scholarship is not a model of moral exegesis.[19]

FACING THE TRUTH

A moral inquiry into the relationship between the biblical narrative and the establishment of the State of Israel must take account of both the real intentions of the Zionist ideologues and the actual policies of the state with respect to the indigenous Arab population of Palestine. Many obstacles make that task more difficult. Western theological and religious discussion on Israel-Palestine has been distorted by one of the most successful disinformation campaigns in modern times carried out by the State of Israel and its supporters abroad, as well as by the parameters within which the highly desirable dialogue between Christians and Jews

---

[18] *From the Stone Age to Christianity: Monotheism and the Historical Process*, Doubleday, New York, 1957, 280-81. Prior to Keith Whitelam's critique (*The Invention of Ancient Israel. The Silencing of Palestinian History*, Routledge, London, 1996, p. 88), no commentator had drawn attention to Albright's undisguised racist attitudes, which were typical of virtually every Western colonial enterprise which predicated that the 'superior' peoples of the West had the right to exploit, and in some cases exterminate the 'natives'. Reflecting conventional values, Albright also judged that through Zionism Jews would bring to the Near East all the benefits of European civilisation ('Why the Near East needs the Jews', *New Palestine* 32 [1942]: 12-13).

[19] While in his *The Gospel and the Land* (1974) and *The Territorial Dimensions of Judaism* (1982) W.D. Davies considers 'the land' from virtually every conceivable perspective, little attention is given to broadly moral and human rights' issues, in particular the rights of the indigenous peoples. On the wider plea for a moral exegesis see my *The Bible and Colonialism*, pp. 216-86 and *Zionism and the State of Israel*, 168-80.

A Living Stone—Selected Essays and Addresses

in fact comports itself.[20] The benevolent assessment of Zionism and the State of Israel is due in no small measure to the success with which the ideologues of Zionism and the historiographers of the state have concealed the real intentions of the Zionist enterprise and the realities surrounding the establishment of the state and its behaviour since.

Until recently, Israeli propaganda had convinced many that the dispossession and dispersion of another people was only forced upon Israel by circumstances. The fabricated official version of history claims that the Zionists intended no ill to the Arabs of Palestine; that, nevertheless, Israel was born into an unreasonably hostile environment; that all Zionist efforts at compromise were rejected by the Arabs; that the altogether more powerful Arabs lost the 1947-49 war; that, in the course of that war, the Palestinian leadership ordered their people to quit their homes. The land had a kind of civilisational barrenness—it was 'empty' in the sense that its inhabitants were without deep roots in the land, and, in any case, being 'natives' scarcely counted; that the neglected land was 'redeemed' by Jewish labour, which 'made the desert bloom'; that Zionism benefited the natives, who nevertheless remain ungrateful; that the few unsavoury actions in 1947-49 were the result of the stresses of war; and that all Israel's wars and invasions, and its actions against the Palestinians were purely defensive, and so forth. That fabricated history has moulded the perceptions of much of the international community. Even in the face of overwhelming evidence to the contrary,[21] the cant is repeated, not least in religious and theological circles. Indeed, the denial of the Palestinian *Nakba*, coupled with the insistence that Israel is virtually above reproach and without responsibility for restitution, appears to be virtually a necessary tenet of Jewish-Christian dialogue.

Any judicious, and every moral discussion of the issue must consider the extent of the Palestinian *Nakba*. The 'return of the Jews to their homeland' had as a necessary Zionist corollary the expulsion of most of the Palestinian Arabs in 1947-49 and again in 1967. At the first

---

[20] Consideration of the origins of Zionism and of the birth of the State of Israel in much Christian-Jewish dialogue betrays either ignorance, naiveté or dishonesty, and contradicts both the theory of Zionism and the reality of the expulsion of the Palestinians. It distorts facts of history, omits core elements of the discourse, and makes claims that lack substance. See my *Zionism and the State of Israel*, 123-31.

[21] See my discussion of the foundational myths of the State of Israel in *Zionism and the State of Israel*, 187-221.

214

opportunity (1947–49), the Zionists dispossessed and dispersed some three quarters of a million Palestinians. Their forcible removal was no accident, but was the result of elementary Zionist intentions from the beginning, and of systematic planning from the mid 1930s. With few exceptions, the major urban centres, including substantially Arab towns, were emptied of their Palestinian residents, with their assets falling to the Zionists. The estimates of the Palestinian Arabs displaced in 1947–49 fall between 700,000 and 800,000. This constituted 54 per cent of the total Palestinian population of Mandatory Palestine, and has grown to create a Palestinian diaspora in excess of five million.[22] Moreover, hundreds of Arab villages were depopulated and destroyed—to ensure that their inhabitants would never return[23]—and even their sacred places were profaned.[24]

The war of June 1967 brought on a further catastrophe for the Palestinians. In its immediate aftermath, Israeli Premier Eshkol convened secret meetings of the cabinet (15–19 June) to discuss the demographic problem arising from the fact that, unlike the situation in 1948, the majority of the Palestinians remained *in situ*, even though some 300,000 fled or were expelled. The disjuncture between what actually happened to the indigenous Arab population of Palestine in 1947–49, and later in

---

[22] See Elia Zureik, 'Palestinian Refugees and Peace', in *Journal of Palestine Studies* 93(1994): 5–17, Table 3, 11. Salman H Abu-Sitta argues for a total figure of 935,000 expelled Palestinians (p. 14), and calculates that the maximum estimate of Palestinians in 1998 is 8,415,930, of which 5,477,745 are refugees (p. 15) (*The Palestinian Nakba 1948. The Register of Depopulated Localities in Palestine*, with accompanying map, *Palestine 1948 50 Years after Al Nakba. The Towns and Villages Depopulated by the Zionist Invasion of 1948*, The Palestine Return Centre, 1998, London).

[23] Walid Khalidi's research team examined the remains of 404 of the 418 destroyed villages, half the total number of Arab villages in Mandated Palestine (*All that Remains. The Palestinian Villages Occupied and Depopulated by Israel in 1948*, Institute for Palestine Studies, Washington D.C., 1992). Abu-Sitta names 531 destroyed villages.

[24] Khalidi's photographs show theme parks or recreation grounds constructed on the sites of some of the destroyed villages. Moreover, an Orthodox Church in 'Ayn Karim was converted into public toilets, the mosque in Safad into an art gallery, and one in Caesarea and 'Ayn Hud into a restaurant and bar, etc. Moreover, the Hilton Hotel in Tel Aviv and the Plaza Hotel in Jerusalem, and the adjacent parks, both called Independence Park, were constructed over Muslim cemeteries (Uri Davis, *Israel: An Apartheid State*, Zed, London/New Jersey, 1987, 24). The case of the Christian village of Biram is particularly poignant (see Elias Chacour, *Blood Brothers. A Palestinian's Struggle for Reconciliation in the Middle East*, Kingsway Publications, Eastbourne, 1985: 36–38, 71, and Sami Aldeeb, *Discriminations contre les non-juifs tant chrétien que musulmans en Israël*, Pax Christi, Lausanne, 9). The remains of Deir Yassin—the scene of the most significant massacre of 1948—have been converted into a mental hospital.

1967, and the official Israeli version is striking.[25] The 'transfer' of the Arab population was promoted by virtually the whole pantheon of Zionist ideologues, albeit mostly in strict secrecy, a fact which comprehensively unmasks the myth of the benevolent and peaceful intentions of Zionism.[26]

Moreover, much has happened during the fifty years of the state's existence to concentrate the mind. In addition to the wars of 1947–49 and 1967, Israel participated in wars in 1956, 1973, and 1982, as well as in the earlier assault on Lebanon in 1977, and subsequent ones in 1993 and 1996. In addition, there is the challenge to moral serenity involved in the ongoing Palestinian diaspora, the emigration of Christians from the Holy Land, the unfulfilled creation of an Arab state, and the uncertain future of Jerusalem.

Israeli appeal to an exclusively 'defensive ethos' is merely a public relations device, as well as an exercise in conscious self-deception, assuaging both world opinion and the consciences of Zionists. Moreover, the consistency with which the State of Israel is excused from having to conform to decent behaviour is one of the great eccentricities of twentieth-century political ethics. Whereas elsewhere the perpetrators of colonial plunder would be charged with war crimes and crimes against humanity, the Zionist conquest is judged widely to be a just and appropriate political accomplishment. Several of the leaders of the state, including at least four Prime Ministers (Begin, Shamir, Rabin and Peres), three of them honoured by the award of the Nobel Peace Prize in an Orwellian farce, have perpetrated crimes against humanity, as have at least two members of former Prime Minister Netanyahu's cabinet (Ariel Sharon and Rafael Eitan). But most alarmingly from a moral perspective, the injustice to the indigenous population is passed over in most Western discourse, including biblical and theological scholarship, and in some religious circles is even clothed in the garment of piety.

---

[25] The Israeli government pamphlet on the refugee question, first published in 1953, proclaims that the Palestinian Arabs were incited to leave temporarily by express instructions broadcast by the president of the Arab Higher Executive and surrounding Arab states, to afford the Arab forces the opportunity to defeat the Zionist invaders without Palestinian losses. The charge is a component of the standard Israeli myth of origins, notwithstanding the absence of corroborating evidence, and the presence of abundant proof to expose it as false. The destruction of the villages of the displaced Palestinians is passed over in the Zionist myth or origins, and their remains are systematically covered over. See my *Zionism and the State of Israel*, 27-33, 204-206.

[26] See the evidence in my *Zionism and the State of Israel*, 190-204.

Indeed, in some quarters, the Zionist conquest is accorded unique religious significance, despite the catastrophic consequences for the people of the region. Much of the rationale for such benevolent appraisal of the Zionist colonial plunder derives from engagement with particular traditions of the Bible, and with a literalist interpretation of the biblical traditions of land and of some of its messianic texts. In most Western Christian and Jewish theological and religious circles the Zionist prize is viewed as being no more than what the Jewish people deserve in virtue of the promises of God outlined in the Bible. This has not always been the case. Indeed it appears that the coming into existence of the State of Israel, and the reality of its ongoing position among the nations of the world demands an ongoing estimation of its theological significance.

Before the state was declared in 1948 there was little enthusiasm in the mainstream Churches for its establishment. Yet today, in some quarters, Christians are required to embrace the reality of the state since it is alleged to be an inseparable ingredient of Jewish self-definition, while in other quarters it is accorded profound religious significance, and is even related to the Second Coming of Christ and the events of the end-time. It is a matter of some scholastic interest to enquire into how the altogether secular ideology of political Zionism, virtually universally despised by both the Orthodox and Reform wings of Judaism until the 1930s,[27] has come to have invested in it such religious significance.

Except in some evangelical Christian circles, prior to its coming into being, there was little Christian enthusiasm for the foundation of a Jewish state. This was certainly the case among Christians in communion with Rome, as reflected in the views of the Holy See since the emergence of political Zionism. The World Council of Churches too—a body formed in the same year as the foundation of the State of Israel—has seldom been more than lukewarm towards Israel. There is today, and there has been throughout the last fifty years, a striking coalescence of views between these two major wings of Christianity, and the leadership of the Jerusalem Church. In addition to concern about specifically religious issues, there is widespread concern for the human and national rights of both peoples. These cluster around concern for equality for the three religions and the

---

[27] See my *Zionism and the State of Israel* (67-102) for an account of the changing religious estimation of Zionism, from being a despised secular enterprise to being clothed in sacred garments.

two nations. The fact of Israel's existence and its hitherto unchallengable power is rather taken for granted, and the religious leadership by and large has settled for an approximate justice for the Palestinians, without demanding the rolling back of the Zionist aggression and the full compensation which a full justice requires.

CONCLUSION

While the Bible is not the only provider of alleged moral legitimacy for Zionism it is the most powerful moral one, without which the Zionist conquest would be no more legitimate than any other colonial plunder. The Bible read at face value provides not only a moral framework which transposes Jewish claims into a divinely sanctioned legitimacy, but postulates the taking possession of the Promised Land and the forcible expulsion of the indigenous population as the fulfilment of a biblical mandate. However, the appeal to the Bible is mainly to those traditions which portray Yahweh as a promoter of an ethnicist and xenophobic 'nationalism', premised on attitudes of racial dominance and exclusion. While these attitudes fit easily with those of nineteenth century European colonialism they do not advance the goal of other traditions within Judaism, such as that inviting the Jewish community to be a light to the nations.

The philosophy of Zionism has succeeded in refracting the whole history of the Israelite-Jewish people through its lens. Moreover, conventional Eurocentric historiography has distorted our view of 'ancient Israel', and virtually silenced the wider history of the region. Political Zionism, a child of the nineteenth-century European colonial age, has successfully portrayed all Jewish aspirations since the biblical period in its terms, and has seduced the mainstream of Western thought also along those lines. Zionist ideology, detested from the beginning by virtually all shades of religious Jews, has been embraced by the establishment of virtually all sectors of Jewish religious opinion.

To a substantial extent the Christian Churches and mainstream Christian Theology, too, have been seduced into accepting a Zionist rendering of all Jewish history. Sectors of these agencies concur, either by direct support or silence, in the ongoing humiliation of an innocent people. The prevailing theological, biblical and religious assessments of

218

Zionism and the State of Israel should be subjected to a critique which reflects the concerns of justice, human rights and international legality. Otherwise one is in danger of according the God of the Bible the dubious accolade of being the great xenophobic, ethnocentric and militaristic ethnic-cleanser.

ETHNIC CLEANSING AND THE BIBLE:
A MORAL CRITIQUE

This 2002 article in Holy Land Studies *identifies the contribution of the biblical narrative to both Jewish and Christian Zionist ideology.*

Zionism's claims to exclusive Jewish title to 'the land of Israel' (*Eretz Yisrael*) rest on the Bible, even though its leading proponents were either non-religious, atheists or agnostics. Although it was a secular ideology and enterprise from the beginning, and was bitterly opposed by the Jewish religious establishment, when it suited their purposes its supporters could look to the Bible for support, particularly the narratives of the promise of land to Abraham and his descendants, and the execution of the promise in the narrative of Joshua's conquest. Even for secular or atheist nationalists uninterested in it as the repository of a theological claim, the biblical narrative could function as the 'historical account' of Jews' title to the land. Thus, for David Ben-Gurion, Israel's first Prime Minister, the Bible was the 'Jews' sacrosanct title-deed to Palestine...with a genealogy of 3,500 years.'[1] For Theodor Herzl (1860-1904), the founder of Political Zionism, the biblical narrative was available to provide legitimising support whenever called upon.

Herzl had no inward relationship to Judaism or to his own Jewishness.[2] Although his aspiration to construct a separate state 'like

---

[1] Ben-Gurion 1954: 100. Ben-Gurion regularly convened the 'Prime Minster's Bible Study Circle', which included President Zalman Shazar. His lecture, 'The Bible and the Jewish People' (Nahalal, 20 July 1964) makes abundant use of biblical texts, especially those dealing with the promise of restoration. While he alludes to the Hebrew prophets and their concern for justice, he does not deal with the injunctions to disinherit the Canaanites, the Joshua legend, nor with the biblical traditions that reflect racist, ethnicist, xenophobic and militaristic tendencies. His sole, oblique reference to the indigenous Palestinians, is that while the whole world regarded Israel with respect and admiration, 'Our Arab neighbours have as yet not made peace with our existence, and their leaders are declaring their desire to destroy us' (1972: 294). See also Moshe Dayan's *Living with the Bible* (1978).

[2] So Martin Buber at Herzl's graveside (1904) - see Wistrich 1995: 30-31. Although Herzl's motivation was utterly secular, at various times people referred to him as the Messiah, or King of Israel, and as the fulfilment of the prophecies of the Jewish Scriptures.

every other nation' linked Zionism with other nineteenth-century European nationalisms his enterprise involved special pleading, since the basic assumption of European nationalisms was the indigenous nature of a specific community, and its desire for independence from the relevant imperial power. Nevertheless, just as 'Pan-Germanism' regarded all persons of German race, blood or descent, wherever they lived as *das Volk* which owed its primary loyalty to Germany, the *Heimat*, so Herzl insisted in his *Der Judenstaat* (1896) that Jews world-wide constituted one people and a *distinctive nationality (Volkspersönlichkeit)* (p. 18), whose problem could be solved only through the *restoration (Herstellung)* of the Jewish state (p. 7).[3] However, despite the anti-religious bias of his Zionism, he acknowledged that the notions of 'Chosen People', and 'return' to the 'Promised Land' would be potent factors in mobilising Jewish opinion.

Although careful to rule out a Jewish theocracy—'We shall keep our priests within the confines of their temples in the same way as we keep our professional army within the confines of their barracks' (p. 71)—Herzl promised that 'The Temple will be visible from long distances, for it is only our ancient faith that has kept us together' (p. 36). He appealed for the support of the rabbis (p. 54), and asserted, 'Our community of race is peculiar and unique, for we are bound together only by the faith of our fathers' (p. 71). Moreover, 'Palestine is our ever-memorable historic home' (*Palästina ist unsere unvergeßliche historische Heimat*), and its very name 'would attract our people with a force of marvellous potency' (p. 30). He ended his pamphlet by promising that 'a wondrous generation of Jews will spring into existence. The Maccabeans will rise again' (p. 79). Later, fearing that the option of establishing a Jewish settlement in East Africa might split the movement, Herzl emphasised that Uganda would only be a staging post to the ultimate goal of Palestine, and lifting his right hand, he cried out, '*Im Yeshkakhekh*

---

[3] The German original was translated by Sylvie d'Avigdor as *A Jewish State*, and in 1946 as *The Jewish State*. The seventh edition, *The Jewish State. An Attempt at a Modern Solution of the Jewish Question*, revised with a foreword by Israel Cohen was published in London (Henry Pordes) in 1993, and it is to that edition that page references are made here. *Der Judenstaat* might be translated more appropriately by 'The State for Jews', to distinguish it from the implications of the Jewish state (*Der Jüdische Staat*). Herzl composed the first draft between June and July 1895, and summarised it in the *Jewish Chronicle* (17 January 1896), 'A 'Solution of the Jewish Question''. The editorial was sceptical of 'a scheme which is the outcome of despair.' For several more years the editor continued to view Zionism as 'ill-considered, retrogressive, impracticable, even dangerous.'

Yerushalayim...' ('If I forget you, O Jerusalem, may my right hand wither'), quoting Psalm 137.5 (Laqueur 1972: 129).

That the Zionist movement would arrogate to itself the agency for the *restoration* of the Jewish people to its ancestral land was, for Orthodox Jews, nothing short of blasphemy. Thus, rabbis representing all shades of opinion denounced Zionism as a fanaticism, and contrary to the Jewish scriptures. 'Zionism, and Herzl himself, were anathema to the most illustrious and influential of eastern European rabbis almost as a matter of course' (Vital 1999: 625). In the west, his own Chief Rabbi, Moritz Güdemann of Vienna, initially a supporter of Herzl's project, objected that the Jews were not a nation, and that Zionism was incompatible with the teachings of Judaism (1897: 42). Likewise, Grand Rabbin Zadok Kahn of France.[4] Moreover, the executive committee of the German Rabbinical Council 'formally and publicly condemned the 'efforts of the so-called Zionists to create a Jewish national state in Palestine' as contrary to Holy Writ'.[5] Belgium's Grand Rabbin, M.A. Bloch, also protested against the First Zionist Congress at Basle, describing its aspirations as 'far from those of Judaism' (Jakobivits 1982: 22 n 17). The British Commonwealth's Chief Rabbi Hermann Adler regarded the Basle Congress as an 'egregious blunder' and an 'absolutely mischievous project', and judged Herzlian Zionism to be 'opposed to the teaching of Judaism'.[6]

The predominantly secular Zionist movement was a rebellion against, and a conscious repudiation of classical Judaism and its theological tenets. For many political Zionists, religion was irrational, non-empirical, imperialistic, and an altogether repressive and regressive force, from which no anthropological validity, social bonding, psychological insight, or existential illumination could be expected. Indeed, in the camp of strident anti-religious secularism one's way to salvation was to escape from the prison of the sacred. Thus, Yosef Hayim Brenner declared, 'From the hypnotic spell of the twenty-four books of the Bible I have been liberated

---

[4] *Diaries,* 18 November 1895. Herzl began his Diaries in 1895, and continued until shortly before his death. Raphael Patai edited an English translation in five volumes (Herzl 1960). His diaries and other writings were published in the original language(s) between 1983 and 1996 (Herzl 1983-1996).

[5] Vital 1975: 336. Herzl referred to the five rabbis, two Orthodox and three Liberal, contemptuously as the *Protestrabbiner* (*Die Welt,* 16 July 1897 – see Jakobivits 1982: 6).

[6] Hermann Adler's writings on political Zionism are limited to a sermon (12 November 1898) published in full in the *Jewish Chronicle* under the title, 'Religious versus Political Zionism' (25 November 1898).

for some time now' (in Diamond 1986: 59, 154, 18). In the estimation of
Karl Kautsky, Judaism was a weight of lead attached to the feet of Jews
who eagerly sought progress (see Laqueur 1972: 420). For such people,
religion was a symptom of Jewry's sickness in exile. For a further minority,
the break with the Jewish past should be not only with religion, but with
Jewish history itself. Zionist Palestine would be new, secular, and
qualitatively different from the past of the diaspora. Its Jewish nationalism
would stand on its own feet, free of its religious modality.

Nevertheless, according to the late Chief Rabbi of the British
Commonwealth, Lord Sir Immanuel Jakobivits,

> The origins of the Zionist idea are of course entirely religious.
> The slogan, 'The Bible is our mandade' is a credo hardly less
> insistently pleaded by many secularists than by religious
> believers as the principal basis of our legal and historical claim
> to the Land of Israel...Modern Political Zionism itself could
> never have struck root if it had not planted its seeds in soil
> ploughed up and fertilised by the millennial conditioning of
> religious memories, hopes, prayers and visions of our eventual
> return to Zion...No rabbinical authority disputes that our claim
> to a Divine mandate (and we have no other which cannot be
> invalidated) extends over the entire Holy Land within its historic
> borders and that halachically we have no right to surrender
> this claim (1982: 19-20).[7]

In the estimation of another of Herman Adler's successors, Chief
Rabbi Jonathan Sacks considers that the State of Israel for many religious
Jews is 'the most powerful collective expression' of Jewry, and 'the most
significant development in Jewish life since the Holocaust'.[8] In the course
of his speech at the Service for Israel's Fiftieth Anniversary, Sacks portrayed

---

[7] Jakobivits goes on: 'But what is questionable is whether we must, or indeed may, assert it
at the risk of thousands of lives, if not the life of the State itself. Any religious law is set
aside...if it involves a danger to life...We are halachically compelled to leave the judgment
on what provides the optimum security for Jewish life in Israel to the verdict of military
and political experts, not rabbis. Included as a major factor in this difficult judgment must
also be the overriding concern to preserve the Jewish character of Israel which may
clearly depend on the proportion of Jews within the State' (pp. 20-21). He asserts the
unique Jewish title to Jerusalem, and accepts the need for an eventual withdrawal 'on
Israeli terms' from territories occupied (p. 21).

[8] *The Daily Telegraph*, 31 December, 1993: 21.

the birth of the state as a coming to the promised land in the line of the biblical stories of Abraham and Sarah, Moses, Ezra and Nehemiah. Adhering to the 'canonical' Zionist reading of Jewish history, he alluded to how the early pioneers who settled the land and built the foundations of the state faced difficulties: 'On the very day of Israel's birth it was plunged into war on all its borders by all neighbours; and it has lived with the threat of war and terror ever since.' While he recalls with sadness the 20,000 men and women who died defending their country so that Israel should exist, he spares no thought for the catastrophe visited upon the native Arab population of Palestine, and the inhabitants of the surrounding states who have paid a severe price for the prize of Zionism. Instead, we learn that the Jewish pioneers created farms and forests 'out of a barren landscape'. Sacks concluded, echoing the Exodus story and bestowing sacral significance on Political Zionism: 'The very existence of the State of Israel after nearly two thousand years of dispersion testifies to the power of hope sustained by prayer. So tonight we give thanks to God for the land and the State of Israel which brought our people from darkness to light, from slavery to freedom, from death to new life.'[9]

The role of the biblical narrative within the Zionist ideology increased significantly in the wake of the 1967 War and the rise of *Gush Emunim*. The biblical paradigm was the backdrop for the Zionist self-portrayal as the (sole) 'descendants of the biblical children of Israel', while the natives were 'Canaanites'. This introduced into the secular discourse a religious authority justifying the new conquest of the land and the maltreatment of its population. Measured against the divine right of the colonisers, appeal to the human rights of the local population, considered to be 'interlopers', 'sojourners' and obstacles to the divine plan, carried no conviction.

More recently, the otherwise forward-looking and ecumenically eirenic statement *Dabru Emet* (Speak the Truth), written by 150 prominent Jews in the USA (12 September 2000), promotes exclusively Jewish claims to Palestine, clothing the Zionist enterprise in the garment of piety, even though its determination to create a state for Jews would require the 'ethnic-cleansing' of the indigenous Arab population. Acceptance of these claims and its contemporary implications is a requirement of the conventional Jewish-Christian dialogue:

---

[9] Speech at the Service for Israel's Fiftieth Anniversary in the Presence of HRH The Prince of Wales, at St John's Wood Synagogue, London, 29th April 1998.

Christians can respect the claim of the Jewish people upon the land of Israel. The most important event for Jews since the Holocaust has been the reestablishment of a Jewish state in the Promised Land. As members of a biblically-based religion, Christians appreciate that Israel was promised—and given—to Jews as the physical centre of the covenant between them and God. Many Christians support the State of Israel for reasons far more profound than mere politics. As Jews, we applaud this support.[10]

Virtually everything, then, rests on the authority of the Bible. While other factors, such as 'endemic', 'irridentist' antisemitism in nineteenth-century Europe, the barbarism of the *Shoah* in the twentieth, etc., could be invoked as justifications for establishing a state, they might not be considered adequate to warrant ethnically cleansing Palestine of its indigenous non-Jewish population.[11] The Zionist conquest would need an 'idea' to redeem it.

Since, as Joseph Conrad's Marlow noted, 'the conquest of the earth is not a pretty thing when you look into it too much,' colonisers invariably sought some ideological principle to justify their actions, and when these involved significant exploitation, the search was all the more intense. Awaiting the turn of the tide on the Thames as he embarked on another colonial expedition, Marlow mused on the enterprise of imperial conquest, whether in Roman Britain or in the European Congo. Conquerors needed only brute force, and grabbed what they could get with violence and aggravated murder on a great scale. What redeemed the 'not-pretty' conquest of the earth—the taking it away from those who have a different complexion or slightly flatter noses than ourselves—

---

[10] However, movement away from 'the physical centre' is a feature in a number of New Testament texts with their centrifugal missionary dynamic moving out from Jerusalem to the ends of the earth. The author of the Gospel of Luke-Acts of the Apostle, for example, has the risen Jesus say, "Stay in the city, until you are clothed with power from on high" (Luke 24.49), and "But you shall receive power when the Holy Spirit has come upon you; and you shall be my witnesses in Jerusalem and in all Judea and Samaria and to the end of the earth" (Acts 1.8). In a similar vein, the Gospel of Matthew ends with the risen Jesus exhorting his disciples to 'make disciples of all nations'. See the discussion in Prior 1995: 52-56.

[11] According to Moshe Menuhin, future Zionist leaders schooled in the Hebrew Gymnasia Herzlia in Palestine had it drummed into their young hearts that 'the fatherland must become ours, '*goyim rein*' (clear of Gentiles-Arabs)' (1969: 52).

is the idea only, something you can set up, bow down before, and offer a sacrifice to (*Heart of Darkness*).

It was not the first time, of course, that the Bible was invoked, usually cynically, to support European colonialism, and to justify inhumane behaviour towards indigenous peoples. As well as Zionist settler-colonialism of Palestine in the 20th century, the invasion of Latin America in the fifteenth century, the 19th- and 20th-century *apartheid* sequel to the Dutch incursion into southern Africa in 1652, have gained the support of a distinctive religious ideology (see Prior 1997a; 1999a and 2000). Earlier, while they ate their meals in silence the Crusader Templars enjoyed public readings from the Bible, with special emphasis on the Books of Joshua and Maccabees. All found inspiration in the ferocious exploits of Judas, his brothers and their war-bands in reconquering the Holy Land from cruel infidels (Seward 1995: 32). More recently, Cotton Mather, in a sermon delivered in Boston in September 1689, charged the members of the armed forces in New England to consider themselves to be Israel in the wilderness, confronted by Amalek: pure Israel was obliged to 'cast out [the Indians] as dirt in the streets', and eliminate and exterminate them (Niditch 1993: 3). Roland Bainton provides numerous examples, from the period of the Crusades up to such eighteenth-century preachers as Herbert Gibbs who thanked the mercies of God for extirpating the enemies of Israel in Canaan (i.e., Native Americans) (1960: 112-33, 168). The Bible, then, has been deployed frequently as *the idea* that *redeems the conquest of the earth* (see Prior 1999b).

Whatever pangs of conscience one might have in the modern period about the expulsion of a million Palestinian Arabs, and the destruction of their villages to ensure they would not return—if one could bring oneself to acknowledge that such was the reality, and indeed the intention of Zionism—the Bible could be appealed to to salve it. It could provide the most authoritative legitimisation for the Zionist conquest, claiming that it was merely restoring the land to the Jews in accordance with the clear intentions of God as narrated in its narrative. The divine provenance of the Bible and the authority that springs from such origins would supply the moral authority that was otherwise lacking. Thus, the normal rules of morality could be suspended, and ethnic cleansing could be applauded by the religious spirit.

But how could such appeal to the Bible be valid on the part of Political Zionism in view of its essentially anti-religious origins? Herzl's

Zionism was a repudiation of core doctrines of Orthodox Judaism, particularly its interpretation of the Exile as a punishment for having sinned while in the land, and the need to wait until the Messiah would reverse it. Moreover, Reform Jewry saw it as contrary to Judaism's universal mission to be 'a light to the nations'. However, Zionism, like a chameleon blending its colour with that of its changing environment, was a most versatile ideology, capable of adapting itself to the most diverse contexts.[12] Nevertheless, that Political Zionism, with its rebellious repudiation of classical Judaism and its theological tenets was eventually able to engage the support of religious Jews, both Orthodox and Reform, and to be now at the core of much religious Jewish self-identification, marks one of the most remarkable ideological metamorphoses of the twentieth century.[13]

The Bible, then, is vital in underpinning exclusively Jewish claims to the land of Israel. This is true whether its land narratives, considered to be substantially historiographical, confer a theological claim, or, whether, as among the secularists, they are viewed as an essential part of Jewish modernity and of the foundation of Israeli society, recalling a period when Jewish sovereignty was taken for granted. Moreover, selected archaeological discoveries from the different eras would confirm Jewish settlement in the land, thus providing Israeli Jews from wherever with a sense of continuity with their ancestors with respect to both space and time.[14] 'Digging, like war, had become politics by other means' (Silberman 1997: 68).

What is striking from a moral perspective is the widespread support which the Zionist enterprise enjoys in the West. Whereas elsewhere the perpetrators of ethnic cleansing would be charged with war crimes and crimes against humanity, the Zionist conquest is widely judged to

---

[12] Zionism is a 'rainbow ideology', with distinctive aspirations, sometimes mutually exclusive: to establish a utopian socialist society, a utopian religious society, a homeland for a renaissance of Jewish culture, a haven from oppression, a state in which Jews could rule themselves, and so on. Some formulations required the expulsion of the indigenous population. Herzl's Zionism is best defined as the movement to establish a state for Jews in Palestine, as outlined at the First Zionist Conference in Basle in 1897.

[13] The ideological foundation for this transformation can be traced to Rabbi Avraham Yitzhak Kook (1865-1935) and his son, Rabbi Zvi Yehuda Kook (1890-1982), who mediated particular teachings of his father (see 'Zionism: from the sacred to the secular', in Prior 1999a: 67-102).

[14] See Elon 1997 and Shavit 1997. Deploying archaeology as an agent of nationalist propaganda is common (see, e.g., Kohl. and Fawcett 1995, Diaz-Andreu and Champion 1996, and Meskell 1998).

be a just and appropriate political accomplishment, and, in some quarters, is accorded unique religious significance. Much of the rationale for such benevolent appraisal derives from a literalist interpretation of the land traditions and some of the messianic texts of the Bible. In most Western theological and religious circles, Christian and Jewish, the Zionist prize is viewed as being no more than what the Jewish people deserve in virtue of the promises of God outlined in the Bible. The claim that the Bible legitimises exclusive Jewish rights to *Eretz Yisrael*—in conformity with the exclusive Israelite rights to 'the land of Canaan'—is so pervasive, not only within the Jewish and Christian Zionist circles, but even within mainstream Christian Theology, and much of university biblical studies, that the very attempt to raise the issue is sure to elicit opposition. The animosity normally takes the form of personal abuse, and the intimidation of publishers and broadcasting corporations. One is seldom honoured by having the substantive moral issues addressed in the usual academic fashion. However, such issues must be raised, if only because the integrity of the scholastic enterprise itself is at stake: Zionism has left its mark even on the biblical academy. The starkness of the moral problematic of the land traditions of the Bible convinces one that a moral critique of them is long overdue.

THE BIBLE AND THE LAND

The Bible narrates God's promise of the land of Canaan to Abraham and his posterity, and to Moses and his fellow escapees from Egypt. The conquest and settlement are recounted in the Books of Joshua and Judges. These traditions are of considerable scholastic interest, and have implications for one's understanding of God, and his relation to the people of Israel, to non-Israelites such as the Canaanites, and, by extension, to all other peoples. Let us review the biblical record: firstly, the narrative of the promise and preparation (Genesis, Exodus, Leviticus, Numbers and Deuteronomy), and then that of the conquest-settlement of the land (Joshua and Judges).

Beginning in Genesis with the divine promise to Abram (Abraham) the biblical narrative affirms his descendants' sole claim to it in perpetuity. By the oak of Moreh at Shechem Yahweh appeared to Abram, and said, 'To your descendants I will give this land'. Already the text gives a hint of problems to come, by noting that 'at that time the Canaanites were in the land' (12.6-7). Abram left the land because of a famine, and sojourned in Egypt. After he and his wife were deported (12.20), they returned to the region of Bethel. Since the land could not support both, Abram and Lot divided it, Lot choosing all the Jordan Valley, and Abram the land of Canaan. After this 'land-for-peace' settlement, Yahweh promised to Abram all the land he could see and an abundance of offspring (13.14-17)—the writer adding ominously, 'At that time the Canaanites and the Perizzites dwelt in the land' (13.5-7)— and so, with divine approval, Abram came to dwell by the oaks of Mamre at Hebron, where he built an altar to Yahweh (13.18).

Yahweh made a covenant with Abram, saying, 'To your descendants I give this land, from the river of Egypt to the great river, the river Euphrates'. Again, the writer alludes to the indigenous inhabitants, 'the land of the Kenites, the Kenizzites, the Kadmonites, the Hittites, the Perizzites, the Rephaim, the Amorites, the Canaanites, the Girgashites, and the Jebusites' (15.18-21). Abram is named Abraham, the ancestor of a multitude of nations, and is promised 'all the land of Canaan, for a perpetual holding' (17. 5-8). Subsequently, the promise is made to Isaac also (26.3-4), and, to guarantee the inheritance, Isaac prayed that the promise to Abraham would be fulfilled in Jacob (28.4; see also 28.13-15; 35.12). In the final verses, Joseph dying in Egypt said to his brothers, 'God will surely come to you, and bring you up out of this land to the land that he swore to Abraham, to Isaac, and to Jacob' (50.24).

The Book of Exodus portrays Yahweh as having compassion on the misery of his people, and as willing to deliver them from the Egyptians, and bring to a land flowing with milk and honey, which, however, belongs to the Canaanites, the Hittites, the Amorites, the Perizzites, the Hivites, and the Jebusites (3.7-8). While the promised land of the narrative flowed with milk and honey, it had no lack of indigenous peoples, and soon would flow with their blood.[15]

---

[15] Ethnic cleansing is a divine imperative also in the Book of Numbers: 'Speak to the Israelites, and say to them: 'When you cross over the Jordan into the land of Canaan, you shall drive out all the inhabitants of the land from before you, destroy all their figured stones, destroy all their cast images, and demolish all their high places. You shall take possession of the land and settle in it, for I have given you the land to possess ... But if you do not drive out the inhabitants of the land from before you, then those whom you let remain shall be as barbs in your eyes and thorns in your sides; they shall trouble you in the land where you are settling. And I will do to you as I thought to do to them' (33.50-56).

In the narrative of the Book of Deuteronomy, after the King of Heshbon refused passage to the Israelites, Yahweh gave him over to them, and they captured and utterly destroyed all the cities, killing all the men, women, and children (2.33-34). The fate of the King of Bashan was no better (3.3). We learn how the invaders were to behave:

> 'When Yahweh your God brings you into the land that you are about to enter and occupy, and he clears away many nations before you - the Hittites, the Girgashites, the Amorites, the Canaanites, the Perizzites, the Hivites...and when Yahweh your God gives them over to you and you defeat them, then you must utterly destroy them. Make no covenant with them and show them no mercy ... Yahweh your God has chosen you out of all the peoples on earth to be his people, his treasured possession' (7.1-11; see also 9.1-5; 11.8-9, 23, 31-32).

In the rules for the conduct of war, when a besieged town surrenders, all its inhabitants shall do forced labour; if not, the Israelites shall kill all its males, and take as booty the women, children, livestock, and everything else in the town (20.11-14). The narrative presents 'ethnic cleansing' as not only legitimate, but as required by the divinity:

> 'But as for the towns of these peoples that Yahweh your God is giving you as an inheritance, you must not let anything that breathes remain alive. You shall annihilate them - the Hittites and the Amorites, the Canaanites and the Perizzites, the Hivites and the Jebusites— just as Yahweh your God has commanded, so that they may not teach you to do all the abhorrent things that they do for their gods, and you thus sin against Yahweh your God' (20.16-18).

The book ends with Moses' sight of the promised land before he dies (34.1-3). Although Moses was unequalled in his deeds, he left a worthy successor, Joshua, who, after Moses had lain his hands on him, was full of the spirit of wisdom (34.4-12).

The Book of Joshua presents its hero as the divinely-chosen successor of Moses, who is destined to complete his work (1). The first part (2.1-12.24) describes in epic style the conquest of the land, concentrating on the capture of a few key cities, and their fate in accordance with the laws of the Holy War. After its wall had collapsed, all the men and women (excepting Rahab's family), the oxen, sheep, and donkeys of Jericho were slaughtered, and Joshua pronounced a curse on anyone who would try to rebuild the city (6.21-27). The marauding party moved on to Ai at Yahweh's command, to do to it what was done to Jericho: not one of the twelve thousand inhabitants survived or escaped, and Joshua burned it, and made it forever a heap of ruins (8.2, 19-29). After the Gibeonites were spared, to become 'hewers of wood and drawers of water for all the congregation' the Israelite elders complained at the lapse in fidelity to the mandate to destroy all the inhabitants of the land (9.21-27). Chapter 10 describes the campaign in the south, and chapter 11 that in the north, in each case ensuring the rigorous enforcement of the ban (*herem*). The author summarises Joshua's destruction of everything that breathed, as Yahweh commanded (10. 40-43). In the northern campaign Israel left no one remaining: Joshua took all the land, utterly destroying its inhabitants (11.1-23). The whole achievement is summed up: Yahweh gave to Israel all the land that he swore to their ancestors he would give them (21.43-45). The exploits of Joshua would be appealed to again.[16]

Clearly, these biblical narratives are problematic in virtue of their very content. G E M de Ste Croix, the authority on the history of class politics in the ancient world, put it this way:

> I can say that I know of only one people which felt able to assert that it actually had a divine command to exterminate whole populations among those it conquered; namely, Israel. Nowadays Christians, as well as Jews, seldom care to dwell on the merciless ferocity of Yahweh, as revealed not by hostile

---

[16] US Televangelist Pat Robertson considered Israel's 1982 Israeli invasion of Lebanon to be a modern Joshua event, and urged American viewers to phone President Reagan offering encouragement to Israel's war. On the night before the signing of the Declaration of Principles on 13 September 1993, President Clinton woke at 3.00 a.m., and resumed work on his speech by rereading the Book of Joshua according (*Washington Post*, 14 September, A1). His address later was a mixture of Bible-based exhortation in the Baptist tradition, and shrewd political manoeuvring. He announced that both the Israelis and the Palestinians pledged themselves to a shared future 'shaped by the values of the Torah, the Koran, and the Bible'. Rabin's speech also referred to the Bible. In the light of the history of reception of these texts one questions whether their values can be relied on to promote justice and peace, and trusts that it will not be the traditions of the President's nocturnal reading which will shape the shared future. Surveying such prospects in December 2001 one respects the prescience of the President's choice of reading.

sources but by the very literature they themselves regard as sacred. Indeed, they continue as a rule to forget the very existence of this incriminating material ... There is little in pagan literature quite as morally revolting as the stories of the massacres allegedly carried out at Jericho, Ai, and Hazor, and of the Amorites and Amalekites, all not merely countenanced by Yahweh but strictly ordained by him...The Greek and Roman gods could be cruel enough, in the traditions preserved by their worshippers, but at least their devotees did not seek to represent them as prescribing genocide (1981: 331-32).

The biblical traditions which glorify 'ethnic cleansing' as a divine imperative are celebrated even in prayer form: 'So he brought his people out with joy, his chosen ones with singing. He gave them the lands of the nations, and they took possession of the wealth of the peoples' (Psalm 105.43-44), and, 'You brought a vine out of Egypt; you drove out the nations and planted it' (Psalm 80.8). It is all the more important, then, that these biblical texts be subjected to an examination based on moral criteria.

ETHICS AND THE LAND TRADITIONS

By modern standards of international law and human rights the land narratives of Exodus-Joshua mandate 'war-crimes' and 'crimes against humanity'. To dismiss the contemporary moral implications of such texts by pleading that they ought not to be judged by the standards obtaining today is not sufficient. Today's readers live in the present, not in the past, and should not be above exercising judgement on the moral validity of the texts—'criticism' (from *krinein*, to pass judgement) implies as much. Nor is it acceptable either to seek refuge in the claim that the problem lies with the predispositions of the modern reader, rather than with the text itself. One must acknowledge that much of the *Torah*, and the Book of Deuteronomy in particular, contains menacing ideologies and racist, xenophobic and militaristic tendencies. Manifestly, the Book of Joshua is a morally scandalous component in a collection of religious writings. The implications of the existence of such dubious moral dispositions and actions, presented as mandated by the divinity, within a book which is canonised as Sacred Scripture invites the most serious investigation.

Nevertheless, biblical scholars show few signs of being overly concerned about these embarrassing facts. Indeed, many retain a high esteem for Deuteronomy, assessing it to be a theological treatise *par excellence*, with its insistence on the incomparability, uniqueness and absoluteness of YHWH—the divine name occurs no less than 561 times in the book—and the focal point of the religious history of the Old Testament.[17] That some of the traditions of Deuteronomy had provided intellectual and moral authority for, among other colonial enterprises, the Iberian devastation of 'Latin America' in the late mediaeval period, for the Afrikaner exploitation of non-whites in southern Africa right up to the 1990s, and was continuing to do so today for Zionists in their ongoing exspoliation of the Arabs of Palestine scarcely dent their enthusiasm (see Prior 1997a).

The Book of Joshua, too, has its admirers. Only a decade after the full horrors of Nazi 'ethnic cleansing' had been revealed, William Foxwell Albright, the doyen of biblical archaeologists, had no qualms about the plunder attendant upon Joshua's enterprise—through which 'a people of markedly inferior type should vanish before a people of superior potentialities'—a project he understood in a largely historically reliable way.[18] Prior to Keith Whitelam's critique (1996a: 88) no commentator

---

[17] Thus, typically, 'this most theological book of the OT' (Blenkinsopp 1989: 95). In the 1995 Lattey Lecture in Cambridge University, Professor Norbert Lohfink argued that Deuteronomy provides a model for an utopian society in which there would be no poor (Lohfink 1996). In my role as the formal proposer of a vote of thanks, I invited Professor Lohfink to consider whether, in the light of that book's insistence on a mandate to commit genocide, the utopian society would be possible only after the invading Israelites had wiped out the indigenous inhabitants. The protocol of the Lattey Lecture left the last word with me, and subsequently I was given a second word, being invited to deliver the 1997 Lattey Lecture, for which I chose the title, A Land flowing with Milk, Honey, and People (Prior 1997b).

[18] 'From the impartial standpoint of a philosopher of history, it often seems necessary that a people of markedly inferior type should vanish before a people of superior potentialities, since there is a point beyond which racial mixture cannot go without disaster...Thus the Canaanites, with their orgiastic nature worship, their cult of fertility in the form of serpent symbols and sensuous nudity, and their gross mythology, were replaced by Israel, with its pastoral simplicity and purity of life, its lofty monotheism, and its severe code of ethics' (1957: 280-81). In a similar vein, George E. Wright, another distinguished American biblical scholar, justified the genocide of the narrative of Joshua in terms of the inferiority of the indigenous culture (1960: 109). In the previous century, Heinrich Ewald, who in his five-volume history of Israel (1843-1855) was determined to demonstrate the Israelites' unique, tireless efforts to achieve true and perfect religion, wrote: 'It is an eternal necessity that a nation such as the majority of the Canaanites then were, sinking deeper and deeper

had drawn attention to Albright's undisguised racist attitudes, which were typical of virtually every Western colonial enterprise which predicated that the 'superior' peoples of the West had the right to exploit, and in some cases exterminate the 'natives'. Reflecting these conventional values, Albright also judged that through Zionism Jews would bring to the Near East all the benefits of European civilisation (1942: 12-13).

Read with a literalist naïveté the land traditions of the Bible predicate a god who is a xenophobic nationalist and a militaristic ethnic-cleanser. Reliance on the authority of a gift of land from such a god, then, is problematic for any reader who might presume that the divinity would entertain the values of the Fourth Geneva Convention and the Universal Declaration of Human Rights, at least. Moreover, at the level of reception, these biblical traditions have fuelled virtually every form of militant colonialism emanating from Europe, resulting in the sufferings of millions of people, and loss of respect for the Bible. Were it not for their religious provenance, such biblical sentiments would be regarded as incitements to racial hatred. On moral grounds, therefore, one is forced to question whether the *Torah* in fact provides divine legitimacy for the occupation of other people's land, and the virtual annihilation of the indigenous peoples.

It is naïve to cleave to the view that God made the promise of progeny and land to Abraham after the fashion indicated in Genesis 15. Recent biblical scholarship, aided by increasing archaeological evidence, makes it impossible to evaluate the biblical narratives of land as pointers to what actually happened in the period portrayed in the text. In the wake of the seminal works of Thomas L. Thompson (1974) and John Van Seters (1975) it is now part of the scholarly consensus that the patriarchal narratives of Genesis do not record events of an alleged patriarchal period, but are retrojections into a past about which the writers knew little, reflecting the author's intentions at the later period of composition, perhaps that of the attempt to reconstitute national and religious identity

into a slough of discord and moral perversity, must fall before a people roused to a higher life by the newly awakened energy of unanimous trust in Divine Power.' Similarly, G.F. MacLear in his commentary on Joshua (1880) could write: 'When...God entrusted the sword of vengeance to Joshua, was ever campaign waged in such an unearthly manner as that now inaugurated by the leader of the armies of Israel?' He ends by quoting a sermon of Thomas Arnold: 'The Israelites' sword in its bloodiest executions, wrought a work of mercy for all the countries of the earth...they preserved unhurt the seed of eternal life' (quoted in Auld 1998: 133).

in the wake of the Babylonian exile, or even later (see further Prior 1997a: 216-23).

Neither do the Exodus-Settlement accounts present empirical facts of history. The archaeology of Palestine shows a picture quite different from that of the religiously motivated writings of the Bible. The evidence from archaeology and extra-biblical literature, supplemented by insights from the independent methodologies of geography, sociology, anthropology, historical linguistics, Egyptology, Assyriology, etc., points in a direction altogether different from that implied by Joshua 1-12. This extra-biblical material suggests a sequence of periods marked by a gradual and peaceful coalescence of disparate peoples into a group of highland dwellers whose achievement of a new sense of unity culminated only with the entry of the Assyrian administration. The Iron I Age settlements on the central hills of Palestine, from which the later kingdom of Israel developed, reflect continuity with Canaanite culture, and repudiate any ethnic distinction between 'Canaanites' and 'Israelites (see further Prior 1997a: 228-47; 1999a: 159-83). The biblical narrative, then, unless read in a naïve, literalist fashion, offers little succour to ethnic cleansers.

The invective one detects in the debate about 'ancient Israel' even—although the new, or 'revisionist' historians (sometimes referred to as 'minimalists') show no particular interest in modern Israel—makes one suspicious that more is at stake than customary objective scholarship in search of an elusive past. The academic transgression, of course, consists in trespassing on a carefully protected discourse on 'Ancient Israel' that has implications for the legitimacy of developments in Palestine in our own time.[19]

---

[19] See, e.g., the 'friendly critique', 'in the hope of fostering a truly interdisciplinary dialogue between specialists', which William G Dever offered to Keith Whitelam's survey of the 'state-of-the-art' on the literature of Israelite origins (Dever 1996). He complains that none of the 'revisionist' historians has any significant credentials in archaeology (p. 5). To Dever's charge of incompetence, H. Shanks elsewhere adds that because 'Whitelam is no kook' his scholarship is insidious, even if it is 'woefully unbalanced and mean-spirited', as well as full of 'considerable cunning'. Whitelam's spirited (and amusing) rejoinder defends his attempt and that of others to challenge the dominant discourse of biblical studies for over a century (1996b; for Shanks' views see n 3). See the discussion on History and Narrative in Prior 1999a: 176-80. See also the *apologia* of Niels Peter Lemche, one of the 'minimalists' (2000).

But even if Patriarchal narratives of Genesis and those of Exodus-Leviticus-Numbers-Deuteronomy-Joshua portrayed the past approximately as it happened one would still have to contend with their ethical stance in portraying Yahweh as the great ethnic-cleanser. Were these narratives acknowledged to belong to the genre of legend rather than history, or to be confined to the realm of mere rhetorical discussion of ancient literature in its various genres, few would object. But when they have vital significance for people's lives even in one's own generation problems arise. As we have seen, much of the legitimacy associated with the establishment of the State of Israel, and the esteem it enjoys in religious circles of having quite distinctive values and even unique religious significance, derives its major moral legitimisation from a particular reading of the Old Testament.

Important conclusions follow from the claim of exclusive Israelite/Jewish rights to Palestine. 'Jews' hailing from any part of the globe, who themselves were never displaced from Palestine, have the 'right of return'. Without the Bible, such a claim to legitimacy would have no currency in the wider world wherein, for one, a communal right of return operates only when a defined community has been subjected to recent expulsion—a *sine qua non* for orderly international behaviour. From a moral perspective there is a more problematic implication. The Jewish 'right of return' easily translates into the 'right to expel' the indigenous population, an aspiration which was at the core of the Zionist enterprise from the beginning. There is, moreover, compelling evidence that the Palestinian *Nakba* (catastrophe) of 1948 (and the subsequent disaster of 1967) were not accidents of war, but were intended, planned for and systematically executed. And, since Jews have sole tenure, a claim deriving from a naïve reading of the biblical narrative, the recently expelled Palestinian Arabs have no right of return (see Prior 2001).

CONCLUSION

Clearly, the land traditions of the Bible pose fundamental moral questions, relating both to their content and to the ways they have been deployed in favour of oppressive ideologies. One might have hoped that the communities which have preserved and promulgated these texts—including the biblical academy which takes upon itself the exegesis of the Bible—

should have some obligation to comment on what has been done in conformity with their values in each generation since their composition. However, not even the fact that the reception of these traditions supported much of the imperialist expansion of the Western world's past has been sufficient to bother contemporary biblical scholars to the point of critical opposition. Yet, to earn some degree of societal acceptability the biblical academy must exercise some level of public responsibility.

While traditional commentators search out whatever can be ascertained about the social, religious, and political context of the biblical writings, they are oblivious to their own contexts, and the impact that these might have on their interpretations of the texts.[20] Moreover, few see it as necessary to evaluate the more morally problematic biblical texts in terms of general ethical criteria, or display any inclination to involve their scholarship in social transformation. Biblical scholars, any more than other academics, do not see themselves as called to become critical transformative intellectuals with a responsibility for criticising systems of oppression on the world scale.[21] Fascination with the unrecoverable past satisfies their intellectual appetites.

Latin American liberation theologians, however, focus on the primacy of the context of one's reflections (*lugar teológico*). Western interpretation, they insist, will always be distorted. The Bible's central message, they claim rather naïvely, is that God is on the side of the oppressed, while interpreters from North America and Europe have never experienced economic, personal, or institutional oppression. Hence,

---

[20] In reflecting upon an aspect of the discipline which is scarcely ever taken into account, namely the ideological baggage of the individual researcher, Burke O Long situates W F Albright's concerns in the apologetic context of protecting Western values from the threat of Communism and totalitarianism. Christianity and 'the Jewish-Christian tradition' were the pinnacle of all religious reflection, and, of course, were enshrined within the American way of life. Albright's efforts had much to do with maintaining social stability and ideological conformity against those movements which threatened the American way of life as he knew it (Long 1997).

[21] In Elisabeth Schüssler Fiorenza's estimation, the biblical academy distinguishes itself by detachment from issues of contemporary ferment, operating as if in a political vacuum, and being accountable only to its 'in-house' fraternity of scholars, who pay no attention to their own social locations, or to how the discipline serves political functions. Thus, in a forty-year period no president of the Society of Biblical Literature used his presidential address to consider the political context of his scholarship: since 1947 no presidential address alluded to any aspect of world or national politics, such as the civil rights movement, liberation struggles, Martin Luther King, the *Shoah*, etc. (1999: 23).

virtually all Western biblical scholars, who live in comfort and guaranteed security, and are respected members of prestigious academic institutions, interpret the Bible from their positions of power. The biblical discourse in the West is in the control of the university departments of biblical studies—as it was in Church/Synagogue circles previously—and it is they that decide upon which questions are important. Such an 'exegetical place', one learns, become an obstacle to an authentic reading of the text (see, e.g., Tamez 1982).

A different dynamic operates in liberation theology circles, where authentic theological endeavour incorporates three elements: reflection, ethical option and action (praxis).[22] Because it arises from being immersed in the concrete situation of people, such a theology introduces a fundamental ethical option, one which properly leads to praxis.[23]

My own 'exegetical place' in Jerusalem imposed certain obligations upon me. It was one thing to learn that the majority of the indigenous Arab population of some 77 percent of Palestine (some 750,000 people) had been expelled in 1948, and that a further 300,000 had been expelled in 1967, since which year the remaining 23 percent of Palestine had been under Israeli military occupation. It was quite another to realise that the Bible allegedly supplied the moral legitimisation for such activity. Even if such concerns appeared to be of little import to the biblical academy, either that *in situ* in the land of the Bible or anywhere else, they provided a unique context for me to pioneer a Moral Exegesis of the Bible. Being sensitive to the victims of various colonial enterprises in recent times, one was led into reading the biblical text 'with the eyes of the Canaanites'.

However late, one detects some recent stirrings in these matters, whether in the literature on post-colonial readings (e.g., Sugirtharajah 1991; 1998; 1999; and 2001), or on the necessity of instituting a Moral

---

[22] In Brazil, for example, the concerns of the poor and exploited predominate, and the reading of the Bible proceeds from their perspectives. Such is the lack of confidence in the methods and concerns of Western biblical studies that the biblical scholars brought up in them are allowed enter the so-called Contextual Bible Study process only as servants, and participate only when they are invited by the people. Rather than being perceived as teachers with an enviable repository of wisdom, gained through expertise in the historical-critical methods of Bible study, biblical scholars are admitted only if they commit themselves to begin with the social reality as perceived, and to engage in socio-political transformation through Bible reading (see Vaage 1991).
[23] On the richness of the historical context of reflection see Ellacuría 1990.

Exegesis of the biblical text. Heikki Räisänen insists that 'a moral evaluation of biblical texts and of their interpretation is indispensable today', and applauds my application of a moral critique to the Zionist enterprise (2000: 207). Peter Miano criticises the biblical academy for virtually ignoring the moral dimensions of the biblical texts and their own real-life contexts. He suggests that when the values of biblical passages go unrecognised they are susceptible to being misappropriated and misapplied, sometimes with damaging consequences. Taking his cue from my Moral Critique, Miano proposes a 'Value Critique', 'the deliberate examination of the value systems presumed by and expressed in the stories of the Bible' (2001: 12).

But while Feminist, or Fundamentalist Exegesis is a fertile field for developing an 'ethics of accountability' in Biblical Studies, the area of Israel-Palestine remains a safe haven. While Elisabeth Schlüssler Fiorenza's programme is scurrilous on those biblical texts which legitimise war, nurture anti-Judaism and misogyny, justify slavery, and promote colonial dehumanisation, etc., it does not rise to the challenge of facing into one of the most blatant uses of the Bible as a charter for oppression, and one for which the domestic politics in, and foreign policy of the USA has a particular responsibility (Schlüssler Fiorenza 1999). Perhaps it is her own 'exegetical location' that prevents her from facing into one of the great scandals of the international biblical community, namely, its silence in the face of Political Zionism's cynical embrace of the biblical narrative as an integral element of its ideological justification for its oppression of the indigenous Arab population of Palestine.

The claim in our own age that the biblical narrative, however repulsive its deployment as part of the ideological support for colonialism in the past, legitimises the 'ethnic cleansing' of the Palestinian Arabs should not remain unchallenged within the biblical academy. Biblical scholars, at least, might be expected to protest against outrages perpetrated in the name of fidelity to the biblical covenant. Biblical research should be conducted with an 'ethics of accountability', i.e., with a concern for exposing 'the ethical consequences of the biblical text and its meanings', especially when these have promoted various forms of oppression, not least through 'colonial dehumanisation', and for making their findings known to a wider public (Schlüssler Fiorenza 1999: 28-29).

Because of the moral seriousness of the debate I make no apology for violating the emotionally-detached, intellectually-dispassionate and rationally value-neutral disposition considered by some to be the appropriate one for biblical scholars.[24] Biblical exegesis, in addition to probing into the circumstances of the composition of the biblical narratives, should concern itself also with the real conditions of people's lives, and not satisfy itself with comfortable survival in an academic or religious ghetto, stimulating only its own 'in-house' constituency.

REFERENCES

Albright, William Foxwell. 1942. 'Why the Near East needs the Jews', *New Palestine* 32: 12-13

Albright, William Foxwell. 1957. From the Stone Age to Christianity: Monotheism and the Historical Process. New York: Doubleday

Auld, A Graeme. 1998. *Joshua Retold. Synoptic Perspectives*. Edinburgh: T&T Clark

Bainton, Roland H. 1960. *Christian Attitudes Toward War and Peace*. Nashville: Abingdon

Ben-Gurion, David. 1954. *The Rebirth and Destiny of Israel*. New York: Philosophical Library.

Ben-Gurion, David. 1972. *Ben-Gurion looks at the Bible* (trans. from the Hebrew by Jonathan Kolatch, 1969). London & New York: W.H. Allen

Blenkinsopp, Joseph. 1989. 'Deuteronomy', in R.E. Brown, J.A. Fitzmyer and R.E. Murphy, *New Jerome Biblical Commentary*. London: Chapman, pp. 94-109

Dayan, Moshe. 1978. *Living with the Bible*. Philadelphia: Jewish Publication Society/ New York: William Morrow

De Ste Croix, G E M. 1981. *The Class Struggle in the Ancient Greek World from the Archaic Age to the Arab Conquest*: London: Duckworth,

Dever, William G. 1996. 'The Identity of Early Israel: A Rejoinder to Keith W. Whitelam', *Journal for the Study of the Old Testament* 70: 3-24

Diamond, James S. 1986. *Homeland or Holy Land? The 'Canaanite Critique of Israel*. Bloomington Indianapolis: Indiana University Press

Diaz-Andreu, M and T Champion (eds). 1996. *Nationalism and Archaeology in Europe*. London: UCL Press

Ellacuría, Ignacio. 1990. *Filosofía de la realidad histórica*. Madrid: Editorial Trotta

Elon, Amos. 1997. 'Politics and Archaeology', in Silberman and Small 1997: 34-47

Enslin, Morton S. 1946. 'The Future of Biblical Studies', *Journal of Biblical Literature* 65: 1-12

Güdemann, Moritz. 1897. *Nationaljudentum*. Leipzig and Vienna

Herzl, Theodor. 1896. *Der Judenstaat. Versuch einer Modernen Lösung der Judenfrage*.

---

[24] See, e.g., the 1945 Presidential Address to the Society of Biblical Literature given by Morton S Enslin (1946).

Leipzig und Wien: M. Breitenstein's Verlags-Buchhandlung

Herzl, Theodor. 1960 (edited by Raphael Patai). *The Complete Diaries of Theodore Herzl,* translated by Harry Zohn. New York: Herzl Press

Herzl, Theodor. 1983-1996. Vol. I, 1983, *Briefe und Autobiographische Notizen. 1886-1895;* Vol. II: 1983, *Zionistiches Tagebuch 1895-1899;* Vol. III, 1985: *Zionistiches Tagebuch 1899-1904* (Vols I-III, ed. Johannes Wachten, *et al.*); Vol. IV, 1990, *Briefe 1895-1898;* Vol. V, 1993, *Briefe 1898-1900;* Vol. VI, 1993, *Briefe Ende August 1900-ende Dezember 1902;* Vol. VII, 1996, *Briefe 1903-1904* (Vols. IV-VII, ed. Barbara Schäfer, *et al.*). Berlin: Propylaen Verlag

Jakobivits, Immanuel (Chief Rabbi). 1982. *The Attitude to Zionism of Britain's Chief Rabbis as Reflected in their Writings.* London: The Jewish Historical Society of England: Lecture delivered to The Jewish Historical Society of England in London, 9 May 1979

Kohl, P L and C Fawcett (eds). 1995. *Nationalism, Politics and the Practice of Archaeology.* Cambridge: Cambridge University Press

Laqueur, Walter. 1972. *History of Zionism.* New York: Holt, Rinehart and Winston

Lemche, Niels Peter. 2000. 'Ideology and the History of Ancient Israel', *Scandinavian Journal of the Old Testament* 14(no. 2): 165-93

Lohfink, Norbert. 1996. *The Laws of Deuteronomy. A Utopian Project for a World without any Poor?* Cambridge: Von Hügel Institute, and in 'The Laws of Deuteronomy. A Utopian Project for a World without any Poor' [without the question mark], *Scripture Bulletin* 26[1996]: 2-19

Long, Burke O. 1997. 'Historical Imaginings, Ideological Gestures: W.F. Albright and the 'Reasoning Faculties of Man'', in Silberman and Small 1997: 82-94

MacLear, G F. 1880. *The Book of Joshua.* Cambridge: Cambridge University Press

Menuhin, Moshe. 1969. *The Decadence of Judaism in our Time.* Beirut: The Institute for Palestinian Studies

Meskell, L (ed.). 1998. *Archaeology under Fire. Nationalism, Politics and Heritage in the Eastern Mediterranean and Middle East.* London: Routledge

Miano, Peter J. 2001. *The Word of God and the World of the Bible. An Introduction to the Cultural Backgrounds of the New Testament.* London: Melisende

Niditch, Susan. 1993. *War in the Hebrew Bible. A Study of the Ethics of Violence.* Oxford: Oxford University Press

Prior, Michael. 1995. *Jesus the Liberator. Nazareth Liberation Theology (Luke 4.16-30).* Sheffield: Sheffield Academic Press

Prior, Michael. 1997a. *The Bible and Colonialism. A Moral Critique.* Sheffield: Sheffield Academic Press

Prior, Michael. 1997b. *A Land flowing with Milk, Honey, and People.* Cambridge: Von Hügel Institute, and in *Scripture Bulletin* 28[1998]: 2-17

Prior, Michael. 1998. 'The Moral Problem of the Land Traditions of the Bible', in Michael Prior (ed.), *Western Scholarship and the History of Palestine.* London: Melisende, pp. 41-81

Prior, Michael. 1999a. *Zionism and the State of Israel: A Moral Inquiry.* London and New York: Routledge

Prior, Michael. 1999b. 'The Bible and the Redeeming Idea of Colonialism', in *Studies in World Christianity* 5: 129-55

Prior, Michael. 1999c. 'The Bible and Zionism', in Naim S. Ateek and Michael Prior (eds), *Holy Land—Hollow Jubilee: God, Justice and the Palestinians*. London, Melisende, pp. 69-88

Prior, Michael. 2000. 'Zionist Ethnic Cleansing: the Fulfilment of Biblical Prophecy?' *Epworth Review* 27: 49-60

Prior, Michael. 2001. 'The Right to Expel: the Bible and Ethnic Cleansing', in Naseer Aruri (ed.), *Palestinian Refugees and their Right of Return*. London and Sterling VA: Pluto Press, pp. 9-35

Räisänen, Heikki. 2000. *Beyond New Testament Theology. A Story and a Programme*. London: SCM

Schlüssler Fiorenza, Elisabeth. 1999. *Rhetoric and Ethic. The Politics of Biblical Studies*. Minneapolis: Fortress

See the discussion on History and Narrative in Prior, *Zionism and the State of Israel*, pp. 176-80. See also the *apologia* of.

Seward, Desmond. 1995. *The Monks of War. The Military Religious Orders*. London: Penguin Books

Shavit, Yaacov. 1997. 'Archaeology, Political Culture and Culture in Israel', in Silberman and Small 1997: 48-61

Silberman, Neil Asher and David B Small. 1997. *The Archaeology of Israel. Constructing the Past, Interpreting the Present* (JSOTSS 237). Sheffield: Sheffield Academic Press

Silberman, Neil Asher. 1997. 'Structuring the Past: Israelis, Palestinians, and the Symbolic Authority of Archaeological Monuments', in Silberman and Small 1997: 62-81

Sugirtharajah, R S (ed.). 1991. *Voices from the Margin: Interpreting the Bible in the Third World*. London: SPCK

Sugirtharajah, R S (ed.). 1998. *The Postcolonial Bible*. Sheffield: Sheffield Academic Press

Sugirtharajah, R S (ed.). 1999. *Asian Biblical Hermeneutics and Postcolonialism: Contesting the Interpretations*. Sheffield: Sheffield Academic Press

Sugirtharajah, R S (ed.). 2001. *The Bible and The Third World: Precolonial, Colonial, and Postcolonial Encounters*. Cambridge: Cambridge University Press

Tamez, Elsa. 1982. *Bible of the Oppressed*. Maryknoll, NY: Orbis

Thompson, Thomas L. 1974. *The Historicity of the Pentateuchal Narratives. The Quest for the Historical Abraham*. Berlin/New York: de Gruyter

Vaage, Leif E. 1991. 'Text, Context, Conquest, Quest: The Bible and Social Struggle in Latin America', in *Society of Biblical Literature Seminar Papers* 30: 357-65.

Van Seters, John. 1975. *Abraham in History and Tradition*. New Haven/London: Yale University Press

Vital, David. 1999. *A People Apart. The Jews in Europe 1789-1939*. Oxford: Oxford University Press

Whitelam, Keith W. 1996a. *The Invention of Ancient Israel. The Silencing of Palestinian History*. London and New York: Routledge

Whitelam, Keith W. 1996b. 'Prophetic Conflict in Israelite History: Taking Sides with William G Dever', *Journal for the Study of the Old Testament* 72: 25-44

Wistrich, Robert and David Ohana (eds). 1995. *The Shaping of Israeli Identity: Myth, Memory and Trauma*. London: Frank Cass

Wistrich, Robert. 1995. 'Theodor Herzl: Zionist Icon, Myth-Maker and Social Utopian', in Wistrich and Ohana (eds) 1995: 1-37

Wright George E and R H Fuller (eds). 1960. *The Book of the Acts of God: Christian Scholarship Interprets the Bible*. London: Duckworth.

THE 'HOLY LAND', ZIONISM, AND THE CHALLENGE TO THE CHURCH

Writing in New Blackfriars *in 2002, Michael challenges the mainstream churches to explain the moral 'double standard' as between Israel and other colonialist enterprises.*

The 'Holy Land' is of particular interest to Christians everywhere, an interest intensified whenever they read their Bibles. There God intervened in human history through his dealings with the Israelites, and in the person of Jesus Christ. Jesus was crucified and raised in, and ascended from Jerusalem, and it was there also that the Holy Spirit descended on the Church.

There has been, of course, an unbroken Christian community in the land from the beginning, and it was those residing there who were the architects of a Christian 'Holy Land'.[1] But Christians outside also have their interests. Well before Constantine, Palestine was a place of pilgrimage. In the middle of the 2nd century, Melito of Sardis went to establish accurately the books of the Old Testament', and to examine the relevant places. Others went 'for the sake of the holy places', and 'to trace the footsteps of Jesus', and pray. Some stayed, living piously near the sites.[2] Nevertheless, however important, the Holy Land never attracted more than a handful of (affluent) pilgrims from abroad, and the practice of pilgrimage was virtually moribund by the end of the 18th century. As we shall see, Western interests from then went beyond the religious.

---

[1] See Robert L Wilken, *The Land called Holy. Palestine in Christian History and Thought* (New York and London: Yale University Press, 1992), 119.

[2] See further my 'Pilgrimage to the Holy Land, Yesterday and Today,' in Michael Prior and William Taylor (eds), *Christians in the Holy Land* (London: WIFT/Scorpion Press, 1994), 169-75; 'A Perspective on Pilgrimage to the Holy Land', in Naim Ateek, Cedar Duaybis and Marla Schrader, *Jerusalem: What makes for Peace?* (London: Melisende, 1997), 114-31, and 'Christian Pilgrimage to the Holy Land', in Duncan Macpherson (ed.), *A Millennium Guide to Christian Pilgrimage to the Holy Land* (London: Melisende, 2000), 25-39.

CONFLICT IN THE HOLY LAND

The ongoing Palestinian-Israeli conflict brings an altogether different dimension to the question. In addition to being one of the most explosive issues in international affairs it constitutes for the Church one of the most significant moral problems of our age. It raises all sorts of questions, concerning not only issues of biblical interpretation, but of the very authority of some biblical traditions. Relationships between religious affiliation and 'nationalism', as well as between the relevant religions also surface. The level of horror in recent months has reached a height unsurpassed since the events of 1948, the date marking the establishment of the State of Israel and the concomitant Palestinian *Nakba* (Catastrophe). The attacks of 11 September 2001 have brought an additional dimension to the explosive atmosphere which erupted with the second *intifada* (September 2000).

The USA's world-wide 'War on Terrorism' and appetite for 'Regime Change' in Iraq confirms that we are living in fearful times. While acknowledging the USA's underlying oil interests one cannot ignore the extent to which the 'Christian Right' influences the administration's world-view. The Christian Right's distinctive interpretation of the Bible accords cosmic significance to 'the return of the Jews', providing Israel with a critical role in ushering in the Second Coming of Christ, and the End of Days. Moreover, in Israel itself, establishing the state and expelling the indigenous population derives its alleged legitimacy primarily from the Bible, even for secular nationalists uninterested in it as the repository of a theological claim to Palestine. Religion and biblical interpretation, then, are central to the conflict, whose origins lay in the plight of Jews in Europe towards the end of the 19th century, and the proposal to address it through establishing a state for Jews in a non-European country inhabited for centuries by another people.

The advent of Political Zionism in 1896 stimulated a renewed Christian interest in Palestine, particularly on the part of the indigenous Christians who feared for their future. As it transpired, such fears were not unfounded. In establishing the State for Jews in 1948 some 80 per cent of the Arab population were driven out, and some 418 of their villages were destroyed to ensure they would not return. To add to the moral problematic, we now know from the Zionist archives themselves that the intention to expel the indigenous Arabs was a core element of the Zionist enterprise from the beginning. It was foreseen as necessary, was systematically planned for, and was executed at the first opportunity, in 1948. We read of the establishment and comportment of the two 'Population Transfer Committees' (1937 through 1944) and the third Population Transfer Committee established by the Israeli cabinet in August 1948, etc.[3]

THE CHURCH WITHIN

In any discussion of Christian estimates of the Holy Land the perspective of the indigenous Christians, those remaining and those either expelled or 'in exile' since 1948 and 1967, must be accorded due significance. Before the current *intifada* the Christian community numbered about 165,000 (114,000 in Israel, and 50,352, in the Occupied Territories), constituting some 41.3 per cent of the Palestinian Christians world-wide (400,000). Living as unequal citizens in the State of Israel since 1948, or as victims of Israel's occupation of the West Bank and Gaza since 1967, the community has experienced high levels of emigration, which surveys demonstrate to be one of the consequences of the ethnocratic nature of Israel.[4] Although small, the 'Church of Jerusalem' lays claim to being the 'Mother Church'. Within that Church, tradition has established a hierarchy, with the three patriarchal Churches (Greek Orthodox, Armenian Orthodox and Latin Catholic) enjoying special authority, but there is also a mosaic of other Churches (Greek-Catholic, Coptic, Syriac Orthodox, Syriac Catholic, Ethiopian, Anglican, Lutheran, Maronite, Quaker, *et al.*). While pilgrims and Christians from outside might be content with free access to the Holy Sites, the Arab Christians have human rights and legitimate political aspirations which also must be respected.

The Churches in the Holy Land, though distinctive in their traditions, liturgies and organisation, manifest virtual unanimity with

---

[3] See Nur Masalha's *Expulsion of the Palestinians: the Concept of 'Transfer' in Zionist Political Thought, 1882-1948* (Washington, D.C.: Institute for Palestine Studies, 1992), his *A Land without a People. Israel, Transfer and the Palestinians 1949-96* (London: Faber and Faber, 1997), and his *Imperial Israel and the Palestinians: The Politics of Expansion, 1967-2000* (London: Pluto, 2000).

[4] See Bernard Sabella, 'Socio-Economic Characteristics and the Challenges to Palestinian Christians in the Holy Land', and Sami Geraisy, 'Socio-Demographic Characteristics: Reality, Problems and Aspirations within Israel', in Michael Prior and William Taylor (eds), *Christians in the Holy Land*, 31-44, 45-55.

respect to the developing situation in Palestine. The first *intifada* which erupted in 1987 stimulated a new sense of unity, marked by ongoing ecumenical co-operation, and issuing in a number of significant joint statements relating to various developments in the changing political circumstances, not least in criticism of the excesses of the Israeli occupation.[5] While such views are mirrored in the mainstream Churches outside, Evangelical Christian Zionists have radically different ones which are important if only because of their influence on the foreign policy of the USA.

EVANGELICAL CHRISTIAN ZIONISM

Whereas none of the mainstream Churches showed any enthusiasm for Zionism, 'Christian Zionists' were enthusiastic in viewing Political Zionism as the instrument of God promoting the ingathering of Jews. Indeed, enthusiasm among such Christians for a Jewish 'return' to Palestine preceded that of the founder of Political Zionism, Theodor Herzl (1860-1904). Now that the State of Israel is established Christian Zionists see it as having even redemptive significance.

'Christian Zionists' number some sixty million world-wide, but their influence is greatest in the USA, especially since the 1970s. When he came to power in 1977, Prime Minister Menachem Begin, realising that the mainstream USA Churches were growing more sympathetic to the Palestinians and were effectively becoming a 'lost cause', directed Israeli lobbyists in the USA to work on the evangelical constituency. His Likud Party began to use religious language, and determined efforts were made to forge bonds between evangelical Christians and pro-Israel lobbies. Such a coalition had enough advantage for each party to co-operate on the single issue of Israel. Recognising that courting the evangelical right was as important as lobbying the White House, Begin's example has been followed by every Prime Minister since.

---

[5] E.g., the Joint Memorandum of the Heads of Christian Communities in Jerusalem on 'The Significance of Jerusalem for Christians' (14 November 1994). The text is reproduced in the appendix to my '"You will be my witnesses in Jerusalem, in all Judaea and Samaria, and to the ends of the earth". Christian Perspectives on Jerusalem', in Anthony O'Mahony (ed.) *Palestinian Christians: Religion, Politics and Society in the Holy Land* (London: Melisende, 1999), 96-140, 136-40.

The effects on USA domestic politics have been significant. The evangelical Christian constituency was a major factor in the election of Jimmy Carter in 1976. However, his call for a 'Palestinian homeland' in March 1977 precipitated his downfall, and the Evangelical Right's switch to Ronald Reagan in 1980 was a major factor in Carter's defeat. The combined efforts of the Israeli lobbies and the Christian Right have continued since, and reached their climax so far in the present incumbent in the White House, whose theological world-view, and that of much of his administration, is very close to the that of the 'Christian Right'.

The evangelicals' emphasis on a literalist fulfilment of biblical prophecy and on its millenarianist eschatology—holding that the Second Coming of Christ will be followed by a thousand-year reign of blessedness after the cataclysmic Battle of Armageddon—leads its proponents to embrace a polity that would otherwise be considered morally repulsive. In translating their theology into modern politics Christian Zionists claim that biblical prophecy finds its fulfilment in Israel, thereby according the state an integral part in the events of the End Time. In their distinctive hermeneutic, when the Bible refers to the past, it does so virtually exclusively as history, ignoring such other literary forms as legend, saga, or myth. At the other end of the time-scale, when they refer to a future, the prophetic oracles are interpreted as finding their fulfilment in a selection of (modern) political developments. Thus, both exclusively 'Jewish' claims to Palestine, and the claims linking modern Israel with God's plans for the End Time are 'validated' by no less an authority than the Bible.

Such views can be traced to excesses developing from the Reformation's new interest in the Old Testament. Its stress on Yahweh's covenant with the Chosen People promoted both the essential separateness of Jews, and their biblically-based link with the Promised Land. Moreover, in such circles the Second Coming of Christ had associated with it the eventual return of Jews. Through these a matrix of belief patterns favourable to subsequent Political Zionism infused Western Protestant thought in the 16th and 17th centuries, and have continued to find expression in millenarian circles ever since. The category of biblical hermeneutics that views prophetic texts as having a literal fulfilment in events as they unfold, can, in its modern form, be traced back to two Englishmen, Revd Thomas Brightman and Sir Henry Finch, MP, with

Finch urging the British people and Parliament to support Jewish settlement in Palestine in order to fulfil Biblical prophecy.[6]

But it was John Nelson Darby (1800-82) who, more than anyone else, laid the foundations for the development of Evangelical Christian Zionism, by stressing the correspondence between biblical prophecy and historical developments. A former minister of the Church of Ireland, Darby renounced the visible Church, and organised a group of 'Brethren' ('Plymouth Brethren'), whose distinctive theology was devised for the final days of history.[7] Darby divided the totality of history into seven epochs ('Dispensations'), beginning with Creation, and ending with the millennial Kingdom of Jesus, following the Battle of Armageddon, views he claims to have derived from Scripture and the proddings of the Holy Spirit.[8]

Israel, for Darby, would replace the Church, which was a mere parenthesis to God's continuing covenant with Israel. Those portions of biblical prophecy and apocalyptic which had not been fulfilled already would be completed in the future. Invoking the apocalyptic language of Col. 3.4 and 1 Thess. 4.15 he postulated a two-stage Second Coming of Christ. The first 'invisible appearing' would involve the 'rapture of the saints': the faithful remnant of the Church, especially his own followers, would go up to meet Christ in the air, before his appearance on earth.[9] The raptured saints would return to earth with the Lord after seven years, as prescribed in 1 Thessalonians.[10] The seven-year long rapture in the air would be marked on earth by the 'Great Tribulation' of natural disasters, wars and civil unrest. After the rapture, a faithful Jewish remnant would observe the Law, and rule on earth for a millennium.[11]

With his authority waning in Britain, Darby concentrated on North America, where he influenced such evangelical leaders as Dwight L. Moody, William E Blackstone and C I Schofield and the emerging Bible and Prophecy Conference movement which set the tone for the

---

[6] Brightman's *Apocalypsis Apocalypseos* was published in London in 1585. Finch's *The World's Great Restauration or Calling of the Jewes* was published in London in 1621.
[7] John Nelson Darby, *The Collected Writings* (edited by William Kelly, Kingston on Thames: Stow Hill Bible and Trust Depot, 1962), Vol. XX, 456.
[8] *The Collected Writings*, Vol. II, 6-7, 108.
[9] *The Collected Writings*, Vol. II, 153-55.
[10] Darby, *Synopsis of the Books of the Bible* (London: G. Morrish, n.d.), Vol. V, 91.
[11] *The Collected Writings*, Vol. I, 94.

evangelical and fundamentalist movements in North America between 1875 and 1920.[12] Typically, Dispensationalism today predicates that the present age, in which the establishment of the State of Israel fulfils biblical prophecy, is the penultimate one, after which Christ will come in glory soon to bring matters to a cataclysmic triumph over the forces of evil at Armageddon.

When Political Zionism appeared in 1896, the prophetic and apocalyptic biblical oracles, interpreted along millenarianist lines, were available to provide theological legitimisation for those of such inclination, despite the fact that Political Zionism was a conscious repudiation of Judaism. The reawakened interest in a 'literalist', as opposed to a more sophisticated literary reading of the Scriptures, contributed to the renewal of interest in a collective 'national' identity of the Jewish 'people', who were desirous of a return to the homeland, producing, virtually for the first time in Western Christianity, a certain Judaeophilia.

The British clergyman, William Hechler, played a significant role in assisting Herzl's plans.[13] Already in 1882 Hechler in his *Die bevorstehende Rückkehr der Juden nach Palästina* had argued for the restoration of Jews to their ancestral land, in fulfilment of the Hebrew prophets. Soon after the publication of *Der Judenstaat* (1896) he presented himself in Herzl's study in Vienna, promising help. Relying on his good standing with the Grand Duke of Baden—he had been a tutor to his children—Hechler arranged Herzl's meeting with him, and later in Jerusalem with the Grand Duke's uncle, Kaiser Wilhelm II. As he explained in a letter to the Grand Duke (26 March 1896), in which he also promised to send three copies of Herzl's pamphlet, Hechler saw a clear correspondence between *Der Judenstaat* and the Hebrew prophetic tradition of Jewish restoration. Indeed, in a letter to a colleague in Jerusalem in 1898, Hechler identified the Zionist Movement with entering Israel's Messianic age, and all Zionist activity (e.g., clearing and irrigating the land) with 'messianic work'.[14] And all of this, despite the fact that the majority of Jews had no interest in Herzl's Political Zionism, and that

[12] Don Wagner, *Anxious for Armageddon: A Call to Partnership for Middle Eastern and Western Christians* (Scottdale & Waterloo, Penn: Herald Press, 1995), 89.

[13] See Paul C Merkley, *The Politics of Christian Zionism 1891-1948* (London/Portland OR: Frank Cass, 1998), 3-34.

[14] In Merkley, *The Politics of Christian Zionism*, 15-16.

the religious establishment thoroughly repudiated his programme as contrary to Holy Scripture and to Judaism.[15]

Darby's legacy, mediated by key supporters, ensured that there would be strong support for the establishment of a Jewish commonwealth among American evangelicals ever since. For William E. Blackstone, as for Hechler, Zionism was 'the fulfilment of prophecy'. He was impressed by the Jewish agricultural settlements in Palestine in 1889, which he saw as 'signs of the times', indicating that the End Time would come very soon.[16] In 1891, Blackstone organised a national campaign urging President Harrison to support the establishment of a Jewish state in Palestine, with the morally-superior USA playing the role of a modern Cyrus speeding the return of the Jews. Hearing that Theodor Herzl was considering Uganda or Argentina for his state, Blackstone sent him a Bible, marking every passage which referred to Palestine, with instructions that it alone was to be the site of the Jewish state. In 1916 Blackstone presented a second petition to the President, this time co-ordinating with American Zionist leaders. The Zionist leaders, of course, passed over the characteristic evangelical disparagement of the Jewish Law as an agent of salvation, and its real hopes for the Jews (their conversion to Christianity), as the price for his support for the Zionist venture.

When it was established in 1948 the evangelical world viewed the State of Israel as the first clear sign of the fulfilment of biblical prophecy and the final countdown to Armageddon. Later, Israel's

---

[15] Herzl and his Zionism were anathema to the most influential eastern European rabbis (see David Vital, *A People Apart: The Jews in Europe 1789–1939,* Oxford: Oxford University Press, 1999, 625). In the West, his own Chief Rabbi in Vienna, Moritz Güdemann, objected that the Jews were not a nation, and that Zionism was incompatible with Judaism (*Nationaljudentum,* Leipzig and Vienna: M Breitenstein's Verlags-Buchhandlung, 1897, 42). Similarly France's Grand Rabbi, Zadok Kahn, protested (Herzl, *Diaries,* 18 November 1895). The German Rabbinical Council publicly condemned the efforts of 'the so-called Zionists' to create a Jewish national state in Palestine as contrary to Holy Writ. Belgium's Grand Rabbi, M A Bloch, also protested, describing Zionist aspirations as far from those of Judaism. The Chief Rabbi of the Commonwealth, Hermann Adler, who had received Herzl in London, viewed his programme as an 'egregious blunder' and an 'absolutely mischievous project.' He considered the Zionist movement to be opposed to the teaching of Judaism (see Chief Rabbi Immanuel Jakobovits, *The Attitude to Zionism of Britain's Chief Rabbis as Reflected in their Writings,* London: The Jewish Historical Society of England, 1982, 4-5).

[16] William E Blackstone, *Jesus is Coming,* (New York: Fleming Revel, 1908, third ed.; first ed. 1878), 210-13, 236-41.

'amazing', even 'miraculous' victory over Arab armies in June 1967 confirmed the prophetic scenario. Hal Lindsey's *The Late, Great Planet Earth* (1970) reflects a mixture of biblical literalism and political analysis, which is typical, with biblical predictions fulfilled in modern events almost to the letter:

—the establishment of Israel (Ezek 30-40);
—the 'fig tree' put forth its first leaves on 14 May 1948 (Matt 24.32);
—Jews' control of all Jerusalem (Zech 12-14);
—the alignment of Arab and Black African states against Israel (Ezek 30.4-5);
—the conversion of Africa to Communism (Dan 11.35-45);
—the Soviet threat in the north (Ezek 38-39), and the Chinese one in the east (Rev 9);
—the rise of the Common Market as the new Roman empire (Dan 7.17), etc.

The October War of 1973 gave further fuel to Armageddon theology. Jerry Falwell's 'Friendship Tour to Israel' in 1983 included meetings with Israeli government and military officials, a tour of Israeli battlefields and defence installations. His 'Prophecy Trips' to Jerusalem heralded the immigration of Jews into Israel as *the* sign of the imminent Second Coming of Christ. Jesus would rapture true Christians into the air, while the rest of humankind would be slaughtered below. Then 144,000 Jews would bow down before Jesus and be saved, but the remainder would perish in the mother of all *Shoahs*. This could happen even while the evangelical pilgrims were in Jerusalem, giving them a ringside seat at the Battle of Armageddon. Biblical prophecy, then, was striving towards its fulfilment in the Middle East today. Thus, Saddam Hussein was reconstructing Babylon to the same specifications of splendour as in the days of Nebuchadnezzar, and the city would ignite the events of the End Times.[17] Against such a divinely-authored and inerrant biblical background it is little wonder that, forgetting momentarily his interests in oil, George W Bush's vulgar rhetoric advocating 'regime-change' gains much unquestioned support in the USA.

---

[17] Thus, Charles H Dyer, *World News and Biblical Prophecy* (Wheaton, Illinois: Tyndale House, 1993), 128-29.

Despite the bizarre nature of such views, broadly shared by Evangelical Christian Zionists in the USA (Hal Lindsay, Jerry Falwell, Pat Robertson, *et alii*), they exert far more influence on USA foreign policies, than do, for example, Jesus' exhortations to 'feed the hungry, etc.' with respect to its attitudes to famine in Africa. But, leaving aside morality concerns and confining one's critique to questions of hermeneutics, one notes that in their determination to insist on the divine provenance of the Bible and its 'inerrancy' Evangelical Christian Zionists neglect the human dimension of the authorship of the books, and ignore altogether the hermeneutical implications of the variety of literary forms within the Bible. Such Christians distort the sophistication of eschatological hope by reducing its expression in symbolic and metaphorical language to precise predictions of future events. Christian eschatology is open-ended, and human language is inadequate to outline the flowering of Christian hope. Humans are no better equipped to define the disposition of the End Time than children in the womb are to describe the world outside. When it comes to the question of hope and the future Christians would do better to enquire into the ramifications of the Passion, Death and Resurrection of Jesus, than to search for a one-for-one conformity between the metaphorical language of an earlier age and contemporary political events, which in our context reduces Christian eschatology to despicable modern barbarisms.

Christian Zionist groups, in general—but one welcomes recent signs of changes of heart—show little concern for issues of human rights and international law when these conflict with their unique understanding of the biblical narrative, and its application to modern Israel. This tendency leads to deviations from any acceptable morality, and certainly one consonant with widely-accepted Christian principles. Thus we had, for example, televangelist Pat Robertson charting the Israeli invasion of Lebanon in 1982, with daily reports on CBN interpreting it according to the end-time fulfilment of biblical prophecy. Israel's attack was a modern Joshua event—by biblical definition, of course, above reproach—and Robertson urged American viewers to phone President Reagan offering encouragement to Israel's war.[18] That

---

[18] Dan O'Neill, and Don Wagner, *Peace or Armageddon? The Unfolding Drama of the Middle East Peace Accord* (Grand Rapids: Zondervan Publishing House, 1993), 84.

the Israeli invasion resulted in some 17,500 casualties, mostly civilian, was of no moral concern.[19]

EUROPE'S SCRAMBLE FOR PALESTINE

The attitudes of the external mainstream Christian Church to the Holy Land reflect changing political circumstances. Prior to the 19th century, the real Palestine was virtually *terra incognita* for Europeans, due to the paucity of Western visitors. In the first thirty years of that century a new appetite for European exploration was developing, which in the succeeding decades reflected religious as well as antiquarian interests. Temporary Egyptian rule in Palestine (1831-1840) under Ibrahim Pasha, was the catalyst for change. In the interests of obtaining Western support for Egyptian control of Syria he opened up Palestine to European exploration and to missionary and cultural activities. Religious explorers confined their interests to relics of antiquity, with the indigenous people and modern settlements being little more than a distraction. The early photography also projected 'a Palestine of stones and relics, mosques, sanctuaries, Crusader remains: a romantic shell, a necropolis, without a single sign of contemporary life,' a deserted landscape, with no sense of a place where people lived, worked, or worshipped.[20]

The 'biblical geography' of Professor Edward E Robinson of Union Theological Seminary, New York, who journeyed to the land in 1837-38, reflected typical Western attitudes to the exotic East, including a general contempt for the locals.[21] He disdained the traditional pilgrimage sites and their 'superstitious practices', supported only by the legendary

---

[19] For a fuller treatment, see my *Zionism and the State of Israel: A Moral Inquiry* (London and New York: Routledge 1999), 137-47. For a perspective on Christian Zionism in the USA, Britain, and Scandinavia, see the articles by Don Wagner ('Reagan and Begin, Bibi and Jerry: The Theopolitical Alliance of the Likud Party with the American Christian "Right"'), Stephen Sizer ('Christian Zionism: A British Perspective') and Göran Gunner ('Christian Zionism in Scandinavia') in Michael Prior and Naim S Ateek, *Holy Land— Hollow Jubilee: God, Justice and the Palestinians* (London, Melisende, 1999), 199-215, 189-98, and 180-88, respectively.

[20] See Naomi Shepherd, *The Zealous Intruders: The Western Rediscovery of Palestine* (London: Collins, 1987), 186-89.

[21] *Biblical Researches in Palestine, Mount Sinai and Arabian Petraea. A Journal of Travels in the Year 1838* (Boston: Crocker and Brewster, 1842).

pieties of the exotic Eastern, and the highly-suspect practices of the Latin Church. His scientific method would refute 'medieval legends', and rescue Palestine for Protestantism, giving a privileged place, of course, to the biblical past.

In that period also, several of the European nations were flexing their colonial muscles around the globe, and with the Ottoman Empire showing signs of disintegration the Middle East was an attractive target for economic, cultural, and political penetration. England, Russia, France, Germany, Austria, and others engaged in a scramble for national presence and influence in Palestine. The open policy of the Egyptians permitted the establishment of consulates in Jerusalem, and, soon after, national societies for the exploration of Palestine were established by Britain (1865), the USA (1870), Germany (1877), and France (1890). There was, of course, an integral relationship between scientific investigation and its imperial supporters, with the charting of the 'new' territory functioning as an aspect of Europe's determination to control other cultures.

Coinciding with the wider European territorial ambitions Western scholars began to investigate the Holy Land from the perspective of the biblical narrative, the cornerstone of Europe's civilisation. Interest was fuelled also by the challenge to the authority of the Bible made by discoveries in the science of fossils, and by Higher Criticism. Science was revealing that the earth was millions, rather than, as the Bible presents it, thousands of years old. Moreover, Higher Criticism was arguing that the first five books of the Bible (the *Torah*, the Pentateuch), previously attributed to Moses, were a much later collection of texts from different periods, containing, in addition, many inconsistencies and chronological impossibilities. However, rather than rejecting outright the discoveries of scholars, it was considered that the assault on the Bible could best be withstood by providing no less rigorous scientific evidence of its accuracy, and no location was more suitable for such a task than the biblical land itself. Inevitably the social and political context of its engagement influenced profoundly Europe's estimation of ancient Palestine: rather than being a region with its own intrinsic value, it was esteemed primarily as the location of events and stories related in the biblical narrative. Concentration on the past was marked by a decided detachment from the contemporary lives of the people. The lifeless mounds enveiling earlier civilisations were much more significant than the throbbing Arab cities and villages scattered throughout the country.[22]

Invariably foreign interest also took the form of establishing Christian institutions, uniting Christian missionary endeavour with national influence. What most distinguished the Dominican foundation, the *École Biblique*, from biblical schools elsewhere was its location. It was the land in terms of its witness to antiquity, rather than the changing demographic circumstances of its contemporary inhabitants, of course, which preoccupied its founder, Père Marie-Joseph Lagrange, OP. Although it was very much a religious and scholastic enterprise, the French government in 1921 effectively constituted it as *École Biblique et Archéologique Française à Jérusalem*, after the fashion of the celebrated French schools in Rome and Athens, and Lagrange considered himself to be entrusted with the charge of assuring for France the prestige in Palestinian antiquities enjoyed by the English and American schools.

In Britain, some circles had advocated that the empire's foreign interests could be advanced by supporting the restoration of Jews to Palestine, aspired to in British (and American) Protestant millenarianist and restorationist circles. As early as 2 August 1840, Viscount Palmerston wrote to Viscount Ponsonby: 'The Jewish *people*, if *returning* under the sanction and protection and at the invitation of the Sultan, would be a check upon any future evil designs of Mohammed Ali or his successor.'[23] Coinciding with the West's cultural and religious colonialism, political Zionism also was beginning to take root in Palestine. Although the European Zionist settlers, for the most part, saw themselves as repudiating the Jewish religion, their enterprise was capable of being viewed in the biblical terms of the promise and conquest of 'the land of Canaan', and restoration to it in accordance with biblical prophecy. There could be, then, a coalescence of goals between secular Zionists and some Christians in the West, for whom the Zionist 'fulfilment of biblical prophecy' coincided with their national foreign interests. The interests of Europeans

---

[22] See Neal A Silberman, *Digging for God and Country* (New York: Knopf, 1982), and 'Structuring the Past: Israelis, Palestinians, and the Symbolic Authority of Archaeological Monuments', in Neil Asher Silberman and David Small, *The Archaeology of Israel. Constructing the Past, Interpreting the Present* (Sheffield: Sheffield Academic Press, 1997, 62-81), 66.

[23] Foreign Office 79/390 [No. 134] Public Record Office (italics added).

can be seen also in the growth in popular Christian pilgrimage to the Holy Land towards the end of the 19th century. Protestant pilgrims, in particular, avoided contact with 'the natives', were disdainful of their customs and pious practices, and were unchanged by the encounter with the region.[24] It was enough that the Holy Land had brought the Bible 'alive' in their imagination, and confirmed them in the assurance of the religious, social, and moral superiority of their Western, Reformed Christianity. That it had modern inhabitants was of no interest.

'GO FROM YOUR COUNTRY': AN ARAB-FREE STATE FOR JEWS

Theodor Herzl outlined his programme to establish a state exclusively for Jews in his pamphlet, *Der Judenstaat* (1896).[25] His Political Zionism was a recourse of desperation. The renewed rise of antisemitism was altogether frustrating the promise held out by European liberalism that Jews would be fully integrated into the mainstream of European humanity, rather than enjoy a pariah-like, second-class status as had been their wont. What mattered for the indigenes of Palestine, of course, were Zionism's demographic consequences for the non-Jewish population, Muslim, Christian and Druze, who at the time accounted for some 95 percent of the population. Herzl was in no doubt that his utopian vision would be a nightmare for the indigenous peoples. An item in his diary entry for 12 June 1895 signals his plans. Having occupied the land and expropriated the private property, 'We shall endeavour to expel the poor population across the border unnoticed, procuring employment for it in the transit countries, but denying it any employment in our own country.'[26] He added that both 'the process of expropriation and the removal of the poor must be carried out

---

[24] See Ruth Hummel and Thomas Hummel, *Patterns of the Sacred. English Protestant and Russian Orthodox Pilgrims of the Nineteenth Century* (London: Scorpion Cavendish, 1995), 3, 13.

[25] *The Jewish State. An Attempt at a Modern Solution of the Jewish Question*, a revised translation, with a foreword by Israel Cohen, was published in London (Henry Pordes) in 1993, and page references in the text refer to this edition.

[26] 'Die arme Bevölkerung trachten wir unbemerkt über die Grenze zu schaffen, indem wir in den Durchzugsländern Arbeit verschaffen aber in unserem eigenen Lande jederlei Arbeit verweigern' (Theodor Herzl, *Briefe und Autobiographische Notizen. 1886-1895*. Vol. II, ed. by Johannes Wachten *et al.*, Berlin: Propylaen Verlag, 1983, 117-18).

discreetly and circumspectly.' Nevertheless, the modern, secular Jewish commonwealth of Herzl's novel *Altneuland* ('Old New Land'), completed in April 1902 but set in 1923 and for European consumption, was a haven of the liberal spirit and a blessing for the natives.[27]

Mirroring typical 19th-century European colonial attitudes, Herzl presented the proposed state as 'a portion of the rampart of Europe against Asia, an outpost of civilisation [*Kultur*] opposed to barbarism'.[28] He reflected elsewhere also typical European colonialist superiority. He assured the Grand Duke of Baden that Jews returning to their 'historic fatherland' would do so as representatives of Western civilisation, bringing 'cleanliness, order and the well-established customs of the Occident to this plague-ridden, blighted corner of the Orient'.[29] To adapt the language of Joseph Conrad, Herzl's state for Jews would be an 'outpost of progress' in 'the heart of darkness'.

THE CATHOLIC CHURCH AND HERZL'S ZIONISM

Despite the significance of Herzl's plans the voluminous Vatican files dealing with Palestine during the last years of Pope Leo XIII's pontificate (1896-1903) do not mention Zionism, nor the growing, but still miniscule immigration of Jews there.[30] Yet as early as May 1896 Herzl had discussed his plans with the Papal Nuncio in Vienna, suggesting to him that Jerusalem, Bethlehem and Nazareth be excluded from his proposed Jewish state, be internationalised, and possibly placed under the protectorate of the Holy See.[31] He attempted in 1901 to secure an audience with the Pope,[32] and two years later tried again,[33] having written already to the

---

[27] *Old New Land*, translated from the German by Lotta Levensohn, is republished by Markus Wiener Publishers, Princeton (third printing, 2000).

[28] *The Jewish State*, 30.

[29] *The Complete Diaries of Theodor Herzl*, translated by Harry Zohn, and edited by Raphael Patai (New York: Herzl Press, 1960), Vol. I, 343. In 1996 the final, seventh volume of all Herzl's writings in the original languages, begun in 1983, was completed (Berlin: Propylaen Verlag).

[30] Andrej Kreutz, *Vatican Policy on the Palestinian-Israeli Conflict. The Struggle for the Holy Land*. Contributions in Political Science, No. 246 (New York, Westport, London: Greenwood Press, 1990), 51 n. 20.

[31] *The Complete Diaries*, 1: 352-54.

[32] *The Complete Diaries*, 3: 1096-97.

[33] 19 October 1903, *The Complete Diaries*, 4: 1566-67.

President of the Italian Zionist Federation: 'We want only the profane earth in Palestine ...The Holy Places shall be ex-territorialised for ever. *Res sacrae extra commercium*, as a right of nations'.[34]

Herzl met Pope Pius X (Rome, 23 January 1904), who refused to support Zionist intentions: 'We cannot prevent the Jews from going to Jerusalem—but we could never sanction it. The soil of Jerusalem, if it was not always sacred, has been sanctified by the life of Jesus Christ'. According to Herzl's account, the Pope also said: 'It is not pleasant to see the Turks in possession of the Holy Places but we have to put up with it; but we could not possibly support the Jews in the acquisition of the Holy Places. If you come to Palestine and settle with your people there, we shall have churches and priests ready to baptise all of you.'[35] If the Pope was more interested in religious than demographic and justice issues the same cannot be said of Victor Emmanuel III, with whom he also had an audience. To Herzl's request for support for a Jewish state in Tripoli, the king replied, '*Ma è ancora casa di altri*' ('But it is already the home of other people').

Up to the Balfour Declaration the primary interest of the Holy See was in the Christian Holy Places.[36] In the face of the prospect of their being 'in the custody of the synagogue', Secretary of State, Cardinal Gasparri, remarked: 'It is hard to take back that part of our heart which has been given over to the Turks in order to give it to the Zionists'.[37] However, the Holy See was also beginning to be sensitive to the aspirations of the indigenous population. On 6 March 1922, Gasparri severely criticised the draft British Mandate for Palestine (7 December 1920), because it would establish 'an absolute economic, administrative, and political preponderance of Jews,' and would act as 'the instrument for subordinating native populations'.[38] One detects here the emergence of a concern for the rights of the Palestinians. The Holy See, however, had little enthusiasm for an Arab government, which it predicted would be unreliable and weak. It was happy to support the social and economic

---

[34] September 1903, in Kreutz, *Vatican Policy* ..., 32. Similarly, in *The Jewish State* (30).

[35] *The Complete Diaries*, 4: 1601-603.

[36] Daniela Fabrizio examines the interplay between religious, cultural and political interests on the question of the Holy Places (*La Questione dei Luoghi Santi e l'Assetto della Palestina 1914-1922*, Milano: FrancoAngeli, 2000).

[37] Sergio I Minerbi, *The Vatican and Zionism: Conflict in the Holy Land, 1895-1925* (New York/Oxford: Oxford University Press, 1990), xiii.

[38] In Andrej Kreutz, 'The Vatican and the Palestinians: A Historical Overview', in *Islamochristiana* 18 (1992): 109-25, 115.

interests of the Palestinians, but not their self-determination, and as late as January 1948, Mgr. G Montini (the future Pope Paul VI) told the British Minister to the Vatican that the Holy See preferred that 'a third power, neither Jew nor Arab ... have control of the Holy Land.'[39]

THE CATHOLIC CHURCH AND THE STATE OF ISRAEL

The establishment of the State of Israel on 78 per cent of British Mandated Palestine, and the expulsion of some 750,000 Palestinian Arabs, including some 50,000 Christians—35 per cent of all Christians who lived in Palestine prior to 15 May 1948—while acknowledged to be a disaster, did not induce the Holy See to make any diplomatic representations. Such was the international support for Zionism in the wake of the *Shoah* that it was virtually impossible for the Holy See to challenge Zionism publicly. In his Encyclicals, *In Multiplicibus* of October 1948 and *Redemptoris Nostri*, six months later, Pope Pius XII did not go beyond the expression of his anguish at the general conditions of refugees, and predictable, broad moral and religious principles, with no explicit political implications. The Palestinian issue was scarcely mentioned publicly for the next twenty years.

The Declaration on Religious Freedom (*Nostra Aetate*) of the Second Vatican Council (1962-65) provided a stimulus to better relations between Christianity and other religions, including Judaism. Parallel with this was the growing sense of the essential link between the Gospel and issues of justice and peace. Translated to the Middle East, there were, then, two, competing tendencies developing, a greater respect for the Jews, and a growing sympathy for the plight of the Palestinians.

The victory of Israel in the war of June 1967 imposed a new sense of the reality and power of the Jewish state. Pope Paul VI expressed his concern at the decrease in the numbers of Christians in the Holy Land, with the fear that 'the shrines would be without the warmth of the living witness of the Holy Places of Jerusalem, and the Holy Land would become like a museum.'[40] In addressing Israeli Jews on 22 December

---

[39] Perowne to Burrows, 19 January 1948—FO 371/68500, in Kreutz, 'The Vatican and the Palestinians', 116.

[40] Apostolic Exhortation, 'Concerning the increased needs of the Church in the Holy Land', 1974.

1975, he appealed for recognition of the rights and legitimate aspirations of the long-suffering Palestinian people, now that Jews after the very recent tragedies had secured safe protection in a state of its own.[41] This was the first time that a Pope had recognised the rights and legitimate aspirations of Jews to a sovereign and independent state, but its establishment brought moral responsibilities.

By 1983 the Holy See recognised the factual existence of Israel, its right to exist within secure borders. After Israeli Prime Minister Shimon Peres' visit to the Vatican (19 February 1985), the Holy See's spokesman referred to differences on essential problems, which included the status of Jerusalem, the sovereignty of Lebanon over all its territory, and the lot of the Palestinian people.[42] The appeal for recognition of the rights of both Jews and Palestinians has been a constant call of Pope John Paul II. The Palestinians' natural rights in justice to a 'homeland' were repeated.[43] During his visit to Austria in June 1988, the Pope called again for equality for Israeli Jews and Palestinians, pointing out that full diplomatic relations between the Holy See and Israel are 'dependent on a solution to the Palestinian Question and the international status of Jerusalem.' The Palestinians had a right to a homeland, 'like every other nation, according to international law.' In his Easter Message of 1991 John Paul II appealed for the rights of oppressed peoples (the Palestinians, the Lebanese, the Kurds) to exist with dignity, justice and freedom.

In the heady atmosphere of the Oslo Accords, the Fundamental Agreement between the Holy See and the State of Israel (30 December 1993) was followed by full recognition of Israel. Finally, in February–March 2000 the Pope made a pilgrimage to the Holy Land, fulfilling a desire since the beginning of his pontificate in 1978. In each country he alluded to different challenges. In Egypt he appealed for the unity of Christians and friendly relations with Muslims. In Jordan he referred to 'peace' thirteen times, and appealed also for unity among Muslims and Christians, as well as for unity among the Christian community. In Israel–Palestine, he referred to 'peace' more than fifty times, and to 'justice'

---

[41] *Acta Apostolicae Sedis*, January–March 1976, 134.

[42] See 'La Santa Sede e lo Stato d'Israele', in *La Civiltà Cattolica*, 16 February 1991, 357-58.

[43] See the communiqué after Yasser Arafat's visit to the Pope (15 September 1982) in *La Documentation Catholique* 73 (1982), 17 October, 921 and 947, and the Apostolic Letter, *Redemptionis Anno* (April 1984), in Secretariatus pro non-Christianis, Bulletin 57 (1984), XIX(3), 254.

twelve times. Reconciliation between Jews and Christians was a recurring theme in the Israel part of the pilgrimage, and mutual respect between Christians and Muslims in the Palestinian areas. Could the Pope in his declining years promote peace? The signs are not promising. Even the inter-faith meeting in Jerusalem's Notre Dame Hotel brought to the surface the depth of the religious and nationalist disharmony, with the Pope looking acutely embarrassed as Ashkenazi Chief Rabbi, Yisrael Lau, proclaimed that the meeting in Jerusalem was tantamount to the Pope's recognition of Israel's exclusive claims to Jerusalem, which was followed by a stinging criticism of Israel's policies in the city by Taysir Tammami, the Head of the Shari'a courts in the West Bank. And shortly after the Pope left Dheisheh Refugee Camp a riot broke out. Soon we had the second *intifada*, and the multiplicity of barbarisms since.

CONCLUSION

It is one of the anomalies of recent Church history that while Christians, embarrassed by past association with colonial enterprises, have supported oppressed peoples virtually everywhere else, there has been little protest against the historic injustice perpetrated on the indigenous population of Palestine by Political Zionism, a movement thoroughly at home in the colonial spirit of 19th-century Europe. The Evangelical Zionist wing in the main, locked into a naïve and fundamentally immoral interpretation of biblical prophetic and apocalyptic texts, shows few signs of moral perturbation. The god of such revelation, of course, is a militaristic and xenophobic genocidist, who is not sufficiently moral even to conform to the requirements of the Fourth Geneva Convention, or any of the Human Rights Protocols which attempt to set limits to barbarism. The grotesque views of Christian Zionists, embracing an essentially ethnic-cleansing enterprise as a fulfilment of biblical prophecy, and clothing Zionism in the garment of piety, would not warrant attention were it not for the influence they have on the domestic and foreign politics of the USA.

Neither has the performance of the mainstream Churches been a model of ethical engagement.[44] Rather than giving a lead in moral

---

[44] There is virtually no difference between the perspectives of the World Council of Churches and the Holy See. With respect to the national churches one detects sympathy for Israel growing the closer they are to Germany. See my *Zionism and the State of Israel*, 103-33.

debate, they fall into line with ongoing political manoeuvres, which in conforming with the demands of the powerful, reflect little contact with recognisable moral principles. The most they appear able to bring themselves to is to subscribe to the 'fallacy of balance'. They offer no critique of the ideology of Political Zionism commensurate with that of *apartheid*, for example, an ideology of far less deleterious consequences than Zionism. To add to the Church's neglect, the evidence is abundant that the damage done to the indigenous population was neither accidental nor due to the unique pressures of war, but was at the heart of the Zionist enterprise from the beginning. Yet, the Churches reflect little appetite to pursue these issues of justice and respect for historical truth.

An individual Catholic has a right to expect better of her/his representative political wing. The absence in the Fundamental Agreement between the Holy See and the State of Israel of any reference to Palestinian Arabs, or to the injustice done them on the establishment of the State of Israel and since, is quite scandalous. The only reference to acknowledged political matters is in Article 11. Both parties commit themselves to the promotion of peaceful resolution of conflicts (par. 1). How exactly, is not spelt out. Instead, we are assured that the prophetic voice of the Church will be silenced: the Holy See solemnly commits itself 'to remaining a stranger to all merely temporal conflicts, which principle applies specifically to disputed territories and unsettled borders' (par. 2).

For religious bodies to 'air-brush' from history, and accord legitimacy to the expulsion of an indigenous population, and the appropriation of their lands is highly problematic, even in consideration of good relations between two religious traditions and their allegedly representative political wings. Invariably, sympathy for the Zionist enterprise, whatever its failures with respect to justice and international legality, is a compulsory requirement for participants in the conventional Jewish-Christian dialogue. Typically, the dialogue is characterised by an uncritical acceptance of the 'canonical' Zionist reading of history, however contradictory that is to historical intentions and realities.[45]

It appears that no Church authority is prepared to insist that Israel apologise for its seminal injustice to the Palestinian Arabs, undo the damage it has perpetrated, honour its obligations with respect to the

---

[45] For a fuller discussion of the proclivities of the Jewish-Christian dialogue see my *Zionism and the State of Israel*, 123-31.

Palestinian right of return, make appropriate compensation for the damage done, and, on the basis of confession and restitution, move towards a less ethnocratic polity. Such exhortations would flow effortlessly from principles of Christian morality, and would be in conformity with elementary justice. What we get instead is the embrace of whatever proposal, however jaded and however lacking in principles of justice, the asymmetric parties to the dispute contrive, as if the Church were content to act on the novel moral principle that the rights of the perpetrators of injustice and its victims are finely balanced.

ANTIZIONISM EQUALS ANTISEMITISM?

Michael here challenges the assertion that criticism of Israel springs from anti-semitism and questions the presupposition behind 'the two state solution' (Doctrine and Life, *Dublin, 2002).*

Virtually as soon as the State of Israel begins to be criticised for its behaviour towards the Palestinians one notices two developments in the West: an immediate increase in the number of media outlets portraying aspects of the *Shoah*—the Nazi's 'Final Solution to the Jewish Problem'— and the resurfacing of the charge of 'antisemitism', directed against critics of Israel's behaviour. While these recurring tendencies are the products of a range of emotions that run deeper than logic they do lock into two common misunderstandings.

The State of Israel is frequently portrayed as simply 'the Jewish response to the *Shoah*'. Thus, the Nazis' horrors prove that Zionism was justified, and Zionist Jews—many Jews are anti-Zionist, post-Zionist, or just tired of the whole business—and the Israelis justify the displacement of the indigenous Palestinians, and exculpate Israel of virtually any maltreatment of the remaining Palestinians. The eccentric nature of such an interpretation of morality, held by even some of the most liberal Israelis, somehow escapes serious analysis.

Secondly, even while being the perpetrator of a gross and ongoing injustice on the indigenous Palestinians, Israel presents itself as an innocent victim above reproach. When criticised, Israelis, then, are casualties of perennial, ubiquitous and irredentist antisemitism. To offset even the most timid Catholic criticism, the saga of 'the Christian contempt of Judaism', and the allegedly despicable performance of Pius XII during the Second World War are played over, again and again.

ZIONISM: A SUBSTITUTE FOR JUDAISM

It is, however, self-deluding for Israelis and their supporters to conclude that criticism of Israel is mostly a manifestation of Jew-hatred, or that

Israel is being singled out simply because it is a Jewish state. It is also naïve to present Political Zionism as a response to the *Shoah*, and it is less than honest to equiparate Zionism with either Judaism or Jewry. It is important to situate the birth of Zionism in its historical context. This reveals its secular, indeed anti-religious nature, evoking virtually universal condemnation from the rabbis, as well as its transparently colonialist nature.

In *Der Judenstaat* (1896)—more appropriately translated 'the state for Jews', to distinguish it from the implications of a Jewish state (*Jüdischer Staat*)—Theodor Herzl (1860-1904) outlined his Political Zionism, and provided the major ideological drive to establish the state for Jews. Herzlian Zionism was a secular ideology from its inception. Herzl had no sense of Jewish culture and no attachment to Judaism. Indeed, while in Vienna in 1881-82, he had considered even mass Jewish conversion to Catholicism as a solution to the problem of being a Jew in Europe. By 1895 he had lost all hope that Jews would ever be fully assimilated into European society, and judged the efforts to combat antisemitism to be futile.

Herzl insisted that Jews world-wide constituted one people and a 'distinctive nationality', whose problem could be solved only through the 'restoration' of the Jewish state. Just as 'Pan-Germanism' proclaimed that everyone of German race, blood or descent, owed their primary loyalty to the homeland, so Jews, wherever they lived, constituted a distinct nation, whose welfare could be advanced only through establishing a Jewish nation-state, preferably in Palestine.

His project immediately ran into opposition from the religious establishment, being perceived as a conscious repudiation of the most fundamental tenets of Judaism. For Orthodox Jews the diaspora was a condition ordained by God, who alone would bring it to an end. That the Zionist movement would arrogate to itself the agency for the *restoration* of the Jewish people to its ancestral land—uniquely the task of the Messiah—was sheer blasphemy. Reform Judaism, for its part, viewing Jewish history as evolutionary, rejected the notion that Jews outside Palestine were 'in exile', insisting that Jews constituted a religious community, rather than a nation, and were citizens of many states.

Zionism was not merely a variant on the Jewish faith, but a very substitute for it. Herzl and his Zionism were anathema to the most influential eastern European rabbis. In the West, his own Chief Rabbi in Vienna, Moritz Güdemann, objected that the Jews were not a nation, and that Zionism was incompatible with Judaism. Similarly France's Grand Rabbi, Zadok Kahn, protested. The German Rabbinical Council publicly condemned the efforts of 'the so-called Zionists' to create a Jewish national state in Palestine as contrary to Holy Writ. Belgium's Grand Rabbi, M A Bloch, also protested, describing Zionist aspirations as far from those of Judaism. The Chief Rabbi of the Commonwealth, Hermann Adler, who had received Herzl in London, viewed his programme as an 'egregious blunder' and an 'absolutely mischievous project.' He considered the Zionist movement to be opposed to the teaching of Judaism.

The Zionist movement was considered to be a rebellion against classical Judaism, and with good reason. For political Zionists, religion was irrational, and a repressive and regressive force. For them, salvation lay in escaping from the prison of the sacred, and the hypnotic spell of the Bible. Judaism was a weight of lead attached to the feet of Jews. For such people, religion was a symptom of Jewry's sickness in exile. Zionist Palestine would be new, secular, and qualitatively different from the past of the diaspora.

Agudat Yisrael, formed in Germany in 1912 to present a united Orthodox front, in the face of the dangers posed by secularisation, assimilation and Herzlian Jewish nationalism was consistently opposed to Zionism because of its arrogating to itself the divine initiative. It considered Zionism to be a pseudo-messianic, satanic conspiracy against God whose responsibility alone it was to gather in the Jews. Moreover, Zionism was bent on removing from Jewish communal life the religious values which had united Jews down the ages. Zionism, then, strove to protect Jewish life, while abandoning the values which had sustained it. The abandonment of what was most characteristically Jewish in the pursuit of purely secular, nineteenth-century European notions of nationhood, was, for them, the ultimate form of assimilation.

Although thoroughly despised as an aspiration by mainstream Orthodox and Reform Judaism until the 1930s and 40s, Zionism, even in its most expansionist and imperialist form, now has virtually unquestioning support in mainstream religious Jewish circles, especially in the wake of the 'miraculous victory' of the 1967 Israeli-Arab war. For many religious Jews, formerly secular, anti-religious Zionism has been metamorphosed and even clothed in the garments of piety. Thus, the late Chief Rabbi of the British Commonwealth, Immanuel Jakobovits, could claim that the origins of the Zionist idea were entirely religious, holding that 'The Bible is our mandate'. And more recently, Chief Rabbi Jonathan Sacks considers the State of Israel to be the most powerful collective expression of Jewry. Its birth was a coming to the promised land, in the line of Abraham and Sarah, Moses, Ezra and Nehemiah. The very existence of the state, he affirms, testifies to the power of hope sustained by prayer. Prayer shawls might sit somewhat uncomfortably on the shoulders of Prime Ministers Begin, Rabin, Peres, Netanyahu, Barak and Sharon.

Despite the *volte-face* of the establishment, both in Israel and abroad, religious opposition to Political Zionism has not altogether been suffocated. Although it still retains some of its ideological non-Zionism, and even anti-Zionism *Agudat Yisrael* has reached an accommodation with Political Zionism. Other more rejectionist religious groups regard the state as an abomination. For the 'ultra-Orthodox' movement—the most undefiled Jews in their own terms—hell had entered Israel with Herzl. Several communities in Israel and elsewhere hold that the state is an act of rebellion against God, because the initiative for 'ingathering' must be God's.

In particular, *Neturei Karta*, founded in Jerusalem in 1938, refuses to recognise the authority of 'the illegitimate so-called 'State of Israel''. For them, Zionism is the most pernicious movement in Jewish history. The *miraculous* event of 1967 is merely the temptation of the righteous to be lured away from authentic salvation. Unlike most participants in the debate who never consider the moral question of the impact of Political Zionism on the indigenous Palestinians, *Neturei Karta* is distressed at the injustices to the Palestinians in the name of Jewishness. It stresses that the Talmud and Midrash explicitly prohibit premature attempts to end exile, and insists that the 'pseudo religion of Zionism' is a product of the abandonment of the *Torah* and a demonising of all nations.

World Jewry, they claim, is implicated in Israel's violence against the Palestinians. Since Israel is now the most dangerous place in the world for Jews, Zionism's 'dismal failure' in solving the 'Jewish question' by 'ending exile' should be acknowledged, and this should lead to the total dismantling of the Israeli state and the transfer of sovereignty to Palestinian rule. Already too much blood has been shed on the altar of a nineteenth-century colonial nationalism, misapplied to the Jewish people. From being a people of faith, Zionism has changed Jewishness to a barren secular, ethnic identity.

True Jews, they insist, are not allowed to dominate, kill, harm or demean another people. They deplore the systematic uprooting of ancient Jewish communities by the Zionists, and the shedding of Jewish and non-Jewish blood for the sake of Zionist sovereignty. After fifty four years, five wars, endless terror and counter-terror, innocent civilians dead on both sides, there is, they bemoan, no solution in sight. They regard Zionism as a tragic experiment. The land belongs to those who have dwelt there for centuries. Whether the Palestinians allow a few or many Jews to maintain citizenship in their state is entirely up to them.

Despite the recent adulation of Zionism in Jewish religious circles—and that constituency has, in one of the most extraordinary ideological metamorphoses of the twentieth century, moved from castigating Zionism as an heresy to embracing it, and being its most enthusiastic supporter—it hardly appears reasonable to equate anti-Zionism with anti-Judaism. Indeed, in the estimation of some religious Jews, Zionism is the very antithesis of Judaism.[1]

THE ORIGINAL SIN OF ZIONISM: ETHNIC-CLEANSING

The religious discourse invariably is an exclusively inner-Jewish one, scarcely moving beyond discussing 'what is good, or bad, for the Jews'. There is inescapably, however, a fundamental moral problem at the core of the Zionist programme which no amount of special pleading, or pretence to innocence, can side-step. This relates to the Zionist determination to establish a state for Jews at the expense of the indigenous Arabs. This resolve, of course, was contrary to the basic assumption of European nationalisms, that the community/nation desiring independence from the imperial power was indigenous to the relevant territory. In Herzl's day, Jews constituted less than five per cent of the population of Palestine. Herzl's claim to construct a state 'like every other nation', then, involved special pleading, of colonial proportions.

In line with stereotypical colonialist prejudices, Herzl dismissed the impact of his plans on the indigenous people. He knew what was needed to establish a state for Jews in a land already inhabited. An entry

---

[1] In my *Zionism and the State of Israel: A Moral Inquiry* (London: Routledge, 1999), pp. 67-102, I trace the metamorphosis of the religious estimation of Political Zionism, from being an anathema, to occupying a position of virtual sacred significance within religious Jewish thinking.

in his diary of 12 June 1895 signals his plans. Having occupied the land and expropriated the private property, 'We shall endeavour to expel the poor population across the border unnoticed, procuring employment for it in the transit countries, but denying it any employment in our own country.' He added that both 'the process of expropriation and the removal of the poor must be carried out discreetly and circumspectly'.

Moreover, there is a 'mountain' of evidence in the Zionist archives tracing the consistency of this line of thinking within the Jewish leadership in Palestine. It demonstrates that the expulsion of the indigenous Arabs was foreseen as necessary, was systematically planned and was executed at the first opportunity, in 1948. From it we learn in detail how prominent was the necessity of 'transfer' in the thinking of the Zionist leadership from the middle 1930s, at least. We read of the establishment and comportment of the two 'Population Transfer Committees' (1937 through 1944) and the third Population Transfer Committee established by the Israeli cabinet in August 1948.[2] The damage done to the indigenous population, then, was neither accidental nor due to the unique pressures of war, but was at the heart of the Zionist enterprise from the beginning. The Zionist archives themselves, then, fundamentally undermine the Zionist pretence that its intentions were altogether innocent, if not indeed altruistic. They demonstrate that the imperative to 'transfer' the indigenous Arab population was at the very core of the Zionist enterprise from the beginning, and was pursued with determination.

The establishment of the State of Israel in May 1948 was preceded and followed by systematic expulsion of 80 percent of the Arab population of what became the state, the destruction of 418 of their villages, to ensure they would not return, and the confiscation of virtually all their land—Jews owned only some 6.6 percent of Palestine before 1948, but, through the application of various 'legal' enactments owned practically all of it within a short time. Of the some 750,000 Arabs expelled in 1948 some 50,000 were Christians, representing 35 percent of all Christians who lived in Palestine prior to 15 May 1948. For the Palestinians, the Zionist War of Independence was their *Nakba*

---

[2] See Nur Masalha's *Expulsion of the Palestinians: the Concept of 'Transfer' in Zionist Political Thought, 1882-1948* (Washington, DC: Institute for Palestine Studies, 1992), his *A Land without a People. Israel, Transfer and the Palestinians 1949-96* (London: Faber and Faber, 1997), and his *Imperial Israel and the Palestinians: The Politics of Expansion, 1967-2000* (London: Pluto, 2000).

(catastrophe). Israel's colonisation policy after the 1967 war has added to Palestinian disaffection to this day.

Palestinians and neighbouring Arab peoples, of course, have most reason to be aggrieved, but outsiders also have reasons for disaffection. This is particularly true of Christians who, at best, are expected either to support the Zionist conquest, even hailing it to be a miraculous act of God, and a victory for freedom and civilised values, or, at least, to remain silent about Israel's behaviour. However, Zionists' failure to 'come clean' on their ethnic-cleansing imperative, and Israel's failure to conform to UN Resolutions and an array of Human Rights Protocols is sufficient to shock many.

The 'canonical' Zionist version of history, of course, plays down, ignores, explains away, denies, or exonerates Zionists of any responsibility for the destruction of Arab Palestinian life. Even the late Chief Rabbi Jakobovits, a distinguished commentator on other aspects of morality, whose conscience was constantly perturbed by the Arab refugee problem, was quick to assert that 'we *(sic)* are neither responsible for their being there nor have a solution for their problems'. Again, while Chief Rabbi Sacks recalls with sadness the twenty thousand who died so that Israel should exist, he spares no thought for the Arabs of Palestine and the surrounding states who have paid an even more severe price for the prize of Zionism. Instead, we learn that the Jewish pioneers created farms and forests out of a barren landscape.

A WAY FORWARD

While Palestine has always been a mosaic transcending ethnic, religious, and national separations—*pace* the biblical legend's embrace of the genocide of the indigenous Canaanites—the *Zeitgeist* since Oslo (1993) has abandoned the presumption of ethnic and political diversity. Imagination, generosity of spirit, courage, and a certain amount of moral thinking are required if Israel-Palestine is to move beyond the all too predictable politics of separation.

Why must the future settle for an arrangement which feeds off the jaded rhetoric of racist and colonialist 19th-century Europe? Why should the Jewish people bind itself inexorably to a controlling ideology which predicates hermetically-sealed separateness as the utopian solution to neighbourliness? The aspiration to a secular bi-national state in the whole of Palestine, espoused by the PLO until 1988, has now also devolved into the option for separation, with two states side by side.

On the surface it might appear that one was dealing with two deeply-rooted, fundamentally irreconcilable nationalist aspirations. The reality, however, is that each of the nationalisms is of recent origin—the late nineteenth-century in the case of Jewish nationalism, and, while the seeds were sown earlier, 1967 in the case of a distinctly Palestinian nationalism. Moreover, the two are not only recourses of desperation, but betray poverty of vision, lack of imagination and moral determination.

The bi-national option within a unitary state has more to commend it in the long run. The formation of a unitary, secular, non-racial state in Mandated Palestine, with equal rights for both peoples (including returned expulsees), and all religions, as in other democracies, would be a bold solution. To achieve it, the essentially discriminatory base and structure of Zionism would have to be dismantled, and Israelis' national goals would have to become inclusive. While not satisfying all nationalist or religious aspirations, a unitary state in Palestine beats throwing the Jews into the sea, or throwing the Palestinian Arabs into the desert. Could it ever happen?

James Diamond considered it as unlikely that Israel would disavow or move beyond Zionism as that the USA would renounce democracy or capitalism, or Russia would forsake Marxism or communism—he was writing in 1986.[3] Since then, the Berlin Wall also has collapsed, South African *Apartheid* has been dismantled, and an agreed settlement in Northern Ireland is almost there. Two separated states is probably the only viable option for the moment, moving perhaps later to a federation of two states with permeable borders, and ultimately to a unified state.

Herzlian Zionism as implemented by Israel since its foundation, and by Ariel Sharon currently is hardly a moral option for Jewry. Disdain for Zionism's exclusivist, oppressive, imperialistic and colonialist essence should not be dismissed as an expression of irredentist hatred of either Jews or Judaism. It should be welcomed as pointing to the necessity of making a better moral future.

---

[3] James S Diamond, *Homeland or Holy Land? The 'Canaanite Critique of Israel* (Bloomington Indianapolis: Indiana University Press, 1986), pp. 126-27.

READING THE BIBLE WITH THE EYES OF THE CANAANITES. IN HOMAGE TO EDWARD W SAID

With the passing on 25 September 2003 of Edward W Said, University Professor of English and Comparative Literature at Columbia University in New York City, humanity and human culture had lost a great champion. One was aware for a number of years, of course, that he had a terminal illness, and that his periods of enthusiastic engagement had to accommodate also bouts of debility. He had 'come back from the dead' a number of times, but now that he was finally dead, one had to come to terms with the fact that one would never see him on a lecture podium again, learn more and more from his scholarly writing, and be constantly stimulated by the freshness of his ongoing commentary on developments in Palestine, and by his theatrical humour. One would have to rest content with the legacy of his literary productions, which, thankfully, are voluminous, including at least fourteen books, and a great number of articles.

In addition to excelling and being an innovator in the worlds of academic and scholarly discourse, Said was also, of course, something of an intellectual superstar: an opera critic, an accomplished pianist, a television celebrity, a media expert, a popular essayist and a public lecturer in great demand. To add to his achievement as a multi-talented 'renaissance man' he was a passionate advocate for truth and justice, and a secular prophet *par excellence*. He was even something of a political theorist, if not also indeed a political activist.

It was, however, only sometime in the first half of the 1990s that I began to be aware of Said, and it was through his public pronouncements on Palestine that I became so aware. I was not at all conversant with what one might now call the industry of postcolonialism. I was pleased to be invited to a Conference on Postcolonialism in Newman College in 1998, for which I chose the title 'Postcolonial Perspectives on the Bible

273

Lands'. Although I had already delivered the Newman Lecture in Newman College in 1994 on 'The Bible, Religion, Politics, and The Holy Land', and the Lattey Lecture at Cambridge University (November 1997), on the subject, '*A Land flowing with Milk, Honey, and People*', and had completed my book, *The Bible and Colonialism* (1997), etc., it had never once struck me that I was engaged in 'postcolonial studies'. Even worse was to come: sometime after I had delivered a lecture on 'Israel-Palestine: A Challenge to Theology' at the Roehampton Institute conference on 'Faith in the Millennium' (2000), a participant assured me that my lecture was a magnificent piece of deconstruction. This, I hoped, was not a terminal condition. The point is that whether or not I was using the appropriate jargon of Literary Theory my locus as a biblical scholar had been encouraging me to 'read the Bible with the eyes of the Canaanites'. It was Said more than most, of course, who gave theoretical underpinning to the influence of one's own *worldliness* on understanding a text in its *worldliness*. Historical Criticism, the dominant mode of Biblical Studies while I was being trained, confined itself to the *worldliness* of the biblical texts. I have over the years moved from that necessary engagement to consider also the *worldliness* of myself and others, especially colonisers and exploiters, who read the biblical text. The outcome for me was the construction of the beginnings of a Moral Critique of the Bible.

ENCOUNTERING SAID

I met Professor Said a number of times—in London, Bethlehem University and Jerusalem—and edited for publication two of his conference speeches. My last conversation with him was on the occasion of the launching in Jerusalem (1999) of *Holy Land, Hollow Jubilee*, which I co-edited with Naim Ateek and which included his Keynote Address to Sabeel's Third International Conference, held on the campus of Bethlehem University, on 10-15 February 1998. Edward had had a most frustrating day. He had been driven from Gaza where he had spent much of the day and arrived quite late in the proceedings, and after both Naim Ateek and I had addressed those gathered for the launch of another significant volume of 'Palestinian' liberation theology.

In private conversation afterwards Edward communicated his obvious delight to me, an Irishman, at his then upcoming award of an honorary doctorate from University College, Galway. As a child of a country colonised by a 'Western people', Edward was being honoured by a college of the National University of Ireland, a country which had enjoyed rather longer than most the benefits of the civilising enterprise of colonialism, so much so, in fact, that it was the first indigenous culture in modern times to reject the beneficence of the colonisers, shake off the shackles of its imperialising neighbour, and exert its independence. It is some irony that the great prophet of Orientalism, who had made his name internationally by drawing attention to the denigratory attitudes of the West towards the East was being honoured by, geographically speaking, the most Western university in Europe, in the most Westerly country which knew a thing or two about the denigratory attitudes of the Easterly neighbour. Said's own *locus scholasticus*—Palestinian Arab, educated in Cairo, Jerusalem (briefly) and the US, and living all his adult life in the US—led him to think that denigratory attitudes to the 'Other' was a peculiarly Western phenomenon vis-à-vis the Orient. When it came to denigrating the 'Other' Westerners showed much greater versatility than even Said recognised. It could indeed be a salutary exercise for English people to revisit the effects of the English and British colonialism of Ireland – including the denigration of its indigenous culture, the attempt to wipe out altogether its Gaelic language, etc. Those of a disposition to welcome such an exercise in catharsis will have an opportunity soon, I hope, of doing so, since a major part of my current work is in extending my reflections of the Bible and colonialism to include the Irish experience. The exercise will have an especial relevance by being written in the Gaelic language, which has just about survived.[1]

Said was, by common affirmation, one of the great, and, perhaps, the most versatile of the public intellectuals of the 20th century. No less striking than the volume of his literary output is the breadth of his contribution. Predictably he wrote a book, his first, on Joseph Conrad (1966), the subject of his doctoral thesis. There followed a number of other studies within the field of literary criticism. First, *Beginnings: Intention and Method* (1975), and some years later, *The World, the Text and the Critic*

---

[1] *An Bíobla agus an Leatrom. Staidéir Comparáideach ar Úsáid an Bhíobla sa Pholaitíocht sa Mheiriceá Laidineach, in Éirinn, san Aifric Theas, agus sa Phalaistín* ('The Bible and Oppression. A Comparative Study of the Use of the Bible in Politics in Latin America, Ireland, South Africa and Palestine') (Series Dán agus Talann, Vol. 11). Maigh Nuad: An Sagart, 2004.

(1983). Nothing very remarkable so far, perhaps, except that, as even the title of the 1983 study suggests, the text and the critic take only second and third place to the world. One ought not to have been too surprised by this change in scholarly orientation, from the critic being immersed in the study of texts to the recognition that all such literary endeavours were being undertaken within the world, and invariably a historically conditioned world. Said was to lay great stress on the *worldliness* of texts. Between 1975 and 1983, after all, Said had written *Orientalism* (1978), which was to establish him forthwith as a major commentator, not merely on technical matters of literary criticism, but on the inescapable relationships between literature, politics and culture.[2] His critique of the hitherto unacknowledged arrogance of the West in its approach to other cultures, a theme resumed in his *Culture and Imperialism* (1993) established him as a champion of the dignity of indigenous cultures around the world, sufficient to merit him the designation the 'Father of Post-Colonialism'.

In between these comments on the general relationship between literature, politics and culture Said had taken up a major issue which resonated well with both his own Arab and Palestinian identity, and with the foreign policy of the country of his residence, the US. The two, he asserted, were critically related. His preoccupation with Palestine (*The Question of Palestine*, 1979) included also his need to comment on the more general Islamic world (*Covering Islam*, 1981), a religious culture he could hardly have known except from the outside.

People will have different reasons to bemoan Edward W Said's passing, and will point to a variety of the characteristics of his person as well as to the significance of his life's work. Two aspects stand out for me: his comments on the responsibilities of the intellectual in the contemporary world, and the exclusively secular nature of his pursuits. His engagement as a fearless intellectual in real-life issues, all the more remarkable in that his engagement brought him away from his academic specialisation, has been inspiring. On the other hand, I could never quite understand Said's apparent assumption that a project such as his could emanate only from a secular, humanistic perspective. I take the view that such engagement

---

[2] Significantly the title of the interviews with Said, edited by *Gauri Viswanathan* is *Power, Politics, and Culture. Interviews with Edward W Said, edited with an Introduction by Gauri Viswanathan* (New York : Pantheon Books 2001), 413-14.

should flow naturally from religious idealism, in my case from Christianity, the religion in which Edward also was brought up and from which he lapsed, a fact which, as I shall show, he seemed to feel obliged to advertise.

The subject of my address, however, is specific: 'Reading the Bible with the Eyes of the Canaanites'. I was well into my own study of the relationship between the biblical traditions on land with colonialism when I came across the phrase, reading the biblical narratives 'with the eyes of the Canaanites'. The first person I read of to use the phrase was the North American Indian, Robert Allen Warrior. It was in Said's collection, *Blaming the Victim* (co-edited with Christopher Hitchens, 1988), as far as I recall, that I first encountered Warrior's sentiment.[3] Since then Warrior has reiterated his position:

> The obvious characters for Native Americans to identify with are the Canaanites, the people who already lived in the promised land ... I read the Exodus stories with Canaanite eyes (Warrior 1991: 289).

I am not aware, however, that Said pursued the exhortation to read the biblical narrative with the eyes of the Canaanites. Instead, he contented himself with quoting the testimony of G E M de Ste Croix, the greatest authority on the history of class politics in the ancient world, who asserts the unprecedented character of the biblical traditions of divinely mandated ferocity:

> I can say that I know of only one people which felt able to assert that it actually had a divine command to exterminate whole populations among those it conquered; namely, Israel. Nowadays Christians, as well as Jews, seldom care to dwell on the merciless ferocity of Yahweh, as revealed not by hostile sources but by the very literature they themselves regard as sacred. Indeed, they continue as a rule to forget the very existence of this incriminating material ...There is little in pagan literature quite as morally revolting as the stories of the massacres allegedly carried out at Jericho, Ai, and Hazor, and of the Amorites and Amalekites, all not merely countenanced by

---

[3] See Edward W Said, 'Michael Walzer's *Exodus and Revolution*: A Canaanite Reading', in Edward W Said and Christopher Hitchens (eds), *Blaming the Victims. Spurious Scholarship and the Palestinian Question* (London/New York: Verso, 1988), 161-78.

Yahweh but strictly ordained by him ... The Greek and Roman gods could be cruel enough, in the traditions preserved by their worshippers, but at least their devotees did not seek to represent them as prescribing genocide (De Ste Croix 1981: 331-32).

Since his seminal work *Orientalism* (1978) had already established Said as a major commentator, normally it was he who was selected to give the Keynote Lecture at international conferences. By the 1990s he had achieved virtually cult status, and in the conferences in which I participated the audience viewed his performance with that kind of reverence one detects in a liturgical setting. His discourse, too, engaged with some of the great themes of religion: truth, critique of power, liberation and justice. While by his own testimony his inspiration derived from altogether humanistic values people of religious sensitivities saw in him also something of a priest, or, perhaps more accurately, a prophet—one who speaks on behalf of God. Yet a secular prophet would wince somewhat at the thought of speaking on behalf of God. Was it not one of the great gains, so to speak, of the European Enlightenment that human beings could dare to think for themselves, having thrown off the shackles imposed by institutional religion with its dependence on God's revelation and the exclusive interpretation of it in the hands of hierarchical authorities. Not even the great godless world wars of the 20th century, the systematic deployment of instruments of mass destruction leading to the deaths of unprecedented numbers of people could even dampen the enthusiasm for exclusively secular solutions to the human condition. Had Said taken upon himself the task of reading the biblical narrative with the eyes of the Canaanites, I suspect, he would have had much to say. Over the last ten years in particular, I have endeavoured to do so, and have the opportunity under God of communicating my views in various publications, not least *Scripture Bulletin,* the journal of the CBA of Great Britain.

THE INTELLECTUAL AS MORAL TRANSFORMER OF SOCIETY

University people seldom distinguish themselves by their commitment to transform the world morally. Usually whatever idealism they once may have had has been well drained out, not infrequently by the imperative of the improvement of their career prospects. They can seldom afford to speak their truth. They have to keep their job, pay the mortgage and other expenses and try to provide what they regard as the best start for their children. Their doctoral studies invariably focus on some specialist and esoteric aspect of a sub-discipline, which can, with a bit of luck be prepared for publication, a *sine qua non* for securing even a part-time lecturing post. Having eventually gained a university position by 'playing the academic game', then, they in turn get down to the business of producing their own academic clones. In such manner the conventional university system goes along its very own emotionally-detached, intellectually-dispassionate and rationally value-neutral way. That, after all, is considered by the university academy and its powers to be the appropriate comportment of scholars, and is the surest way to climb the academic ladder. Even in terms of language, however, a critic who eschews engagement with the forces of domination contradicts the terms of her or his vocation. Criticism, be it Literary or Biblical Criticism, derives from the Greek verb *krinein*, which implies a weighing up and evaluation of things, rather than a pretence to a much safer 'value-free' assessment.

Professor Said also must have understood the term 'criticism' to imply a weighing up and evaluation of things. But he went even further. For him intellectuals had a moral mission, not only to speak truth, however uncomfortable, to criticise systems of structural domination, but even more radically, to work in favour of a moral future for humanity. This was pointing in the direction of a very radical understanding of literary theory. Literary theory as conventionally understood needed not to be more than an engaging mode of research, study and reflection that would bring to the surface an array of exciting ideas that would be self-standing in the world and capable of sustaining a myriad of PhD theses. Or, it would have been considered adequate to have literary theory provide tools for the criticism of texts. Said considered the discipline needed to go much further. It was inextricably bound up with the world. It was not above the conditions of the world, but right at its heart. By employing the art of criticism, then, practitioners could uncover untruth, expose hypocrisy, and do some of those things necessary in preparing the way for change in society. If the text being studied enjoys its distinctive *worldliness*, so does the critic also enjoy its own unique *worldliness*.

Nothing was more reprehensible in an intellectual, in Said's view, than the avoidance of—that characteristic turning away from—

a difficult and principled position which one knew to be right. One would opt instead not to be 'too political' or 'controversial', but to be 'balanced, objective and moderate', and to remain comfortably within the 'responsible mainstream'. These habits of mind, he urged, were not only reprehensible, but were altogether corrupting. The internalisation of such values, he warned, can 'denature, neutralise, and finally kill a passionate intellectual life'. While his admonitions have universal relevance his own life experience made him aware of such dangers in 'the toughest of all contemporary issues, Palestine, where fear of speaking out about one of the greatest injustices in modern history has hobbled, blinkered, muzzled many who know the truth and are in a position to serve it.' Whatever vilification and abuse an outspoken supporter of Palestinian rights evokes, the truth deserves to be spoken, by an 'unafraid and compassionate intellectual.'

Jerusalem in London

And on the question of truth-speaking concerning Palestine there was so much to say. Not only were there many truths to tell, but the spellbinding and hegemonic narrative of half-truths and downright lies had to be challenged, and real people had to take up the challenge, and be prepared to face the consequences. Professor Said was in very lively form as he delivered the Keynote Lecture at the *International Conference on Jerusalem* in London in 1995. He elevated the discussion about Palestinian rights from the customary genre of lamentation to one geared towards mobilizing Palestinian energies in favour of promoting their just cause. He was critical of the PLO negotiators, and censorious also about a certain disposition of passivity among the Palestinian community, at home as well as in the diaspora.

He bemoaned the fact that to this day—he was speaking in 1995, of course—the story of Jerusalem's loss, both in 1948 and 1967, had not been told by the Palestinians themselves: in so far as it had been told at all it had been partially reconstructed either by Israelis, or by foreigners. He attributed that neglect not only to Palestinian powerlessness but also to its collective incompetence. Not only had the Palestinians failed to narrate their story of loss, but they had not created even a collective Palestinian strategy for Jerusalem, thereby depriving themselves of Jerusalem well *before* the fact. The Palestinians, he insisted, have a real historical and cultural claim to Jerusalem, and that that claim must be strenuously made. Israel's plan for Jerusalem was an assault not only on geography, but also on culture, history, and religion, while throughout its history the city had been a seamless amalgam of cultures and religions. To say that Jerusalem was the *eternal undivided capital* of the Jewish state was to exclude the city's present Palestinian population, and to renounce its multicultural past.

Yet the Arabs and Muslims together, and especially the Palestinians, had yet to mobilise their considerable resources to counteract Israel's behaviour in Jerusalem. The Arab League summit, scheduled as a response to Israel's announced expropriations, had been summarily cancelled. Why? And why, despite endless amounts of evidence proving Israel's bad faith, was the Palestine Authority supinely proceeding with its negotiations, while doing absolutely nothing either locally or internationally to mobilise Palestinians against Israel's continued assault on Jerusalem? Why in the *Declaration of Principles* itself was Jerusalem split off from the West Bank and Gaza, and effectively conceded to Israel from the outset of Oslo negotiations? There were two closely related reasons: powerful Israel, with full US backing, could do what it wished with Jerusalem and elsewhere, and the Palestinians were convinced that there was no alternative but to make that, as well as many other concessions. He accused the Palestinian leadership of 'prior moral capitulation', piling up one concession on another. The architect of the accords, the inglorious Abu Mazen, had assured Hanan Ashrawi not to worry about her reservations about the *Declaration of Principles*. 'We shall sign now', he assured her, adding chivalrously, 'you can bargain with them to try to get back the things we have conceded'.

The Palestine Authority, he reminded the audience, usually negotiated without consulting lawyers, with no experience in settling international disputes, and with no real conviction in winning anything at all, except what Israel might deign to throw its way. As if that were not enough, he added, 'The problem of Jerusalem in the peace process today is therefore largely a problem of the incompetence, the insouciance, the unacceptable negligence of the Palestinian leadership, which has in the first instance actually agreed to let Israel do what it wishes in Jerusalem, and in the second instance evinces not the slightest sign that it is capable of comprehending, let alone executing the truly Herculean task that is

281

required before the battle for Jerusalem can really be joined.' And what could be done?

Palestinians needed a clear statement of purpose and principle to guide their way, and if this demanded rethinking and re-doing Oslo, then so be it. In the first place, they must insist that it was not Israel's right to dispose of, or to build in, or to exploit Jerusalem to the exclusion of Palestinians and others. The massive Palestinian-Muslim-Christian multi-cultural reality in Jerusalem should not be subverted by Israel. That, simply, must be inserted into the peace process. It was not sufficient that Mr Arafat merely say so periodically, 'like a schoolchild repeating a lesson by rote, and pretty much without anybody listening'. The saying must be part of a general strategy of negotiating and winning the peace that Palestinians desire. And speaking of East Jerusalem was not enough. The whole city should be a place of co-existence and sharing between the Palestinians and the Israelis, with joint sovereignty and a co-operative vision.

It would never be sufficient merely to lament the facts of dispossession. Facts never speak for themselves, but must be articulated, disseminated, reiterated and re-circulated. And the then Palestine Authority was altogether incapable of ever conceiving, not to speak of doing that, since it had become the prisoner, if not the dutiful enforcer, of the Israeli occupation regime. Mr Arafat—with his chronic disabilities and incompetencies—and his immediate circle, who ran everything unilaterally and undemocratically, would do little more than 'provide Israel with security, leave the settlements alone, and then scramble around looking for development money.' Diaspora Palestinians, who constitute the majority of Palestinians in the world, therefore, must take the initiative on Jerusalem and on the other occupied territories, and do so in a co-ordinated fashion.

Not that Professor Said was arguing against peace. But *real* peace was possible only between equals, who together decide consciously and deliberately to share the land among each other decently and humanely. Israel, in his opinion, had used the peace process as a subterfuge; only to go on holding the land as if it were its sole proprietor, with concessions to Bantustan-like 'separation' and cantonization for the lesser race of human beings. Palestinians, on their part, had accepted Israel as a sovereign state entitled to peace and security. Was it the Palestinian destiny merely to capitulate and accept the dictates of the strong? Surely not.

Rather, the Palestinians must redefine their goals, recognise that they are realisable, and work for them. And since the Palestine Authority was incapable the challenge should be taken up by the Palestinian diaspora, strategically organised, and working in collaboration with a gigantic Islamic and Arab constituency, a Western constituency, a Christian one, and other ones scarcely touched hitherto.

The situation, even in 1995, was desperate: 'The Palestinians are in a state of confusion and despair, caught as they are between the dictatorial whims of their leader on the one hand, and the merciless policies of occupation and humiliation by which Israel maintains its hold on their lives and land.' Diaspora Palestinians, however, were in a stronger position. The support of Palestinian resistance inside Jerusalem, of course, was vital. But, in the first place, speaking the truth was a *sine qua non*.

THE CHALLENGE OF PEACE IN BETHLEHEM

Being neither a politician nor a diplomat, perhaps the most Professor Said could contribute was to speak the truth as he saw it. He was sure that people— even ordinary people—could change the world. He developed that thesis so close to his heart in his Keynote Address to the Third International Sabeel Conference (10-15 February 1998). The theme of the conference was 'The Challenge of Jubilee: What Does God Require?' Edward's slot came on Friday evening (13 February)—the order of the programme had to be changed due to the uncertain condition of his health. And he was so glad to be there, at the heart of a conference on Palestinian Liberation Theology.

The conference was structured around the biblical theme of Jubilee—the breaking of fetters that occurred every fifty years—and its possible relevance to current events in Palestine, fifty years after the Palestinian *Nakba* (catastrophe) of 1948. The earlier papers commented on the relevant biblical texts, reflecting the legacy of the past—my own contribution was on 'The Bible and Zionism'—and subsequent ones considered not only what happened, but how one can deal with the consequent wounds, discussing the interplay between memory, reconciliation and justice. The third batch of papers projected into the future and considered the political visions and spiritual resources for a lasting peace in Palestine.[4] The conference, of course, included more than lectures and workshops. Worship, song, and prayerful reflection were at its heart, and were given quality time at the beginning, during and at the close of each session. A *Worship Program* accompanied the *Conference Program*, and, in addition, Sabeel had prepared a booklet, *Contemporary Stations of the Cross* for a modern *Via Dolorosa* (commemorating Jesus' 'Way of the Cross'). Visiting places of significance, and listening to the testimonies of people who continued to bear the brunt of Zionist colonialism and the Israeli occupation were an integral part of the convention.

The venue was the theatre of Bethlehem University. The audience of the some 900 conference participants packed the hall, while several hundred young Palestinians had to watch the proceedings, courtesy of closed-circuit television, in the basement. Earlier in the day, Professor Said had visited the former home of his family in West Jerusalem, which, ironically, was at that time the headquarters of the fundamentalist group, the 'International Christian Embassy'. The conference participants for their part had spent the afternoon traversing a contemporary *Via Dolorosa*, whether in a refugee camp or on a settlement. Edward had come at a price. He had 'had a session of chemotherapy last week and I did not think I could make it at all.' But he was so grateful 'for providing us all with the opportunity to be together and reflect on issues of importance connected to truth, justice and liberation.' Edward had come into a showpiece of Palestinian Liberation Theology, and seemed very much at home. He relished the opportunity of addressing in particular the young Palestinian university students who were in the basement. The future was theirs.

He began by promising that he would speak freely, irrespective of what offence it might cause. Censorship of speech by the Arab regimes had been a constant cause of Arab impotence. He was now, in 1998, more resolute than ever in classifying the 'peace process' as a further stage in the capitulation of the Palestinians to the advances of Zionism. He was dismissive of the United States' 'even-handedness', and, again, scornful of the Palestinian leadership. The Palestinians were worse off in every respect now than they were before 'the *misery* of Oslo'.

---

[4] For the conference papers and other relevant information see Naim S Ateek and Michael Prior (eds), *Holy Land—Hollow Jubilee: God, Justice and the Palestinians* (London: Melisende, 1999).

Despite all the losses on the ground, however, there should never be an erasing of the historical truth that the existence of Israel was predicated upon the obliteration of the Palestinian people. The scars of the past and of recent times remained unhealed. But what of the future? How could the Palestinians co-exist peacefully with a state that had not even yet declared its boundaries, and that described itself as the state of the whole Jewish people alone? How could they live in peace with Israel as long as it washed its hands of any responsibility for their plight, and pretended to seek peace, while persisting in their exploitation? The oppressive policies of the Israeli government completed the original sin of the *Nakba*. Manifestly such actions were inimical to any real peace. But to aspire to remove Israel and its people was equally fanciful. The first challenge, indeed the moral mission, for the Palestinian people, and for each individual, then, was to extract acknowledgement from Israel of its continued injustice towards the Palestinians. History would never excuse the Palestinians for failing in that enterprise.

Moreover, there was an alternative to the then drastic condition of the Palestinians. Despite the odds, there was a way forward, but it required a resolute national will and a mass movement that was determined to resist injustice. Some form of co-existence could be achieved, whereby both Israelis and Palestinians could live a better life, free of ethnocentricity and religious intolerance. Showing no sympathy for the customary descent into the rhetoric of lament and abject passivity, Professor Said stressed the capacity of people to make their own history.

Thus he introduced the thought of two philosophers of history who had meant a great deal to him over the years, Ibn Khaldun and Gianbattista Vico. Although separated from each other by well over 300 years, and the Mediterranean Sea—Ibn Khaldun, the Arab philosopher died in 1406, while Vico, the Neapolitan philosopher died in 1744— they held astonishingly similar views of history, both of which had great relevance today. Vico's *The New Science* was published a year after his death (1745), and it remained relatively unknown until the late 18th century, when it was discovered by the French historian Jules Michelet, who translated it from Italian into French.

Since that time, major figures in European thought—Hegel, Marx, Nietzsche, Freud, James Joyce, Beckett, Crochet, and many others—were in some way indebted to Vico's profound insight, that *human beings make their own history*, a history that, therefore, can be understood by human beings scientifically, and according to laws of context, development, and understanding. Humankind, Vico said, begins in barbarism, moves to sociability when the family is invented, and then achieves social solidarity—what Ibn Khaldun in the *Muqadimma* calls, '*Al-Asabiyeh*'. Said appears to have stumbled into Vico. It was not on the menu of his intellectual feast at Princeton or Harvard. During his doctoral studies at Harvard 'my own intellectual discoveries were made outside what the regimen required ... such things as Vico's *The New Science*, Lukacs's *History and Class Consciousness,* Sartre, Heidegger, Merleau-Ponty, all of whom shaped my dissertation on Conrad' (*Out of Place* 1999: 290). The tragedy that the Palestinians suffered was, then, the result of human planning and endeavour. It was not a residue of magical forces. Equally, the way forward lay in self-reliance and active resistance—what the Irish nationalists at the beginning of the 20th century called *Sinn Féin* ('Ourselves Alone'). Self-reliance, surely, but never in isolation.

The Palestinians, and their youth in particular, would have to win over international opinion. The reality of Israel challenged the Palestinians to marshal their resources single-mindedly. This would require a massive campaign, in the US and elsewhere, to dispel the Zionist nationalist myths, and undermine the morality of Israel's military occupation. Palestinians, like the ANC-inspired opposition to South African *apartheid*, would have to campaign in universities, churches, corporations and the media. History confirms that although the balance of power is unfavourable, the weaker side can overcome the stronger one, because of the *human* factor, the relentless will to resist injustice. If Palestinians made the case that they were prepared, with the Jews of Israel and Arab people in the surrounding region, to make a new kind of history, based on a new politics of integration and inclusion, they *could* carry the day. Such was Professor Said's unfailing utopian hope. It scarcely allowed for human depravity, and what theologians call sin. Nor did it pay anything like sufficient attention to the obstacles which interested bodies, and in the case of Palestine, Israel and the US, place in the way of people with a will to self-determination.

Reading the Bible with the Eyes of the Canaanites. In Homage to Edward W Said

THE CHALLENGE OF LIBERATION THEOLOGY

Somebody, sometime, perhaps, will turn to inquiring seriously into Edward's engagement with religion. Apart from his *Covering Islam* (1981), here is little, if indeed anything of substance in any of his writings which indicates serious engagement with the question. I have not been able to identify even one article among the hundreds he wrote dealing with Christianity, and nothing specific on the Bible, with the exception of his comments, mostly second hand, which touch upon the narratives of the Exodus and the Israelite conquest. This is surprising in the light of two developments which took place in the nature of Zionism—one 'fundamentalist' Jewish, and the other 'fundamentalist' Christian—particularly since 1967, the events of which year exerted profound influence on Said. 1967 was, indeed, a watershed in his life, providing the stimulus to begin to understand in a novel fashion not only the political implications for his understanding of Palestine, but also for his understanding of both the political dimension of even scholastic endeavour and his understanding of the role of a scholar vis-à-vis the worldliness of the texts being studied. One might have expected some engagement with the Jewish Religious Zionism that developed in the wake of the 1967 war, or with the increasingly prominent and strident role of the fundamentalist Christian Zionist.

The reason for this myopia, I suspect, lies in the presumption within the broader Academy that religious discourse has nothing to contribute any more to human culture. However impressive the contributions of Karl Barth, Karl Rahner, Hans Ur von Balthasar, *et alii*, to in-house theological discourse they have made precious little inroads into contemporary Western society. Theology and Biblical Studies are on the margins of our culture, and their practitioners have done a great deal themselves to merit such disregard for their disciplines. In a world ravaged by hunger and other forms of deprivation, divided by exclusivist nationalisms, driven by the universal imperative to engage flamboyantly in aggressive commercialism, signalled at its worst by how we fuel our economies by the production and sale of weapons of mass destruction, to engage in theoretical speculations about the nature of reality is not only a self-indulgent intellectual irrelevance, but is a sin against one's vocation to be a critic.

Some information does emerge from Said's autobiographical memoir *Out of Place* (1999), both with regard to his early years and the practice of religion into which he was inducted. The narrative is extraordinarily revealing. Although his parents were living in Cairo in 1935 when Edward was due to be born, they ensured that he would be born in Jerusalem. An elder brother, to be called Gerald, was born in a Cairo hospital, but contracted an infection and died soon after birth. Edward was delivered at home in Talbiyah—a part of West Jerusalem lived in exclusively by Palestinian Christians (*Out of Place* 1999: 21)—by a Jewish midwife, Madame Baer (*Out of Place* 1999: 21).

Edward seemed to live in fear of his father, and received no signs of affection from him. Emotional life within the family appears to have been rather restricted, although he never doubted the love of his mother, a love, however, accompanied by her being 'deeply critical of me' (*Out of Place* 45). Little in his childhood would conform to my idea of a normal childhood. Every effort to dislodge him from his natural surroundings appear to have been made, intentionally or not. While his mother did speak to him in Arabic as well as English, it was always in English that she wrote to him, once a week, throughout her life, which Edward reciprocated in like medium. Even his names were problematic: in addition to the oddity of Edward, he never could fathom out where the name Said came from, while his father's name, Wadie, had later become William. His father had been at St George's School in Jerusalem, where he excelled in football and cricket (*Out of Place* 1999: 6-7). Moreover, as a young man Wadie had gone to the US to escape conscription into the Ottoman army. While in the US he signed up for the American Expeditionary Force, in which capacity he served in France for a time, killing a German soldier at point blank range, an incident which produced recurring nightmares. America, he always averred, was his country (*Out of Place* 9-11).

If his father was American by choice, on the basis of his experience in Cairo, Edward assumed that teachers were not only non-Arab, but were supposed to be English (*Out of Place* 36). Little wonder, then, that the fare of the lessons in the GPS, of course, was thoroughly English (Kings John, Canute; Battle of Hastings, etc: 'GPS gave me my first experience of an organised system set up as a colonial business by the British' (*Out of Place* 42). While he liked Cairo, he never felt he belonged there (*Out of Place* 43). But neither was he English. He tells of an incident in which he was walking home, passing through the Gezira Club. The Sec., a Mr Pilley, told him to leave. Even though Edward protested that his family were members Pilley replied: 'Arabs aren't allowed here, and you're an Arab'. Nor did his father challenge Mr Pilley later on the matter: 'there seemed to be a fatalistic compact between my father and myself about our necessarily inferior status' (*Out of Place* 44). Yet, the father would not be happy for his son to be English. He objected in particular to Edward's practising the Cub oath to God and King: 'Why are you saying that ... You're an American, and we have no king, only a president. You are loyal to the President. God and President' (*Out of Place* 49).

If homelife was, by the standards I took for granted in my own childhood, decidedly odd Edward had little ameliorating influence from childhood friends. He could count on one hand the number of times he had set foot in a classmate's apartment or house as he was growing up, and he could not remember any one occasion in which one of his ' friends'—i.e., young boys with whom he had contact—from either school or club came to his house (*Out of Place* 38).

Whether in Jerusalem or Cairo much of his youth was suffused with religion into whose practice he was inducted at each stage. He had a not unimpressive Protestant clerical pedigree.

SAID'S CLERICAL PEDIGREE

—Hilda, Edward's mother, Hilda, was the favourite daughter of an 'unappealing, a fundamentalist Baptist minister in Nazareth—although he was originally from Safad, via a sojourn in Texas (*Out of Place* 1999: 5)—who was both a harsh patriarch and an oppressive husband' (*Out of Place* 1999: 13). Hilda had boarded at two missionary colleges in Lebanon (*Out of Place* 1999: 13-14).

—Hilda's maiden aunt, Emilia ('Matia') Badr, whose father, Edward's great-grandfather, Yousif Badr, was the first native evangelical minister in Lebanon. Matia boycotted church services in Cairo, and doubted whether there was a god (*Out of Place* 1999: 15).

Nevertheless, his grounding in religious practice had little attraction for him.

JERUSALEM AND CAIRO

Although born in Jerusalem, Edward spent most of his early childhood in Cairo.

—Dean Marmoura baptised the young Edward in St George's Cathedral, Jerusalem, and later, his son, Michel, taught him mathematics (*Out of Place* 1999: 109).

—While in Cairo, he attended the Gezira Preparatory School (GPS), from Autumn 1941 till the family left Cairo in May 1942. It was an altogether non-Arab and non-Muslim culture.

—School always began with the singing of hymns—'All Things Bright and Beautiful', etc. (*Out of Place* 38).

—Mrs Bullen's 'daily homilies were simultaneously condescending and cloying' (*Out of Place* 38).

—On rare occasions [only] did the Saids have 'people', i.e., family in for Sunday lunch, 'which enlivened an otherwise monotonous day of enforced piety' (*Out of Place* 50).

—Sundays in Cairo meant Sunday School: 'This senseless ordeal occurred between nine and ten in the morning at GPS, followed by matins at All Saints' Cathedral. Sunday evenings took us to the American Mission Church in Ezbekieh, and two Sundays out of three to Evensong at the cathedral. School, church, club, garden, house—a limited, carefully circumscribed segment of the great city—was my world until I was well into my teens' (*Out of Place* 1999: 22).

—From the age of ten and a half he attended Cairo's School for American Children, which he found particularly agreeable.

—The family spent more and more time in Palestine during the War (rented house in Ramallah)—it was in Ramallah that he first heard talk of his father having had a 'nervous breakdown' (*Out of Place* 1999: 26).

—Being destined to spend most of 1947 in Jerusalem he was enrolled at St George's School, the school attended by his father, and he thought, also by his grandfather and by most male members of his family (*Out of Place* 1999: 108).

—He felt totally at home in the school, 'for the first and last time in my school life', being with boys just like him (*Out of Place* 1999: 108).

—Although on his twelfth birthday (1 November 1947) in Jerusalem, two of his oldest cousins bewailed the day, the eve of the Balfour Declaration, as 'the blackest day in our history', Edward knew nothing of the reference.

—He was confirmed and took his First Communion in early July 1949 in the Anglican cathedral in Cairo, Aunt Nabiha acting as his godmother. Although he felt no great sense of change, at the time of writing he still wore the ring, inscribed with 'ES', given him by Aunt Nabiha on the occasion (*Out of Place* 1999: 145-46).

—He retained an attachment to John's Gospel, and to the Book of Common Prayer, of which he still had his copy, but read now 'only as a way of regretting the pedestrianism of the New Standard Revised Edition, or whatever it is now called' (*Out of Place* 1999: 144).

Why was Said not able to see in religious idealism a way out of misery? Why did he not confront more explicitly the religious dimensions of the Israeli–Arab conflict which, since 1967 at least, virtually dominated his life, particularly in the light of the fact that with the victory in 1967 religion was being accorded more and more significance in the ideological justification for Zionism?

Was Said's 'sidelining' of religion part of the detritus of post-Enlightenment intellectuals for whom the abandonment of religious sensitivities was virtually a *rite de passage* into modernity? Not only had he lapsed from Anglican Christianity, but he found it necessary to publicise the fact, almost as if doing so were the passport into acceptability. Or was this just one more indication of how Edward Said had 'thrown over' much of his own past? He resented from early years the control his parents, especially his father exercised on him: 'I soon began to take secret delight in doing and saying things that broke the rules or took me beyond the boundaries set by my parents' (*Out of Place* 1999: 31).

Was it part of the place that he had to feel 'out of'?

There may also have been some personal matters behind it. In his autobiography he speaks about how his divorce presented a dilemma for his mother—who he had said earlier was 'my closest and most intimate companion for the first twenty-five years of my life. Even now, I feel imprinted and guided by several of her long-standing perspectives and habits' (*Out of Place* 1999: 12): 'If things are so bad between you, then, yes, by all means you should divorce,' but, 'On the other hand for us [Christians] marriage is permanent, a sacrament, holy. Our church will never recognize divorce.' Looking back, Edward commented 'These were statements that often paralyzed me completely' (*Out of Place* 1999: 293)—an intriguing admission.

But then, perhaps, his lapsing had more intellectual roots. Did the Church's alignment with power—and Edward showed little respect for any kind of power, except the power of truth—prevent it from speaking its own truth? Or was it that he considered religion's commitment to the overriding power of God to be destructive of his confidence that people could by their own determination make their own history, could bring about their own redemption? I would love to have had the opportunity of asking him such questions. I would love also to have had the opportunity of pointing out to him points of convergence between the secular and the religious prophet.

University culture, as Edward knew so well, typically isolates intellectuals from the poor and the powerless. Rather than becoming the voices of the poor, then, they opt to became servants of the powerful. The Latin American liberation theologians since the 1970s have made us aware of the problem. Prior to that period, the energies of the Christian leadership tended to express themselves in a form of Christianity that was dominated by the establishment Church, rather than by the idealism of Jesus. The liberation theologians were very critical of the kind of Theology and Biblical Studies—my own field—that were practised in the West. Conventionally the university departments and seminaries decided upon which questions were important, and what was the appropriate training required of practitioners. The poor, and the structural sin that kept them poor, were not high on the agenda.

The liberation theologians, however, complained that Western interpretation of the Bible would always be distorted, since the Bible's central message—they said rather naively—was that God was on the side of the oppressed, while interpreters from North America and Europe did not know the experience of being subject to economic, personal, or institutional oppression, and, therefore, could do no better than interpret the Bible from their positions of power. Consequently, in reflecting on the hermeneutical and exegetical exercise the liberation theologians insisted on the primacy of the scholar's own context or world-view (*lugar teológico*), and required scholars not merely to describe reality as they discover it, but to deploy their scholarship as a transformative agent in the lives of the people. In Brazil, for example, biblical scholars trained in the methods and concerns of Western Biblical Studies were allowed to enter the so-called Contextual Bible Study process only as servants, and participate only when invited by the people. Moreover, whether or not they had dazzling erudition in the biblical languages, they had to be committed to Biblical Studies from the perspective of the oppressed, and commit themselves to socio-political transformation.[5]

Edward Said had some things, but not much, to say even about the biblical narrative. He had been inducted into the Bible, not only through exposure to it in the church services, but also due to his mother and grandmother reading to him 'fairy tales and biblical stories'. He was also given a book on the Greek myths when he was seven (*Out of Place* 1999: 33). Were it his field of enquiry, he would have been scathing on biblical scholars who maintained an academic detachment from significant engagement in contemporary issues, and who continued to seek refuge by expending virtually all their intellectual energies on an unrecoverable past. This was all the more necessary when the biblical narratives had been manipulated by forces of oppression in the interests of various colonial enterprises.[6] Following the exhortation of Robert Allen Warrior, Edward considered that biblical scholars, Church people, and Western intellectuals should read the biblical narratives 'with the eyes of the Canaanites'.[7] Michael Walzer's exegetical appetite had been exhausted simply by his comments on 'the land of milk and honey'.[8] Walzer's mellifluous prose obscured the problem raised by the presence of the indigenous Canaanites, and the requirement of exterminating them in order to be a kingdom of priests and a holy nation (pp. 101-30). The Promised Land of the biblical narrative flowed, indeed, with milk and honey, but it would also, in the narrative, flow with the blood of the indigenous people, all in the name of piety.[9]

---

[5] See L E Vaage, 'Text, Context, Conquest, Quest: The Bible and Social Struggle in Latin America', in *Society of Biblical Literature Seminar Papers* 30(1991): 357-65

[6] See Michael Prior, *The Bible and Colonialism. A Moral Critique* (Sheffield: Sheffield Academic Press, 1997).

[7] See Edward W Said, 'Michael Walzer's *Exodus and Revolution*: A Canaanite Reading', in Edward W. Said and Christopher Hitchens (eds), *Blaming the Victims. Spurious Scholarship and the Palestinian Question* (London/New York: Verso, 1988) 161-78.

[8] *Exodus and Revolution* (New York: Basic Books, 1985).

[9] See Michael Prior, *A Land flowing with Milk, Honey, and People* (The Lattey Lecture 1997) (Von Hügel Institute, St Edmund's College, Cambridge University, 1997), and in *Scripture Bulletin* 28(1998): 2-17.

While the treatment of indigenous peoples of Latin America had presented the Iberian Church with a considerable moral challenge, and had developed the principles of a liberation theology already in the 16th century—with Bartolomé de Las Casas emerging as the champion of the indigenous peoples—it was not until the 1970s that such a theology sprang up again, and on that occasion also in Latin America. Up to then, Christian Theology was somewhat metahistorical, paying little attention to the social conditions of people and the economic structures that determined them. Doing theology among the poor changed all that.

Authentic Christian theology, according to the Jesuit Father, Ignacio Ellacuría, President of the University of Central America in San Salvador, incorporated three elements: reflection, ethical option and action (*praxis*). Reflection was to be on the object of Christian faith, the Reign of God. Because it was immersed in 'the historical reality' (concrete situation) of the people of God, such reflection introduced a fundamental ethical option, one which properly leads to *praxis*. Rather than being considered as separate, or in temporal sequence, the three elements were completely integrated and almost simultaneously present in a dynamic tension in the richness of encountering the weight of reality.[10]

Ellacuría insisted that the *context* of theological reflection was vital to the discipline. His context was that of being among the poor people of Latin America, whom he considered to be crucified on the cross of Latin America.[11] Just as Ignatius of Loyola, the Founder of the Jesuits, had exhorted his disciples to go on their knees at the foot of the cross and ask, 'What have I done, what am I doing, what will I do for Christ crucified?' so Christians today, Ellacuría urged, should reflect on the condition of the poor and ask, 'What have I done, what am I doing for the people on the cross, and what will I do to uncrucify them, and have them raised?'[12] Being among the crucified people was the pre-eminent place of theology, and might well exact a price.

Ellacuría, striving to bring the poor down from the cross, was put up there himself in a dramatic expression of his commitment to

---

[10] See Ignacio Ellacuría, *Filosofía de la realidad histórica* (Madrid: Editorial Trotta, 1990).

[11] See Ignacio Ellacuría, 'Los pobres, "lugar teológico" en America Latina', in *Misión Abierta* (1981, no. 4-5): 225-40, and his 'El Pueblo crucificado. Ensayo de soterología histórico', in *Revista Latinoamerica de Teología* 18(1989): 305-33.

[12] See Ignacio Ellacuría, 'Las Iglesias latinoamericanas interpelan a la Iglesia de España', *Sal Terra* (1982. no. 826) 230.

theological reflection, ethical option and *praxis*. On 16 November 1989 government soldiers murdered him and five other Jesuits of the university, together with a seminary cook and her daughter. For Jon Sobrino also, another Jesuit of the university, who would have been murdered also on that night had he not been out of the country at the time, the task of theology is to bring the poor of Latin America off the cross.[13] Both Ellacuría and Sobrino were theological advisors to Archbishop Oscar Romero, murdered while he was celebrating Mass (24 March 1980). Theologising with a commitment to social transformation could become a matter of the scholar's own life and death.

While Edward Said's death was from a terminal illness he was not spared opprobrium in his lifetime. In addition to being branded 'the Professor of Terror' in a respectable—so to speak—magazine, the President of his own people even banned his books in Palestine. Back in New York his office had been burned and ransacked, and he had had to install a safety button in his own house, which on pressing would bring the police.[14]

THAT HE MAY HAVE FOUND HIS PLACE

While he made much of his dual cultural identity—he was both an Arab and an American: if his surname was Arab, his Christian name was British, in honour of the Prince of Wales, no less—Edward never quite felt at home in either role. It was not, as it was with Baudelaire, that he was permanently restless, 'always content to be in that place in which he was not,'[15] he did have an existential sense of profound exile. He had already absorbed that sense of chronic exile from his early years, and felt compelled to note that

---

[13] See Jon Sobrino, 'The Crucified Peoples: Yahweh's Suffering Servant Today', in Leonardo Boff and Virgil Elizondo (eds) *1492-1992 The Voice of the Victims* (London: SCM; Philadelphia: Trinity Press International, 1990), being *Concilium* 1990(6), 120-29, and his 'Human Rights and Oppressed Peoples: Historical-Theological Reflections', in Michael Hayes and David Tombs (eds), *Truth and Memory. The Church and Human Rights in El Salvador and Guatemala* (Leominster: Gracewing, 2001), 134-58.

[14] *Power, Politics, and Culture. Interviews with Edward W Said, edited with an Introduction by Gauri Viswanathan* (New York : Pantheon Books 2001), 413-14.

[15] 'Il me semble que je serais toujours bien où je ne suis pas', 'Anywhere out of the World. N'importe où hors du Monde' (*Petits Poèmes en Prose (Le Spleen de Paris)* (Paris: Édition Garnier Frères, 1980), 211.

Being myself meant not only never being quite right, but also never feeling at ease … Permanently out of place … Could 'Edward's' position ever be anything but out of place? (*Out of Place* 1999: 19).

For all his sense of being in exile, however, Edward loved music, good food and wine, and smart dressing, and gave every impression of being at home in his oratorical performances, at least.

He had little admiration for politicians, either US or Arab, and was usually equally scathing on the foreign policies of the US and the domestic policies of the Arab states. The Arab states were despotic and tyrannical, while the US was determined to exercise global hegemony. Little wonder that he had never found his place: 'Better to wander out of place, not to own a house, and not ever to feel at home anywhere, especially in a city like New York, where I shall be until I die...With so many dissonances in my life I have learned actually to prefer being not quite right and out of place' (*Out of Place* 1999: 294-95). And again, 'I feel I have no place. I'm cut off from my origins. I live in exile. I am exiled...I don't own any real estate. The flat I live in is rented. I see myself as a wanderer. My position is that of a traveler, who is not interested in holding territory, who has no realm to protect.'[16]

This sense of not being at home, of course, is well attested in the Christian tradition, and in several other traditions as well. Edward, perhaps, might have appreciated the perspective of the anonymous *Letter to the Hebrews* in the New Testament. It is, at one level, a profound reflection on the journey to the Place of Rest. Those on the journey would have to be steadfast. They would be beset by all kinds of problems along the way, and at every turn. They would be tempted to revert to the security of their comfortable past. But they should keep on, never losing sight of the One who has gone before.

---

[16] *Power, Politics, and Culture.* 456.

A DISASTER FOR DIALOGUE

Published in The Tablet *just after Michael's death in 2004, this article rejects the equation of anti-Zionism with anti-Semitism at a recent Catholic-Jewish Liaison Committee.*

After the eighteenth International Catholic-Jewish Liaison Committee met in Buenos Aires earlier this month, it released a joint statement repeating many of the constant emphases of the Jewish-Christian dialogue of recent years. There were wider global concerns too: economic disparity and its challenges, ecological devastation, the negative aspects of globalisation, and the urgent need for international peacemaking. One searches in vain, however, for an interfaith comment on the ever-deteriorating conditions in the Holy Land, and the challenge to justice and charity, or simply to justice and international legality, caused by the situation in Israel. There was not one mention of the Separation Wall dividing Jews and Palestinians.

Two elements above all others of the joint statement are particularly disturbing: the view that anti-Zionism is synonymous with anti-Semitism, and the declaration of commitment to the 'struggle against terrorism'. 'Terrorism' by implication, of course, excludes the multiple forms of state-sponsored outrages in the Middle East and elsewhere, and, even more pointedly, includes any form of resistance to occupation or foreign domination.

Equating anti-Zionism with anti-Semitism marks 'a first' in Catholic thinking, and was quickly noticed by the Israeli newspaper, *Haaretz* (10 July), under the headline, 'Catholic Church equates anti-Zionism with anti-Semitism'. *Haaretz* quoted the director of the World Jewish Congress as saying that the statement marks 'an historic moment: for the first time, the Catholic Church recognises in anti-Zionism an attack ... against the whole Jewish people'. The Anti-Defamation League was also quick to respond and put the joint statement on its website.

It had seemed to me only a matter of time before the equation 'anti-Zionism equals anti-Semitism' would work its way into the religious dialogue, as one of the many fruits of a vigorous campaign to close down any criticism of Israel. Against the background of the almost universal condemnation of the behaviour of the State in the Occupied Territories, the World Zionist Congress (WZC), meeting in Jerusalem in 2002, called upon its supporters everywhere to press the equation of anti-Zionism with anti-Semitism and racism. That was a clever tactic, since the last two are universally despised in humane circles. In accepting the equation, Zionism—unlike any other political ideology, such as nationalism, socialism, Communism, apartheid, or globalisation—would be above reproach, and, by extension, so would the State of Israel. A rhetorical victory, however, would not be enough. The WZC encouraged university students to monitor the lectures of those suspected of criticising Israel, and report back to their masters. Thus, a whole culture reminiscent of McCarthyism has re-entered American campuses. In the Buenos Aires statement we see how the tactic has borne fruit in its inaugural entry into interfaith dialogue. Many Catholics, and not a few Jews, will be dismayed, particularly those with some knowledge of the nature of the ideology of Zionism and those who are distressed by the unfortunate effects of its implementation.

Virtually the entire religious leadership of Jews in nineteenth-century Eastern Europe considered Theodor Herzl, the creator of Zionism, and his creed, to be anathema. Britain's Chief Rabbi considered his programme to be an 'egregious blunder' and an 'absolutely mischievous project'. In Vienna, his own Chief Rabbi judged it to be incompatible with Judaism, a conclusion echoed by the Chief Rabbis of France and Belgium. The German Rabbinical Council condemned the efforts to create a Jewish national state as contrary to Holy Writ. They were not alone.

Agudat Yisrael, formed in Germany in 1912 to present a united Orthodox front against secularisation, assimilation and Herzlian nationalism, considered Zionism to be a pseudo-messianic, satanic conspiracy against God. Zionism would remove from Jewish communal life the religious values which united Jews. While pretending to protect Jewish life it abandoned the values which had sustained it. The abandonment of what was most characteristically Jewish in the pursuit of purely secular, nineteenth-century European notions of nationhood was, for them, the ultimate form of assimilation. The restoration of the Jewish people to its ancestral land was uniquely the task of the Messiah. Basing their stand on Jewish theology, rather than on concern for the indigenous population, such religious Jews saw the Zionist enterprise as a conscious repudiation of the most fundamental tenets of Judaism. A number of religious Jews—far outweighed by the numbers of secular ones who do so—add a humanitarian dimension to their critique.

Unlike those who pass over the moral question of the impact of Zionism on the indigenous Palestinians, the Jewish religious group Neturei Karla—founded in Jerusalem in 1938—continues to be distressed at the injustices to the Palestinians in the name of Jewishness. True Jews, they insist, are not allowed to dominate, kill, harm or demean another people. They regard Zionism as a tragic experiment and a 'dismal failure'. Already too much blood has been shed on the altar of a nineteenth-century colonial nationalism, misapplied to the Jewish people. From being that of a people of faith, Zionism, they charge, has changed being Jewish into a barren secular, ethnic identity. World Jewry, they insist, is implicated in Israel's violence against the Palestinians.

Such religious notables would be bemused to learn that their criticism of Zionism was a manifestation of anti-Semitism. Despite such religiously based criticism of the Zionist enterprise, however, the Jewish religious leadership today, both in Israel and abroad, has been among the most enthusiastic supporters of the Zionist enterprise. Given the consequences for the people of Palestine, I find their moral stance disturbing.

For there is a fundamental moral problem at the core of the Zionist project which no amount of special pleading, or pretence to innocence, can sidestep: it is the determination to establish a state for Jews at the expense of the indigenous Arabs. Herzl and the leadership of the Zionist enterprise were well aware of the ethnic-cleansing imperative of his project. As an entry in his diary of 12 June, 1895, shows, Herzl knew what was needed to establish a state for Jews in a land already inhabited. Having occupied the land and expropriated the private property, he wrote:

> 'We shall endeavour to expel the poor population across the border unnoticed, procuring employment for it in the transit countries, but denying it any employment in our own country ... The process of expropriation and the removal of the poor must be carried out discretely and circumspectly.'

There is also a large body of evidence in the Zionist archives, and in the public domain since the early Nineties, tracing the consistency of this line of thinking within the Jewish leadership in Palestine. In fact, the establishment of the State of Israel in 1948 was preceded and followed by the systematic expulsion of 80 per cent of the Arab population—aided by several massacres and rapes—the destruction of 418 of their villages to ensure they would not return, and the confiscation of virtually all their land. Israel's colonisation policy since 1967 has added to Palestinian disaffection to this day.

There are, then, two reasons for objection to criticism of Zionism being seen as 'an attack against the whole Jewish people'. The first has its roots in Jewish theological considerations, and the second includes consideration of the rights of an indigenous population not to be expelled from, or dominated in their land. If the former concerns preoccupy some religious Jews, then secular Jews, and some religious ones also, are among those most disturbed by the human cost of the implementation of Zionism. Such people should not be dismissed as 'self-hating Jews', nor should those who share their concerns, for either theological or humanitarian reasons, be accused of being 'Jew haters'.

The failure of the Catholic and Jewish leaders to include a thoughtful religious perspective on one of the great moral crises of our time calls the integrity of the actual Catholic-Jewish dialogue into question. How does the evasion of hard truths in any way benefit the noble ideal of inter-religious relations? There are religious and moral considerations of even greater importance than cosy relations with another faith group. One might not unreasonably have hoped that the combined wisdom as reflected in the Buenos Aires joint statement would transcend the liberation rhetoric of Prime Minister Ariel Sharon and President George W Bush.

BIBLIOGRAPHY OF PUBLISHED WORKS

Publications

Note: the original details of works published in this collection are prefixed by an asterisk [*] in the Bibliography.

Books

1. 1989. *Paul the Letter Writer and the Second Letter to Timothy*. (*JSNTSS 23*). Sheffield: Sheffield Academic Press.

2. 1994. (ed. with William Taylor). *Christians in the Holy Land*. London: WIFT/ Scorpion Press.

3. 1995. *Jesus the Liberator. Nazareth Liberation Theology (Luke 4.16-30) (The Biblical Seminar 26)*. Sheffield: Sheffield Academic Press.

4. 1997. *The Bible and Colonialism. A Moral Critique. (The Biblical Seminar 48)*. Sheffield: Sheffield Academic Press. Reprinted in 1999.

5. 1997 *The Bible and Colonialism* and *Zionism, the Bible and Morality*. Bethlehem: Bethlehem University Press.

*6. 1997 *A Land flowing with Milk, Honey, and People* (The Lattey Lecture 1997) Von Hügel Institute, St Edmund's College, Cambridge University.

7. 1998. (ed.). *Western Scholarship and the History of Palestine*. London: Melisende.

8. 1998. *Al-Masihiyyun fi'l-Ard Al-Maqdisa* (Arabic of *Christians in the Holy Land*, translated by Laurence S. Samour). London: Altajir World of Islam Trust.

9. 1999. *Zionism and the State of Israel: A Moral Inquiry*. London and New York: Routledge.

10. 1999. (ed. with Naim S. Ateek). *Holy Land - Hollow Jubilee: God, Justice and the Palestinians*. London: Melisende.

11. 2000. (ed.). *They Came and They Saw. Western Christian Experiences of the Holy Land*. London: Melisende.

12. 2003 *Alkitab wa Alistimar al Istitany Amrika al-latiniyyah, hanoob ifriqyah, filasteen*

(The Bible and Colonialism, Latin America, South Africa, and Palestine). Damascus: Cadmus.

13. 2003 *Bible et Colonialisme. Critique d'une instrumentalisation du texte sacré* (French translation of *The Bible and Colonialism. A Moral Critique*). Paris: L'Harmattan.

14. 2004 *An Bíobla agus an Leatrom. Staidéir Comparáideach ar Úsáid an Bhíobla sa Pholaitíocht sa Mheiriceá Laidineach, in Éirinn, san Aifric Theas, agus sa Phalaistín* ('The Bible and Oppression. A Comparative Study of the Use of the Bible in Politics in Latin America, Ireland, South Africa and Palestine') (Series *Dán agus Talann*, Vol. 11). Maigh Nuad: An Sagart.

15. 2005. *La Biblia y el colonialismo:Una crítica moral* (The Bible and Colonialism: A Moral Critique] (Buenos Aires: Editorial Canaan).

PAPERS PUBLISHED IN COLLECTIVE WORKS

1980. Textual Commentaries in *This is the Word of the Lord* (ed. R. Duckworth), 73-97. Oxford: OUP/BRF.

1988. Biblical Commentaries in *Faith Alive* (ed. R. Pasco and J. Redford) (chaps. 15 and 19). London: Hodder & Stoughton.

1994. 'Pilgrimage to the Holy Land, Yesterday and Today,' in Michael Prior and William Taylor (eds). 1994. *Christians in the Holy Land*. London: WIFT, 169-99; co-authored 'Introduction', 1-7.

1997. 'A Perspective on Pilgrimage to the Holy Land', in Naim Ateek, Cedar Duaybis and Marla Schrader. *Jerusalem: What makes for Peace?* London: Melisende, 114-31.

1998. 'Introduction', and 'The Moral Problem of the Land Traditions of the Bible', in Michael Prior (ed.). *Western Scholarship and the History of Palestine*. London: Melisende, 1-8, 41-81.

1999. 'Introduction', and 'The Bible and Zionism', in Naim Ateek and Michael Prior (eds), *Holy Land - Hollow Jubilee: God, Justice and the Palestinians*. London: Melisende, 1-14, 69-88.

1999. '"You will be my witnesses in Jerusalem, in all Judaea and Samaria, and to the ends of the earth". Christian Perspectives on Jerusalem', in A O'Mahony (ed.) *Palestinian Christians: Religion, Politics and Society in the Holy Land*. London: Melisende, 96-140.

2000. 'Introduction' and 'Studying the Bible in the Holy Land', in Michael Prior (ed.) *They Came and They Saw. Western Christian Experiences of the Holy Land*. London: Melisende, 5-12, 104-27, respectively.

2000. 'Christian Pilgrimage to the Holy Land', and 'A Palestinian Discourse' in

Duncan Macpherson (ed.), *A Millennium Guide to Christian Pilgrimage to the Holy Land*. London: Melisende, 25-39, 99-110, respectively.

2001. 'Israel-Palestine: A Challenge to Theology', in S Porter, D Tombs and M Hayes, *Faith in the Millennium*, Roehampton Institute Studies Series (Sheffield Academic Press), 59-84.

2001. 'The Right to Expel: the Bible and Ethnic Cleansing', in Naseer Aruri (ed.), *Palestinian Refugees and their Right of Return*, London and Sterling VA: Pluto Press, 9-35.

2002. 'Confronting the Bible's Ethnic Cleansing in Palestine', in Harry Wendt (ed.), *Israel, Yesterday and Today*. Minneapolis, MN: Crossways International, 40-62.

2003. 'Speaking Truth in the Jewish-Christian Dialogue', in *A Faithful Presence. Essays for Kenneth Cragg*, ed. David Thomas and Clare Amos (London: Melisende), 329-49.

2003 (June). 'A Moral Reading of the Bible in Jerusalem', in Thomas L Thompson (ed.), *Jerusalem in Ancient History and Tradition*, Sheffield: Sheffield Academic Press East, and West Nexus/Prota (in Arabic).

2003. 'The Bible and the Clash of Civilisations', chapter in book edited by Professor Timothy Niblock. Exeter: Exeter University Press.

2003. '"Out of Zion shall go forth instruction, and the word of YHWH from Jerusalem" (Isa 2.3). Studying the Bible in the Land of the Bible', in Philip R. Davies (ed.), *Zion, Palestine and the Bible* (JSOT Supplements). Sheffield: Sheffield Academic Press.

2003. 'Ebrei, Cristiani e Mussulmani nella Terra Santa. Prospettive future', in *Religioni e Ambiente. Atti del Convegno Internazionale Interreligioso 2000*, Camaldoli: Edizioni Camaldoli.

2003. 'En paz, en el lugar del descanso: Una preciacion de Edward W. Said", in *El Legado de Edward W Said*, edited by Saad Chedid, Buenos Aires: Editorial Canaan, pp.55-82

2004. 'Zionism and the Challenge of Historical Truth and Morality' *Speaking the Truth about Zionism and Israel* (M. Prior ed.) London: Melisende, 13-50.

2005. 'Violence and the Biblical Land Traditions', in (eds) Naim Ateek, Cedar Duaybis and Maurine Tobin, *Challenging Christian Zionism, Theology, Politics and the Israel-Palestine Conflict*, (London: Melisende), 127-44.

ACADEMIC JOURNAL ARTICLES

1979. 'Revisiting Luke'. *Scripture Bulletin* X: 2-11.

1982/83. 'The Bible in Irish', 'The Bible in Irish: Sequel'. *Scripture Bulletin* XIII: 2-4, 37-38.

1984. 'Israel: Library, Land and Peoples'. *Scripture Bulletin* XV: 6-11.

1986. 'A "Copernican" Revolution, or, Griesbach Re-buried?' *Scripture Bulletin* XVII: 14-19.

1988. 'Jesus' Teaching on the Mount'. *Scripture Bulletin* XVIII: 26-33.

1988. 'Paul on "Power and Weakness"'. *The Month* 21: 939-44.

1990. '"Evangelizare Pauperibus Misit Me": Jesus in the Synagogue at Nazareth'. *Colloque* No. 22: 50-62.

1991. 'The Poor in Luke's Gospel'. *Colloque* No. 23: 349-69.

1994. 'Isaiah and the Liberation of the Poor (Luke 4.16-30)'. *Scripture Bulletin* 24: 36-46.

1995. 'The Bible as Instrument of Oppression'. *Scripture Bulletin* 25: 2-14.

1996. 'Jesus and the Evangelization of the Poor'. *Scripture Bulletin* 26: 34-41.

1998. 'A Land flowing with Milk, Honey, and People' (The Lattey Lecture 1997). *Scripture Bulletin* 28: 2-17.

1998. 'Studying the Bible in the Land of the Bible'. *Colloque* No. 38: 122-144.

1999. 'Christian Perspectives on Jerusalem'. *Journal of Islamic Jerusalem Studies* 3: 1-26.

1999. 'The Bible and the Redeeming Idea of Colonialism'. *Studies in World Christianity* 5: 129-55.

1999 'The Liberation Theology of the Lucan Jesus', *Liber Annus* (Studium Biblicum Franciscanum, Jerusalem) XLIX: 79-99.

2000. 'Zionist Ethnic Cleansing: the Fulfilment of Biblical Prophecy?' *Epworth Review* 27: 49-60.

2001 'Revisiting the Pastoral Epistles', *Scripture Bulletin* 31: 2-19.

2001 'Holy Places, Unholy Domination: The Scramble for Jerusalem', *Islamic Studies* 40: 507-30.

2002 'Ethnic Cleansing and the Bible: A Moral Critique', *Holy Land Studies. A Multidisciplinary Journal* 1: 37-59.

2002 'The Israel-Palestine Dispute and the Bible', *Scripture Bulletin* 32: 64-79.

2002 'The "Holy Land", Zionism, and the Challenge to the Church', *New Blackfriars* 83(no. 980, October 2002): 471-89.

2003 'The State of the Art: Biblical Scholarship and the Holy Land', *Holy Land Studies. A Multidisciplinary Journal* 1 (no. 2): 65-92.

2004 'The State of Israel and Jerusalem in the Jewish-Christian Dialogue: A Monologue in Two Voices,' *Holy Land Studies. A Multidisciplinary Journal* 3 (no. 2): 145-171.

2005 'A Disaster for Dialogue: Anti-Zionism, Anti-Semitism and Racism' *Holy Land Studies. A Multidisciplinary Journal* 4 (no. 1): 87-92.

BIBLICAL-LITURGICAL ARTICLES AND COMMENTARIES

1972. 'The Paschal Mystery'. *Scripture in Church* 3: 447-52.

1973. Textual Commentaries, and 'The Epistle to the Hebrews'. *Scripture in Church* 3: 519-32; 614-20.

1974. Textual Commentaries, and 'God Our Father'. *Scripture in Church* 4: 314-17; 386-93.

1975. Textual Commentaries. *Scripture in Church* 5: 140-48; 503-508.

1976. Textual Commentaries. *Scripture in Church* 6: 164-71; 303-305; 334-42; 446-53; 486-95.

1977. Textual Commentaries. *Scripture in Church* 7: 316-32.

1978. Textual Commentaries. *Word in Worship* Aug 1978/Easter 1979: 15-28.

1994. Textual Commentaries. *Scripture in Church* 24: 362-68; 395-407.

1995. Textual Commentaries. *Priests and People*.

1995. Textual Commentaries. *Scripture in Church*.

2002. Celebrant's Guide, and Comments and Reflections on Sundays 27, 28, 29, *Scripture in Church* 128: 386-91; 418-26, respectively.

PUBLIC DISCOURSE ARTICLES

1979. 'Public Examinations in Religious Studies'. *Africa* Aug-Sept, 6-8.

1980. (co-authored with V. Jamset) 'Religion and Music'. *The Simmarian Newsletter* 63: 29-31.

1981. 'Pilgrimage'. *The Simmarian Newsletter* 65: 23-24.

1981. 'Die anglikanische Gemeinschaft'. Part 1. *Heute*, Okt-Dez 19-22, 24-25.

1982. 'Die anglikanische Gemeinschaft'. Part 2. *Heute*, Jan-Mar 19-21.

1983. 'Evangelizare Pauperibus'. *Colloque* No. 8: 134-39.

1984. *The Universe* (Newspaper) 3 Articles: Apr. 27, Sept. 21, and Dec. 7.

1985. *The Universe* 4 Articles: Jan. 25, Feb. 8, 15, 22.

1986. *The Universe* 2 Articles: Nov. 14, Dec. 19.

1987. *The Universe* 2 Articles: Jan 2, 23.

1986-88. Contributor of eight articles to *Faith Alive* (1986-87), *Word* Alive (1987-88).

1988-2000. 'From the Chair'. *Living Stones Magazine*.

★1989. 'Living Stones: A Retreat with Palestinian Christians', *New Blackfriars* 70: 119-23.

★1990. 'A Christian Perspective on the *Intifada*'. *The Month* 23: 478-85.

1992. '*Living Stones*: Christians in the Holy Land'. *Doctrine and Life* 42: 128-34.

★1993. 'Palestinian Christians and the Liberation of Theology'. *The Month* 26: 482-90.

1993. 'Christian Presence in the Occupied Territories.' *Living Stones Magazine*, no. 9: 3-4.

1993. 'Living or Dead Stones? The Future of Christians in the Holy Land' *Living Stones Magazine* 9: 4-6.

★1994. 'The Vatican-Israel Fundamental Agreement' *Living Stones Magazine* 10: 2-4.

★1994. 'Clinton's Bible, Goldstein's Hermeneutics'. *Middle East International* 16 Dec: 20-21.

1995. "If the Torah is from Heaven..." *Living Stones Magazine* 12: 8-12.

1997. 'From Occupation to Universal Redemption'. *Cornerstone* 8: 4-5.

1997. 'Professing in Bethlehem University'. *CAABU* Annual Report: 19-23.

★1997. 'Settling for God'. *Middle East International* No. 565: 20-21.

1998. '"Go from your Country": Israel Fifty Years On'. *The Month* 31: 186-91.

2000. 'Confronting the Bible's Ethnic Cleansing in Palestine', in *The Link* (Americans for Middle East Understanding) 33(5, December): 1-12.

★2002. "Antizionism = Antisemitism?" in *Doctrine and Life* 52 (July-August): 339-47.

2003. "The Holy Land and the Challenge to the Churches" *Living Stones Magazine* 23: 12-15.

2003. "Christians and Zionism: an Interview with Marianne Argobast of the Witness" *Living Stones Magazine* 23: 12-15, and *The Witness*, Vol, 86, Number 3/4, March/April 2003: 19-22.

BOOK REVIEWS (SELECTION)

1974. Hanson, Anthony T. *Studies in Paul's Technique and Theology. Irish Theological Quarterly* 41: 320-21.

1975. Herold, Gerhart. 1973. *Zorn und Gerechtigkeit Gottes bei Paulus. Eine Untersuchung zu Röm 1:16-18. Irish Theological Quarterly* 42: 82-83.

1978. McNamara, Martin (ed.). *Irish Contribution. Proceedings of the Irish Biblical Association.* No. 1. *Scripture Bulletin* IX: 22-23.

1980. Beyerlin, Walter (ed.).1979. *Near Eastern Texts Relating to the Old Testament. Scripture Bulletin* IX: 46-47.

1980. Bammel, E, C K Barrett and W D Davies. *Donum Gentilicium. Scripture Bulletin* X: 39.

1980. Fuchs, Albert (ed.). *Studien zum Neuen Testament und Seiner Umwelt. Scripture Bulletin* XI: 40.

1981. Hagner, Donald A and Murray J Harris. 1980. *Pauline Studies. Scripture Bulletin* XII.

1983. Richards, Hubert J. 1983. *The Gospel in Song. Scripture Bulletin* XV: 39.

1985. *Père Lagrange, Personal Reflections and Memoirs*, translated into English by Henry Wansbrough. *Scripture Bulletin* XVI: 11-12.

1986. Holladay, Carl R. 1985. *Fragments from Hellenistic Jewish Authors. Scripture Bulletin* XVI: 42-43.

1988. Wakefield, Gordon S. 1985. *The Liturgy of St John. King's Theological Review.*

1990. Herbert, Máire and Martin McNamara (eds). 1989. *Irish Biblical Apocrypha. Selected Texts in Translation. Scripture Bulletin.*

1992. Burrows, Mark S and Paul Rorem (eds). 1991. *Biblical Hermeneutics in Historical Perspective. Studies in Honour of Karlfried Froehlich on His Sixtieth Birthday. The Month* 25: 275-76.

1992. Towner, Philip H. 1989. *The Goal of our Instruction. The Structure of Theology and Ethics in the Pastoral Epistles (JSNTSS 34). Heythrop Journal* 33: 334-35.

1993. Cruz, Hieronymus. 1990. *Christological Motives and Motivated Actions in Pauline Paraenesis. Catholic Biblical Quarterly* 55: 145-46.

1994. Wechsler, Andreas. 1991. *Geschichtsbild und Apostelstreit: Eine forschungsgeschichtliche und exegetische Studie über den antiochenischen Zwischenfall (Gal 2,11-14). Catholic Biblical Quarterly* 56: 810-11.

1995. Young, Frances. 1994. *The Theology of the Pastorals. Theology* 98: 489-91.

1996. Richards, E Randolph. *The Secretary in the Letters of Paul. Heythrop Journal* 39: 87-89.

1998. Thurston, Bonnie. 1995. *Reading Colossians, Ephesians and 2 Thessalonians. A Literary and Theological Commentary. Catholic Biblical Quarterly* 60: 385-87.

1998. Whitelam, Keith W. 1996. *The Invention of Ancient Israel. The Silencing of Palestinian History. Heythrop Journal* 39: 189-93.

1999. Dunn, J D G. 1998. *The Theology of Paul the Apostle. Scripture Bulletin* 29: 52-55.

1999. Gilbert, Martin. 1998. *Israel. A History. Heythrop Journal* 40: 479-81.

1999. Lüdemann, Gerd. 1997. *The Unholy in Holy Scripture. The Dark Side of the Bible. Heythrop Journal* 40: 76-78.

2000. Silberman, Neil Asher and David B Small. 1997. *The Archaeology of Israel. Constructing the Past, Interpreting the Present. Heythrop Journal* 41: 329-41.

2000. Hess, Richard S and Gordon J Wenham (eds). 1999. *Zion, City of Our God. Scripture Bulletin* 30: 50-52.

2001 Ellis, Marc H. 1999. *O, Jerusalem! The Contested Future of the Jewish Covenant. The Month* 34(ns): 178-79.

2001. Quinn, Jerome D and William C Wacker, *The First and Second Letters to Timothy,* Eerdmans Critical Commentary (Grand Rapids, MI: Wm B Eerdmans, 1999). *Heythrop Journal* 42: 75-78.

EDITORIAL

1980-84: Joint Editor, *Scripture Bulletin*

1985-89: Editor, *Scripture Bulletin*

1986-87: Editorial Consultant for *The Universe, Faith Alive*

1987-88: Editorial Consultant for *The Universe, Word Alive*

1994: (co-editor) *Christians in the Holy Land.* London: WIFT

1997-: International Editorial Advisory Board of *Journal of Islamic Jerusalem Studies*

1998: (editor) *Western Scholarship and the History of Palestine*. London: Melisende

1999: (co-editor) *Holy Land - Hollow Jubilee: God, Justice and the Palestinians*. London: Melisende

2000: (editor) *They Came and They Saw: Western Christian Experiences of the Holy Land*. London: Melisende

2002-2004: Founding Editor of *Holy Land Studies. A Multidisciplinary Journal* (published by Continuum, 2001-2003 and currently by Edinburgh University Press)

2003-: Editorial Board of *Roczniki Teologiczne. Pismo Swiête* ('Annals of Theology. Holy Scripture', University of Lublin, Poland). ISSN: 1233-1457.